DATE DUE

THE CONSTITUTIONAL PARENT

The Constitutional Parent

Rights, Responsibilities,
and the Enfranchisement
of the Child

JEFFREY SHULMAN

Yale
UNIVERSITY PRESS
NEW HAVEN AND LONDON

Yale University Press books may be purchased in quantity for educational, business,
or promotional use. For information, please e-mail sales.press@yale.edu (U.S. office)
or sales@yaleup.co.uk (U.K. office).

Set in Electra LH type by Newgen North America.
Printed in the United States of America.

Library of Congress Cataloging-in-Publication Data

Shulman, Jeffrey, 1951– author.
The constitutional parent : rights, responsibilities, and the enfranchisement
of the child / Jeffrey Shulman.
pages cm
Includes bibliographical references and index.
ISBN 978-0-300-19189-9 (hardback)
1. Parent and child (Law)—United States.   2. Children—Legal status, laws, etc.—
United States.   3. Domestic relations—United States.   4. Constitutional law—
United States.   I. Title.
KF540.S58 2014
346.7301'7—dc23
2013047823

A catalogue record for this book is available from the British Library.

This paper meets the requirements of ANSI/NISO Z39.48-1992
(Permanence of Paper).

10 9 8 7 6 5 4 3 2 1

For Gretchen
and
Rachel, Sarah, Molly, and Alberta

Mine own, and not mine own
—*A Midsummer Night's Dream*, IV.1.187

CONTENTS

> a grateful mind
> By owing owes not, but still pays, at once
> Indebted and discharg'd; what burden then?
> —*Paradise Lost*, IV.55–57

I owe a great debt—surely, one not soon to be discharged—to my colleagues for their support of this project. Because they are who they are, I bear the burden of gratitude lightly and happily. Robin West's encouragement could not have been more enthusiastic. David Wolitz's intellectual camaraderie could not have been more generous. Many of my colleagues at Georgetown Law were once my teachers, as they are today—none more so than Michael Seidman and the late Steven Goldberg.

For a series of research grants from Georgetown Law, my appreciation to Dean William Treanor, former deans Judith Areen and Alex Aleinikoff, and Associate Dean Gregory Klass. The assistance of the Georgetown Law Library Research Services staff (special thanks to Priscilla Day and Michael J. Nelson II), the Office of Faculty Support Services (thank you, Susanna Fix), and the daily support, both administrative and existential, that I receive from Noelle Adgerson have been invaluable. Several research assistants— Catherine Grealis, May Chiang, Carmen Green, Amy Deroo, Akhil Gola, and Andrew Warner—have labored mightily to save me from as much embarrassment as possible.

Georgetown University has been my academic home for three decades. It was my good fortune for many years to teach in the Department of English; it was a particular privilege to share the "duty" of teaching Milton with Jason Rosenblatt, whose generosity of spirit I have never known to falter. It is my good fortune today to work alongside Frances DeLaurentis, Craig Hoffman, and my other colleagues in the Legal Research and Writing program.

I am also happy to have this opportunity to thank my former colleagues William Craft and Robert Ducharme.

I am thoroughly beholden, of course, to those who have made the study of children and the law their scholarly calling. My debts to such pioneering scholars as Barbara Bennett Woodhouse, James Dwyer, and Elizabeth Bartholet will be, I trust, abundantly clear.

Finally, for their confidence in this work, I am profoundly grateful to William Frucht, executive editor at Yale University Press, and to Wendy Strothman, my agent.

Portions of this work, in different form, have appeared previously in *Journal of Law and Family Studies* 7 (2005): 317; *Villanova Law Review* 53 (2008): 173; *Penn State Law Review* 113 (2008): 381; *Nebraska Law Review* 89 (2010): 290; and *Charleston Law Review* 6 (2012): 385.

THE CONSTITUTIONAL PARENT

ONE

Sacred Trust or Sacred Right?

Some natural tears they dropp'd, but wip'd them soon;
The World was all before them, where to choose
Thir place of rest, and Providence thir guide:
They hand in hand with wand'ring steps and slow,
Through *Eden* took thir solitarie way.
        —*John Milton*, Paradise Lost

Edward Walker was a minor when, in 1838, he went to work at sea. Upon his return, his father, Joseph Walker, claimed Edward's wages for his own use. Joseph made what charitably might be called a private settlement with the owner of the *Etna*, the ship on which Edward had served. Edward disputed the settlement, claiming the wages as his own. The federal district court made note of the general proposition that a father was "entitled to the earnings of his child by virtue of his paternal power." On this ground, Joseph had the right to settle matters on such terms as pleased him. The general proposition, however, was not as legally dispositive as he would have hoped.[1]

The court distinguished between the rights and duties of a father. While a father's duties were "indissolubly attached to the paternal relation," the same could not be said of a father's rights. The rights of the father, according to the court, are given to him by the state to enable him to fulfill his parental duties ("to provide for his child a home, to protect, to maintain, and to educate him according to the measure of his ability"), and, as a more concrete compensation, the father is allowed "to take the fruits of his child's labor." But this paternal power is not a "sovereign and independent authority." It is not, to use the court's comparison, like the *patria potestas* enjoyed by the father in ancient Rome, "whose law held children to be the property of the father, and placed them in relation to him in the category of things instead of that of persons." This sovereign paternal authority, the court declared, "has never been admitted by the jurisprudence of any civilized people." Rather, the father holds only a contingent authority, "subject to the restraints and regulation of law," contingent because it is "inseparably connected with the parental obligations, and arises out of them." In short, paternal power rests on the fulfillment of paternal duty. Relying on a deep pool of legal theoreticians, treatise writers, and jurists, including "[t]he soundest and most esteemed commentators upon the common law," the court affirmed what, by the time of this dispute, was a well-settled legal precept: The power of the parent, because it derives directly from the duty to benefit the child, is limited in scope and duration. It is only as great as is needed to secure the child's welfare: "It is not a power granted to the parent for his benefit, but allowed to him for the benefit of the child, and it ceases when the faculties of the child have acquired that degree of maturity, that it may safely be trusted to its own resources. When, therefore, the parent abuses this power, or neglects to fulfil the obligations from which it results, he forfeits his rights."[2]

For, at bottom, the child does not belong to the parent. The court stressed that Edward, like all children, was endowed with a social nature and was destined for the enjoyment of a social life. As a member of what the court called "the human family," Edward was invested—endowed by birthright, as it were—with all the rights that belong to other members of this universal family. The court explained,

> The Creator of man, in giving to [the child] a social nature and endowing him with those qualities which fit him for the enjoyment of social life, has imposed upon the parent, as one of the conditions of his being, the obligation of providing for his offspring while they are incapable of taking care of themselves. But his children are not on that account born slaves. They do not become the property of the parent. As soon as a child is born, he

becomes a member of the human family, and is invested with all
the rights of humanity.

Thus, when the parent fails to fulfill his duty, when he fails to honor the
human rights and social nature of the child, the "protecting justice of the
country" will interpose and deprive him of his authority. The court was
"not aware of any doubt" that the state could take children from their parents and place them "under the care of persons proper to have the control
of them, and to superintend their education." Indeed, it was the legal and
moral responsibility of the court "to remove a guardian who is unfaithful to
his trust."[3]

It is commonly assumed, by academic and lay audiences alike, that parents have long enjoyed a fundamental legal right to control the upbringing
of their children, but this reading of the law is sorely incomplete and anach-
ronistic. Cases like that of Edward Walker suggest that if by "fundamental"
we designate rights with a deep historical pedigree, the right to parent free
from state interference cannot be numbered among them. What *is* deeply
rooted in our legal traditions and social conscience is the idea that the state
entrusts parents with custody of the child, and the concomitant rule that
the state does so only as long as parents meet their legal duty to take proper
care of the child. Whether custodial authority was called a power or a right,[4]
it was made contingent on the welfare of the child and the needs of the
state. "[T]he right of parents, in relation to the custody and services of their
children," Joseph Story wrote in 1816, "are rights *depending upon the mere
municipal rules of the state*, and may be enlarged, restrained, and limited as
the wisdom or policy of the times may dictate." Custodial authority, maintained the nineteenth-century libertarian treatise writer Christopher Tiedeman, "is not the natural right of the parents; it emanates from the State, and
is an exercise of police power."[5]

These assertions of the ordinariness of parental authority are not isolated
instances. Reviewing the case law of the nineteenth century, Lewis Hochheimer, whose treatise on the law of child custody was a familiar reference
for courts in the late nineteenth and early twentieth centuries, concluded
that "[t]he general result of the American cases may be characterized as

an utter repudiation of the notion, that there can be such a thing as a proprietary right of interest in or to the custody of an infant."[6] It is true of our legal past—as it is true today—that claims of right (natural and civil) were advanced in support of parental power.[7] But, as Hochheimer tells us, the prevailing legal current, driven by the equitable force of trust principles, swept away such "narrow contentions": "The entire tendency of the American courts is, to put aside with an unsparing hand all technical objections and narrow contentions whereby it may be attempted to erect claims of supposed legal right, on a foundation of wrong to persons who are a peculiar object of the solicitude and protecting care of the law."[8]

Traditionally, for both legal scholars and jurists the very word "trust" was something of a linguistic charm to ward away rights-thinking. For James Kent, the duty to provide for the maintenance and education of the child is "a sacred trust"; it is the "true foundation of parental power," the source of the authority that the law "*has given*" to parents. The parent is "absolutely bound" to serve the child. For Story, parents are only "entrusted with the custody of the persons and the education of their children" and only as long as they properly take care of the child. "Why," Story asks, "is the parent by law ordinarily entrusted with the care of his children?" His is a simple answer: "Simply, because it is generally supposed, that he will best execute the trust reposed in him; for, that it is a trust, and of all trusts the most sacred, no one can well doubt." For Hochheimer, proprietary principles were a legal remnant of an antiquated family law; in their place the law had substituted "the idea of trust as the controlling principle in all controversies in relation to such custody." "In true legal conception," he writes, "[the parent] is simply the agent or trustee of the government." For Tiedeman, "[t]he parent has no natural vested right to the control of the child"; parental control is "in the nature of a trust, reposed in [the parent] by the State . . . , which may be extended or contracted, according as the public welfare may require."[9] Likewise, and quite early in our juridical history, courts were equally committed to the word and the concept.[10] By the mid-nineteenth century the jurisdiction of the courts "to remove infant children from the custody of their parents, and to superintend their education and maintenance" was not only "well established" but also considered "indispensable to good order and the just protection of society." This jurisdiction "proceed[ed] upon the theory that the right of guardianship is a trust for the benefit of the child, and the parent is not at liberty to abuse it."[11]

On this basis, the *Etna* court was fully prepared to protect the interests of Edward Walker against the claims of his father. When parents fail "to fulfil the obligations from which [parental power] results," the court observed, the state—as *parens patriae*, as parent of the country—has a "deep interest" to ensure that its grant of authority is not abused.[12] Joseph Walker, it turned out, had not fulfilled the responsibility entrusted to him, and the court awarded Edward his just compensation.

Under a trust model of parent-child relations, biology does not beget rights. It begets responsibilities. The trust model is built on the Lockean principle that it is the child who has a fundamental right (what William Blackstone called a "perfect *right*"): the right to appropriate parental care, including the entitlement to an education that will prepare the child for eventual enfranchisement from parental authority. To Locke, the "right of *Tuition*" is "rather the Priviledge of Children, and Duty of Parents, than any Prerogative of Paternal Power."[13] (It is a noteworthy piece of American legal history that the child's entitlement to a proper education and the consequent affirmative duty of the state to provide a proper public schooling—a striking break with negative constitutionalism—have long been enshrined in our states' political charters.)[14] What biology begets is a duty to ensure the child's best interests. "The terms 'right' and 'claim,' when used in this connection [that is, the custody of children]," declared Hochheimer, "according to their proper meaning, virtually import the right or claim of the *child* to be in that custody or charge which will subserve *its* real interests."[15] In this connection, then, custodial authority is not a right at all. It is, Hochheimer tells us, "a grant of power flowing from the state, a portion of the state's protective care and guardianship."[16]

The idea that, historically, American law embodied a strict regime of parental rights is not easily dislodged. As formidable a scholar as Martha Fineman has written that, "[h]istorically, fathers were entitled to possession of their children. . . . In essence, fathers had an absolute right to their

5

children, 'owning' them as if they held 'title' to them."[17] Yet the American legal tradition is one that treated paternal absolutism and its rights foundation as barbaric.[18] "That the father had any such absolute right to the care and custody of his children," that the state lacked the authority to "control the conduct of the father in the education of his children"—these propositions, Story wrote, "would strike all civilized countries with astonishment."[19] This confident delimitation of the parent's "ordinary" rights is nowhere better seen than in child custody cases, where courts challenged, first, paternal authority and, then, parental control of the child generally. At common law the father was entitled to the value of his minor children's labor and services, a valuable asset, no doubt;[20] but he was entitled to the benefit of the child's labor "in order the better to discharge his duty."[21] Custody courts would not presume that, in fact, the parent was appropriately fulfilling the demands of his role; instead, they would "act according to sound discretion," consulting the child "if it be of sufficiently mature age to judge for itself."[22] Where the child was too young to choose for itself, it was a judicial commonplace that "the real interest of the child is the principle which must govern."[23] The parent retained custody of his—or, as the law evolved, her—minor children, but this privilege was granted on the presumption that parents act in the best interests of the child—and this was a rebuttable presumption. The parental entitlement was good only "so long as [the parent] discharges the obligation imposed upon him by social and civil law."[24] It is sometimes argued that the paramount right of the parent to direct his child's upbringing without state intervention, absent a showing of harm, was so basic as not to need express constitutional protection. In fact, what was so basic was parental obligation—"[T]he obligation of parental duty is so well secured by the strength of natural affection," as Kent wrote, "that it seldom requires to be enforced by human laws"[25]—and American custody courts, only too content to compare their law with the harsh and technical rules of the English cases, had little taste for a harm standard.[26]

Far from being absolute, the right of the parent was not even the custody courts' primary consideration. "The true view," as one mid-nineteenth-century court put it, "is that the rights of the child are alone to be considered, and those rights clearly are to be protected." The very idea that parents have rights *as parents* was called into question. The New York Court for the Correction of Errors was not alone when it declared that "there is no parental authority independent of the supreme power of the state. But the former is derived altogether from the latter." If parental authority is derived from the state, the parent does not obtain rights merely by virtue of being a parent. "It is an entire mistake," Story concluded, "to suppose the court is at all events bound to deliver over the infant to his father, or that the latter has an absolute vested right in the custody." Similarly, the Supreme Court of Pennsylvania: "[T]he right of parental control is a natural, but not an unalienable one."[27]

Rather, the parent obtains authority, however it is styled, over the child by virtue of *acting as a parent*. Indeed, it is the child's entitlement—the child's right "to be surrounded by such influences as will best promote its physical, mental, and moral development"—that was thought to be in the way of a natural vested right. In contrast, the right of the parent "to surround the child with proper influences [was] of a governmental nature," in the sense that parental authority over the child was considered a benefit granted by the state in return for parental care of the child.[28] This benefit was subject to the principle—again, the debt is to Locke—that what is due the child is defined, in a general sense, by basic developmental needs and, more particularly, by the developmental needs of the child destined from birth to be a member of a liberal constitutional order. Accordingly, the metes and bounds of parental duty were not considered a matter solely for private determination. (Nor, for that matter, were the legal parameters of filial duty.)[29] Parents in a liberal society, it was assumed, have no right to parent as they see fit.

In the law, there are rights and then there are rights. Not all rights are created equal. Most laws or other forms of state action receive a deferential review from the courts, despite the fact that they might impinge upon a host of personal prerogatives. Under rational basis review, courts presume the constitutionality of legislation. The party trying to overcome this presumption must show (1) that the law serves no legitimate purpose or (2) that the means employed by the law has no rational relation to the law's stated goal.

7

But laws or other forms of state action that impinge upon rights considered to be fundamental get a far more skeptical judicial reception. Under a strict scrutiny standard, courts will presume that such a law is unconstitutional. To overcome this presumption, the government must show (1) that the law serves a compelling purpose and (2) that the means employed by the law are as narrowly tailored as possible to achieve the law's stated goal. Because the hurdle of strict scrutiny is so difficult to clear ("strict in theory and fatal in fact," it is commonly, if not entirely accurately, said), the level of review employed by the court can easily dictate the outcome of a case.[30] So it is a high-stakes determination whether a right is fundamental or not.

The right to parent would be considered an unenumerated right, implicitly protected by the Fifth and Fourteenth Amendments of the United States Constitution (and, both before and after the passage of the Fourteenth Amendment, by state constitutional analogues).[31] The "liberty" of the Due Process Clauses safeguards those substantive rights "'so rooted in the traditions and conscience of our people as to be ranked as fundamental.'" These are rights, like the enumerated freedom of speech, that are considered "of the very essence of a scheme of ordered liberty."[32] Inevitably, whether an unenumerated right is so rooted and so essential will be a contested, and probably fiercely contested, question. Inevitably, this is a query with both descriptive and normative dimensions. Has the right to parent traditionally been treated as fundamental? Should the right to parent be treated as fundamental? This book answers no to both questions.

The right to parent as a matter of constitutional law is especially tenuous. The Supreme Court has echoed the popular assumption that the right of parents to make decisions concerning the care, custody, and nurture of their children is a fundamental one, time-honored ("perhaps the oldest of the fundamental liberty interests recognized by this Court") and honored by the work of the Court ("[W]e have recognized the fundamental right of parents to make decisions concerning the care, custody, and control of their children").[33] But no Supreme Court holding supports this claim. No decision, including the case that is the source of the far-reaching assertions just parenthetically quoted, has held that the right of parents to make decisions concerning the care of their children is a fundamental one. If the rigor of the Court with regard to the regulation of parental authority has varied,[34] its scrutiny has never been strict. In fact, as Justice Antonin Scalia has observed, there is little decisional support for the notion that the right to parent is a "substantive constitutional right" at all, let alone a fundamental one.[35] More than once, the Court has declined the opportunity to adopt this position.[36]

In 1923, in *Meyer v. Nebraska*, the Court struck down a Nebraska law that prohibited both the use of foreign languages as a medium of instruction and the study of foreign languages before the eighth grade. These restrictions applied to any school, public or private. In 1925, in *Pierce v. Society of Sisters*, the Court struck down Oregon's Compulsory Education Act, which required attendance at public schools. Neither case was really brought to the Court as, primarily, a matter of parental rights—a litigation choice that itself should call into question the well-rootedness of such rights; nonetheless, in both cases the Court concluded that, under the Due Process Clause of the Fourteenth Amendment, the state laws unreasonably interfered with the liberty of parents to direct the upbringing and education of their children.[37]

But *Meyer* and *Pierce* both accept as uncontroversial the principle that the state can define and enforce the parental duty to educate. The *Meyer* Court did not question the authority of the state "to compel attendance at some school and to make reasonable regulations for all schools, including a requirement that they shall give instructions in English."[38] Here, the Court reviewed a law that "sought not to require what children must learn in schools, but to prescribe, in the first case, what they must not learn."[39] The question *Meyer* considers is how far the state can go in dictating what *the parent* can and cannot do.[40] The Court answered that the state may not set up a standard of education and then prohibit any additional or supplemental instruction. If there is a fundamental right at stake in *Meyer*, it is the right of the parent, "after he has complied with all proper requirements by the state as to education, to give his child such further education in proper subjects as he desires and can afford."[41] In *Pierce*, the Court pointedly noted that the case raised no question "concerning the power of the state reasonably to regulate all schools," a power that included a very substantial measure of curricular control ("that certain studies plainly essential to good citizenship must be taught, and that nothing be taught which is manifestly inimical to the public welfare").[42] If there is a fundamental right at stake in *Pierce*, it is the right of the parent "to provide an *equivalent* education in a privately operated system."[43] Broad claims are made for the legacy of these seminal due process cases,[44] but, as Justice Byron White put it, *Meyer* and *Pierce* "lend[] no support to the contention that parents may replace state educational requirements with their own idiosyncratic views of what knowledge a child needs to be a productive and happy member of society."[45]

Meyer and *Pierce* were as much about rhetorical reach as legal doctrine. Their anti-statist sentiment would serve as a constitutional banner for those marching in support of parental rights. That the Court's support of a right to parent was the product of judicial activism at its most active—indeed, the product of a "modern" jurisprudence (built on "more correct ideas" and "a truer conception" of the proper functions of government) that would, in a self-conscious break with legal tradition, set the stage for a new era of unenumerated privacy rights—did not (and does not) deter conservative advocates of parental rights from celebrating the cases that rested on this due process basis.[46] That this right was the product of a *Lochner*-era constitutionalism bent on restricting the police powers of the state—indeed, the product of a narrow, natural law individualism (built on the rejection of a centuries-old common law legacy of "paternal government") that would strike down basic health and safety regulations—did not (and does not) much bother liberal proponents of the right to parent. To parental advocates on both sides of the political spectrum, the prerogatives of parenting apparently ease concern about doctrinal consistency.[47]

Meyer and *Pierce* involved only the general interest of parents in the nurture and education of their children. Where nothing more is at stake, the Court has said, the state's authority outweighs due process objections. Often, though, more is at stake. Legal claims based on the right to parent often come packaged with claims based on other constitutional protections, most frequently and forcefully the Free Exercise Clause. Today, religious parenting rights enjoy a special constitutional protection from state regulation. State action that burdens religious parenting *is* subject to heightened judicial scrutiny.

Why are restrictions on religious parenting rights subject to heightened judicial review? The obvious answer is that the right of religious freedom is considered fundamental, but this is only partially correct. The Supreme Court has said that state action restricting religious practice is constitutionally permissible unless such action directly targets religious practice or discriminates against religious groups. This is the core principle—a controversial one, to be sure—of *Employment Division, Department of Human Resources of Oregon v. Smith*. Decided in 1990, *Smith* held that where state regulation burdens religious freedom only incidentally—that is, where the burden is the incidental effect of regulation that is neutral and generally applicable, restricting secular and religious activity alike—the courts will presume its constitutionality.[48] Thus, for example, a law that makes illegal the use of peyote because of safety and health concerns would be subject to and would survive rational basis review, even though it burdened the beliefs and perhaps effectively prohibited the practices of some religious groups.

Separately, then, neither the right to parent nor the right of religious freedom would trigger strict scrutiny. Combined, however, these rights form a tough legal firewall that protects parents from state interference in the religious upbringing of their children. For the Court has also said that when the interests of parenthood are combined with a free exercise claim, "more than merely a 'reasonable relation to some purpose within the competency of the State' is required to sustain the validity of the State's requirement under the First Amendment."[49] This is the core principle, also a controversial one, of *Wisconsin v. Yoder*. Though *Yoder* was decided in 1972, its invention of a hybrid parenting/free exercise claim survived *Smith*, as did other variations on the hybrid rights theme. So, even after *Smith*, the First Amendment does require heightened scrutiny for claims that involve "not the Free Exercise Clause alone, but the Free Exercise Clause in conjunction with other constitutional protections," such as the right of parents to direct the upbringing and education of their children. In religious parenting cases, by some abstruse constitutional calculation, strict scrutiny becomes the norm, despite the fact that state action does not target religion or impinge upon a fundamental right. Under a strict scrutiny standard, courts will uphold state regulation of religious parenting only where "it appears that parental decisions will jeopardize the health or safety of the child, or have a potential for significant social burdens."[50] Thus, a law that requires parents to send their children to some form of secondary schooling would be subject to and might not survive strict scrutiny if the parents' objections to the compulsory education requirement are religiously motivated.

Writing for the Court in *Smith*, Justice Scalia cautioned that our society would be courting anarchy if every law or regulation of conduct that negatively affected someone's religious belief had to be supported by a compelling state interest. To excuse conduct contrary to a general law "'would be to make the professed doctrines of religious belief superior to the law of the land, and in effect to permit every citizen to become a law unto himself.'"[51] Accordingly, the *Smith* Court discussed hybrid rights as an exception to general constitutional principles. Yet in the universe of religious parenting cases, the exception swallows the rule; because such cases are hybrid by definition, strict scrutiny becomes the norm. The result, if hardly anarchy, is the creation of a separate sphere of the law—a constitutional anomaly, as Scalia described it—where the government's ability to protect children *is* subject to an individual parent's religious beliefs. (Unable to escape this unacceptable conclusion, the *Yoder* Court made a fainthearted attempt to limit its holding to the specific and peculiar facts of the case before it.)[52]

If *Yoder* delivered a special right to religious parents, it did so at some cost to the parentalist cause. (I take the term "parentalist" from the strongly argued essay by Stephen Gilles titled "On Educating Children: A Parentalist Manifesto."[53] I use the term broadly to designate those who advocate a legal and moral regime of considerable deference to parental rights.) For the Court's decision means that the right to parent, by itself, does not enjoy a fundamental status, at least where state regulation of education is concerned. Only where the legal question involves the absolute termination of parental rights has the Supreme Court required that state action (specifically, a declaration of parental unfitness) meet the tough test of justification associated with strict scrutiny[54]—though even here, as David Meyer has pointed out, the balancing of interests undertaken by the Court "is difficult to square neatly with the traditional strict-scrutiny formula."[55] In

2000, the Court had the opportunity to give parental rights a constitutional upgrade. In *Troxel v. Granville*, the Court considered whether a parent has the right to deny visitation rights to a child's grandparents.[56] The decision badly disappointed those hoping for a fundamental rights victory. Though the Court used the language of fundamental rights, it did not conclude that strict scrutiny was the proper standard of review, settling instead for a mere presumption in favor of a fit parent's visitation choices.

With the Court speaking in uncertain tones, lower courts must contend with the fact that "the Supreme Court has yet to decide whether the right to direct the upbringing and education of one's children is among those fundamental rights whose infringement merits heightened scrutiny."[57] Protection for parenting rights varies from jurisdiction to jurisdiction and from claim to claim;[58] and courts have more than enough leeway to decide the merits of a case by choosing whether to apply a standard based on the best interests of the child (rational basis review) or a strict scrutiny harm standard.[59] Given this state of affairs, it is not surprising that some parental rights advocates seek to amend the United States Constitution. The Parental Rights Amendment would declare that "[t]he liberty of parents to direct the upbringing and education of their children is a fundamental right," and, consequently, that strict scrutiny would be the standard of review in cases of alleged infringement.[60]

There are good reasons why the right to parent has not enjoyed a fundamental status in the law. To begin with, the right to parent is not one but many things, a bundle of different interests, each implicating the authority of parent and state in different ways and to different degrees. No surprise, then, that "[f]ar from the absolutist's assumption of strict scrutiny for every incursion, the Court's cases reveal a willingness, at least implicitly, to tailor the nature and strength of judicial scrutiny to the facts of each family privacy controversy." Yet all parental rights cases have one thing in common that even more emphatically cautions against strict scrutiny: They involve a third party, and one who is unable to defend its own interests. Other liberty interests establish a constitutional shield against governmental impairment of individual rights, but conflicts involving parental rights—Justice John

Paul Stevens made this important if, one would think, self-evident point—
"do not present a bipolar struggle between the parents and the State over
who has final authority to determine what is in a child's best interests."[61]
The interests of the child—who may well need the protection *of* the state,
not protection *from* the state—and the state's interest in the child invariably
affect the legal reckoning.

By its very nature, the supposed right to parent is a different creature
from, say, the right of free speech. No one is required to speak responsibly.
No one is required to speak at all. Yet would anyone object to the proposition that parents are required to exercise the right to parent responsibly? Or
that a parent has no right not to parent?[62] By definition, then, the parent's
right to be let alone, to parent free from governmental interference, is and
must be conditional and limited.[63] Far from carrying with it a fundamental
right, the decision to parent is inevitably a choice to forego rights otherwise
available to adults. It is always a choice to give up to some extent, and often
to a great extent, the right of individual choosing. There are compelling reasons why parents want to assume the weighty burden of child rearing, and
there are good reasons why the state wants to give parents plenty of room
to do their job; but parental authority over the child is not justified, not in
our legal tradition and culture, by the proprietary interests of the parent as
a rights-holder.

Obviously, not every break with the past is a bad thing; and, as Martha
Minow reminds us, the case against rights can too easily be "levied by people
who do not want to change existing patterns of hierarchy and domination."[64]
Just as clearly, and our history unhappily bears more than sufficient testimony to this fact, the parens patriae authority of the state can be badly
abused. To say that a parental rights orientation is not deeply rooted in our
traditions, even to say that parental rights as a normative matter *should* not
be considered fundamental, is not to declare that a particular policy decision is right or wrong. It is simply to say that it *is* a question of policy whether
and how the state should regulate parent-child relations. Should we allow,
say, parents to homeschool their children? Is homeschooling in the best interests of the child? Perhaps, perhaps not. Should we allow parents to spank
their children? to compel religious observance, against the wishes of the

child or against the wishes of a former spouse? to restrict visitation from third parties? The questions are as varied as the myriad duties parents undertake. If we think of parenting as a set of responsibilities, not rights, we will not all miraculously reach the same legal and cultural prescriptions — fiduciary principles do not inexorably lead in an antiparentalist direction;[65] individually, the prescriptions we reach may not always fall into neat ideological (conservative or liberal) categories — but we will think of these questions as matters fit for democratic deliberation. To say that a parental rights orientation is not deeply rooted in our traditions is not to answer these questions. It is to ask them. But by giving parents the right to homeschool children or compel religious observance or restrict third-party visitation — or, more generally speaking, by giving parents the right to bring up their children as they want to — parental rights advocates would forestall public debate on contentious questions relating to the care and welfare of children. They would take these questions out of the public domain by keeping the home under constitutional lock and key.[66] The question would no longer be one of the child's welfare but of parental entitlement.

This book looks at four related areas of the law: parental custody, state regulation of education, religion and parental rights, and nonparental third-party rights. In each,

1. historically, the authority of the parent has been treated as a sacred trust, a delegation of state power made on the presumption that it will be employed to promote the eventual enfranchisement of the child (this is the subject of chapter 2);

2. the emergence of a rights orientation has threatened to uncouple the traditional linkage of rights and responsibilities, subordinating the best interests of the child and the legitimate needs of the state to parental preferences (this is the subject of chapter 3); and

3. a renewed reliance on the trust model of parent-child relations would better serve both the developing personhood of the child and the civil society to which he or she belongs (this is the subject of chapter 4).

In each area of the law, we face the same historical reality: It is the rights orientation that breaks with deeply rooted legal traditions and cultural values, rejecting time-honored trust principles of family law meant to protect both private and public interests. For the common law's careful calculation of privileges and duties; for its vision of children's needs as a source of positive claims on the state; for its sensitivity to evolving cultural mores—a focus on parental entitlement substitutes a negative rights wall behind which parents may bring up their children free from both state and nonstate interference. In this way, the "presentist" assumption that parental rights were always thus creates the entitlement mistakenly assumed to be a long-standing legal legacy. If we better understand that, as a descriptive matter, the right to parent is at odds with a cultural tradition of shared responsibility for the welfare of the child, we might be more ready to ask whether, as a normative matter, the right to parent should have a fundamental status in the law. We might be more willing to consider how old equitable principles can lead to new ways of accommodating the interests of parent, child, and state.[67]

On occasion the Supreme Court has put the trust model to productive use. In adjudicating the due process claims of unmarried fathers, for example, the Court has said that the rights of parents "are a counterpart of the responsibilities they have assumed."[68] This linkage of right and duty, according to the Court, is the true legacy of its seminal due process parenting cases. Constitutional parenthood embraces the Lockean principle that "[c]hildren are born to reason," and the law of nature commands a parental duty to secure for them "that *equal Right* that every man hath to his Natural Freedom, *without being subjected to the Will or Authority of any other Man.*"[69] On this commitment to the child's self-determination is predicated the Founders' theory of human dignity and, of particular salience for parent-child relations, the parallel theory of human development—the normative psychology of the law, we might say—that, taken together, sustain the Constitution's promise of personal as well as political freedom.[70] It is the carrying out of this commitment that defines the trust assumed by parents and against which parental efforts must be constitutionally measured and rewarded. Our political charter does not allow for "a utopian conception of society according to which an order having been laid down all that remains to do is to conform to it," in or outside the home.[71]

"Parental rights do not spring full-blown from the biological connection between parent and child," Justice Potter Stewart has said. "They require relationships more enduring."[72] But it is not every enduring parent-child relationship that merits constitutional protection. If this were the case, then compulsory schooling laws would fail against constitutional challenges brought by caring parents. Yet few would disagree that all parents are obligated to look after the educational welfare of their children. It is the trust model of parent-child relations that directs us to the particular charge that is the sine qua non of parental power: to secure the child's "equal Right" to intellectual and moral autonomy (Locke's "Natural Freedom"); or, more simply, to see that children, when they become adults, can choose what life they want to lead, what values they want to honor, what god they want to worship.

This duty presupposes that the child is free to form relationships with those outside the circle of the nuclear family. Hovering over the right to parent is the long-lingering shadow of a property entitlement. Today, the right to parent is fashioned as a right to personal autonomy, a right of privacy; yet it remains, essentially, a right to do what one wants with what is "mine." But if the child, at birth, "becomes a member of the human family," then parents are not free to seclude the child from outside influence. "If we ask ourselves what actually enables people to be autonomous," Jennifer Nedelsky writes, "the answer is not isolation, but relationships—with parents, teachers, friends, loved ones—that provide the support and guidance necessary for the development and experience of autonomy." Thus, our children are not and cannot be "ours," at least not exclusively, not permanently.[73] (We ought to be as careful as Shakespeare with possessive pronouns. When Helena awakes from her tumultuous midsummer night's "dream," she finds Demetrius "like a jewel,/Mine own, and not mine own.")[74] From birth, children are members of a familial community outside and beyond the nuclear family; from birth, they are members of a political community outside and beyond the family. It is only by belonging that children can learn, by and for themselves, where they want to belong.

A trust model of parenting, with its assumption of shared authority over the child, need not evoke the specter of state paternalism. With regard to the child's upbringing, the state also is and also must remain merely an educational trustee. The liberal state holds what Locke calls a "Fiduciary Power to act for certain ends."[75] Like the parent's authority, the state's power over the child is conditional and limited. Ideally, the state, like the ideal parent, would cultivate the child's capacity to think and choose freely; it would foster the child's courage to challenge any closed set of values, public or private, liberal or conservative. The liberal state wants to pass on its traditions of freedom, equality, and tolerance, and no doubt the state, like real parents, can behave less than liberally toward its young people; but the surest way not to pass on these traditions would be to present them as moral absolutes to be accepted uncritically.[76]

For children, though, the threat to freedom of choice and conscience is no less grave when it comes from private orthodoxies, and the injury to the child caused by private coercion is no less grievous. In *Meyer* and *Pierce*, the Court feared that the state, through a regime of mandatory public education, would "standardize its children."[77] Yet children sent to private schools or those kept at home might more easily suffer this fate. We are well cautioned by the pioneering scholar and children's advocate Barbara Bennett Woodhouse that "[s]tamped on the reverse side of this coinage of family privacy and parental rights are the child's voicelessness, objectification, and isolation from the community."[78] For this reason, courts should look skeptically at any educational scheme that seeks to restrict "the right to receive information and ideas."[79] The realm of intellect and spirit is invaded when children are forced to believe what other people believe, or kept from believing what other people do not believe, even if—and, perhaps, especially when—these others are their parents or educational and religious mentors. Thus, if we are not "to strangle the free mind at its source," the state's parens patriae duty must "cut[] against the differential regulation of public and private schools."[80] All children are entitled to an education that is, in the fullest sense, public: that transports them beyond familiar boundaries; that provides a check on the narcissism of their guardians, both public and private; that burdens them with the necessity of moral judgment; and that, finally, makes them truly free, free to stand and free to fall. A public education is the portal by which children find a place or places on "the great sphere" that is their world and legacy.[81] It is their means of escape from or free commitment to the social group to which they were born. It is their best guarantee of an open future.[82]

On this basis, the courts should refuse to allow parents to opt out of state-mandated educational requirements they consider morally objectionable. On this basis, too, the courts should not allow parents to make the public school classroom a forum for their personal religious agenda. Yet if the classroom really is, as the Supreme Court has said, "peculiarly the 'marketplace of ideas,'" the voices of religious children must be allowed to be heard, too.[83] The educational market is a poorer place when school officials cleanse the classroom of religious references or deny children freedom of religious expression. To this end, the study of religion should be a regular part of a common curriculum. The public school classroom at every level should be a forum where students are exposed to diverse viewpoints, secular and religious. The idea that students benefit from exposure to otherness makes sense only if this benefit flows in all directions.

A truly public education may well divide child from parent. We should be entirely forthright and unapologetic about this. The state as educator is no ideologically neutral actor.[84] The philosophical foundations supporting a public education are the liberal biases of our nation's intellectual forebearers, biases in favor of a nonauthoritarian approach to truth, of free argument and debate—what Thomas Jefferson called truth's "natural weapons"—and of a healthy sense of human fallibility.[85] The open world of public schooling should be a place where children use these "weapons" to think about values, whether those values belong to parent or state, or to the "omnivorous peer-culture," or to the cultural oligarchs of the marketplace and the media.[86] We should admit as well that these biases will be more compatible with the beliefs of some religious groups than others.[87] Still, it would be a misrepresentation of trust principles to associate them with antireligiosity. Indeed, a commitment to the child's open future may be the best guarantee of a society with rich and robust religious traditions. Children are natural religious seekers. (Recently, there has been talk of a religious generation gap, or, perhaps better put, a reverse religious generation gap, with children choosing lives of faith, much to the concern, if not dismay, of their more secular-minded parents.)[88] As young adults, some will choose new spiritual paths and some will choose to abandon religious ways altogether, but many, if not most, will find their faith in traditional places, arriving where they started and perhaps knowing the place for the first time.[89] For religious freedom to flourish, however, these choices must be genuine ones, based on knowledge and experience gathered, as it were, out of a multitude of tongues. For the child's sake, for its own sake, the state that protects the freedom of adults to choose a religious or a nonreligious path must also ensure that the freedom of children to choose their path will not be taken from them. Like adults, children must be free to seek as well as to find a spiritual home.

The Constitution's guarantee of personal freedoms is meaningful only if we, as parents, accept the responsibilities from which parental authority arises, and the constitutional strength of parenting privileges should depend on our willingness to do so. The real question is whether parenting furthers the prospective independence of the child. No doubt, there are many ways to achieve this goal. Treating parental authority as a trust does not mean denying parents the opportunity, in the words of the political theorist William Galston, to introduce their children "to what they regard as vital sources of meaning and value."[90] It does mean that parents may not deny their children the opportunity to be introduced to new sources of meaning and value; it does mean that parents may not as a matter of right refuse to share authority for the upbringing of their children. There is, after all, more than one form of unlimited government to which children are vulnerable, and Justice Stevens is certainly correct to caution that "[t]he constitutional protection against arbitrary state interference with parental rights should not be extended to prevent the States from protecting children against the arbitrary exercise of parental authority that is not in fact motivated by an interest in the welfare of the child."[91]

The trust model of parent-child relations heeds this admonitory note. In their consideration of parenting claims, courts ought not to treat the legal question as one of parental rights divorced from parental duties.[92] Our legal traditions teach that parenthood is first and foremost a responsibility, a fiduciary duty owed equally to the child and the state. This time-honored tenet has great room for play in modern times.[93] If allowed to, the form this responsibility takes will evolve, for our understanding of children's best interests—indeed, our very conception of childhood—evolves. Our duty to the child, however, will remain unchanged.

Like a doctrinal will-o'-the-wisp, the fundamental right to parent continues to beckon constitutional travelers. It is a pursuit driven more by psychology than law. The rhetoric of parental rights speaks to a yearning for control, for possession of something that is "mine."[94] It evokes some Edenic time when parents, by right, could tell the state to mind its own business. It evokes some Edenic place where parents, by right, could command obedience from their children. But there never was such a time and place, certainly not in the law. In *Meyer*, the attorney Arthur Mullen stood before the Supreme Court to denounce the power of the state "to take the child from the parent." No state, Mullen argued, should "prescribe the mental bill of fare" the child will follow.[95] His argument supposes that by legal tradition the child is the parent's to begin with, that the parent can prescribe the child's mental bill of fare. To the contrary, trust principles of parenting testify to the "moral fact that a person belongs to himself and not to others nor to society as a whole."[96]

Though John Milton protested prepublication censorship, Milton's God was less troubled by restrictions on the spectrum of available knowledge. When God's children disobey his sole commandment—a commandment, interestingly enough, that would deny Adam and Eve the knowledge of good and evil—they are cast out of their childhood home and sentenced to death for their disobedience. In Milton's telling, their fall, it turns out, is a fortunate one, their disobedience a prerequisite to "[a] Paradise within . . . , happier far."[97] The law of parent-child relations has long embodied a similar belief that education (a "leading away from") is the path away from childhood and toward intellectual and moral enfranchisement. Unless children are to live under "a perpetual childhood of prescription," unless we are to deny them the pursuit of happiness, perhaps in the fond hope of providing happiness, they must be exposed to the dust and heat of the race, intellectually, morally, spiritually.[98]

With all its attendant joys, parenting is a somber task, for it entails, in a profound and poignant way, the loss of the child. It is the parent's task—it is a political as well as a personal obligation—to enable each child to form his or her own self-image rather than merely to conform to some parental likeness. If we could, we might shield our children from the sufferings that accompany individuation. If we could, we might shield ourselves from the pain that accompanies the child's separation from our hands. Is it any wonder that we would want to transform the sacred trust of parenthood into a sacred right? But such a right comes at too great a cost. When Adam and Eve leave Paradise, as Milton recounts the story, they shed some natural tears, but "the World was all before them," as it should be for all children as they enter on the path to adulthood.

TWO

Parenting as a Sacred Trust

Who owns the child? If the parent owns him—mind, body, and
soul—we must adopt one line of argument; if, as a free-will human
being, he owns himself, we must adopt another. In my thought,
the parent is simply a divinely appointed guardian; who acts for
his child until he attains what we call the age of discretion.
—*Kate Douglas Wiggin (1892)*

Doctrinal Beginnings and Byways: Who Owns the Child?

John Locke and the Scepterless Parent

In his *Second Treatise of Government* (1689), John Locke begins his discussion of paternal power (chapter 6) by reminding his readers that "the Power of Parents over their children" does not exist "wholly in the *Father*."[1] The mother, he states, has an equal share in this power, and so this authority ought not to be thought of as naturally paternal. It is "more properly called *Parental Power*."[2] It is a useful reminder, so Locke thought, that we often use names and words carelessly and that adhering to language merely because it has obtained currency is an easy way to lead ourselves into gross mistakes. In this instance, we might forget that the obligations of parenthood bind father and mother equally.

Locke's real interest lies well beyond the distinction between paternal and parental power. His business is more radical, though distinguishing the power of the father from the power of the parent would be consequential enough. It is to demonstrate the difference between parental power and parental right. Striking at the heart of Sir Robert Filmer's defense of hereditary and absolute patriarchalism in government,[3] this distinction rests on the premise that "there can be no reason, why naturally one Man should have any claim or pretence of Right over that in another." If, for Filmer, the prerogative of kings derives from Adam's sovereignty over his own children, from, that is, a *"Right of Fatherhood"* passed down from the first to succeeding patriarchs; if, for Filmer, the *"Fountain of all Regal Authority"* is the subjection of children to generation after generation of fathers, then Locke's critique of parental power as some form of hereditary entitlement attacks the justification for absolute monarchy at its familial root.[4]

In Locke's view, the fact that the mother enjoys an equal share in parental authority is evidence that such power is not absolute. The power of parents bears the name of "Absolute Dominion, and Regal Authority" because we forget that that power is not wholly appropriated to the father. The assertion of parental absolutism, Locke observes, would sound odd "if this supposed Absolute Power over Children had been called *Parental*, and thereby have discover'd, that it belong'd to the *Mother* too."[5] Shared power, the argument runs, is poor support for a regime of unchecked domestic authority.

Whatever the scope of parental power, Locke contends that neither parent gains domestic authority merely by begetting a child. Against the argument that biology conveys rights, Locke responds with a preemptive existential foray, making an ultimate religious claim to deny derivative claims to parental prerogatives: "They who say the *Father* gives Life to his Children are so dazled with the thoughts of Monarchy, that they do not, as they ought, remember God, who is *the Author and Giver of Life: 'Tis in him alone we live, move, and have our Being.*" It is the "All-wise Contriver" who makes a living creature. It is the Contriver who has "so visible a claim to us as his Workmanship" that his fatherhood "utterly excludes all pretence of Title in Earthly Parents" (and thus all pretense of title in earthly monarchs), "for he is *King* because he is indeed Maker of us all, which no Parents can pretend to be of their Children." Our sons and daughters are given to us by God, but there can be only one Patriarch who holds good title to them.[6]

Though, from the standpoint "[t]*hat all Men by Nature are equal*," there can be no reason why "naturally one Man should have any claim or pretence of Right over that in another," Locke is not so unworldly as to assert that children are born in a full state of equality. Because they are not,

"Parents have a sort of Rule and Jurisdiction over them when they come into the World, and for some time after." Children, Locke writes, are born without the use of reason. In opposition to Filmer, Locke views this "imperfect state" as the true source of parental authority. The law of nature does not command filial obedience absolutely, without regard to the state of the child's knowledge or understanding.[7]

But if not born in a state of equality, children "are born to it." The state of full equality is every child's birthright, and so the rule of the parent is "but a temporary one": "The Bonds of [the child's] Subjection are like the Swadling Cloths they are wrapt up in, and supported by, in the weakness of their Infancy. Age and Reason, as they grow up, loosen them till at length they drop quite off, and leave a Man at his own free Disposal."[8] Because children are born to reason, the law of nature commands the parental duty to secure for them "that *equal Right* that every man hath, *to his Natural Freedom,* without being subjected to the Will or Authority of any other Man." Parents are obligated to supply the defects of the child's imperfect state; they are duty-bound to bring children to the state of reason that is every child's birthright. It is the Maker who has entrusted parents with the responsibility to teach children how to govern their actions "according to the Dictates of the Law of Reason which God has implanted in [them]." It is to the Maker of these children that parents will be held accountable: "*Adam* and *Eve,* and after them all *Parents* were, by the Law of Nature, *under an obligation to preserve, nourish, and educate the Children,* they had begotten, not as their own Workmanship, but the Workmanship of their own Maker, the Almighty, to whom they were to be accountable for them."[9]

Thus, it is education, not generation, that justifies parental authority.[10] The power that parents have "arises from that Duty which is incumbent on them, to take care of their Off-spring, during the imperfect state of Childhood." Parental power allows for the fulfillment of parental duty, and, accordingly, its scope is defined by that duty: It reaches "no farther" than necessary to satisfy that duty. In this regard, parental power is like governmental power, which is "only a Fiduciary Power to act for certain ends." Properly speaking, then, parental authority is not a right at all; the right of "tuition" belongs to the child, not to the parent:

The subjection of a Minor places in the Father a temporary Government, which terminates with the minority of the Child: and the *honour due from a Child*, places in the Parents a perpetual right to respect, reverence, support and compliance too, more or less, as the Father's care, cost and kindness in his Education, has been more or less. . . . The want of distinguishing these two powers; viz. that which the Father hath in the right of *Tuition*, during Minority, and the right of *Honour* all his Life, may perhaps have caused a great part of the mistakes about this matter. For to speak properly of them, the first of these is rather the Priviledge of Children, and Duty of Parents, than any Prerogative of Paternal Power. The Nourishment and Education of their Children, is a charge so incumbent on Parents for their Childrens good, that nothing can absolve them from taking care of it.

Indeed, the prerogative of paternal power is so far from a natural right that its continuation depends on how well the parent serves the child: "Nay, this *power* so little belongs to the *Father* by any peculiar right of Nature, but only as he is Guardian of his Children, that when he quits his Care of them, he loses his power over them, which goes along with their Nourishment and Education, to which it is inseparably annexed." The authority of our governors, both parental and political, is "*Power given with trust* for the attaining an *end*, being limited by that end," and when this end is neglected or opposed, "the *trust* must necessarily be *forfeited*." That the power of the parent may be transferred, in which case "it belongs as much to the *Foster-Father* of an exposed child, as to the Natural Father of another," is testimony to how "little power . . . the bare *act of begetting* give[s] a Man over his Issue."[11]

It is discretion that "leave[s] a Man at his own free Disposal." In due time the child will develop "an Understanding to direct his actions," and once arrived at a state of reason the child is enfranchised. "[W]hen he comes to the Estate that made his *Father a Freeman*," Locke says, "the *Son is a Freeman* too." The "*Father's Empire* then ceases," and the child is free "to dispose of his Actions and Possessions according to his own Will." For Locke, this liberty is entirely consonant with the "Law of Reason" and the laws that reasonable men enact so as to be "free from restraint and violence from others." This freedom is not unbounded license but is grounded in reason, "which is able to instruct [man] in that Law he is to govern himself by, and make him know how far he is left to the freedom of his own will." In a state of maturity, the child has come "to know that Law, that so he might keep his Actions within the Bounds of it." The adult child is self-governing, equally free with other adults from the dominion of the patriarch and equally subject with other adults to the dominion of the law.[12]

Locke concedes that in the first ages of the world it was easy for a familial jurisdiction to become a political one, that is, "for the *Father of the Family* to become the Prince of it." But this "resigning up to [the father] a Monarchical Power" was "by the express or tacit Consent of the Children, when they were grown up," not, he insists, "by any *Paternal Right*." In this way, the foundation for hereditary kingdoms was laid: as a matter of custom, chance, contrivance, or constitutional law, but not as a reflection "of the natural *Right of Fathers* to Political Authority." It is also true that children have an obligation to honor their parents, but, Locke insists, "this is very far from giving Parents a power of command over their Children, or an Authority to make Laws and dispose as they please, of their Lives or Liberties." It is one thing "to owe honour, respect, gratitude and assistance" and quite another "to require an absolute obedience and submission." Filial gratitude "puts no Sceptre into the Father's hand."[13]

It was critically important for Locke to establish that parents do not have a right to govern their children and most certainly not a right to govern their children as they see fit, a right, that is, to "dispose as they please"[14]— important not only to undermine Filmer's patriarchal genealogy (the first treatise) but to prepare the ground for a consensual theory of political power (the second treatise). Far from being free to do what they like, parents bear an absolute obligation ("nothing can absolve them") to guide the child to the "*Understanding* of his own to direct his *Will*." This obligation is not merely a personal one; it is a debt each parent owes to society to ensure that no one is "subjected to the Political Power of another, without his own *Consent*." In Locke's view, the parent ought to be a bulwark against the kind of authority that Filmer would have the parent/monarch personify. If the child is destined to be a freeman, then he must be provided with an education befitting a freeman.[15]

In this respect, Locke's feud with Filmer is more than a matter of political philosophy. In defining parental power as a privilege rather than "a natural Right of Dominion,"[16] Locke may have targeted absolutist notions of political obligation, but he struck a mortal blow to the patriarchal family as well. Gordon Schochet has described the Stuart family as "an authoritarian institution in which great power was concentrated in its patriarchal head."[17] The subordination of child to parent, according to Schochet, was a model for all social relationships, one that was "supported by an official and regularly taught ideology."[18] The power of the political patriarch is prefigured by that of the parent, and thus the repudiation of governmental absolutism rightly begins at home.[19]

In opposition to patriarchal absolutism, Locke tethered parental power to parental duty. It was certainly possible for Locke to attack political absolutism without undermining domestic patriarchalism. As other populist writers did, he could have left the family untouched by differentiating kingly from fatherly power. But Locke turns the analogical argument for political patriarchy on its head by repudiating the absolute power of the domestic patriarch. The Lockean parent is not a household autocrat but a deliberate, patient teacher required by fundamentally fiduciary principles to protect the child's future freedom.[20]

For Locke, the business of education is to equip children with "a variety and freedom of thinking":

> The business of education . . . is not, as I think, to make [children] perfect in any one of the sciences, but so to open and dispose their minds as may best make them capable of any, when they shall apply themselves to it. If men are for a long time accustomed only to one sort or method of thoughts, their minds grow stiff in it, and do not readily turn to another. It is therefore to give them this freedom, that I think they should be made to look into all sorts of

knowledge, and exercise their understandings in so wide a variety
and stock of knowledge. But I do not propose it as a variety and
stock of knowledge, but a variety and freedom of thinking, as an
increase of the powers and activity of the mind, not as an enlargement of its possessions.[21]

As James Axtell explains, Locke meant for education "to develop the child's
potentiality, not to gather actual 'mental' possessions." The educator "must
prepare the child's mental, moral, and physical capabilities to meet any
situation."[22] The child, Locke advises, must be put "in the right way of knowing and improving himself, when he has a mind to it." Put more broadly, the
controlling principle of family education, as of social arrangements more
generally, is that of self-governance: the child learning to guide himself by
reason's light, the parent learning to trust the self-determining capacities of
the child. The difference between a child and an adult "lies not in having
or not having Appetites, but in the Power to govern, and deny our selves in
them."[23] Because self-governance requires self-denial, Locke insists, as we
are reminded by Jacqueline Reinier, that parents must "gradually relax their
authority."[24] By weaning the child from the *strict Hand* of authority, the
Lockean parent fosters the child's free and rational self-mastery, not "slavish" obedience to the imperious temper of the parent.[25]

Because there is no generic child, there can be no generic way to achieve
this goal. Locke's educational prescriptions, though based on a universal
theory of human understanding, nonetheless stress "that children [are] human beings, with their own particular needs, abilities, and patterns of development." So, while a Lockean education pays close attention to the ways
in which children in general gain a variety and freedom of thinking, it does
not lose sight of real children, of "their different temperaments and rhythms
of development"; and it works to "accommodat[e] the educational program
to the child, not the child to the program."[26] For Locke, accommodation is
the heart of parental duty and care. All parents assume this responsibility,
though the ways in which they fulfill the charge will be as varied as children
themselves.

William Blackstone: The Law as Relation

For William Blackstone, as for Locke, the parent is only entrusted with custody of the child. This trust makes sense because it was presumed in Blackstone's time, as it is today, that natural affection will lead parents to take care of their children. But, as Blackstone tells us approvingly, the law is not content to leave the child at the mercy of the parent's good nature. Instead, the parent is obligated to assume responsibility for the welfare of the child. In return, the law provides the parent with a specific set of privileges, with, that is, the instruments of power that enable the parent "more effectually to perform his duty." Like Locke, Blackstone understands parenthood as begetting responsibilities, not rights. It is the child who has rights, and however strong the hold of natural affection, the state stands ready to enforce these rights if the parent fails to do his duty. Because the power of the parent is derived solely from duties owed to the child, parental privileges are only conditionally granted. Natural affection should ensure that parents fulfill their obligations, but the municipal laws of the state provide a more fail-safe enforcement mechanism. If the parent fails to do his duty, "*judex de ea re cognoscet* [the judge will take notice of it]." This portrait of the parent-child relation is hardly one drawn in absolutist strokes.[27]

In his *Commentaries on the Laws of England* (1765–69), Blackstone translates Lockean theory into family law doctrine. Blackstone breaks his discussion of parent-child relations into three sections: (1) the duties of parents to their children, (2) the power of parents over their children, and (3) the duties of children to their parents.[28] The order itself illustrates the principle that parental authority is based on and bounded by parental obligation. Or, as Blackstone says, "The *power* of parents over their children is derived from . . . their duty." Parental power is in the nature of a civil stipend earned by the parent "as a recompence for his care and trouble in the faithful discharge" of parental duty.[29]

Blackstone discusses three types of parental duty: maintenance, protection, and education. The duty to provide maintenance is a principle of natural law (Blackstone describes it as an absolute as opposed to a relative duty), but it is also premised on the core principles of contract law. By begetting children, the parent has voluntarily assumed this obligation.[30] Thus, children have what Blackstone calls "a perfect *right*" to maintenance from their parents.[31]

Discussing the duty of protection in quick order,[32] Blackstone moves on to the parental obligation he considers "of far the greatest importance of any," that of providing an education suitable to the child's station in life. Here, again, the law operates on the principle that the parent has obligated himself voluntarily. Having brought a child into the world, the parent does little good "if he afterwards entirely neglects [the child's] culture and education." The parent has no right to suffer a child "to grow up like a mere beast, to lead a life useless to others, and shameful to himself." Blackstone notes that the municipal laws of most states are "defective in this point, by not constraining the parent to bestow a proper education upon his children." He does not entirely exempt the laws of England from this general censure, but he takes pride in the fact that under English law the children of the poor "are taken out of the hands of their parents" and, for their good and the good of the state, bound to apprenticeships: "Our laws, though their defects in this particular cannot be denied, have in one instance made a wise provision for breeding up the rising generation; since the poor and laborious part of the community, when past the age of nurture, are taken out of the hands of their parents, by the statutes for apprenticing poor children; and are placed out by the public in such a manner, as may render their abilities, in their several stations, of the greatest advantage to the commonwealth."[33] This "wise provision" of binding children to third parties would be the state's basic child welfare provision in the eighteenth century, both in England and in pre- and postrevolutionary America. No doubt suspect to a modern temperament, reflecting as they do historical prejudices about class, race, and ethnicity,[34] apprenticeship laws also express a genuine concern for children who were perceived to be disadvantaged. The well-being of children, however understood or misunderstood, was a matter of deep public interest, linked closely to the welfare of the state. In separating child from parent, apprenticeship treated children as a precious public good.[35]

Because it derives from the duty entrusted to him, the power of the parent is only as great as is needed to secure the child's welfare. Blackstone observes that, though sufficient to keep a child in order, "[t]he power of a parent by our English laws is much more moderate" than that prescribed by the municipal law of other nations. He rejects a "very large and absolute authority" for the parent, insisting that the parent may "lawfully correct his child," but only "in a reasonable manner." Correction must be "for the benefit of [the child's] education"; it must serve the child, not the will, and certainly not the unbridled will, of the parent.[36] The power of the parent is finite in duration as well as scope, for it is directed toward the enfranchisement of the child, toward the time, that is, when "the empire of the father . . . gives place to the empire of reason." The child is "enfranchised by arriving at years of discretion." With regard to the child's monetary estate, Blackstone states that "[a] father has no other power . . . than as his trustee or guardian; for, though he may receive the profits during the child's minority, yet he must account for them when he comes of age," but it would be with regard to the child's intellectual and moral estate that the representation of parenthood as a trust would have its greatest resonance. When the child comes of age, the parent must account for, and be held accountable for, the child's arrival at years of discretion.[37]

Blackstone sets his discussion of parent-child relations against a broad consideration of the difference between absolute or natural rights (and duties) and relative or civil rights (and duties). Absolute rights and duties are established by God and nature. They are part of the presocial liberty of humankind; they belong to humankind in the state of nature.[38] Blackstone describes natural liberty as the power of acting as one sees fit, without restraint or control. Though such liberty may be "one of the gifts of God," we readily surrender some of it when we enter into society. It is a good bargain:

> But every man, when he enters into society, gives up a part of his natural liberty, as the price of so valuable a purchase; and, in consideration of receiving the advantages of mutual commerce, obliges himself to conform to those laws, which the community has thought proper to establish. And this species of legal obedience and conformity is infinitely more desirable, than that wild

and savage liberty which is sacrificed to obtain it. For no man, that considers a moment, would wish to retain the absolute and un-controlled power of doing whatever he pleases; the consequence of which is, that every other man would also have the same power; and then there would be no security to individuals in any of the enjoyments of life.

To the degree that natural liberty is not consistent with the liberty we enjoy as members of society, the law restrains us in our private inclinations. We sacrifice some of our natural liberty for "public convenience," but the loss is not unrewarded. The civil liberty we enjoy is a set of privileges "which society hath engaged to provide, in lieu of the natural liberties so given up by individuals." Civil liberty is thus "natural liberty so far restrained by human laws (and no farther) as is necessary and expedient for the general advantage of the publick." But this is a liberating restraint. The wild and savage liberty of nature is but a form of servitude to the harsh insecurity of Hobbesian competitiveness; thus, the constraints of the civil law, Blackstone concludes, are "by no means subversive but rather introductive of liberty." If the law is conducive to the public advantage, it increases the civil liberty of humankind, even if it should diminish natural liberty.[39]

Blackstone describes absolute rights as those that we are entitled to enjoy "whether out of society or in it." They are what remain after the state has restrained natural liberty by human law "as is necessary and expedient for the general advantage of the publick," a "*residuum* of natural liberty"—natural liberty as far as it is consistent with civil liberty.[40] Such rights are few and simple: life, or, more precisely, the right of personal security; the right of personal liberty, by which Blackstone means freedom from unjust confinement; and the right of private property.[41] With regard to these rights, the civil law has no force. They do not depend on the handiwork of the legislative power: "[They] need not the aid of human laws to be more effec-tually invested in every man than they are; neither do they receive any ad-ditional strength when declared by the municipal laws to be inviolable." In delineating absolute rights, Blackstone writes, the legislature "acts only . . .

in subordination to the great lawgiver, transcribing and publishing his precepts." There is no need for law with regard to actions that are "intrinsically right or wrong."[42]

But most actions are not intrinsically right or wrong. In themselves, they are things indifferent. The rights that pertain to things indifferent (and they are numerous and anything but simple) Blackstone designates as "relative." Relative rights depend entirely on the work of the legislature. They are right because the legislature has made them so for the public convenience. They are relative in two senses: first, they are not right or wrong by some absolute measure, and, second, they arise out of the need to order social relations.[43] They do not "belong to a man considered as an individual"; they belong to him "considered as related to others." They belong, that is, to one of the many social roles by which we conduct our mutual commerce. Blackstone offers this illustration: "Thus our own common law has declared, that the goods of the wife do instantly upon marriage become the property and right of the husband; and our statute law has declared all monopolies a public offense: yet that right, and this offense, have no foundation in nature; but are merely created by the law, for the purposes of civil society." Whereas absolute rights "appertain and belong to particular men, merely as individuals or single persons," relative rights, like the rights pertaining to coverture, are incident to men (quite literally in the case of coverture) "as members of society," as they stand in various relations to each other. (The relational nature of the civil law also affects our treatment of absolute rights. There are times when a right arises from nature, but "the particular circumstances and mode of doing it become right or wrong, as the laws of the land shall direct.") Because relative rights arise from relationships, their substance and scope vary, determined by the social meaning of the specific role from which they emerge. Thus, Blackstone discusses not the rights of parents as a distinct topic, as though parental rights preexisted the social role of parent, but the rights and duties that pertain to the relation of parent *and* child, just as he does for husband *and* wife, and guardian *and* ward.[44]

Blackstone's reference to coverture as the mere creation of civil law, with no foundation in nature, illuminates the historical (or antihistorical) treatment of parental rights. By making absolute what was once relative, we manufacture legal dogma, sometimes out of bits and pieces of the historical fabric, sometimes out of whole cloth. In his account of marital law in America, Hendrik Hartog describes how coverture, understood by Blackstone as part of the "body of evolving man-made rules and policies" that compose the common law (that is, the municipal or ordinary law), came in time to be viewed as "the legal expression of God's will in mandating marriage." Both those in favor of and those opposed to this peculiar legal construct "shared . . . a particular historical (or anti-historical) consciousness." They took the law as "complete, a frozen structure," "a finished product," as the revelation of "a 'true' or 'false' or 'received' or 'unchanging' law," not as a description of evolving policies and practices.[45] It is much the same with the reification of the right to parent. We undo the fluidity of the case law past, we ignore the gap between legal pronouncements and legal practices, we skip over whatever is soft and sentimental, in order to make history stand for a body of coherent, hardened doctrine.

In his treatment of relative rights as nuanced, Blackstone underscores a core thematic current of the common law tradition: the idea of relation. "[T]he idea of relation, and of legal consequences flowing therefrom," observed Roscoe Pound, "pervades every part of Anglo-American law."[46] Protesting against the tide of individualistic, rule-based law ("the law in the books," a law at odds with the collectivist tendencies of modern thought and feeling, "the law in action") and writing just a few years before the United States Supreme Court would fix the star of parental rights in our constitutional constellation, Pound rejected the principle that the end of all law is liberty "conceived in the sense of the widest possible individual self-assertion." This doctrine of "ultra-individualism"—a product, as Pound saw it, of equal parts natural law theory, Reformation and Puritan theology, and contractarian economics—"gave rise to a conception of the function of law as a purely negative one of removing or preventing obstacles to such individual self-assertion, not a positive one of directly furthering social progress."[47] Negative liberty eroded the "feudal" idea that rights and duties arise from the relations we embrace, from the moral obligations we choose to accept. For Pound, this was an unhappy departure from the common law's account of rights as relational in character.

In contrast to negative liberty, the freedom of the common law takes into account the reality that we do not live, in Pound's phrase, as "abstract individual[s]" or, to borrow from Michael Sandel, that we do not live "unencumbered."[48] Common law rights and duties arise from and attach to the specific relationships we form. To illustrate, Pound contrasts the Roman law concept of patria potestas with the common law concept of paternal authority. The authority of the Roman father "is legally quite one-sided." His almost absolute power is a function of his status as the head of the household. But where rights arise out of the relation between parent and child and are thus predicated on the duty of protection, contractually implied by the act of begetting a child, the scope of paternal authority is duly circumscribed.[49]

What we call family law was first cast as the law of domestic relations. The law of household status asks, "What rights and duties belong to the husband or wife, to the parent or child?" The law of household relations asks, "What rights and duties are incident to the relationship of husband and wife, of parent and child?"[50] In the law of domestic relations, no man is a juristic island, and no family exists as a world unto itself. The most private family matters may have the most profound public consequences; thus, Pound asserts, to secure for the child "a moral and social life," social interests at times will take precedence over parental preferences. Before the individual interests of the child, "the parent's claim to the custody of the child and to control over its bringing up has come to be greatly limited in order to secure these interests." As a matter of fact, according to Pound, "[t]he individual interest of parents . . . has come to be almost the last thing regarded as compared with the interest of the child and the interest of society."[51]

Pound celebrated the common law's "feudal" belief that rights arise from and are dependent upon social relations. The same principle has been more recently studied (and, it is fair to say, celebrated) by William Novak, whose study of the well-regulated society presents us with a nineteenth-century America where courts routinely upheld state action against claims of individual rights. This was a jurisprudence "based primarily on the principles and doctrines of the common law," based, that is, on a "legal worldview that fostered and legitimated . . . the common law vision of a well-regulated society."[52] Central to this vision is the principle of sociability: the premise, as stated by one court in 1784, that "man was made for *society*—that society is absolutely necessary for *man*—that the *public good* ought always to be the supreme rule."[53] With roots in the natural law theory of the seventeenth century and the moral philosophy of the Scottish Enlightenment, the principle of sociability treats society as the true state of nature and duty to others as the true source of rights. Aaron Garrett provides a good summation of this "sociable" moral scheme: "We have various duties and roles as humans, as parents, as parishioners, etc., which arise from different features of our human 'frame'; they are natural to us, as sociable human beings who seek and need other human beings. We have rights in order to fulfill these duties. We are granted a right to property, in order to feed our families and ourselves. We have a right over our children, in order to teach them and help them to grow."[54] For moral theorists like Francis Hutcheson, whose influence on the founding generation was considerable, benevolence is the basis of rights.[55] Garrett continues: "What is right, in other words, and what one has a right to [according to Hutcheson] is that which is right for the common good." In other words, rights enable social beings to carry out their social duties. Novak quotes Mark Hopkins, a professor of moral philosophy at Williams College from 1836 to 1872, to this effect: "A man has rights in order that he may do right."[56]

From the principle of sociability emerged legal decision making far removed from the individualistic, rights-against-society orientation that would strike down public welfare regulation at the beginning of the twentieth century. As Locke taught that personal freedom lies in rational governance of the self, so civil liberty lies in the social restraints of the law. The common law right, Novak writes, was not "something to be exerted against society" but something "intimately connected to the duties and moral obligations incumbent on social beings."[57] On this point, Novak quotes the jurist and legal scholar Nathaniel Chipman (1752–1843): "The rights of man are relative to his social nature, and the rights of the individual exist, in a coincidence only with the rights of the whole, in a well-ordered state of society and civil government."[58] For a contemporary statement of this theme, we might again turn to Sandel: "The morality of right . . . speaks to that which distinguishes us, the morality of the good corresponds to the unity of persons and speaks to that which connects us."[59]

Thus, under common law principles, rights are construed as relative, not absolute, as social, not individualistic. In this view, the law best promotes the claims of self and society by treating them as a unified field, by taking as its natural jurisdiction the self-in-society. Thus, rights are construed as positive, not negative, as "the central source and rationale of legal and governmental power," not as "a shield to protect individuals from society and government." In this view, the restraints of law are not restraints on liberty but the embodiment of liberty, the civil liberty that liberates humankind from a presocial world of possessive individualism. Thus, rights are construed as dynamic, not static, as the product of "an ongoing calculation of the reciprocal rights and duties of others and the good of the whole in a constantly changing society." In this view, it is the common law, with its sensitivity to the complexity of human experiences, with its conscious commitment to historical process, with its embrace of truths that are at best uncertain, that nourishes the soil in which civil liberty thrives. It is the idea of law as relation—rather than, in Novak's nice phrase, "the timeless, external truths of God, Reason, Sovereign, or Text"—that invests government with the authority to regulate the myriad interactions of social life.[60]

Pound thought that the idea of relation was "a living force for justice in the society of today and of tomorrow."[61] This sentiment has been captured by a number of modern scholars writing about family law. Looking beyond the atomistic orientation of rights-based approaches to legal disputes, a relational approach to family conflict serves, to borrow from Milton Regan, the "ethic of relational obligation" that holds together the intricate web of domestic bonds. Looking toward, to borrow from Robin West, the "communal essence" of family life, a relational approach to rights serves as a living force for domestic justice and does so by honoring principles with deep roots in our legal heritage.[62]

In the eighteenth and nineteenth centuries American jurists would create a novel common law of child custody on the basis of relational principles. Freely departing from fixed, general rules, "[t]he American courts . . . from the earliest periods, with certain exceptions, adopted the view, that in all cases affecting the custody of infants, the determination, based upon a consideration of the facts and circumstances of each particular case, must be in accord with the demands of actual justice and right."[63] In this, they outpaced their British counterparts (a fact in which American jurists and legal scholars took no little pride), travelling, to quote the family law treatise writer Joel Bishop, "more rapidly toward the light than in England."[64] However deeply enshrined paternal prerogatives were in ancient common law, parental rights found tough purchase in American soil. By the last quarter of the nineteenth century, one American court could confidently proclaim — though too confidently, to be sure — that "[t]he substantial reality of the old common law right [of custody] has faded almost to fiction under the ameliorating influence of the modern common law."[65] Though the notion of parental authority as a form of entitlement would never quite fade to fiction, the entire tendency of the American courts would be, in Hochheimer's apt phrase, to reject the assertion of parental rights erected on a foundation of wrong to the child.

A Family Law Revolution:
Parental Custody and the Best Interests of the Child

The principle that the parent is only entrusted with the custody and care of the child, and then only until the child reaches the age of discretion, translated easily to colonial and postcolonial shores. The American Revolution was described by both sides as a conflict between parent and child.[66] While Tory writers criticized the wayward colonists for their filial ingratitude, the rebellious children framed the war as one against the empire of the father, citing the duty of the parent to foster the child's enfranchisement. The colonial protest resounded with Lockean themes: the colonies owed respect to their mother country, but not absolute obedience and submission; by failing to fulfill his parental duty, the king had surrendered his parental authority; the colonists had reached a state of maturity and were no longer subject to the strictures of parental authority. The relationship between the governed and their governors, as Locke proposed, was like that of a trusteeship—Peter Hoffer suggests that the Declaration of Independence reads like a bill in equity, with Jefferson "rais[ing] equitable principles of trusteeship to the level of constitutional principles"—and the king/parent had broken his fiduciary commitment.[67] The same themes were heard on a more domestic front. If political rebellion could be portrayed as a family affair, it was partly because the American family was undergoing a revolution of its own.[68]

The new order of the ages brought with it "a new and different type of family life, one characterized by solicitude and sentimentality toward children and by more intimate, personal and equal relationships."[69] This is well-charted territory. Under the influence of the era's "antipatriarchal ethos," to use Michael Grossberg's phrase, the family was thought of as "a collection of individuals each with his or her own needs and rights."[70] More particularly, with regard to the bond of parent and child, it was, as Mary Ann Mason writes, a transformational era.[71] The idea of childhood itself was reenvisioned, according to Steven Mintz and Susan Kellogg; what was "previously conceived as a period of submission to authority, was increasingly viewed as a period of growth, development, and preparation for adulthood." Within the family collection of individuals, the child was considered to be "a special being with distinctive needs and impulses," and chief among these needs was education, specifically, the kind of mentorship that fosters the child's natural drive for self-determination.[72]

Even before the Revolution of 1776, "parents were advised to train their children in independence." While children were still young and malleable, "they had to develop a capacity for self-reliance, self-assessment, and self-direction, in the hope that this would prepare them for a world in which they would have to make independent choices of a career, of friends, and of a spouse."[73] In the outpouring of parenting guidebooks that followed the birth of the new republic—and that beleaguered a new generation of parents, as future guidebooks would beleaguer future generations—"[n]early every work of the age . . . dwelt on issues of familial responsibility and warned against the evils of parental tyranny and the harsh and arbitrary modes of child-rearing of an older, more savage age."[74] More authoritarian voices were to be heard as well,[75] but it is hardly surprising that under this democratic pressure the parent's power "evolved from a property right to a trust tied to his responsibilities as a father."[76] In his influential *Legal Outlines* (1836), the University of Maryland law professor David Hoffman summed up this evolutionary process, maintaining that parental power did not arise from "some fancied property given to the parent in his offspring, by the act of propagation," but from principles of implied consent. Parental authority, as Hoffman saw it, is founded on "the presumed consent of the offspring":

> The parent shows himself ready, by the care and affection manifested to his child, to watch over him, and to supply all his wants, until he shall be able to provide for himself. The child, on the other hand, receives these acts of kindness; a tacit compact between them is formed; the child engages, by acts equivalent to a positive undertaking, to submit to the care and judgment of his parent so long as the parent, and the manifest order of nature, shall coincide in requiring assistance and advice on the one side, and acceptance of them, and obedience and gratitude on the other.[77]

Unsurprisingly, no figure did more to foster this notion of family compact than John Locke. (Less the political Locke of the *Two Treatises* than the pedagogical Locke of the *Essay Concerning Human Understanding* and *Some Thoughts Concerning Education*.)[78] In his review of the republican push against patriarchalism, Jay Fliegelman describes how "Locke's educational theory redefined the nature of parental authority in very much the way that the Revolution of 1688, which replaced an absolute monarchy with a constitutional one, redefined the rights and duties of the crown."[79] For Locke, as we have seen, the controlling principle of family education, as of social arrangements more generally, is that of self-governance. Like Milton before him, Locke would not praise "a fugitive and cloistered vertue, unexercis'd and unbreath'd."[80] More than knowing how to read and write, education was a matter of moral exercise. In a world of temptation, a fallen world where "the tares and wheat shall grow together to the end of the world," only the educated mind is free to make the right moral choices.[81]

This mélange of educational theory and Protestant moral injunction would raise questions of freedom and authority that were both personal and political. Fliegelman reads popular eighteenth-century educational guidebooks as making the point that parents "thwart the development of their children's reason by insisting that they accept without examination or inquiry all doctrines taught them." In so doing, they "put their children's salvation in jeopardy; for saving faith is, by definition, that faith one freely and rationally chooses to embrace."[82] Gordon Wood likewise points to the popular didactic literature of the era as attesting to the metamorphosis of the "true" parent from biological progenitor to moral preceptor: "Being a parent was no longer simply a biological fact; it was also a cultural responsibility. . . . [A] child's true parents were not his blood relatives, but those moral preceptors [like Fénelon's Mentor] who shaped his mind and raised him to become a reasoning moral adult in a corrupt and complex world. Children were no longer merely dependents but moral beings to be cared for and educated."[83]

The upshot of this stress on rational freedom was a pedagogical scheme that "concern[ed] itself less with content, doctrinal or otherwise, than with perfecting the mind's ability to evaluate and judge." The point was not "to secure a child's obedience," Fliegelman writes, "but to prepare a child for his eventual emergence into the world—in effect, to prepare him for the death of his parents." Put a bit less morbidly, the proper task of the ideal mentor was to "train[] his charges in the free use of their judgment that they might eventually become independent not only of his authority, but of the authority of all others."[84] This antiauthoritarian pedagogy was too much for the republican ideologue Benjamin Rush, who, writing in 1786, dissented from "opinions with which modern times abound: that it is improper to fill the minds of youth with religious prejudices of any kind and that they should be left to choose their own principles after they have arrived at an age in which they are capable of judging for themselves."[85]

In a revolutionary era, it is not surprising that the pedagogical and the political merged with apparent seamlessness, and the parent's task—"not to instill submission to authority but to develop a child's conscience and self-government" (Mintz and Kellogg); "to make authority and liberty compatible, to find a surer ground for obligation and obedience than 'the fear of the rod'" (Fliegelman)—became a matter of public moment, both a domestic and a civic duty. "The anti-patriarchal family," writes Reinier, "would become the basic unit of the new republican society."[86] For a revolutionary family, the child's passage to autonomous adulthood was the parent's foremost responsibility; for a revolutionary polity, it was one of the state's foremost concerns.

Indeed, for some republican educational theorists the new nation was the new family. Samuel Harrison Smith's essay on education, which, in 1795, won the contest sponsored by the American Philosophical Society of America for contributions on educational reform, urged "the establishment of a [national educational] system which shall place under a control, independent of and superior to parental authority, the education of children." It is "the duty of a nation," argued Smith, "to superintend and even to coerce the education of children."[87] This duty is "so momentously important [that it] must not be left to the negligence of individuals" or, we might say, in Justice White's cautionary phrase, to the "idiosyncratic views of what knowledge a child needs to be a productive and happy member of society."[88] A common schooling would replace what Melvin Yazawa calls the "old ligaments of the familial commonwealth" with national bonds of affection; collective determination would supersede personal and local prejudices.[89] With regard to the child's self-rule, to be sure, how these new ties beyond the family might differ from the bonds of the familial past—how, in other words, the law's republic might differ from the father's empire—was a question sometimes lost amid speculations of a bright republican future. It was not uncommon for the pedagogical precepts of the new world order to sound familiar patriarchal notes. "Let our pupil be taught that he does not belong to himself, but that he is public property," advised Rush. "Let him be taught to love his family, but let him be taught at the same time that he must forsake and even forget them when the welfare of his country requires it."[90] With less ideological fervor but no less patriotic spirit, George Washington, who also advocated a federal university, declared that "[the] more homogenous our citizens can be made [in principles, opinions, and manners], the greater will be our prospect of permanent union."[91]

As patriarchal models of family governance receded before the republi-can tide, "education became increasingly a matter of 'public concernment.'" The parental duty to educate had long been enjoined by public regulation. Statutes for the promotion of education, as the historian Lawrence Cremin reports, legally "compel[ed] households to do what in England they had long been accustomed to do." Beginning in 1642, Massachusetts law em-powered selectmen "to take account from time to time of all parents and masters, and of their children, concerning their calling and employment of their children, especially of their ability to read and understand the prin-ciples of religion and the capital laws of this country." In 1647, Massachu-setts ordered that "every township in this jurisdiction, after the Lord hath increased them to fifty households shall forthwith appoint one within their town to teach all such children as shall resort to him to write and read, whose wages shall be paid either by the parents or masters of such children, or by the inhabitants in general"; by the same act, the "Old Deluder Act," every town of one hundred families or householders was required to "set up a grammar school, the master thereof being able to instruct youth so far as they may be fitted for the university." Other colonies adopted similar com-pulsory education statutes: Connecticut in 1650; New Haven, 1655; New York, 1665; Plymouth, 1671; Pennsylvania, 1683.[92]

These measures reached beyond the traditional audiences of colonial welfare. In his family law treatise of 1816, Tapping Reeve noticed that the duty to educate "is not enforced by the law of England, any farther than that overseers of the poor have, by statute, a power to bind out the children of paupers to masters, where they may receive a proper education."[93] The colonies, too, and the states after them, had poor laws, under which the children of pauper parents were separated from their parents and bound out as apprentices. These statutes targeted the children of "undeserving" parents—that is, for the greater part, poor parents. In part, compulsory edu-cation laws served a similar purpose, enforcing a parental duty that, as James Kent pointed out, would provide children with a means of economic self-sufficiency: "Without some preparation made in youth for the sequel of life, children of all conditions would probably become idle and vicious when they grow up, either from the want of good instruction and habits, and the means of subsistence, or from want of rational and useful occupation. A parent who sends his son into the world uneducated, and without skill in any art or science, does a great injury to mankind, as well as to his own family, for he defrauds the community of a useful citizen, and bequeaths to it a nuisance." Where parents could not or would not adequately educate their children, the state was free to employ the same coercive mechanisms that separated parent from child under the poor laws.[94]

But compulsory education laws also suggest the broader moral focus of early child welfare efforts. The duty of the parent to educate was not just a matter of the poor child's economic self-sufficiency and the economic welfare of the community, but of every child's rational self-sufficiency and the political welfare of the community.[95] Such laws had always expressed a Protestant concern with the individual's direct knowledge of the Bible.[96] For Reeve, the point of education was not to keep down relief costs but to raise children who "may be able, for themselves, to search scriptures of truth."[97] Children need an education not only to join the community as contributing members but also to pursue truth by and for themselves. Yet truth may lie outside the boundaries of the father's empire, and, as Cremin writes, what was meant to be the key to salvation could well open the door to other opportunities.[98] Accordingly, then, as now, state control of education could be seen to undermine parental authority in a way that other welfare measures did not. The Connecticut compulsory education law, Reeve noted, "has, by some, been branded as tyrannical, and as an infringement of parental rights."[99] For the child's growing intellectual and moral autonomy might be far more alarming than any political infringement of parental rights. Once children begin to think for themselves, they may find truths that to their parents are foreign and unsupportable.

To those who built a nation on the liberal legacy of Milton and Locke, the stress of accommodating multiple truths was a cost of true freedom. Jefferson thought governmental efforts to coerce moral agreement "tend only to beget habits of hypocrisy and meanness."[100] He would leave the mind free to follow the dictates of reason and conscience. The Virginia Statute for Religious Freedom testifies to Jefferson's confidence that Truth will prevail "if left to herself."[101] The coercive unification of opinion, he declared, is "a departure from the plan of the holy author of our religion, who being Lord, both of body and mind yet chose not to propagate it by coercions on either."[102] Though apprehensive lest succeeding generations depart from the path of religious freedom, Jefferson nonetheless stayed true to the belief that the only saving faith is the one that is freely chosen.[103]

A collection of rights-bearing individuals is not the likeliest of recipes for family stability. With increasing frequency, postcolonial courts were called upon to settle conflict within the family, and they did so with decreasing deference to paternal authority. In 1816, considering the case of a youth whose military enlistment was made without parental consent, Justice Joseph Story declared that parental rights "are rights depending upon the mere municipal rules of the state, and may be enlarged, restrained, and limited as the wisdom or policy of the times may dictate, unless the legislative power be controlled by some constitutional prohibition." While, by common law, the father has a right to the custody of his children during their infancy, such custodial authority is a limited one. Following Blackstone and subsequent cases, Story remarked that the custody of minors "is given to their parents" for the benefit of the child. It would be hard to maintain "upon the mere footing of the common law," he wrote, that a father is entitled to apprentice his child on terms injurious to the child's interests or, more generally, to disregard the maintenance, protection, and education of the child "to answer his own mercenary views, or gratify his own unworthy passions."[104] (Here Story relied on *Respublica v. Kepple* (1793), in which the Pennsylvania Supreme Court held that the common law did not permit a father to bind out his child as a servant. The child, Benjamin, fourteen years old, had been bound "to *serve*, and not to learn any trade, occupation, or labour." This indenture, according to the court, could not be supported upon the principles of the common law. "[N]o parent, under any circumstances," the *Kepple* court insisted, "can make his child a *servant*.")[105] A father's entitlement, in other words, is part of a bargain made in consideration of the father's fulfillment of his parental responsibilities. No less true, the custody of minors "is given to their parents" for the benefit of the state. It is a "granted power," always subject to legitimate governmental needs; it may be abrogated as the discretion of the state dictates. If the exercise of a valid legislative power, in this case, the congressional power to enlist minors in the naval service, "should sometimes trench upon supposed private rights, or private convenience," Story concluded, "it is to be enumerated among the sacrifices, which the very order of society exacts from its members in furtherance of the public welfare."[106]

As early as 1796, American courts began to exact such sacrifices, employing equitable principles to erode the law's biases in favor of paternal custody. Indeed, a growing concern with child nurture would prejudice courts in favor of maternal custody rights. "By the 1820s," Grossberg writes, "traditional paternal custody rights had declined so precipitously that some judges began to seek a means by which fathers could be given presumptive but not absolute rights."[107] American courts might acknowledge the principle that "[t]he wife, by the common law, has no right to the children against the husband." [108] But this presumed paternal right was far from absolute. No court would award a child to an unfit father. The absoluteness of a fit father's right as against the mother might depend on the father having possession of the child.[109] Or on whether a wife had "voluntarily" separated herself from her husband.[110] And on the age and gender of the child. Beyond these specific doctrinal caveats, the rigor of the paternal presumption, however rigorously the conventional precepts were pronounced, was always mitigated by a dedication to equitable practice. This focus on fairness, in the grand words of one state supreme court, was "the jurisprudence of a refined race, one that had emerged from its barbarism":

> This difficulty [of adjudicating custody conflicts] is not lessened, but increased, by the difference of the sources from whence our law is derived; . . . By the one, women and children of immature years, held as they always have been by uncivilized people as the property of the husband and father, and having no will of their own, no rights in contradiction to his power and authority, and only considered, through him, as a portion of the community in which they lived. By the other, with more regard to the harmony of nature, looked upon as beings created, not only by the same

power, but with exceptions resulting from the subordinate position in which the laws of nature place them, as having equal rights to all the enjoyments of life, and as safe and adequate protection for them as the husband and father.[111]

In time, judicial and legislative regard for the subordinate position of women and children led not just to a devaluation of the father's claims. The law would "reduce[] the rights of parenthood generally." Even in quite early custody cases, we observe the first doctrinal steps—the best interests of the child doctrine, the tender years doctrine, the infant discretion rule—that courts took not only to forgo legal presumptions favoring paternal custody but "to take the ultimate decision of child placement out of the hands of both parents."[112] Among these early cases were the following:

- The case *Nickols v. Giles* (1796), heard by the Superior Court of Connecticut, is short enough to be recited in full:

  William Nickols exhibited his motion for a *habeas corpus* to take a daughter of his, about three years old, from one Thomas Giles, who as he said, unjustly detained and withheld her from him, and unlawfully imprisoned her; and also to bring said Giles, before this court to show reason why he thus detained and imprisoned his daughter, etc.—Upon inquiry it appeared that the child was with its mother, who lived with her father the said Thomas Giles; that the child was well provided for; and said Nickols having no house and very little property, and very irregular in his temper and life, his wife had left him and went and lived with her father, where both she and her child were well provided for. Upon which the court refused to grant said writ.[113]

  The case has a significance that outstrips its brief description. Beyond its suggestion of a judicial willingness to challenge legal presumptions favoring the father, the case presents the key procedural mechanism that would allow courts the leeway to develop a custody standard based on the best interests of the child. Nickols had brought the dispute before the court on a writ of habeas corpus, presumably to avoid adjudication in equity. But, despite republican suspicion toward judicial discretion, American courts did not stand much upon the law / equity distinction.[114] The great precedent regarding the proper response of the court was Lord Mansfield's twofold declaration in *Rex v. Delaval* that "[i]n cases of writs of habeas corpus directed to private persons, 'to bring up infants,'" (1) "the Court is bound, ex debito justitiae, to set the infant free from an improper restraint," but (2) "they [i.e., the courts] are not bound to deliver them over to any body nor to give them any privilege." The child's deliverance was not an abstract question of rights. It was a matter that "must be left to [the courts'] discretion, according to the circumstances that shall appear before them"; and if the child were of sufficient age, it was a matter on which the court would defer to his or her discretion.[115] Though British law wavered with regard to the Mansfield principles (until reforms were codified in the Custody of Infants Act of 1839), the same cannot be said with regard to the American courts, which relied on Mansfield's pronouncement again and again to adjudicate custody cases.[116] In the American cases, the Mansfield principles, to borrow the horticultural imagery of the Tennessee Supreme Court, were quickly "engraft[ed] . . . upon the rude stem of the common law."[117]

By this grafting process American judges followed the antipatriarchal path that British courts had laid out and then abandoned. Danaya Wright has shown that eighteenth-century British custody cases involving third parties, cases, that is, that were not disputes between two living parents, were characterized by a judicial readiness to interfere with paternal rights. Wright isolates four historical strands that "reflected changing views about the origins and scope of patriarchal power and the appropriateness of legal oversight in family affairs": "a gradual decline in the rights and preroga-tives of fathers, a consistent recognition of and protection for mothers as testamentary or socage guardians, a gradual awareness of and protection for children's interests as the courts began to interfere in aspects of childrearing and educational decision-making, and a strong willingness on the part of judges to interfere with familial life in the name of the Crown's role as *parens patriae.*"[118] It was only when interspousal custody litigation reached the courts in 1804, in the persons of Leonard Thomas De Manneville and Margaret Crompton (Mrs. De Manneville),[119] that the courts' liberal approach to custody claims abruptly halted: "When mothers and fathers began suing one another for custody of their chil-dren, the relative leniency of these eighteenth-century cases was rejected in favor of strict paternal rights that were not only a deviation from the prior century, but appeared to be more patriarchal than in any period before."[120] What we witness, then, in nineteenth-century British decisions is the assertion of legal presumptions that, according to Jamil Zainaldin, "had the effect of creating *new* paternal rights, the existence of which had only been vaguely hinted at by previous judges."[121]

This was a deviation that many American courts chose not to follow. In 1840, the Court for the Correction of Errors of New York considered one of the most famous custody cases of the century, that of John and Eliza Barry. Reviewing the history of custody case law, the Court of Errors observed that "the American cases . . . showed it to be the established law of this country that the court, or officer, were authorized to exercise a discretion, and that the father was not entitled to demand a delivery of the child to him, upon habeas corpus, as an absolute right." This was, the court pointed out, "also the law of England at the time of our separation from the mother country." But since that period the decisions of the English courts "appeared to have gone back to the principles of a semi-barbarous age, when the wife was the slave of the husband, because he had the physical power to control her, and when the will of the strongest party constituted the rule of right."[122] In short, the American courts, with evident self-satisfaction—the Court of Errors: "This state has never been disgraced by laws so subversive of the welfare of infant children, of the rights of mothers, and of the morals of the people"[123]—refused to adopt what was "actually a recent innovation."[124]

- In the case *Prather v. Prather* (1809), Jeanette Prather, complaining of ill usage, sued her husband, William, for a separate maintenance and custody of their infant children. On a first hearing of the case, the judge, self-described as "an enemy to innovation," decided he was not "at liberty to take [the children] out of the care and custody of the father." On appeal, the Superior Court of South Carolina admitted that "it [was] treading new and dangerous grounds," but it nonetheless ordered that custody of the couple's infant daughter be surrendered to the mother.[125]

- In *Commonwealth v. Nutt* (1810), neither Levi nor Acha Nutt obtained custody of the daughter who was the focus of their custody dispute. To the court, the father's negligence was too apparent, his place of habitation too unsettled, and his language too indelicate to be repeated. The mother kept house for a tavern keeper and was living in "constant habits of adultery" and engaging in "acts of the grossest indecency." Not to mention that "fiddling, dancing, and frolicking [were] frequent at the house." The court of common pleas was not about to entrust the child to such parents nor would it "set her adrift upon the wide world." Relying on Mansfield, the court sought out the safety of some other domestic harbor.

In the end, they gave custody of the child to her older sister, warning the parents that they interfered with this arrangement "at their peril."[126]

- *In re McDowle* (1811) held that under a state statute an infant may not be bound as an apprentice unless he is a party to and executes the deed. Upon releasing the children from their indentures, the court followed Lord Mansfield's lead by declaring that, once having released the child from confinement, it was not bound to deliver the child to the father (or to any party) but was free to use its discretion to place the child. The *McDowle* court deferred to the custodial preferences of the children, who "expressed a decided and unequivocal desire to return to their masters, and a strong and unaccountable repugnance to go back to their father."[127]

- The same grounds were trod by the Pennsylvania Supreme Court in *Commonwealth v. Addicks*.[128] When this case was first brought before the court in 1813,[129] the court awarded custody of Adelaide and Frances Lee to their mother "on account of the tender age of the infants," despite the fact that she had been "divorced for adultery." In his opinion Chief Justice William Tilghman began by asserting that the court would not be confined "to an abstract question on the rights of guardianship" but would "determine according to our discretion, on the expediency of delivering the infants to the custody of the father." On a second petition, made in 1815, the court returned the children to their father. Now that the children were older, the court reasoned, their best interests were no longer served by a mother's care, at least not the care of a mother who misunderstood "the obligation of the marriage contract." Still, the court cautioned the father "not to be abrupt in their removal, but to conduct the matter so as to avoid a violent shock either to [the children] or their mother."[130]

Writing in 1840, the Pennsylvania Supreme Court observed that by the time of the *Addicks* decision—that is, by
1815—trust principles of custodial authority were already
time-honored. The 1840 case, a high-profile affair brought by
Ellen Sears d'Hauteville against the Swiss aristocrat Baron
d'Hauteville, was also a custody dispute. Counsel for the
father had argued that *Addicks* was a judicial anomaly, and he
asked the court to disregard it. (His language was somewhat
more vigorous: He asked the court "to ride it over and ride it
down.") The court disagreed with this reading of legal history.
"The principle upon which the *Addicks* case was decided,"
the court stated, "did not originate with Chief Justice Tilghman; he but followed in the tracks which both foreign and
American judges had imprinted." For added measure, the
court went on to say that "the safety and wisdom of the path
[taken by Tilghman] have been recognized by all judges who
have followed him." The once new and dangerous custody
grounds had become firm footing for judicial steps.

The *d'Hauteville* court made the important point that
while judges might pay homage to the father's custodial
entitlement, this was often no more than a habitual rhetorical gesture, if one too easily taken as testimony of unfettered
support for parental rights. These same judges did not hesitate
to base their decisions solely on the best interests of the child.
Thus, while some courts stated that the father can forfeit his
custodial rights only by misconduct, "the bulk of the cases
embrace broader grounds; and an examination of even those
which at the first blush seem to support this doctrine, mani-
fests that they furnish no foundation upon which to really
rest the structure of argument attempted to be based upon
them." In fact, "without a single exception," stressed the
court, all of the American cases brought forward to support
the rights of Baron d'Hauteville followed the principles of the

Addicks decision "to the fullest extent."[131] As one example, the court cited the decision of *People v. Nickerson* (1837), a case on which counsel for the father placed great confidence, as "repeat[ing] the principle 'that the father is the natural guardian of his infant children,' [but admitting the court's] right to transfer the custody to the mother whenever it would be 'for the interests of the child.'"[132]

- In 1816, the Supreme Court of New York was asked to decide the fate of Margaret Eliza Waldron, whose custody was sought both by her father and her maternal grandfather. Relying on *Addicks*, the court found "strong corroboration" of the principles that (1) custody "is a matter resting in the sound discretion of the Court, and not [a] matter of right which the father can claim at the hands of the Court," and (2) "[i]t is to the benefit and welfare of the infant to which the attention of the Court ought principally to be directed."[133]

Refusing to be confined "to an abstract question on the rights of guardianship," these courts acted to protect the child's real needs. Parental authority was treated as something earned and therefore something that could be taken away. It was derived not from some timeless truth but from the time-honored commitment to secure the child's natural and equal right to freedom. It was the product not of self-assertion but of self-sacrifice. In the years ahead, the idea that rights arise from caring relationships would produce "a novel custody law of which the highest priority was the child's interests as determined by the judiciary." To be sure, these determinations required the courts to balance the competing interests of parent and child, a weighing that was no doubt a delicate task, but, increasingly, "[a]s the focus of custody disputes became a nurture-based definition of child welfare," the scales tipped in the child's favor. Focused on the child's well-being, courts discarded "[t]raditional paternalistic custody rules and practices," thereby adopting a degree of discretion that "enabled post-Revolutionary state judges to rewrite the common law of custody: first in scattered decisions early in the nineteenth century and then in an increasingly intricate and expansive body of rules as the period came to an end."[134] Peter Bardaglio has charted the evolution of a "child-centered theory of guardianship" among southern jurists in the nineteenth century, a theory that supported "the systematic attempt to link women and children directly with the state rather than through the male head of the family." Though his observations are regionally based, Bardaglio provides a fair assessment of judicial developments throughout the country: "Treating parenthood as a trusteeship rather than a proprietary right, judges developed innovative policies and set new standards for parental behavior that took into consideration the needs of the child and society. Although biological rights remained important, parental supremacy was no longer unchallengeable."[135]

Treating parenthood as a trusteeship allowed American custody courts to construct the intricate and expansive body of rules that would tie parental power to the fulfillment of parental duty. This linkage of rights and responsibilities was built on a coherent set of doctrinal propositions that embraced a Lockean model of parent-child relations. Embodying a common law, relational approach to the question of custodial authority within the family, these premises included:

1. **The child has independent legal interests**.
   For custody courts, the individual child, not the family, is
   the relevant legal unit. The conception which underlies the
   status of minors "is that of the separate legal personality of
   the child. . . . From the very moment of birth the child becomes
   a citizen, or subject of the government under whose jurisdiction
   born, entitled to the protection of that government."[136] (With no
   little complaisance, the courts set themselves in sharp contrast
   with the Roman law system, under which "the identity of the
   child was merged in that of the family."[137] Contrary to the views
   of former ages, "a child is in our modern law regarded as from
   birth entirely a human being, given, by the severance of the
   cord which connected it to its mother, all the rights pertaining
   to man. Its independent circulation is not physical only, but
   legal as well.")[138] The right of custody belongs to the child: It is

"the right or claim of the *child* to be in that custody or charge which will subserve *its* real interests."[139] The child "has its own independent rights, the chief whereof is the promotion of its own well-being; and when they require a change of custody . . . , the custody will be transferred to one who, assuming the duties, will better perform them."[140]

2. **The state has an independent interest in the welfare of the child and plenary power to legislate on behalf of the child. The care owed to the child is a duty the state owes to itself.**

   "[C]hildren are not born for the benefit of the parents alone, but for the country; and, therefore, . . . the interests of the public in their morals and education should be protected."[141] In custody controversies, the child's interests are primary because the health of the state requires such a rule: "This rule is based upon the theory that the state must perpetuate itself, and good citizenship is essential to that end."[142] As parens patriae, the state has plenary power to legislate on behalf of the child.[143] The interest of the state in its children is so broad "as to almost defy limitations."[144] The parental responsibility to educate the child properly is a duty "owe[d] not to the child only, but to the commonwealth."[145] It is a duty the state owes to itself to see that "each man should be reared and educated under such influences that he may be qualified to exercise the rights of a freeman and take part in the government of the country."[146]

3. **The power of the state to secure the child's welfare is superior to parental claims of right to control the child. The extent of state power is a matter of social policy and legislative expediency, not constitutional right.**

   "The natural rights of a parent to the custody and control of his infant child are subordinate to the power of the state, and may be restricted and regulated by municipal laws."[147] Natural rights notwithstanding, "the necessity for government has forced the recognition of the rule that the perpetuity of the state is the first consideration, and parental authority itself is subordinate to

this supreme power."[148] How far state regulation of parent-child
relations "should extend is a question, not of constitutional
power for the courts, but of expediency and propriety, which it
is the sole province of the legislature to determine."[149] Legislation which would, following *Lochner*-like reasoning, interfere
with the due process rights of adults may present no constitutional question when applied to children.[150] "Even the courts
which take a very liberal view of individual liberty and are
inclined to condemn paternal legislation would concede that
such paternal control may be exercised over children."[151]

It imports no diminution "of moral obligation or the extent
of reciprocal natural rights and duties resulting from the relation of parent and child" to observe that the rights and powers
arising out of these relations "derive their sanction from the
state." These rights and powers must "be asserted and maintained upon strictly legal grounds." After making every concession to natural claims, "there still remains a supreme fountain
of authority in such matters from which all other authority
derives its entire sanction and existence. This is known as the
paramount authority of the state over all its citizens, to which
every other claim must yield."[152]

4. **It is the sole province of the legislature to determine how far
to regulate or restrict the authority of the parent. Where judicial intervention is allowable, the custody of children must
always be determined by the best interests of the child.**
Because the control of children by parents "is subject to the
unlimited supervisory control of the state,"[153] it is the sole
province of the legislature to determine how far to regulate or
restrict the authority of the parent. On the matter of parent-
child relations, "[t]he judiciary has no authority to interfere
with the exercise of legislative judgment."[154]

In the absence of any statutory mandates, however, the custody of children "must always be regulated by judicial discretion, exercised in reference to their best interests."[155]

5. **The legal status of the parent is purely that of a trustee. All parental power is a function delegated by the state. This grant may be limited by and is revocable by the state without a showing of parental misconduct.**

"[A]ll power and authority over infants are a mere delegated function intrusted by the sovereign state to the individual parent or guardian . . . to be at all times exercised in subordination to the paramount and over-ruling direction of the state."[156] The state delegates its power because it does not possess the "requisite knowledge" necessary to care for the individual child.[157] Parents are entrusted with the upbringing and education of their children, but only "upon the natural presumption, that the children will be properly taken care of."[158] Thus, the authority of the parent is "inseparably connected with the parental obligations, and arises out of them."[159] It is "subject to such restrictions and limitations as the sovereign power of the nation think proper to prescribe."[160] "The law recognizes the parent as the natural guardian of, and entitled to the custody of, his minor child . . . ; [i]t does not, however, recognize in him any property interest in his child, but merely accords to him the benefits resulting from the child's services during minority."[161] In short, the legal status of the parent is "purely that of a trustee—his trust differing from other trusts only in this respect, that it is of all trusts the most sacred."[162] There is no inalienable right to parent.[163]

The doctrine of the American courts is that "gross cruelty or ill-treatment, immorality or depravity of the most pronounced type, is not necessary to be shown, in order to warrant the interference of the courts of chancery." It is not necessary, that is, to make out a case of misconduct against the parent. "The courts will take into consideration all the circumstances and render their decision on principles of justice and natural equity, having in view primarily the welfare of the child and attaching sleight weight to mere technical considerations."[164]

On this point, as has been noted, American jurists and legal theorists set themselves in proud contrast to English courts of the post-Mansfield era, which refused to keep children from a legal guardian unless he was demonstrably "unfit."[165]

Illustrating these trust principles and their application is the case *Ex parte Crouse* from 1839. This was a habeas case in which the father of Mary Ann Crouse sought her release from the state's House of Refuge, a juvenile reformatory where she had been committed upon her mother's petition. The court declared that "[t]he right of parental control is a natural, but not an unalienable one. It is not excepted [by the state constitution] out of the subjects of ordinary legislation; and it consequently remains subject to the ordinary legislative power." The authority of the parent is held at the sufferance of the public, and thus, when circumstances dictate, the parent can be superseded by the state operating as "the guardian of the community."[166]

In the court's view, the object of the House of Refuge was reformation, not punishment.[167] The institution made reform possible "by training its inmates to industry; by imbuing their minds with principles of morality and religion; by furnishing them with means to earn a living; and, above all, by separating them from the corrupting influence of improper associates." In short, it did the work parents were supposed to do. When parents failed to do their job, there was no bar to prevent the public from assuming the task. "[M]ay not the natural parents, when unequal to the task of education, or unworthy of it," the court asked, "be superseded by the *parens patriæ*, or common guardian of the community?"[168] The court was quick to answer its own question: "It is to be remembered that the public has a paramount interest in the virtue and knowledge of its members, and that, of strict right, the business of education belongs to it."[169]

The State as Common Guardian

Crouse reminds us that custody cases did not always involve intrafamily conflict. Nonetheless, the trust model of parent-child relations made its greatest contribution to the law in cases that pitted one family member against another. In *Mercein v. People*,[170] the New York Court for the Correction of Errors followed "the great principle which runs through nearly all the American and the earlier English cases": that "'[i]t is the benefit and welfare of the infant to which the attention of the court ought principally to be directed.'"[171] As a "necessary result" of this principle, "it follows that the custody of infant children must always be regulated by judicial discretion, exercised in reference to their best interests."[172] The *Mercein* court was tasked with deciding the custodial fate of the child Mary, the subject of a lengthy, bitter dispute between the daughter's biological parents, John and Eliza Barry. In the written opinion of the court,[173] Sen. Alonzo C. Paige, upon a review "of all the [binding] authorities," came to the "undoubting conclusion, that the right of the father to the custody of his child is not absolute." Even in cases "which uphold to the greatest extent the right of the father," Paige noted, "it is conceded that it may be lost by his ill usage, immoral principles or habits, or by his inability to provide for his children." But, according to Paige, the law did not make custody dispositions turn on the father's fitness. He maintained that the child's benefit should be the deciding factor: "The interest of the infant is deemed paramount to the claims of both parents. This is the predominant question which is to be considered by the court or tribunal before whom the infant is brought. The rights of the parents must in all cases yield to the interests and welfare of the infant."[174]

Paige found support for his position in the law of nature,[175] but his argument rested firmly on case law precedent, from which he drew confirmation that custody cases should be settled according to a trust model of guardianship. He maintained, against John Barry's tireless defense of his paternal rights, that the welfare of the child is properly a portion of the sovereign power; and because the sovereign lacks "the requisite knowledge necessary to a judicious discharge of the duties of guardianship and education of children, such portion of the sovereign power as relates to the discharge of these duties, is transferred to the parents." But "[t]here is no parental authority independent of the supreme power of the state," and the delegation of state duties is "subject to such restrictions and limitations as the sovereign power of the nation thinks proper to prescribe." In all cases, Paige concluded, "[t]he rights of the parents must . . . yield to the interests and welfare of the infant."[176]

The convoluted history of the *Mercein* case, with its litany of opinions, created a precedent that defined the contours of custody case law in the second half of the nineteenth century. Hartog describes how "litigants and judges constantly claimed the various opinions in *Mercein* for every side and position": "The case was authority for the state's interest in child care. It was also authority for parental autonomy and authority. It was relied on by women asserting the propriety and legality of a court determination in their favor. It was also cited by courts and lawyers that wished to reaffirm a father's rights." Still, as Hartog concludes, the predominate meaning of the case was "that the authority of courts and other public officials to determine the best interests of the child stood superior to any parental rights, distinctively those of fathers."[177] In his *Treatise on the Constitutional Limitations* (1868), Thomas Cooley, discussing the writ of habeas corpus, cited *Mercein* for the proposition that the courts "do not go further in these cases than to inquire what is for the best interest of the child, and they do not feel compelled to remand him to any custody where it appears to be not for the child's interest." The right of the father, Cooley declares, is not a controlling factor: Though the father's right "is generally recognized as best, . . ; [t]he courts have a large discretion in these cases, *and the tendency of modern decisions has been to extend rather than to limit*" this judicial authority.[178] Not a few of these cases—like *In re Gregg* (1847), to cite one decision—relied on *Mercein* as evidence of the fact that "[i]t is a matter of frequent occurrence that this supposed absolute right [of the father to the custody of the child] is made to yield to the mere will of the child." If the child is of sufficient discretion, the court defers to his or her choice, even where "this choice is . . . opposed to the wishes and claims of both parents, the child preferring to place itself in the care and custody of strangers." The question of a father's superior right, then, arose only when the child was unable to choose for itself. In such cases, and infant Gregg's was one of these, Judge Thomas J. Oakley declared,

> [T]he real question . . . is not what are the rights of the father or mother to the custody of the child, or whether the right of one be superior to that of the other, but what are the rights of the child; . . . The true view is that the rights of the child are alone to be considered, and those rights clearly are to be protected in the enjoyment of its personal liberty, according to its own choice, if arrived at the age of discretion, and if not, to have its personal safety and interests guarded and secured by the law acting through the agency of those who are called upon to administer it.[179]

After *Mercein*, Hartog writes, "[a] structure of understandings that had once been hegemonic—tacit and presumptively true—was on its way to becoming ideological—contested, challenged, and recognizably partial." It is true, as Hartog acknowledges, that paternal legal rights "were not simply atavisms from a rejected past."[180] The father's assertion of a paramount custodial right—to be defeated only by a showing of harm to the child—would remain a feature of custody litigation, and at times a winning feature.[181] Yet, he continues, "[e]ven when courts reaffirmed paternal rights, they did so in a context where those rights had to be asserted noisily, aggressively, in a context where rights were contested, partial, and indeterminate." The paternal presumption men once relied on "could no longer be taken as a given."[182] But American custody courts were never quite so hegemonically predisposed. In all of the cases reviewed by the *Gregg* court, "even those in which the superior right of the father seems to have been most strongly maintained, the principle is clearly recognized that there may be circumstances *irrespective of the personal disqualification of the father* which may defeat his claim."[183] It was not in the atavistic past that courts laid a foundation for the structure of parental rights; this task had to await the post-Lochnerian future, in which the rhetoric of private parental rights would more aggressively challenge the tradition of public parental responsibilities. Most nineteenth-century courts were not easily distracted from the real question: "[N]ot what are the rights of the father or mother to the custody of the child, or whether the right of one be superior to that of the other, but what are the rights of the child."

The courts' presumptions about the welfare of children were bound to reflect the moralistic prejudices of a moralistic era. Children were so often seen through the glass of race/ethnicity/class that they remained largely unprotected from the kinds of mistreatment that today we define as abuse and neglect. It has been suggested that the child welfare measures of the nineteenth century were "bifurcated" along class lines: The private realm of the home was invaded only when families were poor; the state was disinclined to look for parental misconduct among nonpoor families.[184] But nonpoor families were not shielded by parental or privacy rights. The state had always claimed the authority to protect children from abusive and neglectful parents, regardless of class distinctions.[185] That this authority rarely reached the middle- and upper-class home was not a function of personal rights; rather, it is testimony to the all-too-obvious public wrongs—wrongs that both private and public agencies understood as constituting abuse and neglect—that afflicted poor children. Though child mistreatment was often (mis)understood as a social problem attributable to "failed" families, nonetheless, as Grossberg writes in an essay that captures well the contradictions of the child reform movement, child protection efforts became "the primary way to conceptualize a new sense of the public responsibility to the nation's young." Inevitably, as child welfare measures "legitimated a new balance between public interests and family autonomy," the law would separate the interests of children from those of their guardians. If, as Grossberg writes, child protectors deferred to notions of parental control over children "by emphasizing that they were concerned only with failed families," even so their efforts "reduced the deference accorded parental authority."[186]

In fact, an increasing deference to the sanctity of the private home was accompanied by—as Stephanie Coontz argues, it *relied* on—an increasing dependence on public intervention to take over traditional family functions. For Coontz, this "apparent paradox" is explained by "the limited definition of privacy within the middle class":

> Unlike today, when those who preach the sanctity of the private family most vehemently are also those most deeply suspicious of public institutions such as schools and government agencies, it

was the middle-class *supporters* of domesticity who most enthusiastically embraced the construction of specialized extra-familial
institutions to deal with education, crime, mental illness, and
poverty. . . . The privacy demanded by the middle class was social, not personal—the right to non-interference by the rich or the
poor, and most especially the right to reject claims put forward by
the lower classes. In the nineteenth century, many public institutions could be seen as means to extend this right rather than as
threats to it.[187]

In similar fashion, Reva Siegel remarks that the privacy accorded the
nineteenth-century family home was not a privacy of personal rights.[188]
When a blind judicial eye was turned to marital violence, it was done in full
awareness that chastisement was not a spouse's legal prerogative; indeed,
courts endeavored "quite self-consciously" to disassociate themselves from
such a rights-oriented position, focusing instead on the "evils of publicity"
that would attend judicial review of family matters.[189] Siegel discusses the
case *State v. Rhodes* (1868) on this point. The North Carolina Supreme
Court would not inflict this evil upon society:

> It will be observed that the ground upon which we have put this
> decision, is not, that the husband has the *right* to whip his wife
> much or little; but that we will not interfere with family govern-
> ment in trifling cases. We will no more interfere where the hus-
> band whips the wife, than where the wife whips the husband; and
> yet we would hardly be supposed to hold, that a wife has a *right* to
> whip her husband. We will not inflict upon society the greater evil
> of raising the curtain upon domestic privacy, to punish the lesser
> evil of trifling violence.[190]

It was not moral rights but a grotesque distortion of manners that kept the
domestic curtain closed in the nineteenth century. Most striking about talk
of a personal right of domestic privacy, according to Jill Elaine Hasday, is
"how much of a rarity such discourse was."[191]

If courts continued to state, as a matter of course, that the right to the custody of the infant is generally in the father; if some courts stated this principle with great vigor, and some increasingly so as the reform efforts of the last quarter of the nineteenth century gathered steam,[192] nonetheless, they almost always qualified the right to take into account the welfare of the child,[193] and, as in the case *Verser v. Ford* (1881),[194] often decided against a fit biological parent.

In *Verser*, a father demanded the return of his three-year-old daughter, who, from birth, had been in the care of the infant's grandmother. The case is cited as a not-atypical, pro–parental rights case, evidence that nineteenth-century courts allowed the legal claims of the father to outweigh the best interests of the child.[195] From the *Verser* court, there was, indeed, tough talk about the father's entitlement to the child:

> It is one of the cardinal principles of nature and of law that, as against strangers, the father, however poor and humble, if able to support the child in his own style of life, and of good moral character, cannot, without the most shocking injustice, be deprived of the privilege by any one whatever, however brilliant the advantage he may offer. It is not enough to consider the interests of the child alone. . . .
>
> Any system of jurisprudence which would enable the Courts, in their discretion and with a view solely to the child's best interests, to take from him that right and interfere with those duties, would be intolerably tyrannical, as well as Utopian.

Yet, there are, the court continued, "exceptional cases, depending on their own circumstances, in which the sovereign power of the State as *parens patriæ*, acting through the Chancellor, has interfered so far as may be necessary to afford the child reasonable protection." Here, though the father had remarried, was a moral man, and had the means to meet his parental obligations, the *Verser* court found exceptional circumstances in the "ties [that had] been woven between the grand-mother and grand-daughter." Using its "delicate discretion," the court left the child in the home where "[t]here has been all of a mother's care, and scarcely less than a mother's affection."[196] In like manner, most nineteenth-century custody courts would find ways to take a soft approach to hard doctrine. As Hartog, writing about spousal relations, reminds us, "[t]he internal dialogue of the law—the discourse produced by judges and treatise writers—took blanket statements of patriarchal authority and interrogated them, exploring qualification and limitations in the black-letter rules"—and it was not unusual for the interrogation to rout the statement of authority.[197]

The remarkable fact of nineteenth-century custody cases is the great agility with which many judges undertook the necessary, common law work of case-by-case, fact-based inquiries. They did so for the most part without a prerequisite of harm and, being sensitive to each child's preferences and to evolving conceptions of child nurturance, with a readiness to consider the specific circumstances of each child's history.[198] Perhaps most notably, the maternal preference of the tender years doctrine eroded paternalistic control of the child. By custody adjudications and by statutory law, parents were placed, as one court put it, "on an equality as to the future custody of the child."[199] Even a fit father, one whose reputation "may be stainless as crystal," one "who was not afflicted with the slightest mental, moral, or physical disqualification from superintending the general welfare of the infant," could be denied custody if the best interests of the child required it.[200] Yet with equal force the same concern for the child's nurturance could work against the mother's claims.

What the custody law doctrine of the nineteenth century really challenged, then, was parental control of the child. Even when parents reached agreement about custody, the court might choose to settle matters in its own way.[201] The law had given to courts "the most unbounded jurisdiction over minors": "Fathers may be preferred to mothers—mothers to fathers—relatives to parents—or strangers to either, for the custody and care of minors, where the interests of the child require its exercise."[202] As Lee E. Teitelbaum writes, "[R]esort in the nineteenth century to a 'best interests' test made these determinations depend not on either parent's wishes or even their joint wish, but upon a court's assessment of where the public interest lay."[203]

Questions relating to parental custody were to be decided, not by procrustean rules (Rollin Hurd's phrase), but by the broad principle that the well-being of the child was first and foremost a matter of public concern.

While the trust model of parent-child relations was enthusiastically embraced by the child advocates of the nineteenth century,[204] it was not the intellectual property of welfare reformers alone. In his treatise of 1886 on the constitutional limits of the state's police power, Christopher Tiedeman similarly contends that "[t]he authority to control the child is not the natural right of the parents; it emanates from the State, and is an exercise of police power."[205] Tiedeman was anything but partial to the assertion of state authority. For him, popular government was a repudiation of absolutism "in its most repulsive form": the divine right of kings. Because the king obtained his authority "from above," there were no definite limitations on government power:

> The king ruled by divine right, and obtaining his authority from above he acknowledged no natural rights in the individual. If it was his pleasure to give to his people a wide room for individual activity, the subject had no occasion for complaint. But [the subject] could not raise any effective opposition to the pleasure of the ruler, if he should see fit to impose numerous restrictions, all tending to oppress the weaker for the benefit of the stronger.

When divine right was replaced by a theory of popular government, Tiedeman goes on to say, "the opposite principle [was] substituted, that all governmental power is derived from the people." Now "the king and other officers of the government were the servants of the people, and the people became the real sovereign." This principle, too, was subject to abuse. For many years after popular government was established, "there was no marked disposition manifested by the majority to interfere with the like liberties of the minority." "On the contrary," Tiedeman continued,

> the sphere of governmental activity was confined within the smallest limits by the popularization of the so-called *laissez-faire*

doctrine, which denies to government the power to do more than to provide for the public order and personal security by the prevention and punishment of crimes and trespasses. Under the influence of this doctrine, the encroachments of government upon the rights and liberties of the individual have for the past century been comparatively few.[206]

But, according to Tiedeman, the economic pressures of the nineteenth century had weakened doctrines of governmental inactivity and subjugated the rights of the minority (presumably what Tiedeman refers to as the conservative classes) to a constitutionally impermissible "assumption by government of the paternal character altogether." For Tiedeman, it was as though the state, acting as parens patriae, was a too-generous father, too solicitous of its many weak children:

> Governmental interference is proclaimed and demanded every-where as a sufficient panacea for every social evil which threatens the prosperity of society. Socialism, Communism, and Anarchism are rampant throughout the civilized world. The State is called on to protect the weak against the shrewdness of the stronger, to determine what wages a workman shall receive for his labor, and how many hours daily he shall labor. Many trades and occupations are being prohibited because some are damaged incidentally by their prosecution, and many ordinary pursuits are made government monopolies. The demands of the Socialists and Communists vary in degree and in detail, and the most extreme of them insist upon the assumption by government of the paternal character altogether, abolishing all private property in land, and making the State the sole possessor of the working capital of the nation.
>
> Contemplating these extraordinary demands of the great army of discontents, and their apparent power, with the growth and development of universal suffrage, to enforce their views of civil polity upon the civilized world, the conservative classes stand in

constant fear of the advent of an absolutism more tyrannical and more unreasoning than any before experienced by man, the absolutism of a democratic majority.

Tiedeman's goal is to demonstrate that this new form of the patriarchal principle—democratic absolutism—is "impossible in this country, as long as the popular reverence for the constitutions, in their restrictions upon governmental activity, is nourished and sustained by a prompt avoidance by the courts of any violations of their provisions, in word or in spirit."[207] The proper object of government is to protect private rights. These rights "do not rest upon the mandate of the municipal law as a source. They belong to man in a state of nature." The object of government, through its police power, is "to impose that degree of restraint upon human actions, which is necessary to the uniform and reasonable conservation and enjoyment of private rights"—but only to that degree: Any further use of the police power is "a governmental usurpation." "Any law which goes beyond that principle, which undertakes to abolish rights, the exercise of which does not involve an infringement of the rights of others, or to limit the exercise of rights beyond what is necessary to provide for the public welfare and the general security, cannot be included in the police power of the government."[208]

What, then, about laws restricting parental authority? Here, Tiedeman distinguishes the family as a political institution (a subdivision of the body politic) from the family as a "domestic relation." In "early history" the family was an independent political entity, with the father as autocrat. During this "patriarchal age," the father ruled "without constraint, could command the services of the child, make a valid sale of the adult children as well as the minor, and punish them for offenses, inflicting any penalty which his wisdom or caprice may suggest, even to the taking of life." The father was the king of the family, reigning with the same absolutism as the monarch whose authority was of divine provenance. But this absolute control, as Tiedeman would have it, derived from the political character of the family as an institution of government; absolute paternal authority was part of a larger political arrangement, and that authority was taken away as part of new political arrangements. When the family "ceases to be a subdivision of the body politic, and becomes a domestic relation instead of a political institution, . . . this absolute control of the children is taken away." The children become autonomous members of the polity and "acquire political and civil rights, independently of the father":

> By the abolition of the family relation as a political institution, the child, whatever may be his age, acquires the same claim to liberty of action as the adult, viz.: the right to the largest liberty that is consistent with the enjoyment of a like liberty on the part of others; and he is only subject to restraint, so far as such restraint is necessary for the promotion of the general welfare or beneficial as a means of protection to himself. *The parent has no natural vested right to the control of his child.*

The father's "supreme control" is "transferred to the State, the father retaining only such power of control over his children during minority, as the promptings of nature and a due consideration of the welfare of the child would suggest." Thus, the parent's power over the child "is in the nature of a trust, reposed in him by the State . . . , which may be extended or contracted, according as the public welfare may require."[209] What the state gives, it can take away. Parental control of the child can be extended or contracted because it is only "as a police regulation"—not as a right—"that the subjection of minor children to the control of parents may be justified under constitutional limitations." The authority to control the child emanates from the police power of the state, not from the natural right of the parent.[210]

Tiedeman was not alone among libertarian-minded social theorists in his treatment of family history and parental rights. Indeed, his views were shared by the nineteenth century's most celebrated libertarian, Herbert Spencer. Like Tiedeman, Spencer treats parent-child relations as part of history's grand procession. Social progress occurs, simultaneously and at the same pace, on two fronts: the family and the state. "Despotism in the state," Spencer asserts, "is necessarily associated with despotism in the family. The two being alike moral in their origin, cannot fail to coexist." He argues that the law of equal freedom—*"Every man has freedom to do all that he wills, provided he infringes not the equal freedom of any other man"*—"is fully as complete when used on behalf of the child, as when used on behalf of the man." "The child's happiness, too, is willed by the Deity," Spencer maintains; "the child, too, has faculties to be exercised; the child, too, needs scope for the exercise of those faculties." Therefore, the child "has claims to freedom—rights as we call them—coextensive with those of the adult. We cannot avoid this conclusion, if we would." Spencer saw signs in modern society and the modern family that times were changing. "[T]he decline in the rigour of paternal authority and in the severity of political oppression," he remarks, "has been simultaneous." The rapid growth of "democratic feeling" was accompanied "by a tendency toward systems of non-coercive education—that is, toward a practical admission of the rights of children," but not, Spencer hastens to add, the rights of parents. Whatever claims parental care establishes for the parent, it establishes "no title of dominion." However careful parents are in the fulfillment of their obligations, they obtain no right thereby "to play the master" over the child.[211]

Of course, as Tiedeman cautions, though "there is no constitutional limitation to the power of the State to interfere with the parental control of minors," not every denial of parental authority would be "enforcible or beneficial." Tiedeman would trust that "[t]he natural affection of parents for their offspring is ordinarily the strongest guaranty that the best interests of the child as well as of society will be subserved." State interference with the natural bond between parent and child should be reserved for exceptional cases. Quoting Philemon Bliss's treatise *Of Sovereignty* (1886), Tiedeman returns to his anticommunistic theme, this time focusing on the abolition of private familial rights: "Constitutions fail when they ignore our nature. Plato's republic, abolishing the family, making infants but the children of the State, exists only in the imagination." To ignore human nature is to invite popular discontent. ("[A] law, which interferes without a good cause with the parental authority, will surely prove a dead letter.")[212] It would be startling, Tiedeman writes, if the police power were to be "carried to its extreme limit in laying down the proposition, that . . . the State may take away the parental control altogether, and assume the care and education of the child, whenever in the judgment of the legislature such action may be necessary for the public good, or the welfare of the child." But these are policy considerations, "considerations by which to determine the wisdom of a law," and as such are not the concerns of the courts: "[T]hey cannot bring the constitutionality of the law into question, enabling the courts to refuse to carry the law into execution in any case that might arise under it."[213]

Tiedeman concludes his discussion of the parent-child relation with a brief review of the compulsory school attendance question.[214] By midcentury, child rescue schemes had broadened out beyond the law of apprenticeship and institutional commitment. In 1852, Massachusetts became the first state to make school attendance compulsory. By 1900, more than thirty states had enacted compulsory attendance statutes. The impact of this legislation was to make state regulation of the parent-child relation a matter that affected all parents. Who controlled the child's education was no longer a concern primarily for marginal communities. Tiedeman accepted that it is within the police power of the state to establish free schools—only "the most radical disciple of the *laissez-faire* doctrine" would deny to the state this authority—but he considered it a serious question whether the state could require public school attendance against the wishes of the parents. The question of compulsory public schooling laws would turn on whether the control of children were viewed as a right or a privilege. If a right, then the state is not "authorized to interfere with parental authority." If a privilege or duty, then not only could the state compel parents to send their children to school, it could as well "deny to the parent his right to determine which school the child shall attend." Thus, it would be constitutional "to force every child to partake of the State bounty, against its will and the wishes of its parents, perhaps against the honest convictions of the parent that attendance upon the public schools will be injurious to the child." His ideology tempered by reality, Tiedeman thought it probable that "under the influence of the social forces now at work" the view that parental authority is a privilege, a duty entrusted to the parent by the state, would prevail, "and compulsory education [would] become very general."[215]

Tiedeman was right, of course. Compulsory education would become very general—universal, in fact. But the reformers' success would spur contrary social forces, prompting the disciples of the laissez-faire doctrine to bring to the courts their view of parental control as a natural vested right. Mandatory school attendance and, more particularly, mandatory curricular requirements would be subjected to legal challenge, and for the last quarter of the nineteenth century and the first quarter of the twentieth (and beyond), education would be at the forefront of a great cultural and constitutional debate to determine the scope of parental authority to direct the upbringing of the child.

Whose Education Is It, Anyway?: The Curricular Requirements Cases

By 1918, all states had passed compulsory school attendance legislation, and enforcement mechanisms were increasingly efficient.[216] The success of attendance laws prompted novel, rights-based constitutional challenges to governmental control of education. For the most part, these challenges saw only modest success.[217] Direct assaults on the state's power to mandate compulsory school attendance were rejected on the familiar ground that "[t]he natural rights of a parent to the custody and control of his infant child are subordinate to the power of the state, and may be restricted and regulated by municipal laws."[218] Indeed, as one state supreme court stated, what was truly "natural" was the fiduciary educational duty of the parent: "One of the most important natural duties of the parent is his obligation to educate his child, and this duty he owes not to the child only, but to the commonwealth. If he neglects to perform it or willfully refuses to do so, he may be coerced by law to execute such civil obligation. The welfare of the child and the best interests of society require that the state shall exert its sovereign authority to secure to the child the opportunity to acquire an education."[219]

Indirect assaults on compulsory education, which asked the courts to declare a parental right to pick and choose from state-mandated curricular requirements, were received with greater, though hardly unanimous, enthusiasm. In *State v. Webber* (1886), the Indiana Supreme Court found nothing arbitrary in the enforcement of state educational requirements. "The power to establish graded schools carries with it, of course," the court pointed out, "the power to establish and enforce such reasonable rules as may seem necessary to the trustees, in their discretion, for the government and discipline of such schools, and prescribing the course of instruction therein." It was the will of the parent that smacked of arbitrariness, and the state was under no obligation to accommodate it:

> The important question arises, which should govern the public high school of the city of La Porte, as to the branches of learning to be taught and the course of instruction therein, the school trustees of such city, to whom the law has confided the direction of these matters, or the mere arbitrary will of the relator [i.e., the parent], without cause or reason in its support? We are of opinion that only one answer can or ought to be given to this question. The arbitrary wishes of the relator in the premises must yield and be subordinated to the governing authorities of the school city of La Porte, and their reasonable rules and regulations for the government of the pupils of its high school.[220]

For the Supreme Court of New Hampshire, it was novel doctrine that "each parent had the power . . . to decide the question what studies the scholars should pursue, or what exercises they should perform." This would be a power "of disorganizing the school, and practically rendering it substantially useless"; and "however judicious it may be to consult the wishes of parents, the disintegrating principle of parental authority to prevent all classification and destroy all system in any school, public or private, is unknown to the law."[221]

Yet the principle was not entirely unknown. Several late nineteenth-century courts, seeking some libertarian check on state regulation of the family, did uphold parental challenges to specific courses that were a (sometimes required, sometimes optional) part of the public school curriculum.[222] In doing so, they relied on a reading of the common law that paid scant attention to traditional notions of parental power as limited and conditional. In these cases, the parent was given a "paramount right" to choose what courses his child would take from those dictated by the state-mandated curriculum.[223] Though the presumption was that the parent would make "a wise and judicious selection,"[224] the rights of the parent, not the best interests of the child, were the focus of judicial attention.

Typical of cases upholding curricular requirements is *School Board District No. 18, Garvin County v. Thompson*.[225] In *Thompson*, school officials expelled several children who, "under the direction of their parents," refused to take singing lessons, which were part of the prescribed course of study. In its judgment for the parents, the Supreme Court of Oklahoma began its analysis with a restatement of basic common law principles:

> At common law the principal duties of parents to their legitimate children consisted in their maintenance, their protection, and their education. These duties were imposed upon principles of natural law and affection laid on them not only by Nature herself, but by their own proper act of bringing them into the world. It is true the municipal law took care to enforce these duties, though Providence has done it more effectually than any law by implanting in the breast of every parent that natural insuperable degree of affection which not even the deformity of person or mind, not even the wickedness, ingratitude, and rebellion of children, can totally suppress, or extinguish.

Oklahoma state law was "in the main declaratory of the common law," and compulsory school laws had no doubt "modif[ied] more or less the authority of the parent over the child in school matters." Yet the court insisted that the parent's paramount right to determine what studies his child shall pursue is consistent with the common law duty to provide children with a suitable education. This selection right of the parent "is superior to that of the school officers and teachers."[226] Generally, courts that were favorably inclined to parental prerogatives deferred to school authorities when the parent refused to offer any reason for his objection to a curricular requirement.[227] The

Thompson court, however, was not prepared to make even this concession to state authority. It thought the better rule was "to presume, in the absence of proof to the contrary, that the request of the parent was reasonable and just, to the best interest of the child, and not detrimental to the discipline and efficiency of the school."[228]

The *Thompson* court was defending more than a parent's right to take his child out of singing lessons. Underlying these cases was the fear that the parents' educational authority was being made subject to what Tiedeman called the "assumption by government of the paternal character altogether." Where Blackstone saw the absolute control of the child by the parent as barbaric, these courts saw exclusive state control of the child as the hallmark of despotism.[229] Where Kent saw the child's proper education as a prerequisite for social and political engagement, these courts looked to the autonomous family as "the keystone of the governmental structure."[230]

Yet for the courts that struck down educational requirements, all forms of the paternalistic principle were not created equal. Their vision of the home was hardly that of an educational forum where children learned to think for themselves. "In this empire," the *Thompson* court pronounced, "parents rule supreme during the minority of their children."[231] Thus the reminder of the Wisconsin Supreme Court that "it is one of the earliest and most sacred duties taught the child, to honor and obey its parents."[232] While for most jurists and commentators the scope of state authority to regulate the family was considered a question, not of constitutional power for the courts, but of legislative expediency and propriety,[233] the courts that upheld requests for curricular exemptions were protecting rights they considered superior to ordinary legislation.

Especially the rights of the father. In these cases, to borrow from Tiedeman, the family as a domestic relation was replaced by the family as a political institution, in which, said the *Thompson* court, "the parent, and especially the father, is vested with supreme control over the child." The state could not take from the father his right of parental control, any more than it could deprive him of more tangible property rights. If the courts were to uphold required courses against the will of the parent, the state as educator would have "the right to enforce obedience even as against the orders of the parent." The effect "would be to alienate in a measure the children from parental authority."[234] And who other than the father knows what is best for the child? "Now who is to determine what studies she shall pursue in school?" the court asked. "A teacher who has a mere temporary interest in her welfare, or her father, who may reasonably be supposed to be desirous of pursuing such course as will best promote the happiness of his child? The father certainly possesses superior opportunities of knowing the physical and mental capabilities of his child."[235]

Even when the best interests of the child were threatened, the father might rule supreme. In *Board of Education v. Purse*, the Supreme Court of Georgia went so far as to uphold the suspension of a child because the child's parent had disrupted the classroom. The court acknowledged that "it is hard upon the child to be deprived of the benefit of an education because his parent will not submit himself to the reasonable rules, regulations, practices, and customs incident to the system providing for the education of his child," but to grant the child an independent right to an education would be to undermine "established institutions." In a remarkable reversal of the idea that the parent's duty to educate his child is owed to the state, the *Purse* court concluded that the public ought not to be deprived of the benefits of parental absolutism:

> It would be contrary to the policy of our law, based, as it is, upon the common law, to bestow upon the child, in the matter of its education, any right independent of the parent. It needs no argument to sustain the proposition that the father is, and ought to be, the head of the family, and the public has the right to look to him to control his children. A law which would take from him this control, and deprive the public of the benefits to be derived from such control, would be in conflict with our established institutions.

To reach this conclusion, the *Purse* court, like other courts that struck down education requirements, had to read the common law in absolutist terms. The child was no worse off, according to the court, than he would have been at common law. The common law left the child completely at the mercy of the parent's will, so far as obtaining an education was concerned; in fact, the status of the child is the same. At common law he was at the mercy of an arbitrary parent whether he should be placed at school or not; placed at school in [the state of] Georgia he is still at the mercy of an arbitrary parent, who may so conduct himself as to deprive the child of the benefits to be derived from an education.[236]

By ceding to the parent a "paramount right" to select courses from the prescribed state curriculum, the courts fabricated the right they purported to find. The common law did not propose a legal regime that made children's educational best interests secondary to parental rights. Not only was the matter of education deemed a legitimate function of the state,[237] but parental custody itself was made "to depend upon considerations of moral fitness in the parent to be entrusted with the formation of the character of his own offspring."[238] Thus, consistent with common law principles, state compulsory attendance statutes not only set minimal educational requirements for the public schools, but required private schools to offer equivalent instruction.

Though nineteenth- and early twentieth-century courts, notwithstanding the success of some curricular challenges, commonly deferred to the regulatory discretion of school authorities, such deference would be sorely tried as state efforts to regulate education took on more monopolistic features. In 1919, Nebraska and sixteen other states passed statutes prohibiting the teaching of foreign languages in private as well as public schools.[239] To the Nebraska Supreme Court, hearing a challenge to the state language prohibition law, the salutary purpose of the legislation was clear and well within the sphere of the state's police power.[240] In dissent, Judge Charles B. Letton protested that the measure upset the proper allocation of educational control between parent and state, and thereby "infringe[d] upon the fundamental rights and liberty of a citizen protected by the state and federal Constitutions."[241] Letton conceded that the state could manage and control private schools but had no right "to prevent parents from bestowing upon their children a full measure of education *in addition to the state required branches*": "Has it the right to prevent the study of music, of drawing, of handiwork, in classes or private schools, under the guise of police power? If not, it has no power to prevent the study of French, Spanish, Italian, or any other foreign or classic language, unless such study interferes with the education in the language of our country, prescribed by the statute."[242] Letton relied on *State ex rel. Kelley v. Ferguson* (1914), in which the Nebraska Supreme Court *had* upheld a parent's paramount right to select what classes he wanted his child to take from the state-prescribed course of studies. In that case, the parent objected to his child's attendance at a domestic science class. Letton concurred, but in the judgment only. Unwilling "to go so far with respect to the right of parental control" as the state supreme court did, Letton based his concurrence on the fact that domestic science was not a "plainly essential" course. He would extend the right of parental control "only to such studies as are not plainly essential or which are not at least impliedly required to be taught in the grade of school in which the pupil may enroll."[243]

Letton was trying to accommodate the competing concerns of parent and state. Parents had no right to prevent the state from mandating a common curriculum; giving them a veto power over minimal educational requirements threatened to upset the balance of power in favor of parental control. Letton supported the state's authority, though he would have limited it to mandatory subjects. But no principle of law gave the state authority to prevent parents from teaching their children subjects *"in addition to* the state required branches." When Nebraska passed its language prohibition statute, the balance of power was upset in favor of state control. Here, Letton drew his line, knowing that it would likely fall to the United States Supreme Court to sort out the proper allocation of educational control between parent and state.

Rights, Responsibilities, and Religion: *Prince v. Massachusetts* (1944)

Betty Simmons was nine years old when she accompanied Sarah Prince, her aunt and guardian, to distribute religious literature on the streets of Brockton, Massachusetts. Prince did not ordinarily permit Betty to engage in preaching activity on the streets at night, but on the evening of December 18, 1941, she reluctantly yielded to Betty's entreaties. Both Prince and Betty were Jehovah's Witnesses, for whom street preaching is a religious duty. For Betty, street preaching was work commanded by the Lord, but it was work she loved to do. It was a way of worshipping God. For the legislators of Massachusetts, however, Betty's religious work was something else entirely: a violation of the state's child labor laws. These statutes prohibited children from selling or offering to sell "any newspapers, magazines, periodicals or any other articles of merchandise of any description . . . in any street or public place." Criminal sanctions were imposed on parents and guardians "who compel or permit minors in their control to engage in the prohibited transactions." Sarah Prince was convicted on several counts, and, for the most part, the judgment of the trial court was affirmed by the Supreme Court of Massachusetts. Prince appealed to the United States Supreme Court.[244]

Prince v. Massachusetts is well known for its conclusion that "the family itself is not beyond regulation in the public interest, as against a claim of religious liberty." In *Prince*, the Court stressed that the state is responsible for the general welfare of young people. As parens patriae, the state may protect children against the misconduct of their own parents and guardians. The state's parens patriae authority, according to the *Prince* Court, is "not nullified merely because the parent grounds his claim to control the child's course of conduct on religion or conscience."[245]

From Prince's point of view, the state of Massachusetts had struck a blow at the parent's—or, in this case, the guardian's—right of religious mentorship. This, she claimed, the state did not have the authority to do. She rested her case, the Court stated, on two liberties: "[Prince rests her case] squarely on freedom of religion under the First Amendment, applied by the Fourteenth to the states. She buttresses this foundation . . . with a claim of parental right as secured by the due process clause of the latter Amendment." This parental rights buttress was built partly on the law of the state and partly on the law of a higher authority. Prince cited the Court's seminal due process parenting cases as countering "the totalitarian precept that children are the exclusive property of the state." But to her these precedents were hardly as compelling as the call of a duty, to borrow from James Madison, "precedent, both in order of time and in degree of obligation, to the claims of Civil Society."[246]

For Prince, the family is beyond the reach of the state; the family precedes and transcends the state's authority. She argued: "The family and home are institutions in their own right. They do not depend upon government for their creation. Long before organized government was established these institutions prevailed to secure the perpetuation of humanity." In fact, it is the state that depends upon family, which is "the backbone of all orderly governments." The role of the democratic state, accordingly, is "to protect and conserve the parental authority over children, regardless of how misguided others may think that appellant [that is, Prince] is in the spiritual education of the child and the practice of preaching according to the dictates of her conscience." Prince could not follow the dictates of her conscience if she allowed Betty to stray from the true path. Really, then, for Prince, there were not two liberties at stake; rather, the right of religious freedom and the right to parent were inseparably wound together. The state could not strike at one without damaging the other.[247]

Relying on Blackstone, Massachusetts argued that the federal Constitution offered no protection for "the liberty of parents to bring up their children in the religious beliefs of the parents." Natural liberty "consists properly in a power of acting as one thinks fit, without any restraint or control." It is this liberty, as Blackstone taught, that we give up by entering society. Civil liberty is natural liberty "so far restrained by human laws (and no farther) as is necessary and expedient for the general advantage of the public." It is this liberty that is constitutionally protected against unreasonable state encroachment. "The liberty of parents to bring up their children in the religious beliefs of the parents," the state contended, "is a natural and personal liberty; not a civil liberty." This freedom to parent as one thinks fit may be restrained when the welfare of the state requires it. Some restrictions on personal liberty are inevitable, intrinsic as they are to human relationships; some "spring from the helpless or dependent condition of individuals in the various relations of life, among them being those of parent and child." Legislation for the protection of minor children—a "'just restraint[] upon personal liberty'" — is the necessary by-product of the state's status as parens patriae.[248]

For these propositions the state cited a case from 1907 decided by the Supreme Judicial Court of Massachusetts. In *Purinton v. Jamrock*, the court upheld the constitutionality of a state statute that allowed adoption by parents who adhered to a religion different from that of the biological parents. At the outset, the court rejected the notion that parents have "any inherent right of property in their minor child, of which they can in no way be deprived without their consent." Parents are, indeed, "the natural guardians of their child, entitled to its custody, with the right to appropriate its earnings, and may recover damages for any interference with their rights by a wrongdoer." But the right to parent "is not an absolute and uncontrollable one"; it is not a right that will be "enforced to the detriment or destruction of the happiness and well being of the child." Rather, the right to parent "is in the nature of a trust reposed in [parents], and is subject to their correlative duty to care for and protect the child; and the law secures their right only so long as they shall discharge their obligation." In the event that parents fail to discharge their obligation, the child has the right to call upon the state for help: "As the child owes allegiance to the government of the country of its birth, so it is entitled to the protection of that government, which must consult its welfare, comfort, and interests in regulating its custody during its minority."[249]

This protection, as the *Purinton* court would have it, might extend to cases in which a parent's religious beliefs were compromised. The court acknowledged that "[t]he wishes of the parent as to the religious education and surroundings of the child are entitled to weight." But these parental preferences are trumped by the welfare of the child, which "must be first of all regarded and its requirements must be treated as paramount." Indeed, the general policy that "the parents' religion is prima facie the infant's religion" is grounded on the rights of children: on "the right to be brought up, where this is reasonably practicable, on the religion of their parents."[250] For the state of Massachusetts, *Purinton* was strong testimony in support of "the principle of the competency of the state as *parens patriae* to enact laws looking to the establishment of [child] protection." Protective laws are not an unconstitutional interference with freedom of religion, the state argued, "even though such legislation runs *contra* to a particular parent's religious beliefs."[251]

In effect, both Prince and the state of Massachusetts asked the Supreme Court to decide whether a Lockean model of parent-child relations applied to religious parenting claims. Rejecting heightened scrutiny, the *Prince* Court rendered a judgment squarely supporting basic trust principles:

1. While "the custody, care and nurture of the child reside first in the parents," and while parents enjoy the right "to give [children] religious training and to encourage them in the practice of religious belief," neither rights of religion nor rights of parenthood are beyond limitation.[252]

2. While there is a "private realm of family life which the state cannot enter," the state may protect its interest in the well-rounded growth of young people "against impeding restraints and dangers, within a broad range of selection."[253]

3. The state's authority over children's conduct "is broader than over like actions of adults." Thus, the same regulation might be invalid when applied to adults and valid when applied to children.[254]

4. The fact that a complaint combines the interests of parenthood with a free exercise claim does not elicit heightened constitutional protection. The Court took seriously the hybrid nature of Prince's claim: "The parent's conflict with the state over control of the child and his training is serious enough when only secular matters are concerned. It becomes the more so when an element of religious conviction enters." But, as the Court decided, the fact that "two claimed liberties are at stake" does not confer "a broader [constitutional] protection"; the alliance of religious freedom and parenting claims does not narrow the state's "wide range of power for limiting parental freedom and authority in things affecting the child's welfare." Against this hybrid claim, the family remains subject to regulation in the

public interest: "[N]either rights of religion nor rights of parenthood are beyond limitation."[255]

5. A "clear and present danger standard" for cases involving children is not required as a matter of constitutional law or desirable as a matter of social policy.[256]

6. In cases of religious parenting, the rights of the parent and
child, though they may be aligned, are not identical. In *Prince*,
the Court was careful to assign the ownership of the rights at
issue: "[T]wo claimed liberties are at stake. One is the parent's, to bring up the child in the way he should go, which for
appellant means to teach him the tenets and the practices of
their faith. The other freedom is the child's, to observe these
[tenets and practices.] . . . [T]his Court has sustained the parent's authority to provide religious with secular schooling, and
the child's right to receive it."[257] The Court did not address the
question of whether the parent's right to provide religious training (or, presumably, not to provide religious training) trumps
the child's right to receive or reject it. The question would
hover in the wings of several Supreme Court decisions on the
scope of parental rights,[258] but to date it has yet to be presented
on the main stage.

The Court's application of these principles was straightforward, if not
entirely convincing. Pointing to a long line of cases upholding state statutes that might abridge parental rights (such as compulsory schooling laws)
and religious parenting rights (such as compulsory vaccination laws),[259] the
Court rejected Prince's position that such regulations could be justified
only by a threat of harm to the child. No such showing was necessary where
children are involved. The state was required to demonstrate only that it
had a legitimate (not a compelling) interest to promote the public welfare
and that it had used a means—here, a restriction on commercial activity by
children—reasonably related to its purpose (not the least restrictive means
possible). Child protection laws served "the interest of youth itself, and of
the whole community, that children be both safeguarded from abuses and
given opportunities for growth into free and independent well-developed

men and citizens." For the Court, it was simply too late to doubt that legislation designed to safeguard children is within the state's police power, "whether against the parent's claim to control of the child or one that religious scruples dictate contrary action." On the assumption that street preaching was dangerous work for children—the majority was content to rely upon the "harmful possibilities . . . of emotional excitement and psychological or physical injury" that attend upon street preaching—the Court held that Prince was not entitled to an exemption from the general law of the state regulating child labor.[260]

The *Prince* Court limited its holding to the facts before it.[261] (Interestingly, the Court would make the same minimalist gesture in *Wisconsin v. Yoder*, where it distinguished *Prince* to protect parental control over the religious training of children. In both cases, the cabining effort was doomed from the start.) In broader effect, the *Prince* Court sustained the proposition that the welfare of the child is a public good. For its continuance, "[a] democratic society rests . . . upon the healthy, well-rounded growth of young people into full maturity as citizens, with all that implies." This was not a principle that could be restricted to religious pamphleteering. But what does it imply? What is "healthy, well-rounded growth"? What does "full maturity" mean? The Court's answer was decidedly nonauthoritarian: "It is the interest of youth itself, and of the whole community, that children be both safeguarded from abuses and given opportunities for growth into free and independent well-developed men and citizens." If religious parenting rights foreclose these opportunities, they come at too great a cost. The Supreme Court famously said as much to Sarah Prince: While parents may be free to become martyrs themselves, "it does not follow they are free, in identical circumstances, to make martyrs of their children before they have reached the age of full and legal discretion when they can make that choice for themselves."[262]

Nonparental Claims: Toward Psychological Parenthood

Beyond placing parents "on an equality as to the future custody of their children," nineteenth-century courts vigorously supported the custody claims of third parties. In such cases—indeed, in all types of custody cases—it was routine for courts to note, as Justice Story did in *United States v. Green* (1824), a dispute between the child's father and maternal grandparents, that "in a general sense" it is the right of the father to have custody of his child; but courts just as routinely added, as Justice Story did, that the "right" of custodial authority was "not on account of any absolute right of the father, but for the benefit of the infant, the law presuming it to be for his interest to be under the nurture and care of his natural protector, both for maintenance and education."[263] As in cases of divorce, so in third-party cases, where parental custody did not serve the child's best interests, the fiduciary duty of the parent was transferred to the court:

> When, therefore, the court is asked to lend its aid to put the infant into the custody of the father, and to withdraw him from other persons, it will look into all the circumstances, and ascertain whether it will be for the real, permanent interests of the infant; and if the infant be of sufficient discretion, it will also consult its personal wishes. It will free it from all undue restraint, and endeavour, as far as possible, to administer a conscientious, parental duty with reference to its welfare. It is an entire mistake to suppose the court is at all events bound to deliver over the infant to his father, or that the latter has an absolute vested right in the custody.[264]

And, as with divorce cases, third-party custodial decisions did not depend on a finding of parental unfitness.[265] Rather, the deciding consideration was whether someone other than the father or mother had assumed the role of parent, whether, that is, a surrogate had formed a new, parent-like attachment with the child, and, of even greater importance, whether the child had formed a new, child-like attachment with the surrogate.[266] Where such ties were established, parental rights in the "general sense" were allowed, as the Kansas Supreme Court put it, to "sink into insignificance."[267]

Typically, third-party cases addressed the custodial claims of other family members. The case *Merritt v. Swimley* (1886) is a good example of judicial sensitivity to the emotional ties that might bind a child and surrogate parent.[268] The plaintiff in this case was a father who sought custody of his daughter Jessica. When Jessica was an infant, her mother died; subsequently, with the consent of the father, the child was raised by her maternal aunt and the aunt's husband. Thirteen years later, the father sought to regain custody.

The court noted that the father had not been an especially solicitous parent: "[D]uring the thirteen years of his daughter's life in Virginia, he has only seen her two or three times, and has never seen her at all except when called to Virginia on business connected with her mother's property. And he has contributed nothing to her support except the nominal rent obtained from the grandmother for the undivided interest of the first wife in the home place." Conceding that, as a general proposition, the legal right was with "a fit and suitable" parent, the court observed that "there are circumstances which take the case out of the general rule." Such circumstances did not have to include a showing that a parent was unfit to "superintend[] the general welfare of the infant." Indeed, the parental claimant may not have the "slightest . . . disqualification": "[T]here may be cases where the reputation of the father is stainless; he may not be afflicted with the slightest mental, moral or physical disqualification from superintending the general welfare of the infant; the mother may have separated from him without the shadow of a pretense of justification; and yet the interests of the child may imperatively demand the denial of the father's right." Though "the legal rights of the parent or guardian are to be respected," the court insisted that "the welfare of the infant is the pole-star by which the discretion of the court is to be guided."[269]

In cases like Jessica's, "the affections of both child and adopted parent [had] become engaged." Jessica wanted to stay in her adopted home, "where the tenderest ties of affection have been wound around her," and she was of sufficient age and judgment to have her own wishes respected. Thus, for the court, "the real question in a case like this is not what are the rights of the father or the other relative to the custody of the child, or whether the right of the one be superior to that of the other, but *what are the rights of the child?*"[270] There was no question of a right of property in the child. If a right was involved, it was the child's right to enjoy a loving relationship.[271] The court ordered that Jessica should stay with the only parents she had ever known.

To decide third-party claims, custody courts relied on what today we would call the concept of psychological parenthood, their chief concern being continuity of affection.[272] Placement of the child was based on "the instinct of childhood to attach itself and cling to those who perform towards it the parental office," notwithstanding parental legal rights and biological connections. Where third parties "have faithfully executed their trust," courts would not regard parental rights as controlling.[273] In most of these "established ties" disputes, the plaintiff was a single parent, often the father, seeking "reclamation" of a child left in the care of other family members. But the claims of married couples, too, might not be supported if the result meant taking a child from the home where "the child has been nursed, and loved, and cherished."[274] "Even when father and mother are living together," one state supreme court declared, "the court has power, if the best interests of the child require it, to take it away from both parents, and commit the custody to a third person."[275] Further, on occasion nonfamily members who had established ties with the child would be awarded custody.[276] In short, if sundering emotional ties would not be in the best interests of the child, the court would use the full scope of its discretionary authority to maintain an established relationship.[277]

In the custody case *Chapsky v. Wood*[278] (1881), the Supreme Court of Kansas reviewed the "questions of law" that should govern cases involving "established ties." Writing for the court, Judge David Brewer (who would go on to become a justice of the United States Supreme Court) declared that the following propositions were "not subject to much doubt":

1. The presumption that the biological parent is entitled to custody of his or her minor children springs from two sources, both of which assume the duty of parental care: "[O]ne is, that he who brings a child, a helpless being, into life, ought to take care of that child until it is able to take care of itself; and because of this obligation to take care of and support this help-less being arises a reciprocal right to the custody and care of the offspring whom he must support; and the other reason is, that it is a law of nature that the affection which springs from such

a relation as that is stronger and more potent than any which springs from any other human relation."[279]

2. "[A] child is not in any sense like a horse or any other chattel, subject-matter for absolute and irrevocable gift or contract."[280]

3. "[A] parent's right to the custody of a child is not like the right of property, an absolute and uncontrollable right."[281]

4. Once the parent has transferred custody of the child, and "new ties have been formed and a certain current given to the child's life and thought," the court will exercise its discretion to select the most suitable home. "It is an obvious fact, that ties of blood weaken, and ties of companionship strengthen, by lapse of time; and the prosperity and welfare of the child depend on the number and strength of these ties, as well as on the ability to do all which the promptings of these ties compel."[282]

5. In cases of this kind, competing interests must be considered: "The right of the father must be considered; the right of the one who has filled the parental place for years should be considered." Though it might not be "technically correct" to speak of the surrogate parent as a rights-holder, it is only "fair and proper" to respect the interests of those "who have for years filled the place of the parent."[283] Above all, "the paramount consideration is, what will promote the welfare of the child?"[284]

The *Chapsky* court was confronted with familiar facts: a child left in the care of relatives, a father who sought to reclaim custody. Chapsky was not unfit to be a father; though the court described him as "a man still and cold," there was no imputation against him "of an unkind nature or an immoral life." Nonetheless, the child's aunt had truly been a psychological parent to her: "[T]he child has had, and has to-day, all that a mother's love and care can give." In accord with its propositions, the court thought it best to "[l]et well enough alone."[285]

The same child-centered principles might lead the court to decide that certain relationships should be fostered even though emotional ties had not yet been established. The concept of psychological parenthood, in other words, could be employed prospectively. This was the case with John Lippincott.

In *Lippincott v. Lippincott*,[286] the Court of Errors and Appeals of New Jersey was called upon to decide the custodial fate of young John Lippincott. John's mother had died when he was two years old, at which time he was sent to live with his paternal grandparents. There he had lived most of his life. Four years after the death of his mother, John's father died, but not before leaving direction (in writing) that, in the event of his death, John's care, custody, and nurture should be delegated to the boy's paternal grandparents. John's maternal grandparents sought custody for two months a year.[287]

The chancery court had acknowledged, as the paternal grandparents conceded, that there was no "appreciable difference in the material advantages" that the parties were able to give John.[288] There were, however, other advantages that John would never know. He would never know "that devotion and love that is materially fostered by the association of one with those in whose affection he should hold a prominent place."[289] When the court considered John's best interests, it weighed that devotion and love and decided that John's father, regardless of fitness, did not get to dictate the boy's happiness. The "essential inquiry" before the appeals court was "whether, exercising its judgment as parens patriae in behalf of the state, the court of chancery, intent alone upon promoting the best interests of the infant, may in the situation confide [John's] custody for two months of the year to his maternal grandparents."[290] This jurisdictional question led the court to consider the nature and scope of state power to interfere in custody disputes.

The Court of Errors and Appeals began its inquiry with a history lesson. Some countries, the court explained, "considered the child as a charge of the state," while others "conceded to the father absolute dominion over the child." But, taking its cue from neither of these historical antecedents, "[t]he English common law . . . presented a composite system." In such a system, the courts protect children from monopolistic legal regimes, both those that (like Sparta) give the state possession of the child and those that (like Rome) give the parent a general power to dispose of his children.[291] This system of shared authority, which was the basis for American custody cases as well, illustrated the long-standing principle that "[e]quity possesses a controlling and superintending power over all guardians . . . and will take the infant from the guardian and deliver it to another whenever the welfare of the infant requires it."[292] A survey of the case law, the court concluded, revealed that "'[t]he power of the court to intervene for the protection of the infant was . . . an inherent power in the court derived from the common law.'"[293]

The court's decision to hear the case, then, merely affirmed well-settled principles of custody law. In cases like John Lippincott's, the touchstone of its jurisprudence "[was] the welfare and happiness of the infant," not the father's parental rights. "It has been quite generally held," the court went on, "that even the natural right of the father to the custody of his child cannot be treated as an absolute property right." Rather, the right of the father to custody of the child should be thought of "as a trust reposed in the father by the state, as parens patriae for the welfare of the infant."[294]

The court ruled that denying visitation to the maternal grandparents was not in "the manifest interest of the child"—this, for the court, was "the material and only ground for judicial interposition." Determining that it was in young John Lippincott's best interests to spend two months a year with his maternal grandparents, the court took a spacious view of the child's welfare: "That it will be for the material and moral interests of the child in its parental isolation to know and enjoy the affection and love of its mother's people will be conceded by all who are so fortunate as to be able to revive the delectable memories of a youth so placed." The day had long since passed, as the chancery court put it, "when the rights of infants to be properly nurtured are subordinate to the strict legal rights of parents."[295]

Whether, in fact, that day had long since passed was more of a question than the court could have suspected. The appeals court handed down its judgment—a distillation of traditional trust principles—in 1925. But a new jurisprudential attitude was emerging, one in which it could no longer be taken for granted that the rights of parents are subordinate to the interests of the child. In that same year, the Supreme Court decided *Pierce v. Society of Sisters*, which (along with its predecessor case from 1923, *Meyer v. Nebraska*) would carry the mysteries of substantive due process from the marketplace to the home. In the liberty guaranteed by the Fourteenth Amendment, the Court would find a doctrinal philosopher's stone, and, in the best alchemical tradition, it began the "great work" of transforming a sacred trust into a sacred right.

THREE

Parenting as a Sacred Right

In this day and under our civilization, the child of man is his parent's
child and not the state's. Gone would be the most potent reason for
women to be chaste and men to be continent, if it were otherwise. It was
entirely logical for Plato, in his scheme for an "ideal commonwealth," to
make women common; if their children were to be taken from them, and
brought up away from them by the state for its own ends and purposes,
personal morality was, after all, a secondary matter. The state-bred monster
could then mean little to his parents; and such a creature could readily
be turned to whatever use a tyrannical government might conceive
to be in its own interest. In such a society there would soon
be neither personal nor social liberty.
— *Brief of Appellee (William Guthrie and Bernard Hershkopf)*
Pierce v. Society of Sisters *(1925)*

Doctrinal Beginnings and Byways: *O'Connell v. Turner* (1870)

Daniel O'Connell was fourteen when he was committed to the Reform
School of Chicago under a city statute that permitted arrest and confinement "of all children, between the ages of six and sixteen years, who are destitute of proper parental care, and growing up in mendicancy, ignorance,
idleness or vice."[1] Upon petition by Daniel's father, the Supreme Court of
Illinois issued a writ of habeas corpus, and the case came before the court.
The year was 1870. For the city of Chicago, the city attorney submitted a
brief that was little more than a direct recitation of the case *Ex parte Crouse*
(1839). In *Crouse*, the Pennsylvania Supreme Court had declared that "the

93

public has a paramount interest in the virtue and knowledge of its members, and that, of strict right, the business of education belongs to it."[2] On behalf of Daniel, the attorney William T. Butler offered, as David Tanenhaus describes it, "a vision of the postbellum world in which the liberty of the individual would reign supreme."[3] For his critique of state paternalism Butler found support in the newly minted Fourteenth Amendment. The liberty guaranteed to "all persons," he asserted, was promised to children, too. In *O'Connell v. Turner*, the legal world received early warning of movement along the fault line between common law tradition and liberal constitutionalism.[4] Though the court pursued a natural law alternative, it was Butler's brief that pointed out the means by which parental rights would make their constitutional appearance.

The *Turner* court echoed Butler's solicitude for the rights of children, but it turned to a more ethereal source of law: "the rights which inhere both in parents and children." Both parent and child enjoy "the inherent and inalienable right to liberty" that is "independent of all human laws and regulations." This liberty, as Sarah Prince would argue some fifty years later, is "higher than constitution and law, and should be held forever sacred." Far from being the product of legislative largesse, the power of the parent is a natural right, "an emanation from God" that the municipal law should not disturb "except for the strongest reasons." Not surprisingly, the court demanded a tough standard of review as a check on undue state regulation. Violations of divine emanations, it would appear, can be justified only by "dire necessity." So, before it could abridge the right to parent, the state was required to prove "gross misconduct or almost total unfitness on the part of the parent." By "parent," the court really meant the father, who "struggles and toils through life" to educate the child. Like the courts that upheld the parent's right to choose what public school courses his child would take, the *Turner* court was alarmed that state interference might "alienate the father's natural affections."[5]

The *Turner* court did not entirely abandon the trust model of parent-child relations, nor did it endorse a rule of arbitrary parental power. The parent (unlike, as the court conceded, the father under Roman law) has only as much authority "as may be necessary to the discharge of his sacred trust."

The law tolerated "moderate correction and temporary confinement." But these concessions only confirmed that, in Daniel's case, the state's commitment statute was itself a product of uncontrolled authority: "If a father confined or imprisoned his child for one year, the majesty of the law would frown upon the unnatural act, and every tender mother and kind father would rise up in arms against such monstrous inhumanity. Can the State, acting as *parens patriae*, exceed the power of the natural parent, except in punishing crime?"[6] The law would not tolerate the despotism of the state any more than it would the despotism of the parent. "The principle of the absorption of the child in, and its complete subjection to the despotism of, the State," the court stated, "is wholly inadmissible in the modern civilized world."[7] The Supreme Court of Illinois ordered Daniel to be discharged, concluding that the confinement statute, which, in its view, made crimes of misfortunes, was hopelessly vague and deprived children of the most basic due process protections.[8]

Though *Turner* would prove to be an outlier, it gained notoriety as compulsory education statutes strengthened state authority over the child. The state had placed Daniel in a reform school. It was a different—if, to its opponents, no less sinister—type of schooling that made *Turner* a case of national interest. For it could be argued that the case's natural law principles applied equally to compulsory school attendance laws. Indeed, the argument was made, and forcefully so, by the notable jurist Isaac Redfield, a former chief justice of the Vermont Supreme Court, whose highly enthusiastic appraisal of *Turner* appeared in the *American Law Register*. For Redfield, compulsory public education was a battleground on which were arrayed two great forces. On one side were those who thought that compulsory education was no more than a form of confinement without due process. On the other side were the forces of reform, whose purpose was "to erect an empire, superior both in character and power to any other, ancient or modern." The hope of the reformers, as Redfield saw it, was to mold a country of diverse nationalities and discordant political and religious viewpoints "into one homogeneous compound of purity and perfection," and one of the "foundation stones" of this progressive empire was to be compulsory education. He applauded the *Turner* court "as striking at the very root and life of one of the most favorite schemes of reform known to the present age; what is called in popular language, legislative moral reform and compulsory public education."[9]

Redfield thought that *Turner* had struck the reformers "a fatal blow at the very foundation of their entire superstructure." His commentary was as colorful as it was hyperbolic. "[T]his decision projects a fatal shaft, which has entered between the very joints of the harness of the most impregnable armor [of the reformers]," Redfield wrote. Such a decision "must, if maintainable, penetrate into the most vital parts of its most indispensable machinery." Once the progress of the empire builders was stopped, all men would be "free to keep their own children at home, and educate them in their own way." This would be "a very wonderful advance in the way of liberty."[10]

One of Redfield's objections to compulsory education measures was that the purity and perfection of reformist schemes had a decidedly Protestant bias. The "non-sectarian" moral majoritarianism of the common schools, he claimed, evinced an "ominous squint" toward Catholic children.[11] True moral reform, Redfield argued, had to begin, and stay, at home. It was bred from within the domestic empire of the family, where children could be trained from earliest infancy to follow the dictates of private authorities: "[A]ll hopeful and reliable moral reforms must be looked for only in a high degree of religious faith and culture, from earliest infancy; and . . . this cannot be expected to come from the common schools, or the reform schools, or any other schools; but exclusively or mainly from family training, and from the authoritative teaching of the church and her ministers, in the daily discipline of a devout and holy life." What Redfield called "text-book-training" would not help children, he claimed, "but rather the contrary." It would lead children to "vain conceit and imperfect comprehension, and the attempt in all classes to handle things which are too high for them."[12] For the educational utopia sought by misguided reformers, Redfield would substitute the pristine setting of the family, a domestic paradise (without low-hanging and far-reaching temptations) where children could be trained by reliable moral authorities. It may be true, as Tanenhaus contends, that *Turner* is "the first modern children's rights case,"[13] but Redfield's commentary should be a reminder that what, for the adult, may appear to be a step forward—an expansive independence from state authority—might be, for the child, little more than a step backward toward complete dependence on private authorities; what appears to be the child's right might do little more than replace one paternalistic threat with another.

Redfield's commentary did not go unnoticed by courts considering similar cases. In 1876, in *Milwaukee Industrial School v. Supervisor of Milwaukee County*,[14] the Wisconsin Supreme Court reviewed the constitutionality of a state statute that allowed children to be transferred from the Milwaukee Poorhouse to the Milwaukee Industrial School. The objection to the law was that it operated as an imprisonment without due process of law. Thus, *Turner* was on point. The Wisconsin court was struck "so forcibly" by the views of Redfield ("that great jurist and gifted man") that, to begin its opinion, it borrowed his picture of a country at war with itself:

> We live in a time of inquiry and innovation, when many things having the sanction of time are questioned, and many novelties jarring with long accepted theories are proposed. In political science, there are those who would reduce government to a mere skeleton of absolutely necessary powers, purely political; and those who favor paternal government, recognizing in the sovereignty much of the authority of patriarchal rule. All this is seen chiefly in political discussions; but the late reports show that these conflicting theories are finding their way into judicial tribunals.

Though the court shared Redfield's distrust of theories that, under the name of reform, tended "to substitute the authority of the state, as *parens patriae*, for parental authority and domestic discipline," it upheld the Wisconsin statute for several reasons. First, the court distinguished between commitment and imprisonment. Parental authority often implies some form of restraint. To secure the welfare of children, the state, acting as parens patriae, was compelled at times to use its "parental" authority to restrain. Second, under the Wisconsin statute, the state assumed this authority only upon "the total failure" of the parent to provide for the child. The *Turner* court had been troubled by the broad sweep of the state's authority to detain children on the basis of ignorance, idleness, and vice. The commitment criteria of the Wisconsin statute, in contrast, were adequately respectful of the primary caretaking role of the family. The court found it difficult "to comprehend the right of a parent to complain that the discharge by the state of his own duty to his child, which he has wholly failed to perform, is an imprisonment of the child as against his parental right in it." Third, the court read the statute "not to foreclose the right of a parent, when competent, to resume the custody and care of his child." Under the statute, the parent's right to custody would be restored upon a showing that "the disability or default on which the child's commitment proceeded was accidental or temporary, and no longer exists." With these protections in place, there was no reason to fear that Wisconsin's commitment statute was a step on the road to the absorption of the child in, and its complete subjection to, the despotism of the state.[15]

When Illinois revised its commitment statute, it was more attentive to children's rights. In the case *In re Ferrier* (1882),[16] the Illinois Supreme Court again considered a statute allowing dependent children to be committed to a suitable industrial school. The court hastened to point out that the statute was drafted with "anxious provision" for the protection of due process. Like the court in *Milwaukee Industrial School*, the Illinois Supreme Court rejected the notion that confinement must mean punishment. The Industrial School for Girls was not a prison, it declared, but a school, "and the sending of a young female child there to be taken care of, who is uncared for, and with no one to care for her, we do not regard [as] imprisonment." Some restraint was essential to the proper education of children; thus, commitment statutes were "in no just sense an infringement of the inherent and inalienable right to personal liberty."[17]

The *Ferrier* court took pains to justify its jurisdiction over cases involving dependent children. Its power to commit children to proper placements outside the family was "but of the same character of the jurisdiction exercised by the court of chancery over the persons and property of infants, having foundation in the prerogative of the Crown, flowing from its general power and duty, as *parens patriae*, to protect those who have no other lawful protector." In describing the scope of its authority, the court, echoing Story, restated the basic features of the trust model of parent-child relations:

> [The court's] jurisdiction extends to the care and person of the infant, so far as is necessary for his protection and education, and upon this ground that court interferes with the ordinary rights of parents in regard to the custody and care of their children, for although, in general, parents are intrusted with the custody of the persons and the education of their children, yet this is done upon the natural presumption that the children will be properly taken care of, and will be brought up with a due education. But whenever this presumption is removed, and the parent is grossly unfit and fails in this respect, the court of chancery will interfere, and deprive him of the custody of his children, and appoint a suitable person to act as guardian, and to take care of them, and to superintend their education.[18]

The rights of the parent, according to the court (following Blackstone), are ordinary rights, an aspect of civil, not natural, liberty. Of course, the state may impose "restrictions . . . upon personal liberty." The very survival of society depends upon it: "The right to liberty which is guaranteed is not that of entire unrestrainedness of action. Civil government in itself implies an abridgment of natural liberty." As does the survival of the child. Restrictions on the personal liberty of parents "spring from the helpless or dependent condition of individuals in the various relations of life, among them being those of parent and child, guardian and ward, teacher and scholar." These "are legal and just restraints upon personal liberty which the welfare of society demands." And, citing Cooley, the court concluded they "entirely consist with the constitutional guaranty of liberty."[19]

Newton Bateman was unperturbed by the outcome of *O'Connell v. Turner*. As the superintendent of public instruction of the state of Illinois and a leading champion of compulsory school attendance laws, Bateman was well aware that the natural law footing of the *Turner* decision could be relied upon, as he wrote, "by those who deny the competency of a legislature to meddle with the question of school attendance." In his report of 1872 on the condition of Illinois' free school system, Bateman struck a glancing blow at Judge Redfield's commentary on the case. The logic of Redfield's argument, Bateman wrote, swept too broadly: It not only demonstrated the unconstitutionality of compulsory school attendance laws, but "even create[d] a doubt of the power of the legislative department to establish and maintain a system of free schools!"[20]

Bateman turned *Turner* upon itself. He was fully prepared to support the notion that deprivation of liberty without due process violated "the inherent and inalienable right of all men to their personal liberty." In Bateman's view, though, there was no comparison between Daniel O'Connell's confinement and compulsory school attendance. In fact, Bateman himself used the idea of inherent rights, employing the higher law language of the *Turner* court to declare that "education is a natural and inalienable right" of every child; it is, he asserted, with a familiar rhetorical flourish, "a right independent of all human laws and regulations; higher than constitution and law; and . . . it should be held forever sacred." The appeal to natural law was thus a double-edged sword, capable of being wielded by both sides in the war of educational reform. "We believe that the same bill of rights which so firmly buttresses the opinion of the [*Turner*] court," Bateman declared, "is also the impregnable bulwark of our position." Among the inherent and inalienable rights of children, Bateman found "not only 'life, liberty, and the pursuit of happiness,' but *education*, also."[21]

In this contest for a natural law imprimatur, neither side would prevail. Bateman would not get a declaration that education is a fundamental right.[22] But the Supreme Court has clearly stated that public education is more than some mere "governmental 'benefit' indistinguishable from other forms of social welfare legislation." The distinction, according to the Court, is marked by "the importance of education in maintaining our basic institutions, and the lasting impact of its deprivation on the life of the child."[23] For his part, Redfield would be disappointed by continued state restrictions on parental authority, though no doubt pleased with the ruling of the *Milwau-*

kee Industrial and *Ferrier* courts that due process requires proof of parental unfitness before the state can assume custody of a child (and no doubt very pleased to learn that the modern Supreme Court has confirmed that termination of parental rights must be premised on a clear and convincing showing of unfitness). *Turner* did not project a fatal shaft at state efforts to regulate child welfare.[24] But it was, clearly enough, a warning shot, putting the state on notice that the battle had been engaged. The reformers would win the day: Compulsory education statutes would be adopted by all states. Yet, as *Turner* reminds us, the armor of the "child savers" was not impregnable.

Whose Education Is It, Anyway?:
Meyer v. Nebraska (1923) and *Pierce v. Society of Sisters* (1925)

The *Pierce* Court famously pronounced that the child is not the mere creature of the state. It is a peculiarly understated proposition, seemingly defensive in its negative assertion. When *Pierce* is set against a tradition of cases that support a trust model of parent-child relations, however, the Court's carefulness makes good sense. For the courts had said time and again that the child is "primarily a ward of the state."[25] *Meyer* and *Pierce* have been read to affirm the fundamental nature of parental rights, but, in fact, they stand for a much more modest proposition: that the state does not have *exclusive* authority over the child's education, or, more particularly, that the state cannot prohibit parents from teaching their children subject matter outside the scope of a state-mandated curriculum or from teaching them outside the public school system.[26]

There was nothing new in the alarm that the state was claiming exclusive control of education. The mid-nineteenth century had witnessed a protracted and, at times, even violent struggle to decide the fate of public school funding.[27] Protesting that the common schools had "assumed the exclusive right of monopolizing the education of youth," Catholic leaders argued that the purportedly secular education provided by the schools was really instruction in the "sectarianism of infidelity." They warned that state control of education would lead to even more ominous monopolies:

Should the professors of some weak or unpopular religion be oppressed today, the experiment may be repeated tomorrow on some other. Every successful attempt in that way will embolden the spirit of encroachment and diminish the power of resistance; and, in such an event, the monopolizers of education, after having discharged the office of public tutor, may find it convenient to assume that of public preacher. The transition will not be found difficult or unnatural from the idea of common school to that of a common religion.[28]

The Catholics lost this battle, but the war against "the monopolizers of education" would remain a hotly contested one. In the curricular requirements cases, opponents of state-controlled education took a more targeted approach. We have seen that some courts tried to swing the pendulum of educational authority back to the parent. The Wisconsin Supreme Court asked, "Whence, we again inquire, did the teacher derive this exclusive and paramount authority over the child, and the right to direct his studies contrary to the wish of the father?"[29] In these cases, though, the state was not prohibiting parents from teaching their children subject matter beyond that required by the state, or prohibiting parents from teaching their children outside the public school setting. This is precisely what the state tried to do in *Meyer* and *Pierce*. In *Meyer*, the state had prohibited the teaching of modern foreign languages to children in the primary grades of all schools, public and private. (The state statute also had imposed restrictions on the use of a foreign language as a medium of instruction.) In effect, the state was claiming the authority to establish a curricular monopoly, at school and, as a practical matter perhaps, at home. In *Pierce*, the monopoly demanded by the state was institutional. The state wanted to prohibit private schooling for children between the ages of eight and sixteen. In both cases, the concern, broadly stated, was whether the state had "carr[ied] the doctrine of governmental paternalism too far."[30] But regardless of its allusion to fundamental rights,[31] the Court did not declare a general parental right to direct the education of children. Indeed, it decidedly declined the invitation to embrace a spacious, natural rights position in support of parental authority, walking instead in the well-worn path of basic trust tenets.[32]

As David Upham writes, the Court "indicated that the right to direct a child's education results not from a natural familial relation, but simply as a necessary concomitant to the power of custody, however defined and assigned. For the Court, it was not natural parenthood that gave both custodial and educational rights; it was custodial power—whether resulting from biology, positive law, or otherwise—that gave educational rights."[33] What the Court did acknowledge, in *Meyer* (and its companion cases),[34] was the right to teach something *in addition* to what the public schools required, and, in *Pierce*, "the right of parents to provide an *equivalent* education in a privately operated system."[35] More particularly, neither *Meyer* nor *Pierce* rejected the government's authority to enforce and regulate the parental duty to educate. The *Meyer* Court did not question the authority of the state "to compel attendance at some school and to make reasonable regulations for all schools, including a requirement that they shall give instructions in English." In *Pierce*, the Court remarked that the case raised no question "concerning the power of the state reasonably to regulate all schools." The question that these cases considered is how far the state can go in dictating what the parent can and cannot do.[36]

Meyer teaches that the state may not set up a standard of education for children and prohibit any additional instruction. The Court's reasoning was based on the arbitrariness of the language prohibition. The state had argued that the statute would have a salutary effect on children that "'outweighed the restriction upon the citizens generally, which, it appears, was a restriction of no real consequence.'"[37] The Court asked, however, not what good the statute would do, but what harm it might prevent. It answered that the mere knowledge of a foreign language could not reasonably be regarded as clearly harmful. Thus, in proscribing foreign language instruction in private schools, the legislature had exceeded its police powers, and in so doing, it had infringed "rights long freely enjoyed," including the right to supplement the state's educational prescriptions.[38] (Privately, Chief Justice William Howard Taft confirmed the limited reach of the Court's assertion of parental rights. He wrote that *Meyer*, though it does not prevent the state from regulating private schools, "does prevent the Legislature from forbidding a parent to employ a private school or a private school teacher to teach his child any subject matter which is not in itself vicious.")[39] If there is a fundamental right at stake in *Meyer*, it is the right of the parent "after he has complied with all proper requirements by the state as to education, to give his child such further education in proper subjects as he desires and can afford."[40]

This is the narrow entitlement for which Arthur F. Mullen, on behalf of Robert Meyer, argued before the Court. Mullen was careful to concede that the state, under its police power, could enforce curricular requirements. But this was as far as he was prepared to go: "I do not concede for a moment that the legislature has the power, when we comply with the curriculum of study prescribed by the State, to deny us the right to teach a foreign language as an optional subject." What the plaintiff in error wanted was the "right to teach these foreign languages and other branches in addition to the curriculum required by the public schools."[41] (The plaintiff in error, who was a teacher at a parochial school, had framed the case as implicating his due process rights to pursue a calling and to enter into contracts. Here, as in *Pierce*, the parents of schoolchildren were not parties to the litigation.[42] But the Court took a broader view of the interests at stake: "Evidently the Legislature has attempted materially to interfere with the calling of modern language teachers, with the opportunities of pupils to acquire knowledge, and with the power of parents to control the education of their own.")[43] If such teaching did not disrupt the required curriculum, Mullen argued, there was no sound reason under the police power to prohibit it:

> The only objection they can make to the teaching of foreign languages in a private or parochial school is this: I can conceive that if it was done in such a way as to interfere with the regular course of study, there might be reasonable objection to it. But when we get above the minimum requirements in our State, qualifications of teachers, equipment, and everything else, it is none of the state's business what we teach the child, so long as we do not teach it

sedition, or something of that kind. We have a right to teach any useless or harmless study—gymnastics, dancing, or anything else; and languages as well as anything else; because there is nothing inherently bad about learning a foreign language.[44]

Central to Mullen's argument was the question of whether the statute merely regulated or actually proscribed the teaching of foreign languages. This distinction between the power to regulate and the power to destroy was a standard feature of due process cases.[45] Though, as the Court conceded, regulation may be proper where there is "abuse incident to an occupation ordinarily useful," abolition requires more: some sort of emergency, in fact.[46] This point was doubly important because Oregon's recent enactment of a statute *prohibiting* private schooling for the primary grades was clearly a secondary object of the *Meyer* Court's deliberations. Before the Court, and at the virtual invitation—indeed, insistence—of Justice James Clark McReynolds, Mullen put forward a slippery slope argument: that the elimination of foreign language teaching would inevitably lead to the abolition of private schools.[47]

Both sides agreed that teaching children while they were young was the key to educational success. The state argued that the law was regulatory in character, pointing to the fact that the statute did not "forbid the use of foreign languages by persons of maturity or prevent the study of foreign languages by persons who have passed the eighth grade." The purpose of the law was not to prohibit foreign language instruction, but "to prevent children reared in America from being trained and educated in foreign languages and foreign ideals before they have had an opportunity to learn the English language and observe American ideals." The state's interest was based on the "well known fact that the language first learned by a child remains his mother tongue and the language of his heart." By forcing children to wait until they passed the eighth grade, the law worked "to insure that the English language shall be the mother tongue and the language of the heart of the children reared in this country who will eventually become the citizens of this country."[48] For Nebraska, both educational success (learning the English language) and civic success (learning the language of the

American heart) were well within the state's police powers and superior to the rights of the parent:

> If it is within the police power of the state to regulate wages, to legislate respecting housing conditions in crowded cities, to prohibit dark rooms in tenement houses, to compel landlords to place windows in their tenements which will enable their tenants to enjoy the sunshine, it is within the police power of the state to compel every resident in Nebraska to so educate his children that the sunshine of American ideals will permeate the life of the future citizens of this republic. A father has no inalienable constitutional right to rear his children in physical, moral or intellectual gloom.[49]

Mullen fully accepted the state's pedagogical premises. However, artfully drawing upon Pharaoh's edict to the Hebrews to make bricks without straw,[50] he countered that because the law prohibited children from studying a foreign language "when they are most impressionable," it amounted to a total abolition of foreign language instruction. Mullen reasoned, "[I]t is more difficult for a child to learn a language after it gets into high school than it is in the lower grades; and [the statute's] purpose is to discourage the study of foreign languages; that is the only theory upon which it was enacted."[51]

The Court found that the statute was a prohibition flatly denying parents the right to supplement the mandated curriculum. It would require some "adequate foundations" to justify a blanket ban on foreign language teaching; otherwise, the state law was without "reasonable relation to any end within the competency of the State." Two years later, the *Pierce* Court would similarly find that private schools were not harmful; that the result of enforcing the state legislation would be their destruction; and, finally, that there were no interests sufficient to justify the state's exclusive institutional control of the child's education.[52]

If the doctrinal results of *Meyer* and *Pierce* were modest, the same cannot be said of the Court's rhetoric. The Court's homage to "rights long freely enjoyed" was as much an anxious response to the prospect of a liberty-denying future as it was an accurate picture of a liberty-protecting past.[53] The shadow of socialist child-rearing was never far from the legal debate.

In 1922, when the voters of Oregon approved an initiative mandating public education, it became clear that the Supreme Court would enter the fray. The next year, in *Meyer*, the law professor William Dameron Guthrie filed an amicus brief specifically to address the Oregon compulsory public school law. Guthrie described the Oregon act as "a revolutionary piece of legislation," evoking images of Bolshevik menace:

> It adopts the favorite device of communistic Russia—the destruction of parental authority, the standardization of education despite the diversity of character, aptitude, inclination and physical capacity of children, and the monopolization by the state of the training and teaching of the young. The love and interest of the parent for *his* child, such a statute condemns as evil; the instinctive preferences and desires of the child itself, such a law represses as if mere manifestations of an incorrigible or baneful disposition.[54]

The law was not only communistic; perhaps worse, it was Platonic. Guthrie deplored "[t]he notion of Plato that in a Utopia the state would be the sole repository of parental authority and duty and the children be surrendered to it for upbringing and education."[55] Likewise, on behalf of the defendants opposing Nebraska's language prohibition, Mullen had portrayed the case as one about "the power of a legislative majority to take the child from the parent." This, he warned, was "the principle of the soviet."[56] (Proponents of compulsory public schooling could also play the communist card. In *Pierce*, the state argued that "[i]f the Oregon School Law is held to be unconstitutional, it is not only a possibility but a certainty that within a few years the great centers of population in our country will be dotted with elementary schools which instead of being red on the outside will be red on the inside.")[57]

It was strong rhetoric—and it was effective. Striking down Nebraska's foreign language prohibition, Justice McReynolds followed, and bettered,

Guthrie's dislike of classical models of education. He compared the language prohibition statute to the communistic parenting measures of ancient Sparta ("In order to submerge the individual and develop ideal citizens, Sparta assembled the males at seven into barracks and intrusted their subsequent education and training to official guardians") and Plato's *Republic* ("[T]he wives of our guardians are to be common, and their children are to be common, and no parent is to know his own child, nor any child his parent"). For the Court, such measures rested on an allocation of educational control wholly at odds with the letter and spirit of the Constitution.[58]

Then, in 1925, the Supreme Court struck down Oregon's compulsory education law, finding that it "unreasonably interfere[d] with the liberty of parents and guardians to direct the upbringing and education of children under their control." Again writing for the Court, Justice McReynolds made the case one about the power of the state "to standardize its children by forcing them to accept instruction from public teachers only." Thus his declaration that "[t]he child is not the mere creature of the State."[59] His antistatist fervor on high display, McReynolds drafted what the Supreme Court, in *Wisconsin v. Yoder* (1972), would cast as "a charter of the rights of parents to direct the religious upbringing of their children."[60]

Yet these cases are hardly a "ringing endorsement of religious freedom and of limited government dominion over citizens."[61] Concerned that the state was assuming "the paternal character altogether," the Court, its rights rhetoric notwithstanding, sustained only the limited proposition that neither parent nor state enjoyed absolute authority over the child. And even if *Meyer* and *Pierce* were doctrinally more ambitious, reliance on them would pose a difficulty for supporters of parental rights. *Meyer* and *Pierce* required only that the state not restrict the right to parent—or more precisely, the right of parents to direct the education of their children—unreasonably or arbitrarily. In other words, the Court applied a reasonableness test, not the strict scrutiny that today is afforded to fundamental rights.[62] To be sure, *Meyer* and *Pierce* were decided before the Supreme Court had delineated degrees of constitutional scrutiny, but the reasonableness standard of these early due process cases shows little of the rigor of heightened review.[63]

For parentalists who view judicial activism with suspicion, the comfort offered by *Meyer* and *Pierce* is especially cold. For these are substantive due process cases, decided at the height of the Court's constitutional campaign against "unreasonable" social and economic regulations. This was a wide-open judicial crusade, little less than a call to change "the whole theory of the relations of the State and Federal governments to each other and of both these governments to the people."[64] For *Lochner's* author, Justice Rufus Peckham, the seventeenth and eighteenth centuries—and here his history is not far from the mark—were a time "when views of governmental interference with the private concerns of individuals were carried to the greatest extent."[65] Modern times, however, called for a modern jurisprudence. While for Blackstone the due process right of liberty "consists in the power of locomotion, of changing situation, or removing one's person to whatsoever place one's own inclination may direct,"[66] the *Meyer* Court would not be so restrained, declaring that the liberty guaranteed by the Fourteenth Amendment denotes much more than mere freedom from bodily restraint.[67] Whatever due process denotes, the freedom that *Meyer* and *Pierce* establish is entirely dependent on court-created rights. (This point is not lost on parental rights advocates. Consider the concern voiced by Michael Farris, the founder of the Home School Legal Defense Association: "In short, Scalia believes that no right is protected unless it is expressly stated in the text of the Constitution. While most of us like this theory if it is used to reverse *Roe v. Wade*, we would be quite alarmed if parental rights were suddenly no longer a protected constitutional right.")[68] Thus, the right to parent, as far as the cases establish one, stands on the same constitutional footing as the rights to use contraception, to terminate a pregnancy, or to engage in consensual homosexual sodomy. For that matter, the right to parent as a matter of due process stands on the same footing as the right of a minor to use contraception or to terminate a pregnancy without parental consent or notification.[69] Though the antistatist sentiment of *Meyer* and *Pierce* would long resonate with those seeking a fundamental right to parent, the reality is that these cases, and their resurrection in the modern era of substantive due process, give advocates of parental rights good reason to be careful with their constitutional wishes.

Rights, Responsibilities, and Religion: *Wisconsin v. Yoder* (1972) and Hybrid Rights

Wisconsin v. Yoder is by all measures an odd case. Its facts are, to borrow a word that echoes throughout the decision, idiosyncratic. Its reasoning is a strange brew of romantic projection and conscious self-deception, something akin to infatuation from a court old enough to know better. Its holding is uncertain; it is limited to the facts of the case, yet it has been a steady prop for those seeking religious exemptions from generally applicable law. And though its legacy is tied to the doctrine of hybrid rights, it is not clear why the Court bothered with such a creation. Or even *whether* it did.

It is clear that the *Yoder* Court, on the unique set of facts before it, repudiated the trust model of parent-child relations. Whereas the Court's seminal parenting cases established a due process right to direct the upbringing of children, *Yoder* grants much more authority than the word "direct" suggests. It gives religious parents a right to *control* the upbringing of their children, and to do so by keeping them cut off from foreign ideas and influences. *Yoder* goes well beyond the rule of *Pierce* that state educational regulation must "yield to the right of parents to provide an equivalent education in a privately operated system." The Amish parents refused to send their children to secondary school altogether. Like *Meyer* and *Pierce*, *Yoder* reflects a deep disquiet about the state's power to influence its children, but, really, here the Court sought to protect a religious community from nonstate forces. Secondary schooling, the Court stated, would bring "[t]he Amish mode of life . . . into conflict increasingly with requirements of contemporary society exerting a hydraulic insistence on conformity to majoritarian standards."[70] To secure this way of life from the (hydraulic?) pressures of modernity, *Yoder* granted a particular group of religious parents not just the right to supplement the state-mandated curriculum (*Meyer* did that) or the right to choose a private educational option (*Pierce* did that), but an outright exemption from the fiduciary responsibility to prepare young people for the "additional obligations" of adult life. *Yoder* is itself the charter of religious parenting rights it levies upon precedent.

The *Yoder* Court made a heavy analytical investment in the Amish way of life. The Court considered a claim that Wisconsin's compulsory secondary school attendance law violated the Free Exercise Clause. The case was brought by members of the Old Order Amish congregation, who believed that "their children's attendance at high school, *public or private*, was contrary to the Amish religion and way of life." By sending their children to high school, Amish parents "would not only expose themselves to the danger of the censure of the church community, but . . . also endanger their own salvation and that of their children." The Amish way of life, the Court noted, is centered on "a fundamental belief that salvation requires life in a church community separate and apart from the world and worldly influence. This concept of life aloof from the world and its values is central to their faith." As the Court saw it, the *entire* Amish way of life and education is inseparable from the basic tenets of the community's faith—"indeed, as much a part of their religious belief and practices as baptism, the confessional, or a Sabbath may be for others." A related feature of Amish life is the community's "devotion to a life in harmony with nature and the soil." A deep reverence for things natural, the Court opined, "require[s] members of the community to make their living by farming or closely related activities."[71]

From these core beliefs arose the Amish objection to secondary schooling. Education beyond the eighth grade would involve "impermissible exposure" to worldly influences in conflict with Amish values: "The high school tends to emphasize intellectual and scientific accomplishments, self-distinction, competitiveness, worldly success, and social life with other students. Amish society emphasizes informal learning-through-doing; a life of 'goodness,' rather than a life of intellect; wisdom, rather than technical knowledge; community welfare, rather than competition; and separation from, rather than integration with, contemporary worldly society." Beyond the threat that high school would bring "pressure to conform to the styles, manners, and ways of the peer group," secondary schooling would take the Amish children "away from their community, physically and emotionally, during the crucial and formative adolescent period of life":

> During this period, the children must acquire Amish attitudes favoring manual work and self-reliance and the specific skills needed to perform the adult role of an Amish farmer or housewife. They must learn to enjoy physical labor. Once a child has learned

basic reading, writing, and elementary mathematics, these traits, skills, and attitudes admittedly fall within the category of those best learned through example and "doing" rather than in a classroom. And, at this time in life, the Amish child must also grow in his faith and his relationship to the Amish community if he is to be prepared to accept the heavy obligations imposed by adult baptism. In short, high school attendance with teachers who are not of the Amish faith—and may even be hostile to it—interposes a serious barrier to the integration of the Amish child into the Amish religious community.[72]

At the outset of its analysis, the Court acknowledged "'the power of a State, having a high responsibility for the education of its citizens, to impose reasonable regulations for the control and duration of basic education.'" To this extent, the Court adhered to the reasoning and reach of *Meyer* and *Pierce*. Yet even this "paramount responsibility," the Court continued, must be balanced against any impingement on fundamental rights and interests. Where compulsory education interferes with religious belief and practice, the state must demonstrate an interest "of sufficient magnitude to override the interest claiming protection under the Free Exercise Clause." The great question, then, is, what magnitude is sufficient to override a challenge brought under the Free Exercise Clause?[73]

The Court settled on a strict scrutiny standard—sort of. Only interests of "the highest order" would be of sufficient magnitude. The Court relied on *Sherbert v. Verner* (1963), which had concluded that "no showing merely of a rational relationship to some colorable state interest would suffice" to overcome a challenge under the Free Exercise Clause.[74] But *Sherbert* did not deal with the scope of parental authority. Perhaps this is why the Court felt the need to strengthen the constitutional footing on which it set the right of the *Yoder* parents. For whatever reason, the Court declared that it would apply strict scrutiny "when the interests of parenthood are combined with a free exercise claim of the nature revealed by this record." This combined right may be limited only "if it appears that parental decisions will jeopardize the health or safety of the child, or have a potential for significant social burdens." (*Yoder*'s strict scrutiny standard, it should be noted, has two prongs, one directed toward the child and one toward society at large. The latter prong has been all but forgotten.)[75]

The *Yoder* Court was confronted with two relevant lines of cases: The Due Process Clause protected the right to parent, which included the right to direct the upbringing and education of the child, and the Free Exercise Clause guaranteed religious freedom. But neither line offered complete protection for religious parenting rights. The Court did rely on *Meyer* and *Pierce*, but these cases had involved "nothing more than the general interest of the parent in the nurture and education of his children." *Pierce* may stand, as the Court declared, as a charter of the right of parents to direct the religious upbringing of their children; nonetheless, it is a charter of parenting, not religious, rights, and where nothing more is involved, the *Yoder* Court stipulated, "it is beyond dispute that the State acts 'reasonably' and constitutionally in requiring education to age 16 in some public or private school meeting the standards prescribed by the State." A parenting claim by itself would not outweigh the state's interest in universal compulsory education.[76]

Moreover, the Supreme Court's parenting cases had made the right to direct the upbringing of children contingent on the parental duty to provide children with a proper education. The state's high responsibility may be made to yield to a parent's right to choose private schooling, but, the *Yoder* Court granted, private schooling must provide an equivalent education to that of the public system. *Meyer* and *Pierce* had established that the state "may not pre-empt the educational process," but *Yoder* presented the Court with difficult facts. The Amish parents themselves were asserting a personal right to preempt the educational process.

Writing for the Court, Chief Justice Warren Burger had good reason not to rely too heavily on the Due Process Clause. Only two months before, he had inveighed against the Court's willingness to strike down state legislation on substantive due process grounds. His dissent in *Eisenstadt v. Baird* (1972) admonished the Court for "seriously invad[ing] the constitutional prerogatives of the States and regrettably hark[ening] back to the heyday of substantive due process." Burger drew attention to the fact that the Massachusetts state law at issue, which restricted the distribution of contraceptives to unmarried persons, merely regulated but did not ban the use of contraceptives:

> I see nothing in the Fourteenth Amendment . . . that even vaguely suggests that these medicinal forms of contraceptives must be available in the open market. I do not challenge *Griswold v. Connecticut* . . . despite its tenuous moorings to the text of the Constitution, but I cannot view it as controlling authority for this case. The Court was there confronted with a statute flatly prohibiting the use of contraceptives, not one regulating their distribution. I simply cannot believe that the limitation on the class of lawful distributors has significantly impaired the right to use contraceptives in Massachusetts. By relying on *Griswold* in the present context, the Court has passed beyond the penumbras of the specific guarantees into the uncircumscribed area of personal predilections.[77]

Now writing for the majority, Burger refused to strike down, as a violation of due process, a state compulsory education law that merely regulated secondary education, unlike the statute in *Pierce*, which flatly prohibited private schooling. Besides, the prospect that any parent, for reasons however virtuous, could displace the educational regime on due process grounds alone was surely an unacceptable outcome. Parenting concerns could then be interposed as a barrier to reasonable state regulation of education even if they were based on purely secular considerations. The Court knew too well that "the very concept of ordered liberty precludes allowing every person to make his own standards on matters of conduct in which society as a whole has important interests."[78] It was not about to give a constitutional pass to the Henry David Thoreaus of the world.[79]

But why not resolve *Yoder* solely on free exercise grounds? The Court accepted it as settled that "only those interests of the highest order . . . can overbalance legitimate claims to the free exercise of religion."[80] In fact, the *Yoder* parents had not made any due process claims arising from the Fourteenth Amendment. Their case was based on the Free Exercise Clause standing alone.[81] Yet the Court devoted little attention to cases based on the Free Exercise Clause, perhaps because there was little case law to which it could be devoted and perhaps because what case law existed was of little help. The controlling case, as the state argued, was *Prince v. Massachusetts*, and the *Yoder* Court was well aware that *Prince* "might be read to give support to the State's position."[82]

The *Yoder* Court confined *Prince* to a narrow scope, as it had to. The Court said that prior decisions had limited *Prince* to circumstances involving "harm to the physical or mental health of the child or to the public safety, peace, order, or welfare."[83] This reading of the case law is questionable (What threat to the public welfare makes Sunday closing laws constitutional?),[84] and it only begs the question of whether such harm could be inferred from the refusal to comply with compulsory education laws. In concluding that it could not, the *Yoder* majority simply read the children out of the case.

The state offered two justifications for compulsory secondary schooling, both of which addressed the educational welfare of the child: (1) "that some degree of education is necessary to prepare citizens to participate effectively and intelligently in our open political system if we are to preserve freedom and independence," and (2) that "education prepares individuals to be self-reliant and self-sufficient participants in society."[85] While the Court accepted these propositions in general, it disagreed that secondary education would do much good for Amish children. If the value of education "must be assessed in terms of its capacity to prepare the child for life," the Court insisted, "[the Amish] alternative mode of continuing informal vocational education"—by which the Court meant, of course, no schooling at all—was equivalent to the schooling mandated by the state: "It is one thing to say that compulsory education for a year or two beyond the eighth grade may be necessary when its goal is the preparation of the child for life in modern society as the majority live, but it is quite another if the goal of education be viewed as the preparation of the child for life in the separated agrarian community that is the keystone of the Amish faith."[86]

Here, the Court misrepresented the goals of the state by equating them to the choices made possible by state-mandated education. The task of the state as educator is not to prepare a child for life in a separatist religious community, nor is it to prepare a child for life in modern society as the majority live. As the state of Wisconsin argued, education is the instrument that prepares young people to participate meaningfully in society, even if this participation takes the form of a choice not to live in modern society as the majority live.[87] It may well be that "[t]he Amish alternative to formal secondary school education has enabled them to . . . survive and prosper in contemporary society as a separate, sharply identifiable and highly self-sufficient community," but such separatist success is hardly "strong evidence they are capable of fulfilling the social and political responsibilities of citizenship without compelled attendance beyond the eighth grade."[88] The common law obliged parents to provide "an education *suitable to the child's station in life.*"[89] The *Yoder* Court read this proviso with remarkable illiberalism. It concluded that the Amish way of life was itself an education suitable for children who were destined to live . . . the Amish way of life.

Because the children were not parties to the litigation, the Court was not called upon to determine "the proper resolution of possible competing interests of parents, children, and the State."[90] But it left little doubt as to how it would resolve such a conflict:

> Recognition of the claim of the State in such a proceeding would, of course, call into question traditional concepts of parental control over the religious upbringing and education of their minor children recognized in this Court's past decisions. . . . Indeed it seems clear that if the State is empowered, as parens patriae, to "save" a child from himself or his Amish parents by requiring an additional two years of compulsory formal high school education, the State will in large measure influence, if not determine, the religious future of the child. Even more markedly than in *Prince*, therefore, this case involves the fundamental interest of parents, as contrasted with that of the State, to guide the religious future and education of their children.

If the state's argument was that "exemption of Amish parents from the requirements of the compulsory education law might allow some parents to

act contrary to the best interests of their children by foreclosing their opportunity to make an intelligent choice between the Amish way of life and that
of the outside world," then the same argument could be made "with respect
to all church schools short of college." (A curious concern this, considering
the Court's contention that the Amish community was uniquely qualified to
provide an alternative mode of education that satisfied the state's interests.)
This argument suggested that parents generally ought to consult with their
minor children before making a church-school placement, and this suggestion was too much for the Court.[91]

Yet it was equally too much for the Court to hold that parents generally
ought to be allowed to foreclose their children's educational opportunities.
The Court's sociological discursions were analytically necessary because
it was going to grant the Amish, and only the Amish, a constitutional release from the Lockean duty to bring their children to a state of educational enfranchisement. The radical open-endedness of such a step had to
be countered by an equally complete closure of this fiduciary loophole. So
the Amish model of informal vocational education met *precisely* the educational interests advanced by the state. If predestined to live in a separated
agrarian community, Amish children do not need secondary education. If
Amish children decide to leave the church, their agricultural training and
habits of industry and self-reliance will keep them from becoming a burden
on the state. One way or the other, a democratic society will always find use
for more sturdy yeomen.[92]

It is not unusual for the Court to limit a holding to the facts before it, refusing to speculate about future applications of problematic doctrine. The
Prince Court took this approach to its declaration that "the family itself is
not beyond regulation in the public interest, as against a claim of religious
liberty." The *Yoder* Court went a step further, solidifying its holding by an-
ticipating that "probably few other religious groups or sects" could make
the showing necessary to secure an Amish-type exemption.[93] Wisconsin's
compulsory education statute was a burden for reasons peculiar to one religious sect: an entire way of life inextricably bound to religious belief, the
continued survival of a long-established and self-sufficient agrarian community, an informal mode of vocational education that precisely parallels

state interests, etc. Strict scrutiny is required "when the interests of parenthood are combined with a free exercise claim of the nature revealed by this record."[94] It is also not unusual for the Court to make law that, in effect, benefits (or burdens) a specific religious group, but in such cases the law will have, if only in theory, a general application. It *is* a strange business for the Court to make what amounts to private constitutional law. By subjecting restrictions on religious parenting—or, at least, one subset of religious parenting—to strict scrutiny, the *Yoder* Court presided over the creation of a separate sphere of the law where some individuals enjoy a private right to be exempted from generally applicable civic obligations.

On its own terms, then, *Yoder* is essentially sui generis.[95] Yet, practically, the Court did more than rescue Amish parents from state educational requirements. In a real sense, under *Yoder*, parenting did at last become a sacred right. The heightened status of religious parenting was novel law when the Court announced it in *Wisconsin v. Yoder*, and it remains doctrinally fragile. But the spirit of strict scrutiny, once summoned, would not be easily cabined. *Yoder* would become the precedential port from which a number of religious parenting cases would be launched, asking courts to apply a rationale that "contradicts both constitutional tradition and common sense"—and undermines the basic premises of the trust model of parent-child relations.[96]

In *Employment Division v. Smith*, the Court rejected the application of strict scrutiny to religiously motivated claims for exemption from the general laws of the state. There was to be no separate sphere of the law where the government's ability to enforce generally applicable law is subject to an individual's religious beliefs. Yet, by not overturning *Yoder* (and a handful of other cases that had been reviewed under strict scrutiny), the *Smith* Court did in fact what it declined to do in theory: It left intact a sphere of the law where personal religious imperatives trump countervailing public interests. For the Court also said, this time explicitly, that heightened scrutiny had been applied to claims that involved "not the Free Exercise Clause alone, but the Free Exercise Clause in conjunction with other constitutional protections."[97] The Court did little to clarify why this hybrid rights loophole is justified, however, and the result has been a legacy of doctrinal confusion and much judicial scrambling.

In *Smith*, the Supreme Court was faced with a challenge to Oregon's antidrug laws. The case was brought by two members of the Native American Church who had been fired from their positions as drug counselors for using peyote, even though it had been used for sacramental purposes. When the state denied them unemployment benefits on the ground that their drug use was work-related misconduct, the plaintiffs argued that they were entitled to an exemption from the state's substance abuse statutes. The Court held that the First Amendment does not bar the application of a neutral, generally applicable law to religiously motivated action.[98] A state law that does not target religious belief or practice is subject only to rational basis review, even if the law has the incidental effect of burdening, or perhaps effectively prohibiting, religious activity.

Controversially, the Court concluded that it was not making new doctrine: "We have never held," Justice Scalia wrote for the Court, "that an individual's religious beliefs excuse him from compliance with an otherwise valid law prohibiting conduct that the State is free to regulate."[99] The Court had applied strict scrutiny to some claims based on the Free Exercise Clause, but these cases, the Court decided quite after the fact, had involved the Free Exercise Clause and some other constitutional provision. Scalia pointed to *Yoder* as an example of such a case. Rather than overrule *Yoder*, the *Smith* Court distinguished it: *Yoder*, unlike *Smith*, involved a hybrid rights claim. With undisguised exasperation, critics of the decision complained that rather than overrule anything and perhaps lose his majority, Scalia "distinguished everything away."[100] But whether or not Scalia's reading of precedent "borders on fiction,"[101] it is clear that some kind of hybrid rights doctrine survives *Smith*.

Smith is as controversial for what it did not say as for what it did. First, in a neat bit of jurisprudential legerdemain, Scalia never explicitly approved of the hybrid rights doctrine; rather, he used it to explain in descriptive terms why the Court was not overruling cases that had subjected general laws to heightened scrutiny.[102] Second, like any good magician, Scalia did not reveal how the hybrid rights doctrine actually works.[103] Is strict scrutiny triggered when a litigant makes a Free Exercise Clause claim in conjunction with any other companion constitutional claim? Or is there a viable hybrid rights claim only when the companion claim itself would trigger strict scrutiny? There is a fair measure of inscrutability to each option. Much religious practice involves conduct that implicates other constitutional rights. But, as Justice David Souter would later point out, "[i]f a hybrid claim is simply one in which another constitutional right is implicated, then the hybrid exception would probably be so vast as to swallow the *Smith* rule." Yet (and, again, Souter) if each conjoined right "is one in which a litigant would actually obtain an exemption from a formally neutral, generally applicable law under another constitutional provision, then there would have been no reason for the Court in what *Smith* calls the hybrid cases to have mentioned the Free Exercise Clause at all."[104] The Ninth Circuit nicely summed up the problem: "[T]he application of the hybrid-rights exception can turn neither upon the fact that a companion right is 'implicated' (else the central holding of *Smith* vanishes) nor upon the existence of a fully protected, independently viable companion right (else the Free Exercise Clause itself vanishes)."[105] So, while it is clear that the hybrid rights doctrine survives *Smith*, it is not clear what the proposition means in the first place. What is a hybrid right?

As would be expected, it became the unhappy task of the lower courts to sort out the doctrinal details, and it has proved to be a difficult assignment, generating no shortage of discussion and disagreement.[106] The courts have taken several routes through the uncertain terrain of hybrid rights:

1. **There is no general doctrine of hybrid rights.**
   This approach is, if nothing more, the path of least resistance. Some courts stay out of the doctrinal arena entirely, taking refuge in the fact that the Supreme Court's discussion of hybrid rights was mere dictum. Under this approach, the Second Circuit has decided that it is not bound to apply heightened scrutiny to hybrid claims.[107] More candidly, the Sixth Circuit considers the doctrine too nonsensical to apply. In the court's view, it is "completely illogical" to conclude "that legal

standards under the Free Exercise Clause vary depending on whether other constitutional rights are implicated." Putting the doctrine on hold, the Sixth Circuit has decided that it is the better part of judicial discretion to follow the rule of *Smith* until the Supreme Court clarifies its intentions.[108]

To be sure, ignoring the *Smith* exception to honor the *Smith* rule has the virtue of simplicity, but it requires the court also to ignore the fact that cases like *Yoder*, where the Supreme Court *did* hold that a hybrid rights claim subjects a law to a higher level of scrutiny, remain on the books and are binding precedent. As the Ninth Circuit has remarked, lower courts do not always have the option of throwing up their hands in doctrinal despair: "Our job is not to critique or to deconstruct; ours is to make sense of a confusing doctrinal situation—to make the pieces fit."[109]

2. **A hybrid rights claim exists only when a Free Exercise Clause claim is made in conjunction with a claim that would independently require an exemption**.
One way to make the pieces fit is to require a companion claim that independently triggers strict scrutiny. This appears to be the approach of the First Circuit.[110] But, as Justice Souter said, if a litigant's due process claim independently requires heightened scrutiny, there is no need to join it to a claim based on the Free Exercise Clause. This approach works only by ignoring the *Yoder* Court's assertion that strict scrutiny is not required "where nothing more than the general interest of the parent in the nurture and education of his children is involved." It was by invoking the Free Exercise Clause in conjunction with a parenting rights claim that the *Yoder* Court somehow made the whole of the parents' claim greater than the sum of its constitutional parts. It is mysterious arithmetic.[111] But, as has been pointed out (again the Ninth Circuit), the repeated references to the Free Exercise Clause in the so-called hybrid cases leave little doubt "that, whatever else it did, the

Court did *not* rest its decisions in those cases upon the recognition of independently viable free speech and substantive due process rights." Lower courts, the Ninth Circuit cautioned, should not lightly presume that the Supreme Court "was wasting its breath."[112]

3. **A hybrid rights claim exists only when a Free Exercise Clause claim is made in conjunction with a colorable claim.**
If a hybrid rights claim requires an independently viable companion claim, the Free Exercise Clause vanishes. If a hybrid rights claim requires only that the companion claim implicate another constitutional right, the *Smith* rule vanishes. Few laws would be subject to the *Smith* rule if the mere allegation of a companion right is enough to trigger strict scrutiny. To salvage some utility for the *Smith* rule, the Ninth and Tenth Circuits adopt a colorable claim doctrine.[113] To make a hybrid rights claim, a litigant must do more than merely allege the violation of a companion right, but there is no requirement that the companion claim would independently trigger strict scrutiny. The conjoined claim must have "a 'fair probability' or a 'likelihood,' but not a certitude, of success on the merits." The court must decide "whether either the claimed rights or the claimed infringements are genuine."[114] In theory, this approach would allow some hybrid claims to proceed where the companion claim is based on the parents' due process rights—but only where the due process claim involves a genuine infringement of a genuine constitutional right, whatever that means. Far easier to state than apply (and it is not all that easy to state), the colorable claim approach requires courts "to make difficult, qualitative, case-by-case judgments regarding the strength of companion-claim arguments."[115]

It may not be clear what the hybrid rights theory really means—and, for now, it may mean different things to different courts—but it remains good law. Thus, on the same day, the Michigan Supreme Court, applying rational basis review, could reject one claim brought by homeschooling parents who had run afoul of a teacher certification requirement;[116] and, applying strict scrutiny, it could uphold the claim of a second set of homeschooling parents who also failed to meet the certification requirement.[117] In the first case, the parents brought their claim under the Due Process Clause of the Fourteenth Amendment alone; in the second case, the parents brought their claim under the Due Process Clause and, because the parents' objections to state regulation were religiously based, under the Free Exercise Clause. In the court's judgment, the state had a legitimate interest in requiring a teaching certificate for homeschoolers (thus it survived rational basis review) but not a compelling one (thus it failed strict scrutiny).[118] The results of bringing forward a hybrid rights claim speak for themselves. As do the results of not bringing forward such a claim. "Regardless of the intellectual merits of the hybrid theory," Richard Duncan advises, "it is still law until the Court holds otherwise, and it is malpractice not to plead hybrid claims in free exercise litigation."[119]

The *Yoder* Court's defense of "traditional concepts of parental control" was challenged by justices agreeing or disagreeing with the result. Justice Stewart wrote separately to suggest that had the religious beliefs of the children differed from those of their parents, it would have been a different case.[120] Justice White, joined by Justices William Brennan and Stewart, also concurred, stating that, for him, it would have been a different case had the parents "forbade their children from attending any school at any time and from complying in any way with the educational standards set by the State." Because the children were allowed to acquire the basic tools of literacy, White stated, there was only a "relatively slight" deviation from the state's compulsory education law. On this relatively slight basis, White agreed with the Court's decision. In a much bolder assertion, he declared that parents have no exclusive right to decide "what knowledge a child needs to be a productive and happy member of society." In his view, the Court's seminal parenting cases stand for no such entitlement:

[*Pierce*] lends no support to the contention that parents may replace state educational requirements with their own idiosyncratic
views of what knowledge a child needs to be a productive and
happy member of society; in *Pierce*, both the parochial and military schools were in compliance with all the educational standards that the State had set, and the Court held simply that while
a State may posit such standards, it may not pre-empt the educational process by requiring children to attend public schools.[121]

The educational system, White observed, is not merely about basic literacy. The school system is "rather attempting to nurture and develop the
human potential of its children, whether Amish or non-Amish: to expand
their knowledge, broaden their sensibilities, kindle their imagination, foster a spirit of free inquiry, and increase their human understanding and
tolerance." Perhaps for those Amish children who wished to continue living the life of their parents, "their training at home will adequately equip
them for their future role." But White cited evidence that some children
choose to "desert" their Amish faith when they come of age. Some may
wish "to become nuclear physicists, ballet dancers, computer programmers,
or historians, and for these occupations, formal training will be necessary."
A proper education should develop the latent talents of children; at a minimum, it should "provide [children] with an option other than the life they
have led in the past." The state has an interest that encompasses more than
preparing children for life choices that have been made for them. It has an
interest in helping children develop the capacity to make life choices for
themselves.[122]

More famously, Justice William O. Douglas, the Court's lone dissenter,
took the case on its own terms and proposed that it be remanded so that
the children could have the opportunity to present their views. For Douglas, the case was not a contest merely between parent and state. The children, he wrote, "have constitutionally protectable interests" of their own. If
parents are granted a religious exemption from state educational requirements, Douglas cautioned, "the inevitable effect is to impose the parents'
notions of religious duty upon their children." With a strong, if perhaps not

entirely appropriate, image, Douglas objected that Amish children cannot simply be "harnessed" to the religious preferences of their parents. If they are, and their education "is truncated," their "entire life may be stunted and deformed."[123]

Douglas advanced his own list of career options shut to students with a limited education. The Amish child "may want to be a pianist or an astronaut or an oceanographer. To do so he will have to break from the Amish tradition." Douglas was bothered that the Wisconsin Supreme Court had "brushed aside the students' interests with the offhand comment that '[w]hen a child reaches the age of judgment, he can choose for himself his religion.'" In other proceedings, especially where family conflict is brought before the court, he noted, children are "regularly permitted" to testify as to their wishes. Before making a decision that might stunt and deform a child's future life, Douglas wanted to hear the voices of the Amish children:

> It is the future of the student, not the future of the parents, that is imperiled by today's decision. If a parent keeps his child out of school beyond the grade school, then the child will be forever barred from entry into the new and amazing world of diversity that we have today. The child may decide that that is the preferred course, or he may rebel. It is the student's judgment, not his parents', that is essential if we are to give full meaning to what we have said about the Bill of Rights and of the right of students to be masters of their own destiny. If he is harnessed to the Amish way of life by those in authority over him and if his education is truncated, his entire life may be stunted and deformed. The child, therefore, should be given an opportunity to be heard before the State gives the exemption which we honor today.[124]

For Douglas, the maturity of the child was the key question: "Where the child is mature enough to express potentially conflicting desires, it would be an invasion of the child's rights to permit such an imposition without canvassing his views." Douglas cited studies by child psychologists and sociologists to show that the moral and intellectual maturity of minors "approaches that of the adult." Writing a century earlier, Judge Oakley had come to the same conclusion that "the rights of the child . . . are to be protected in the enjoyment of its personal liberty, according to its own choice, if arrived at the age of discretion."[125] It was a common law commonplace. And it would become constitutional law. Writing a few years later, the Court itself (Justice Harry Blackmun writing) would agree that "[c]onstitutional rights do not mature and come into being magically only when one attains the state-defined age of majority."[126]

Nonparental Claims: *Troxel v. Granville* (2000)

The Reverend John Robinson had cautionary advice for parents about "the possibility of a pernicious influence being exerted over children by overly indulgent grandparents." He warned that "children brought up with their grandfathers or grandmothers, seldom do well, but are usually corrupted by their too great indulgence." The year was 1620, and Robinson was pastor to a group of Pilgrims soon to leave Holland for the New World. The Old World was being left behind, in more ways than one. But apparently grandparents were a bother in the New World, too.[127] In the nineteenth century, the court considered many cases like that of John Lippincott, and quite often with a result in favor of grandparent custody or visitation.

The Supreme Court finally considered the issue in *Troxel v. Granville* (2000).[128] If merely denominating a right as "fundamental"—multiple times—could make it so,[129] then Justice Sandra Day O'Connor's plurality opinion would have guaranteed a securely fundamental future for the right to parent. "[T]he interest of parents in the care, custody, and control of their children," O'Connor wrote, "is perhaps the oldest of the fundamental liberty interests recognized by this Court."[130] But adjectival excess aside, there is nothing in *Troxel* to support the conclusion that state regulation of parenting choices should trigger strict scrutiny. Quite the opposite. The Court's ruling that the visitation preferences of legal parents are entitled only to "some special weight" deeply disappointed advocates of parental rights, spurring the pursuit of a constitutional amendment to settle the question.

The Washington State visitation statute was "breathtakingly broad." It provided that "[a]ny person may petition the court for visitation rights at any time, and the court may grant such visitation rights whenever visitation may serve the best interest of the child." For Justice O'Connor, this language "effectively permit[ted] any third party seeking visitation to subject any decision by a parent concerning visitation of the parent's children to state-court review." The defect of the statute was that it "contravened the traditional presumption that a fit parent will act in the best interest of his or her child":

> In an ideal world, parents might always seek to cultivate the bonds between grandparents and their grandchildren. Needless to say, however, our world is far from perfect, and in it the decision whether such an intergenerational relationship would be beneficial in any specific case is for the parent to make in the first instance. And, if a fit parent's decision of the kind at issue here becomes subject to judicial review, the court must accord at least some special weight to the parent's own determination.[131]

The Washington Supreme Court had held that "the Constitution permits a State to interfere with the right of parents to rear their children *only to prevent harm or potential harm to a child.*" But, despite its repeated description of the right to parent as fundamental, the Supreme Court did not subject the statute to this type of strict scrutiny harm standard. Resting its judgment on the "sweeping breadth" of the state statute, the Court declined to consider "whether the Due Process Clause requires all nonparental visitation statutes to include a showing of harm or potential harm to the child as a condition precedent to granting visitation."[132]

Justice O'Connor cited "extensive precedent" to support her assertion — "[I]t cannot now be doubted," she wrote — that the right to parent is a fundamental one.[133] In fact, the cited cases show only that the right to parent is constitutionally protected. Only *Santosky v. Kramer*, which concerns the absolute termination of parental rights, contains anything resembling a description of fundamental rights.[134] Indeed, the other cases cited by O'Connor suggest that the Court has been disinclined to cast the right to parent as fundamental. *Meyer v. Nebraska* is cited for the proposition that "the 'liberty' protected by the Due Process Clause includes the right of parents to 'establish a home and bring up children' and 'to control the education of their own'"; *Pierce v. Society of Sisters* for the proposition that "the 'liberty of parents and guardians' includes the right 'to direct the upbringing and education of children under their control'"; *Prince v. Massachusetts* for the proposition that "there is a constitutional dimension to the right of parents to direct the upbringing of their children"; and so on.[135]

It is no secret that there is a constitutional dimension to parental rights. The question is, what are the dimensions of this dimension? The problem is not so much that O'Connor quotes her precedents selectively, though this is problem enough, as that she misses what is most significant in these cases: the linkage of rights and responsibilities. This should not have been hard to miss. Prior to *Troxel*, the Supreme Court had already put these cases to their proper use:

> In [these] cases, . . . the Court has emphasized the paramount interest in the welfare of children and has noted that the rights of the parents are a counterpart of the responsibilities they have assumed. Thus, the "liberty" of parents to control the education of their children that was vindicated in *Meyer v. Nebraska* and *Pierce v. Society of Sisters* was described as a "right, coupled with the high duty, to recognize and prepare [the child] for additional obligations." The linkage between parental duty and parental right was stressed again in *Prince v. Massachusetts*, when the Court declared it a cardinal principle "that the custody, care and nurture of the child reside first in the parents, whose primary function and freedom include preparation for obligations the state can neither supply nor hinder."

This was the Court's assessment in *Lehr v. Robertson* (1983), one in a line of cases where the Supreme Court asked who qualifies as a parent for constitutional purposes. Instead of asking the negative rights question, "What rights belong to the father (or mother)?" the *Lehr* Court asked the relational question, "What rights and duties are incident to the relationship of parent and child?"[136]

In *Lehr*, the defendant, Lorraine Robertson, was the biological mother of a child born out of wedlock. The plaintiff, Jonathan Lehr, was the child's biological father. Eight months after the child's birth, the defendant married Richard Robertson, and when the child, Jessica, was two years old, the couple filed for adoption. The plaintiff, who had not received notice of the adoption proceeding, filed a petition to vacate the adoption order on due process and equal protection grounds. In finding that the biological father's rights had not been violated, the Court set out the parameters of constitutional parenthood:

1. "When an unwed father demonstrates a full commitment to the responsibilities of parenthood by 'com[ing] forward to participate in the rearing of his child,' his interest in personal contact with his child acquires substantial protection under the due process clause"; but

2. "[T]he mere existence of a biological link does not merit equivalent constitutional protection."

The Court reached its conclusion by rehearsing the basic premises of the trust model of parent-child relations. Parenthood, the Court said, is an opportunity to develop a relationship with one's child. Nonetheless, it is only an opportunity, not a guarantee against state interference: "If [the parent] grasps that opportunity and accepts some measure of responsibility for the child's future, he may enjoy the blessings of the parent-child relationship and make uniquely valuable contributions to the child's development. If he fails to do so, the Federal Constitution will not automatically compel a State to listen to his opinion of where the child's best interests lie."[137]

In *Lehr*, the Court read its seminal parenting cases to stand for the principle that "the rights of the parents are a counterpart of the responsibilities they have assumed."[138] This traditional "linkage between parental duty and parental right" was the doctrinal backbone of the Court's line of putative father cases. Culminating in *Lehr*, these cases were decided as follows:

- In *Stanley v. Illinois* (1972),[139] the Court invalidated an Illinois state statute conclusively presuming that the father of a child born out of wedlock is unfit to have custody of his children. Under Illinois law, the children of unwed fathers became wards of the state upon the death of the mother. The nature of the actual relationship between parent and child, the Court stressed, was considered irrelevant. In this regard, the father "is treated not as a parent but as a stranger to his children."

  The *Stanley* Court underscored the fact that, in the case before it, there was nothing in the record to indicate that the plaintiff "is or has been a neglectful father who has not cared for his children." Stanley had lived with the mother and their children intermittently for eighteen years. Though the state had legitimate interests—first, to protect "the moral, emotional, mental, and physical welfare of the minor and the best interests of the community" and, second, to "strengthen the minor's family ties whenever possible"—the Court concluded that the destruction of the custodial relationship by automatic presumption was hardly a rational way to secure these ends: "We observe that the State registers no gain towards its declared goals when it separates children from the custody of fit parents. Indeed, if Stanley is a fit father, the State spites its own articulated goals when it needlessly separates him from his family."[140]

- In *Quilloin v. Walcott* (1978),[141] the Court upheld a Georgia state statute that required only the mother's consent for the adoption of a child born out of wedlock. In this case, the mother and the child's father "never married each other or established a home together." The child's mother eventually married and consented to the adoption of the child by her husband.[142] Though Quilloin was not found to be an unfit parent, the adoption was granted over his objection. The trial court determined that the adoption had been in the best interests of the child. Upholding the judgment, the Georgia Supreme Court based its decision on Quilloin's failure "to support or legitimate the child over a period of more than 11 years." Unlike the father in *Stanley*, Quilloin, "had never been a *de facto* member of the child's family unit."[143]

The Supreme Court agreed with this conclusion and its reasoning: Quilloin "ha[d] never shouldered any significant responsibility with respect to the daily supervision, education, protection, or care of the child." Nor was he now seeking custody of the child. In the Court's view, the state acted constitutionally when it tied the strength of Quilloin's parental rights claim to "the extent of [his] commitment to the welfare of the child."[144]

• In *Caban v. Mohammed* (1979),[145] the Court again sounded the depth of a father's commitment to the welfare of his child. The Court upheld a challenge to a New York State statute that permitted an unwed mother, but not an unwed father, to block the adoption of their child simply by withholding consent. Here, the parents had lived together, representing themselves as husband and wife, though they were never legally married. The couple had three children together, and both mother and father had participated in their care and support. The mother, who had adopted the children, sought to make biology a stand-in for commitment, asserting that "a natural mother, absent special circumstances, bears a closer relationship with her child . . . than a father does."[146]

Rejecting the claim that "the broad, gender-based distinction of [the state statute] is required by any universal difference between maternal and paternal relations at every phase of a child's development," the Court found no reason to believe that the children "had a relationship with their mother unrivaled by the affection and concern of their father." It would have been a different case had Caban, the father, not "come forward to participate in the rearing of his child." It would have been a different case, that is, had Caban failed "to act as a father toward his children."[147]

"Parental rights," Justice Stewart stated in *Caban*, "do not spring full-blown from the biological connection between parent and child. They require relationships more enduring." Constitutional parenthood comes into being when enduring relationships come into being. Thus, the relationship between an unwed father and his biological child may acquire constitutional status if "the actual relationship between father and child [is sufficient] to create in the unwed father parental interests comparable to those of the married father."[148] The *Lehr* Court agreed. The Constitution protects not parental rights, but "certain formal family relationships." In *Meyer, Pierce*, and *Prince*, the Court "ha[d] found that the relationship of love and duty in a recognized family unit is an interest in liberty entitled to constitutional protection." Today, as in the past, parents have rights in order to do right by their children.[149]

The idea that parental rights and responsibilities are constitutional counterparts was not missed entirely by the *Troxel* Court. In separate dissents, Justices Anthony Kennedy and Stevens borrowed from the *Lehr* line of cases to argue that the linkage of right and duty is well adapted to changing family conditions. Kennedy's "principal concern" was that the Court's holding "seem[ed] to proceed from the assumption that the parent or parents who resist visitation have always been the child's primary caregivers and that the third parties who seek visitation have no legitimate and established relationship with the child." This assumption is no truer today than it was in the nineteenth century. "For many boys and girls," Kennedy observed, "a traditional family with two or even one permanent and caring parent is simply not the reality of their childhood." Given the realities of modern family life, the conventional nuclear family cannot serve to establish a visitation or custody standard. A harm standard is simply not appropriate for the many cases that are sure to arise "in which a third party, by acting in a caregiving role over a significant period of time, has developed a relationship with a child which is not necessarily subject to absolute parental veto."[150]

Stevens also spoke to modern times, observing that "[t]he almost infinite variety of family relationships that pervade our ever-changing society strongly counsel against the creation by this Court of a constitutional rule that treats a biological parent's liberty interest in the care and supervision of her child as an isolated right that may be exercised arbitrarily." Beyond this, however, Stevens made the point that the right to parent has "never been regarded as absolute." If rights arise from the responsibilities that parents assume, then these rights "are limited by the existence of an actual, developed relationship with a child, and are tied to the presence or absence of some embodiment of family." Even where an actual, developed relationship with a child exists, the right to parent is limited by the fact that parenthood takes place within a web of complementary interests: "These limitations have arisen, not simply out of the definition of parenthood itself, but because of this Court's assumption that a parent's interests in a child must be balanced against the State's long-recognized interests as *parens patriae*, and, critically, the child's own complementary interest in preserving relationships that serve her welfare and protection." Unlike other rights, the right to parent cannot establish "a rigid constitutional shield" that would keep the state from reaching the child absent a showing of harm. The child's interests are stronger than that. As Stevens cautioned, "[W]e should recognize that there may be circumstances in which a child has a stronger interest at stake than mere protection from serious harm caused by the termination of visitation by a 'person' other than a parent." We should recognize as well that there may be circumstances in which a child has a stronger interest at stake than protection from an unfit parent. "[E]ven a fit parent," Stevens reminds us, "is capable of treating a child like a mere possession."[151]

When the dust of this fragmented decision settled, there was no clear voice in support of a fundamental due process right to parent, the restriction of which warranted strict scrutiny. The Court declined to address whether the Due Process Clause requires all nonparental visitation statutes to include a showing of harm or potential harm. Both Kennedy and Stevens directly challenged the harm requirement.[152] In his concurrence, Justice Souter would go only so far as to say that "a parent's interests in the nurture, upbringing, companionship, care, and custody of children are generally protected by the Due Process Clause of the Fourteenth Amendment." And Justice Clarence Thomas, also concurring in the judgment, argued from precedent that strict scrutiny applies to the infringement of parental rights, though he did not accept the proposition that, read correctly, the Due Process Clause actually protects unenumerated rights.[153]

Justice Scalia was alone in forthrightly rejecting the Court's jurisprudence of unenumerated rights. In a decision that disappointed many, his brief dissent was the unkindest cut of all. For parentalists could have no better friend on the Court. In Scalia's view, "a right of parents to direct the upbringing of their children is among the 'unalienable Rights' with which the Declaration of Independence proclaims 'all men . . . are endowed by their Creator.'" This right, he continued, "is also among the 'othe[r] [rights] retained by the people' which the Ninth Amendment says the Constitution's enumeration of rights 'shall not be construed to deny or disparage.'" Yet, as Scalia had to concede, the Declaration of Independence "is not a legal prescription conferring powers upon the courts; and the Constitution's refusal to 'deny or disparage' other rights is far removed from affirming any one of them." And even if the Constitution could be construed to affirm "other rights," Scalia warned (as had Justice James Iredell more than two hundred years earlier), it would be beyond the wisdom of judges "to identify what they might be."[154]

As Locke maintained, parenthood does not beget personal rights; it begets great responsibility, a new world of private and public obligation. This duty can take many forms, and a liberal society will create a wide berth for parental preferences. But a just society will hold parents to a high standard of care. Traditionally, the right to parent has been circumscribed by doctrinal strictures far more stringent than those required for the protection of children from abuse and neglect. While a harm standard may allow for the categorical resolution of parental claims, it is ill suited to the resolution of family law disputes.[155] From the time of Mansfield, custody courts have wisely insisted on judicial discretion, not judicial certainty.

Soon after *Troxel* was decided, Justice O'Connor repeated the formulation that parents have a "fundamental liberty interest . . . in the care, custody, and management [as opposed to control?] of their child." Whatever O'Connor might have meant by "fundamental," she did not mean the kind of interest that mandates strict scrutiny. The sorting out of family rights and responsibilities is not a matter susceptible to bright-line judgments. In O'Connor's words,

> But the adjudication of constitutional disputes does not necessarily translate to the effective resolution of family disputes. While constitutional due process doctrine is primarily concerned with the relationship of individuals to the State, the resolution of family disputes focuses primarily on the relationship of individuals with each other. In family cases, the rights of individuals are intertwined, and the family itself has a collective personality. Thus, the due process model may not be the best framework for resolving multi-party conflicts where children, parents, professionals, and the State all have conflicting interests.
>
> Accordingly, family law is—and must be—a collaborative enterprise. While the Supreme Court is well positioned to articulate general principles of constitutional law, there is much more to family law than the setting of constitutional rules. Underlying each family law case that reaches us are issues of state law and policy, as well as an actual family with its own dynamics, challenges, and problems.[156]

For more than two centuries the "actual family" has remained at the center of family dispute resolution. It is no small irony that parental rights advocates would undo a collaborative enterprise that for so long has sought to serve the best interests of the child. To this end, it is asserted that, historically, parents enjoyed a fundamental personal right to control the upbringing of their children and, accordingly, that state interference with the right to parent must pass the rigors of strict scrutiny. This assertion is fundamentally wrong.

FOUR

Toward Constitutional Parenthood

The child is not put into the hands of parents alone. It is not born to hear
but a few voices. It is brought at birth into a vast, we may say an infinite,
school. The universe is charged with the office of its education.
— *William Ellery Channing*

Whose Education Is It, Anyway?: The Parent as Educational Trustee

Opting Out: The New Curricular Requirements Cases

A deep distrust of the state as educator is the resounding note in Turk Leebaert's complaint against the public school system.[1] Leebaert wanted his son
Corky excused from attending health education classes that were required
as part of the seventh grade public school curriculum.[2] By law, Leebaert was
permitted to excuse his child from classes related to instruction in family life
and AIDS education, but health instruction, too, he contended, is a matter
of "character development education," a subject that, in his view, properly
belongs only to the parent.[3] Leebaert did not object to "normal curriculum
subjects such as reading, writing and arithmetic"; his objection was to those
portions of the curriculum that, he thought, needed to be taught from a religious perspective.[4] For Leebaert, the right of the parent to mold his child's
moral character was a matter of religious faith. "I believe," he testified, "that
God has empowered human beings with the right to bring their children
up with correct moral principles in dealing with the issues taught in this
course, not the school system."[5]

This is a fight that has been waged before. Leebaert's brief relied heavily on the curricular requirements cases of the late nineteenth and early twentieth centuries. He borrowed the outrage of the Nebraska Supreme Court ("Now who is to determine what studies the child shall pursue in school? A teacher who has a mere temporary interest in her welfare, or her father, who may reasonably be supposed to be desirous of pursuing such course as will best promote the happiness of his child?"); the California Court of Appeals ("Has the state the authority to alienate in a measure the children from parental authority?"); and other courts that repudiated state interference with "the right of parents to control their own children—to require them to live up to the teachings and the principles which are inculcated in them at home under the parental authority."[6] He borrowed the rhetoric of *Meyer* and *Pierce*. For Leebaert, these cases "not only declare[] that parents have the affirmative, fundamental constitutional right to direct the education of their children, but also contain[] the important pronouncement that states lack the power to *standardize children*." A bulwark against state-mandated uniformity, the Constitution, as Leebaert read it, serves as a parentalist manifesto in opposition to the "intellectual roots of the 'It takes a village to raise a child' philosophy." This philosophy would produce sons and daughters who grew up "like 'Stepford children,' mere carbon copies of all the other students . . . when it comes to their values and their character." Above all, Leebaert borrowed the assumption (and its accompanying dismay) that parents are in danger of suffering a great loss—the loss of some preconstitutional, common law right; the loss of control over the child—at the hand of the state:

> If the Plaintiffs are right—and parents are still the primary teachers of core values of their children—then parents should be allowed to opt their children out of any course that reasonably encroaches on these core values. If the Defendants are right, then parents of public school children have lost control of their children's upbringing in these core values and have lost even their pre-Constitutional, common-law right to direct the upbringing including the education of their children.[7]

It is a fight that has continued to be waged. In the fall of 2009, with a new school year beginning, President Barack Obama planned to make a speech to welcome back public school students. Though previous presidents, Republicans among them, had made such addresses, President Obama's proposal generated heated opposition, and many school districts made some form of accommodation to those offended by the president's plan. In fact, some schools, in a wealth of accommodating spirit, decided simply not to air the speech. This protest reflected something more than knee-jerk political contrarianism. As in the 1920s, the opposition was driven by a profound suspicion that the public school system is a primary agent in Big Government's efforts to indoctrinate children in a left-wing ideological agenda. The chairman of the Florida Republican Party spoke for many when he said that the speech was an effort to "spread President Obama's socialist ideology." Indeed, the fear that our schools were being "turned over to some socialist movement" was the inescapable undercurrent of objection to the president's speech.[8] This protest was not about the takeover of our nation's industries. The concern—more grave than soviet-style economic planning—was that our children's values, if not their very souls, were being collectivized.

It is a fight that will continue to be waged. The latter-day curricular requirements cases are at the center of a perfect storm of questions that occupy the attention of educational, social, and legal theorists. Swirling around Leebaert's simple opt-out request are heady concerns about the nature of liberalism in a pluralistic society, the definition of good citizenship, the formation of individual identity and moral agency, the legitimacy of group rights, and the role of the state and its schools in fostering a national unity around democratic values. One question that encapsulates much of this discussion is often posed as, Do we, as members of a liberal, pluralistic society, have to tolerate the intolerant? This framing allows us to think of the argument as one of adult rights against state interference with adult choices. But, both theoretically and practically, children have a way of complicating things. The tougher question is, Do we have to tolerate individuals and groups who insulate their children from exposure to diverse values and beliefs? More starkly stated, the question might be, Do individuals and groups have a right to protect their beliefs and traditions—to protect the continuity and perhaps the very survival of these beliefs and traditions—by rejecting a model of education that, to quote Stephen Gilles's parentalist manifesto, "promotes values contrary to their own"?[9]

Leebaert did not contest that the mandatory health curriculum would pass rational basis review. Relying on *Troxel* (due process alone) and both *Yoder* and *Smith* (a hybrid right), he argued that "to pass constitutional muster, the mandatory nature of the curriculum must withstand strict scrutiny."[10] The court did not reach Leebaert's hybrid rights claim,[11] but its decision is a good example of how modern courts, when considering challenges to the state's educational authority, defeat strict scrutiny by dismantling one or both of a litigant's hybrid claims. Reluctant to second-guess the state as educator, most courts ask only whether state regulation has a rational basis, even where litigants, in *Yoder*-like fashion, join due process and free exercise claims. To avoid strict scrutiny, however, as Leebaert's case illustrates, they have to go a long and rather results-oriented way around the doctrinal barn. Thus, the shadow of *Yoder* is heavy even when courts find their way to rational basis review.

With regard to the due process prong of the hybrid claim, courts routinely hold that parents enjoy no right to direct the education of children free from reasonable state regulation. The Second Circuit rejected Leebaert's primary due process contentions. Here, the court relied on the work of other circuits. The First Circuit had considered a similar claim in *Brown v. Hot, Sexy and Safer Productions, Inc.*, where the court held that a challenge to a public school's sex education program was not rooted in a constitutionally protected entitlement.[12] Reading the Supreme Court's seminal parenting cases as doctrinally restrained, the *Brown* court distinguished the right established in *Meyer* and *Pierce* (which the court construed as the right of parents to choose a specific educational program) from the right asserted by the parent plaintiffs (which the court construed as the right to dictate the public school curriculum).

The First Circuit accepted that *Meyer* and *Pierce* "evince the principle that the state cannot prevent parents from choosing a specific educational program—whether it be religious instruction at a private school or instruction in a foreign language." This constitutional limitation on the state's educational authority means more generally that "the state does not have the power to 'standardize its children' or 'foster a homogenous people' by completely foreclosing the opportunity of individuals and groups to choose a different path of education." Put a little less fervidly, the state has no monopoly on educational authority. But, as *Meyer* and *Pierce* make clear, neither do parents, and the *Brown* court made much of this limit on the reach of due process:

> We do not think, however, that this freedom encompasses a fundamental constitutional right to dictate the curriculum at the public school to which they have chosen to send their children. We think it is fundamentally different for the state to say to a parent, "You can't teach your child German or send him to a parochial school," than for the parent to say to the state, "You can't teach my child subjects that are morally offensive to me." The first instance involves the state proscribing parents from educating their children, while the second involves parents prescribing what the state shall teach their children.

It would be absurd, the court thought, to force the public schools "to cater a curriculum for each student whose parents had genuine moral disagreements with the school's choice of subject matter."[13] The same conclusion was reached by the Tenth Circuit in *Swanson v. Guthrie Independent School District No. I-L* (also cited in *Leebaert*), where the court rejected a challenge to the public school's policy against part-time attendance.[14] The *Leebaert* court followed the lead of its sister circuits, agreeing that due process does not protect "'the right of parents . . . to pick and choose which courses their children will take from the public school.'" Curricular decisions, the court said, "'are uniquely committed to the discretion of local school authorities.'"[15]

Equally unavailing was Leebaert's reliance on *Troxel*. Leebaert argued that *Troxel* was dispositive because it "specifically held that the right of a parent to direct the upbringing of his child is a *fundamental* constitutional right and that it includes a child's education." The court, however, observed that there is nothing in *Troxel* to support this conclusion: "[T]here is nothing in *Troxel* that would lead us to conclude from the Court's recognition of a parental right in what the plurality called 'the care, custody, and control' of a child with respect to visitation rights that parents have a *fundamental* right to the upbringing and education of the child that includes the right to tell public schools what to teach or what not to teach him or her." Once the Second Circuit had dismissed Leebaert's assertion of a fundamental right, the court subjected his parenting claim to rational basis review—with the predictable result. There was no doubt that "[r]equiring students to attend health education classes serves a legitimate state interest and is reasonably related to that interest."[16]

It is safe to say that there is as much expediency as principle at work here. The court framed the question so boldly that it would be hard to argue that Leebaert's claim was fundamental. No matter what the precise scope of parental authority, courts can safely decide that due process does not include something as uncontainable, say, as the "right of every parent to tell a public school what his or her child will or will not be taught."[17] Yet it is no less difficult to contend that the parenting claim is fundamental when courts define the question too ungenerously, say, as the right to opt out of a community service requirement[18] or a school uniform policy.[19] For parents like Turk Leebaert, the due process road to strict scrutiny is carefully guarded by the gates of this constitutional catch-22.

With regard to the free exercise prong of the hybrid claim, courts routinely find that a litigant's specific complaint does not rise to the level of a *Yoder*-like constitutional problem. The less a litigant's claim resembles the facts of *Yoder*, the less likely that state regulation imposes a significant burden on religious freedom. In this way, courts return to the proposition that there is no free exercise exemption from generally applicable laws.

Leebaert maintained that his claim was based on the same configuration of rights as that of the *Yoder* parents. In both cases, the state would require the parents "to abandon their religious beliefs and assimilate their convictions with that of the Defendants, as espoused in the [public school] curriculum." In both cases, the gist of the complaint was that state control of education enforces a regime of religious conformity: "The real threat in *Yoder* is the same type of threat hurled at Plaintiffs—'either accept the standards taught in the Health curriculum, or move your child to a private school.' That is the ultimate choice given to Plaintiffs by Defendants. But that choice is unacceptable under the law of *Yoder*."[20] Having demonstrated that the health curriculum conflicted with his sincerely held religious beliefs,[21] Leebaert made the indisputable point that it is not for the courts to say that some religious beliefs are more important than others:

> Government's province cannot include the authority to say that Plaintiffs' sincerely held religious belief, which is completely woven with Plaintiffs' way of life, is not as important as those of the Amish. . . . Plaintiffs take their religious beliefs extremely seriously, and have gone to great lengths to avoid inculcation of morals from any other standpoint. Whether part of a particular religious sect in existence for almost 300 years, as the Amish, or whether the religious belief espoused by an individual Christian family (and Christianity has been in existence for approximately 2000 years), the sincerity, sanctity, and respect afforded by government ought to be the same.[22]

Leebaert thus challenged the court to address directly why the *Yoder* rationale does not apply to any way of life threatened by restrictions on religious commitment. Certainly, the Old Order Amish are not the only group for whom "religion is pervasive—[for whom] everything in their lives is religiously significant."[23] If anything, according to Leebaert, the Court's reasoning in *Yoder* was *more* applicable to his claim. The *Yoder* parents had won a right to withdraw their children completely from school requirements beyond the eighth grade whereas Leebaert was asking only for an exemption from part of the school's health curriculum. This request was a reasonable one, Leebaert maintained, especially so in light of the nature of the course from which he sought relief. In his view, "this portion of the Health curriculum proposes to teach morality rather than, e.g., substantive mathematical or grammar skills."[24] Not objecting to "normal curriculum subjects," Leebaert returned to the compromise position of Judge Charles

Letton in *Meyer v. State*.[25] Like Letton, Leebaert made a constitutional distinction that would extend the right of parental control "to such studies as are not plainly essential or which are not at least impliedly required to be taught in the grade of school in which the pupil may enroll."[26]

The Second Circuit followed a secure course and cabined the holding of *Yoder* to its own set of facts:

> [The] threat to the Amish community's way of life, posed by a compulsory school attendance statute, was central to the holding in *Yoder*. We have no reason to doubt either Leebaert's sincerity or the depth of his convictions. But because of the comparative breadth of the plaintiffs' claim in *Yoder*, we do not think that Leebaert's free exercise claim is governed by that decision: He has not alleged that his community's entire way of life is threatened by Corky's participation in the mandatory health curriculum. Leebaert does not assert that there is an irreconcilable *Yoder*-like clash between the essence of Leebaert's religious culture and the mandatory health curriculum that he challenges.[27]

This, it would also be safe to say, is a dangerous line of reasoning. To set the threshold for burdensomeness by reference to a claim so comparatively broad (*Yoder's* "entire way of life" standard) "creates an intolerable risk of discrimination against unconventional religious practices and beliefs, and threatens to narrow the protection of religious liberty overall."[28] Little wonder the Supreme Court presumed that "few other religious groups or sects" could make the same case for constitutional deference. Extending *Yoder* would require courts to make distinctions that border on the theological, such as the centrality of a religious belief.[29] (What is the essence of Leebaert's religious culture?) Yet not extending *Yoder* requires the same forbidden evaluation. It is equally outside the judicial ken to find that other religious claimants do *not* suffer from regulation in the same way or to the same degree as the *Yoder* parents. Intent upon salvaging yet not extending *Yoder*, the Second Circuit comes perilously close, as did the Supreme Court itself, to favoring some religious ways of life—or, more accurately, one religious way of life—over others.[30]

It is one thing to declare a right fundamental. It is another to live with the consequences of this declaration. If strict scrutiny is to be strict; if, as Scalia writes, "'compelling interest' really means what it says," it will be the unhappy lot of the courts to "leave public education in shreds."[31] This is a prospect they are not prepared to face. By one circuitous route or another, then, most courts treat public school opt-out cases as an occasion to render the hybrid rights doctrine a nullity; they dismantle the fundamentalness of the hybrid claim and make a comfortable, if not entirely credible, retreat to rational basis review. The result does not come without a high price to pay: in doctrinal convolution and inconsistency, in the disingenuous treatment of rights claims, in the threat of discrimination against minority religious groups. It comes with a savings of a sort, too. Amid all this discussion of rights and burdens, there is little room to worry about the welfare of the child.

In *Yoder*, the Supreme Court thought that its high regard for the "idiosyncratic separateness" of the Amish way of life was compatible with "the diversity we profess to admire and encourage." This reasoning would seem to call for a greater dedication to pluralism, not a restriction of *Yoder* to its own facts. The *Yoder* Court stepped back, with due caution, from this position, but the call has been answered by social theorists who support a policy of strong deference to separateness, however idiosyncratic; of deference, most significantly, to individuals and groups who themselves have little admiration for and interest in encouraging diversity. For liberal pluralists, autonomy is only "one possible mode of existence in liberal societies." It is a way of life, William Galston acknowledges, that must be respected, "but the devotees of autonomy must recognize the need for respectful coexistence with individuals and groups that do not give autonomy pride of place."[32] In the absence of this recognition, it is argued, a commitment to autonomy can become its own kind of uniformity. Galston makes the case that a commitment to autonomy "tugs against specific kinds of lives that differ fundamentally . . . from many others and whose disappearance would reduce social diversity."[33] With regard to the education of children, however, the opposite equation is no less true. Social diversity can easily tug against the autonomy of the child. When diversity fosters educational communities of like-minded parents and teachers, it, too, becomes its own kind of uniformity. It may be true that civic order does not require everyone to lead autonomous lives as long as enough people do so "to yield a threshold level of stability."[34] But one need not quarrel with the virtue of respectful coexistence to ask about the fate of children whose families and communities do not give autonomy pride of place.

Parentalists maintain that state regulation of schooling threatens educational pluralism. Yet it is the absence of state regulation that is more likely to do so. Without some kind of common education, there is pluralism only in the sense that different schools are each free to teach a closed set of values, not in the thicker sense that each child's world is opened to a range of viewpoints.[35] The case of Turk Leebaert and his son Corky makes the point. What Leebaert wanted, his brief states, was "to impart to his sons *his* own religious, moral and ethical values free of interference or preemption by school officials."[36] While Leebaert objects to the public school system as ideologically monolithic, his children are to be regarded as "closed-circuit recipients" of only that which he chooses to communicate.[37]

Many of us would agree that there is some place for state regulation of the parent as educator. (Not all of us, though. Under Virginia state law, religious parents who opt out of public schooling may do so completely free from state regulation, without any requirement to show that their children "are being home-schooled or otherwise educated."[38] This allows for the possibility that "some children [perhaps as many as seven thousand children in Virginia] will receive absolutely no education at all.")[39] The difficulty is to decide where to draw the line beyond which parents may not go, and here the parentalist position has faltered, wavering between an interventionist window so tightly closed that it would prohibit the state from addressing all but the most egregious threats to the child's welfare, and one so wide open that it would be difficult to stake out any clear limit to state action.

Galston sets out to offer an account of liberalism "that gives diversity its due." He acknowledges that some core liberal purposes would justify public interference with private group practices, but identifies these purposes narrowly; critically, they need not include the protection and promotion of autonomy "understood as choice based on critical rationalism." One purpose is the protection of human life. Galston would allow the state "to intervene against religious worship that involves human sacrifice." A second purpose is "the protection and promotion of normal development of [the child's] basic capacities."[40] This is a fairly open-ended proposition. How does a parent who does not want to protect/promote the child's autonomy protect/promote the normal development of the child's basic capacities? The answer is to have a rather stunted view of human development. Galston's illustration: He would allow the state "to intervene against communities that bind infants' skulls or malnourish them in ways that impede physical growth and maturation."[41] It would be hard to deny that this concession to governmental oversight of parenting practices does give diversity its due.

Yet, if the line is not drawn at skull binding and malnourishment, then even the most ardent parentalists struggle to limit the scope of legitimate state authority over private child-rearing decisions. Shelley Burtt takes the position that we don't owe children an open future.[42] In her view, parents may "raise their children to understand themselves as in some important way lacking a choice about what they do and who they are." Indeed, parents may "exercise *decisive influence* over their children's worldviews and values." Like Galston, though, Burtt concedes that adults may wield this influence only "as long as they concomitantly meet their children's developmental needs." Children must be allowed to achieve "some minimal level of autonomy." This qualification, it turns out, might well put at risk the very authority it is meant to sustain. First, Burtt explains, children must be allowed to think independently "about questions of identity and morality," though it is hard to square this with her claim that parents may "teach their children that there is a right way of life for them and that their flourishing as individuals depends on assuming certain roles or affirming certain beliefs or living by certain traditions." Second, and somewhat startling, parenting practices may be constrained in order to promote political interests. Burtt would allow the state "to prevent parents from raising individuals with a deep-rooted antipathy to the state's constitutional order and/or a settled indifference to widely held principles of international law and human rights."[43] (Perhaps the parentalist "indifference" to the Convention on the Rights of the Child is itself evidence that its principles are not widely held.) Similarly, for Stephen Gilles, parents must be free to share their worldview "unless it rejects basic moral or liberal-political norms on which there is a general consensus among reasonable people in our society."[44] This degree of trimming might be too much for the most fiercely antiparentalist.

It is not only parentalists who have a problem with fine lines. Some child-sensitive educational theorists try to accommodate parents like Turk Leebaert by defining autonomy "down." For example, Harry Brighouse supports educational programs that merely facilitate autonomy as opposed to those that actively promote it.[45] Under his Solomonic recommendation, children would be taught that diversity is a fact, but they would not be taught that diversity is desirable. They would not be taught that differing views deserve respect or even tolerance. With the faith of a Horace Mann in what amounts to a latter-day nonsectarian sectarianism, Brighouse would have schools focus on knowledge and skills rather than the substantive teaching of values. This basic education would "equip[] people with the skills needed rationally to reflect on alternative choices about how to live"—skills which are "a crucial component of providing [children] with substantive freedom and real opportunities." Brighouse hopes, with frankly less than complete confidence, that an autonomy-facilitating education will be less likely to alienate deeply religious parents from mainstream society: "In refraining from teaching substantive civic values, autonomy-facilitating education refrains from putting Mammon before God. While religious parents may remain distrustful of the authorities, autonomy-facilitating education does not actually teach values that contradict their own."[46] If only we put substantive questions aside (Brighouse speaks of "disarming religious parents"), the classroom can be a haven of Rawlsian public reasonableness.

Likewise, Rob Reich (following Eamonn Callan) demands only the degree of autonomy needed for the child to escape ethical servility.[47] The condition of servility "implies dutiful slavishness or submissiveness to others, an unwillingness or incapacity to make decisions or judgments for oneself." This is Reich's pedagogical bottom line: "Neither parents nor the state can justly attempt to imprint indelibly upon a child a set of values and beliefs, as if it were an inheritance one should never be able to question, as if the child must always defer and be obedient." This negative obligation brings with it a positive duty to "develop[] through education a basic capacity for critical deliberation." It is only by exposure to and engagement with unfamiliar values and beliefs that "a child learns to think for him or herself enough to surpass the threshold of ethical servility." Understood in this way, "the degree of autonomy necessary to escape ethical servility is extremely minimal."[48]

This may be minimal, perhaps extremely minimal, but even so it will prove to be too much. In some spiritual lives—the pluralists get this right—it is autonomy that is slavishness (the enslavement to selfhood); it is in ethical servility that real freedom lies (in the selfless obedience to truth). Surely, for some parents, there is good reason to worry about the kind of education that promotes or even facilitates freethinking. If truth has been found, there are no choices—at least not right ones—to be made, and critical deliberation can mean only doubt or confusion where there should be certainty. Reich himself observes that "to expose children to and engage students with values and beliefs other than those of their parents"—and this, he says, is the function of the school setting "even in a minimal construal of autonomy"—is a bottom line that will be threatening to some parents.[49]

The attempt to define autonomy minimally, so as to make some kind of peace between the dictates of the private, that is to say, the parental, conscience and the constitutional commitment to the child's prospective freedom of choice, takes neither conscience nor choice seriously enough. Amy Gutmann urges public schools to "be careful not to confuse teaching children the virtue of mutual respect with teaching them . . . skeptical reflection on ways of life inherited from parents or local communities." A liberal education, she insists, "does not entail either moral or metaphysical skepticism." Yet Gutmann would have children learn skills of political reflection, even though these "cannot be neatly differentiated from the skills of evaluating one's life." Teaching children to think about social justice means "teaching them that it may be reasonable to disagree with their parents and teachers—and every other authority—on politically relevant matters"—and this teaching, as Gutmann well knows, "is threatening to the moral convictions of many parents (and teachers and other authorities) and to their way of life."[50]

We cannot have it both ways. Children will not be satisfied with one bite of the apple. K. Anthony Appiah suggests a compromise by which "parents are permitted to insist that their children not be taught what is contrary to their beliefs [at least where "identity-related propositions are at stake"]; and, in return, the state will be able to insist that the children be told what other citizens believe, in the name of a desire for the sort of mutual knowledge across identities that is a condition of living productively together." Thus, Appiah concludes, we can "teach children about the range of religious traditions . . . without requiring that they assent to any of them, so that, to begin with, at least, they will assent only to the religion they have learned at home."[51] As though children need to be taught to question authority. (They need to be taught not to.)[52] As though critical reasoning will not lead to critical reflection. There is simply no way to teach children to be a little bit autonomous. And even a little bit of autonomy may run contrary to what some parents believe. This is the lesson we should have learned from Vicki Frost and Robert Mozert.

In *Mozert v. Hawkins County Board of Education*, the most well-known of modern curricular requirements cases, a group of parents objected to the textbooks used as part of a schoolwide critical reading program.[53] The parents' religious beliefs compelled them to refrain from exposing their children to viewpoints not consistent with strict adherence to biblical teaching. Frost, one of the lead plaintiffs, testified that "she did not want her children to make critical judgments and exercise choices in areas where the Bible provides the answer." Accordingly, the parents sought to opt out of the reading program. The Sixth Circuit concluded that mere exposure to opposing viewpoints is not constitutionally burdensome, reasoning that the reading curriculum did not require students "to affirm or deny a religious belief or to engage or refrain from engaging in a practice forbidden or required in the exercise of a plaintiff's religion." The court dismissed the plaintiffs' reliance on *Yoder*, deciding that "*Yoder* rested on such a singular set of facts that we do not believe it can be held to announce a general rule that exposure without compulsion to act, believe, affirm or deny creates an unconstitutional burden." The parents in *Mozert*, so the court determined, were not put to a *Yoder*-like crisis of conscience:

> The parents in *Yoder* were required to send their children to some school that prepared them for life in the outside world, or face official sanctions. The parents in the present case want their children to acquire all the skills required to live in modern society. They also want to have them excused from exposure to some ideas they find offensive. Tennessee offers two options to accommodate this latter desire. The plaintiff parents can either send their children to church schools or private schools, as many of them have done, or teach them at home. . . .
>
> *Yoder* was decided in large part on the impossibility of reconciling the goals of public education with the religious requirement of the Amish that their children be prepared for life in a separated community. . . . No such threat exists in the present case, and Tennessee's school attendance laws offer several options to those parents who want their children to have the benefit of an education which prepares them for life in the modern world without being exposed to ideas which offend their religious beliefs.[54]

Some scholars of the case object to a portrait of the appellants that paints them as being unreasonable. John Tomasi, for one, suggests that the *Mozert* case record can be read to suggest that the parents objected merely to "the repetitive and unbalanced presentation of the reader as a whole." Thus, Frost's lengthy list of objectionable material. Tomasi writes, "[T]he complainants indicated that—despite even their objections about repetitiveness and depth—they were willing to have their children use the reader, provided that the lesson made explicit and clear to the children that they were not being encouraged to view any of these philosophies or religions as true."[55] This reading of the complaint is overly generous to the plaintiffs and underappreciative of their religious principles. The *Mozert* parents would be content with nothing less than an *unbalanced* treatment of moral values.[56] Both of the primary witnesses, Frost and Mozert, testified that they "objected to passages that expose their children to other forms of religion and to the feelings, attitudes and values of other students that contradict the plaintiffs' religious views *without a statement that the other views are incorrect and that the plaintiffs' views are the correct ones.*" This is not a request for respect and evenhanded treatment. What the *Mozert* plaintiffs really wanted was for the state to shape its public educational requirements so as to support a regime of private religious indoctrination. If successful, they would reshape First Amendment jurisprudence "to require the Government itself to behave in ways that the individual believes will further his or her spiritual development or that of his or her family."[57]

In his *Mozert* concurrence, Judge Danny Boggs, too, argued that the plaintiffs were not politically unreasonable:

> A reasonable reading of plaintiffs' testimony shows they object to the overall effect of the Holt series, not simply to any exposure to any idea opposing theirs. . . . Their view may seem silly or wrong-headed to some, but it is a sincerely held religious belief. By focusing narrowly on references that make plaintiffs appear so extreme that they could never be accommodated, the court simply leaves resolution of the underlying issues here to another case, when we have plaintiffs with a more sophisticated understanding of our own and Supreme Court precedent, and a more careful and articulate presentation of their own beliefs. The district court specifically found that the objection was to exposure to the Holt series, not to any single story or idea.[58]

Yet the plaintiffs were not careless or inarticulate. It is clear enough that their quarrel was not, as Boggs notes, with a specific reading and certainly not with any suggestion that their children were being asked to believe this or that story. They objected, with more than adequate articulation, "to the very principles—tolerance and evenhandedness—traditionally used to justify liberal education." Nomi Maya Stolzenberg gets this exactly right:

Although the *Mozert* plaintiffs identified particular offensive "teachings," such as evolutionary theory and the alleged illiteracy of Jesus, their quarrel with the assigned series of textbooks was broader than that. They explicitly objected to the school's presentation of differing values and beliefs. It was not exposure to a particular hostile value or belief, such as Darwinism, but rather exposure to the diversity of values and beliefs that, to the plaintiffs, represented a violation of the Free Exercise Clause. In other words, the plaintiffs objected to the very principles—tolerance and evenhandedness—traditionally used to justify liberal education.[59]

Nor was there, as the superintendent of the school system suggested, perhaps with a thought to building bridges, a "misunderstanding" on the part of the parents that "exposure to something [could] constitute teaching, indoctrination, opposition or promotion of the things exposed."[60] Boggs was on more solid ground when he argued that the reading program was, in fact, a substantial burden on the religious liberty of the plaintiffs. The parents stated that they would face "eternal damnation" for letting their children read the books and that the children "will be punished with eternal damnation if they read the books."[61] What greater burden could there be?

In her concurring opinion, Judge Cornelia Kennedy was able to sidestep the question of burdensomeness because she decided that any imposition on religious belief was justified by compelling governmental interests. Some of these interests were administrative (e.g., avoiding classroom disruption and religious divisiveness),[62] but Kennedy also considered the needs of the schoolchildren. "Teaching students about complex and controversial social and moral issues," she wrote, "is . . . essential for preparing public school students for citizenship and self-government." Kennedy understood the religious burden well enough. Many of these difficult issues, she noted, "will be subjects on which [the parents] believe the Bible states the rule or correct position."[63] Yet, she concluded, there was simply no way to accommodate the plaintiffs' beliefs and to meet the school system's educational goals.

Kennedy's opinion points in the right direction. The *Mozert* plaintiffs might argue that the public schools should teach "only normal curriculum subjects" or basic skills (Frost said, "I thought they would be learning to read, to have good English and grammar, and to be able to do other subject work"),[64] but no minimalist education would satisfy them. We teach children to read and write, to do math, to understand science, to learn a foreign language because we believe it is better for them that they learn to think for themselves. Even "[t]he logic of mathematical argument," says Christopher Eisgruber, teaches a "ruthlessly egalitarian" lesson: "[A] bad geometric proof is a bad proof, no matter how rich your parents are or what church they attend." We teach children these basic skills because we believe it is better for *us* that they learn to think for themselves. Again, Eisgruber on the three R's: "[T]here is an essential connection between these intellectual skills and the virtues needed for good citizenship." Good writers will write good essays, and "[t]o write good essays, students must become reflective about their own views . . . ; [and] they must learn to be sensitive to other people's perspectives." In other words, they must prepare themselves for the "discursive forum" we call liberal democracy.[65]

There is simply no stopping at "normal" curriculum subjects. Someone will have to assign texts, and "most (if not all) texts [including parent-assigned ones] will be open to interpretation that might subvert a particular parent's values."[66] One of the disputed *Mozert* readings, accompanied by a picture of a boy making toast while a girl reads to him, went like this: "Pat reads to Jim. Jim cooks. The big book helps Jim. Jim has fun." Here, Robert Mozert found that "the religion of John Dewey is planted in the first graders [*sic*] mind that there are no God-given roles for the different sexes."[67] It would be futile to look for curricular materials that are more normal. Who would suspect that the Goldilocks story preached secular humanism because the heroine does not pay for her crimes? Or that the story "Freddy Found a Frog" could "seduce a child into a belief in disarmament"?[68] Even if it were possible to render the curriculum value-neutral (and value-neutrality were not itself a moral posture), the learning process itself would interfere with Mozert's ability to control his child's religious upbringing. Girls sit side by side with boys. Gay children take gym with straight children. Women teach. Everything we do as educators, like everything we do as parents, is laden with moral value.

Sadly, nothing could prepare the *Mozert* children more to be agents of state-thought than the closed-mindedness of their parents' world. The parents objected to the reading program both because "it turns the children into cookie-cutter models; it homogenizes and standardizes their values and beliefs" *and* because it "encourage[s] children to believe that they are their own authority"—and "unfetters their imaginations when their imaginations ought to be bounded."[69] This is not as contradictory as it might seem. It is not really objectionable that the children are turned into cookie-cutter models. The harm is that the state, by teaching children to think for themselves, interferes with the parents' own manufacture of cookies pleasing to them. Tomasi writes that "the *Mozert* parents sought only measures to protect their own children's faith."[70] In truth, what the parents sought were measures to protect *their* faith. What they wanted from their children was not faith, but the mere parroting of religious feeling.

Opting In: Religious Viewpoint Discrimination in the Classroom

When Grace Oliva invited her first-grade students to read a favorite story to the class, she placed only one condition on the students' selection of material: She would review the stories selected by the students to "insure that their length and complexity were appropriate for first graders." One student, Z.H., chose to read a story titled "A Big Family," which told part of the biblical account of Jacob and Esau. The story, in its entirety, read as follows:

> Jacob traveled far away to his uncle's house. He worked for his uncle taking care of sheep. While he was there, Jacob got married. He had twelve sons. Jacob's big family lived on his uncle's land for many years. But Jacob wanted to go back home. One day, Jacob packed up all his animals and his family and everything he had. They traveled all the way back home to where Esau lived. Now Jacob was afraid that Esau might still be angry at him. So he sent presents to Esau. He sent servants who said, "Please don't be angry anymore." But Esau wasn't angry. He ran to Jacob. He hugged and kissed him. He was happy to see his brother again.

Though the passage itself was free of any overt religious content, Z.H. was not allowed to read the story to the class because of its biblical lineage. Concerned that young students would not be able "to distinguish messages a teacher specifically advocates from those she merely allows to be expressed in the classroom," the Court of Appeals for the Third Circuit upheld the school's decision. The court was also worried lest the school infringe upon the right of parents to direct the religious upbringing of their children: "It is not unreasonable to expect that parents of non-Christian children would resent exposure of their six-year-old children to a reading from the Bible. Nor is it unreasonable to expect that some parents of Christian first graders would regard a compelled classroom exposure to material from the Bible as an infringement of their parental right to guide the religious development of their children at this stage."[71]

This really ought to be caution to a fault, but it is caution that, regrettably, is not entirely unwarranted; for some parents do seek to make the public school classroom a forum for their personal religious (and political) agendas. To promote a particular religious viewpoint (and to make a constitutional statement), these parents put their religious words in the mouth of a child. In the absence of a fundamental due process right to dictate the public school curriculum, this strategy looks to the Free Speech Clause, and its strong protection against viewpoint discrimination, as a trigger for strict scrutiny.[72]

In *Walz ex rel. Walz v. Egg Harbor Township Board of Education*,[73] a student named Daniel Walz wanted to distribute candy canes at a kindergarten classroom party, an innocuous enough request — except that attached to these candy canes was a religious story titled "A Candy Maker's Witness." The story (an apocryphal one, it turns out) tells how the candy came to "incorporate[] several symbols for the birth, ministry, and death of Jesus Christ." The *Walz* court (again, the Third Circuit) distinguished personal religious observance from outward religious promotion and concluded that Daniel sought to promote a specific religious message.[74]

But Daniel sought no such thing. It was, in the Third Circuit's proper assessment, "[h]is mother's stated purpose . . . to promote a religious message through the channel of a benign classroom activity." Daniel was simply a litigation foil for a parent, one who sought to make her child a spiritual foil, too. The district court had been clear on this point: "The facts leave little doubt that plaintiff's mother, Dana Walz, is the driving force behind the distribution of these items and this lawsuit. It is highly unlikely that [Daniel] . . . was able to independently read and advocate the dissemination of the message[s]. Additionally, Mrs. Walz has consistently inquired about and challenged the school's limitations on the distribution of such items and she is the one who is dissatisfied with the accommodations made by the school." Nonetheless, given the procedural posture of the case, the court had to assume it was Daniel who "was attempting to freely speak and exercise his religious beliefs when distributing these items to his young classmates."[75]

When a public school restricts student religious speech, the question is usually whether the child has been subjected to discrimination on the basis of a religious viewpoint. The resolution of this question may turn on the court's choice of a standard by which to judge the constitutionality of such restrictions. Can schools discriminate on the basis of religious viewpoint if such regulation is reasonably related to pedagogical concerns? Or does the Constitution require that a school's restriction be not only reasonable, but also viewpoint neutral, a standard that would require schools to show a compelling interest for restricting religious speech?[76] Under either standard the court must distinguish between expression that *describes* religious belief— acceptable to the courts—and expression that *promotes* religious belief— unacceptable. This is a tangled legal web that courts need not weave, at least not at the elementary school level. It has long been recognized that elementary school students are an especially impressionable lot[77]—thus, the concerns that young children will think a school endorses speech that it merely permits, and that public schools will capture the hearts and minds of their youngest wards.[78] As the *Walz* court said, as a matter of fact and law, "Kindergartners and first graders are different."[79]

This difference is constitutionally meaningful. When we protect the speech of children as young as Daniel, we are not protecting *their* speech. What we are protecting, it is no secret, is the speech of parents who manipulate their children to make a legal point. (Using children to send adult messages is hardly a practice that belongs solely to religious groups or to one side of the political spectrum. In *Tinker v. Des Moines Independent Community School District*, one of the armband-wearing children was only eight years old. It is hard to believe that protesting the Vietnam War was a matter of conscience for this second-grader.)[80] There is no need to maintain this fiction or to tolerate such selfishness. The right of free speech assumes freedom from coercion, but Daniel Walz, at age four, was not free in this sense. Just the opposite is the case. The language of rights masks—barely, but, in the eyes of the law, effectively enough—the real interests at stake here. It is only the parent who has an interest in free speech. The child's interest is not to test constitutional waters. It is to begin the lifelong process of finding his or her own voice.[81]

The reality is that there is scarce room for free speech in elementary school. The *Walz* court remarked, uncontroversially, that "in the context of an organized curricular activity, an elementary school may properly restrict student speech promoting a specific message." But at the elementary school level, almost all activities are part of some organized curricular activity. The party in *Walz* was a typical holiday party, yet it must have taken little effort by school officials to produce "abundant evidence that the school seasonal parties for these young children were meant to have an educational component, and also that they were highly structured, supervised, and regulated." If this holiday party "had a clearly defined curricular purpose to teach social skills and respect for others in a festive setting," it is hard to imagine what part of the day is not an organized curricular activity for young children. Snack time, perhaps. The court noted that "[w]here a student speaks to his classmates during snack time, he does so as an individual."[82]

This is not to say that the elementary school setting should be cleansed of religious speech. The duty of the state to inculcate "tolerance of divergent political and religious views" is poorly served by such political correctness. Many religious parents are concerned, and rightly so, that school officials sponsor particular religious or political beliefs—not deliberately, perhaps, but by a failure to see their own viewpoints as partial, as subject to criticism; not consciously, perhaps, but by a failure to see that a state-mandated secularism is not a morally neutral starting point. If the classroom is peculiarly the marketplace of ideas,[83] then the voices of religious children must be allowed to be heard, for their sake, and for the educational benefit of the entire class. If children are to learn a civility that goes beyond mere manners, then the state will let them speak for themselves (whether they speak the language of reason or faith) and for their community and culture (whether that background is informed by religious or secular values). In fact, these goals would be better served if teaching about religion were a regular part of the classroom, public or private.[84] Where student speech is responsive to the assignment; where the school has solicited individual views; or where children otherwise are allowed to speak for themselves, school officials may not disfavor religious viewpoints—and the Establishment Clause stands ready to protect young children from discrimination, without the pretense that it is they who are promoting a specific message.

Can schools teach about religion without teaching religion? The Supreme Court thought so, even as it struck down state-mandated religious exercises.[85] Can schools provide a basic education without teaching about religion? The Supreme Court thought not,[86] and, given the place that religion occupies historically and culturally, for good reason. Teaching about religion can be a productive part of a more broadly based civic education. It might, as its proponents contend, help young people better manage the political and moral crosscurrents that accompany religious pluralism. Once admitted to the classroom, the study of religion could strengthen the curriculum more generally. Other social sciences as well as the humanities and the arts cannot be studied successfully without a healthy measure of religious literacy. Few would disagree with Justice Robert Jackson that "for good or for ill, nearly everything in our culture worth transmitting, everything which gives meaning to life, is saturated with religious influences."[87]

Certainly, it would be a mistake to underestimate the challenges that will arise from teaching about religion. We should not assume that parents who object to a "godless" curriculum will not object with equal vehemence to the "objective" study of religious literature and traditions.[88] No doubt, many secular parents will be concerned that the study of religion as a cultural or historical subject is but a step removed from religious advocacy. Yet, if implemented in good faith, teaching about religion should operate on intellectually generous principles. The voices of all children need to be heard, with fairness and respect. But it is *their* voices that need to be heard. What a liberal education seeks to ensure is that, at a minimum, the child learns that there are questions to be asked and choices to be made. "[E]ach of us must learn to ask the question of how we should live," muses Callan; and "how we answer it can be no servile echo of the answers others have given, even if our thoughts commonly turn out to be substantially the same as those that informed our parents' lives."[89]

Toward a Public Education

In *Fields v. Palmdale School District*,[90] the Ninth Circuit declared that "the right of parents to make decisions concerning the care, custody, and control of their children is a fundamental liberty interest protected by the Due Process Clause." However, the court added, this fundamental right is "substantially diminished" when parents choose to send their children to the public schools.[91] The case involved the distribution to elementary school children of a survey containing questions about sexual topics. The parents of several children complained that the administration of the survey "deprived them of their free-standing fundamental right to control the upbringing of their children by introducing them to matters of and relating to sex in accordance with their personal and religious values and beliefs."[92]

The Ninth Circuit did not think that due process reached this far. While parents "have a right to inform their children when and as they wish on the subject of sex," there is no fundamental right, the court held, "to prevent a public school from providing its students with whatever information it wishes to provide, sexual or otherwise, when and as the school determines that it is appropriate to do so." The right to direct a child's upbringing may reside first with parents, but it does not reside with them *"exclusively."*[93] Thus, like the *Leebaert* court, the Ninth Circuit concluded that *Meyer* and *Pierce* do not encompass a right *"'to restrict the flow of information* in the public schools.'"[94]

The court drew a precise boundary line where the right to parent must give way to the state as educator. The right to parent "does not extend beyond the threshold of the school door." Rejecting strict scrutiny, the court found that the survey met several legitimate educational objectives: protecting the mental health of children and reducing barriers to students' ability to learn. The court held that, apart from any educational purposes, the promotion of which is part of the state's plenary police power, the survey was justified as "well within the state's authority as *parens patriae*."[95] But if the welfare of students falls within the state's authority as parens patriae, why should this authority stop at the door of the private schoolhouse? The governmental interest in children's mental health and educational outcomes is no less compelling because students go to private school. How closely private schools ought to be regulated may be a matter fit for public deliberation; but what is not open to debate, at least not as a matter of constitutional law, is that the state may require private schools to "meet[] the secular educational requirements which the state has power to impose."[96] The Supreme Court, in *Board of Education v. Allen*, made this clear enough:

> Since *Pierce*, a substantial body of case law has confirmed the power of the States to insist that attendance at private schools, if it is to satisfy state compulsory-attendance laws, be at institutions which provide minimum hours of instruction, employ teachers of specified training, and cover prescribed subjects of instruction. Indeed, the State's interest in assuring that these standards are being met has been considered a sufficient reason for refusing to accept instruction at home as compliance with compulsory education statutes. These cases were a sensible corollary of *Pierce v. Society of Sisters: if the State must satisfy its interest in secular education through the instrument of private schools, it has a proper interest in the manner in which those schools perform their secular educational function.*[97]

Turk Leebaert enjoys a right of exit from the public school system (from a common schooling), but he enjoys no right of exit from the public school curriculum (from a common education).[98] Still, he is not defenseless against the pressure of the "'It takes a village to raise a child' philosophy." No matter what curriculum is mandated by the state, parents remain free to inculcate their values in the countless formal and informal ways that parents inculcate values. This is the constitutional lesson of *Meyer* and *Pierce*. To support his assertion that only the parent has the authority to teach character education, Leebaert described how, when he teaches his children, he goes beyond the conformist character-building methods of the public schools. He cited as an example a boat trip that he and his sons took down the Connecticut River. They built the boat themselves and traveled more than four hundred miles from the river's source in New Hampshire to Long Island Sound:

> This is not something that the average parent teaches his chil-
> dren, and it demonstrates the extent to which Mr. Leebaert wants
> his sons to go *beyond* the secular teachings of the Fairfield School
> system which he believes reduce the potential of his sons to the
> secular culture's views on the development of character and right
> and wrong. Mr. Leebaert's sons, Corky and Timmy Bruce, are
> both honor students at Roger Ludlowe Middle School and, in
> addition to everything else, are adept at violin, full-contact karate,
> animal tracking and other interests. The flat boat Connecticut
> River trip is just one example of the lengths to which Mr. Lee-
> baert goes to personally build character in his sons.[99]

Leebaert is exactly right, but he proves too much. The state as educator does not replace the parent as educator. The parent remains a private
source of intellectual and moral authority, as do a host of private players
and entities. Indeed, against these private sources, "the state is normally at a
disadvantage."[100] Thus, even if the state were to mandate a common curriculum for all schools, the allocation of educational authority still would be
shared by parent and state. Ira Lupu, among others, approaches the issue of
educational pluralism by thinking in terms of separated powers, comparing
the division of authority over the education of children to the Constitution's
structural division of governmental power.[101] This model of shared authority, Lupu writes, "reduces the risk of tyrannical treatment and domination
of children" by parents as well as by the state.[102]

Most parents who choose private schooling do not do so to gain monopolistic control over the ideas and associations to which their children have access. Many send their children to private secular schools where the curriculum mirrors that of the public system; others, to private parochial schools that provide a broad-based secular education along with religious instruction and training. For some parents, though, there can be no compromising with a curriculum that is not uncompromisingly sectarian; no concession to state regulation is acceptable;[103] and the only option is one of educational and social segregation.[104]

From within the homogeneity of the segregated school, the child will miss the associations and incitements, for good and bad, that accompany a diverse peer group.[105] The child will never meet that teacher who, just by being a nonparental role model, opens the eyes of children to new and unimagined scenes.[106] In the broadest sense, an education that is ideologically or socially reclusive robs children of community. It keeps from them a common intellectual and cultural capital. Even the children of a separatist religious group are members of many other communities: political, historical, philosophical, artistic. They belong to a past as well as a present; they live, geographically and otherwise, in multiple jurisdictions. A liberal education takes heed of this. It respects the rootedness of children's lives, teaching children from the inside, from what Warren Nord has nicely called "the communities of memory which tentatively define them."[107] No topic ought to be a means to discount the history and culture that children bring with them to school. The classroom should be a place where the child's primary commitments can be strengthened. In this sense, a truly liberal education is inherently conservative, reinforcing cultural continuity. A liberal education equally respects the self-directedness of children's lives, teaching children from the outside, from a stance (again, Nord) of "critical distance on the particularities of their respective inheritances."[108] These are not incompatible lessons. We reinforce tradition as we come to understand it and even as we come to reinterpret it.

A public education need not be limited, as a matter of institutional form, to the traditional public school. One promising way to support common education without the uniformity of common schooling is the charter school, and more attention should be paid to the role that religiously based charter schools might play in a public school system. But whatever form a school takes, it needs to be more than a state-supported means of forming a bounded community "within which like-minded parents and teachers can reside."[109] And within which, it apparently goes without saying, students will be expected to be similarly like-minded. One advocate of educational "choice" observes approvingly that a charter school would provide parents "with the opportunity to create a free public school that, while it does not teach their religious beliefs, also does not teach lessons that they find religiously objectionable."[110] Indeed, it has been suggested that "if students are financially empowered to choose among a variety of secular and religious schools, the compulsion to protect their individual consciences from the moral or religious content embodied in the curriculum or environment at any particular school dissipates significantly."[111] It hardly needs to be pointed out that children do not make these choices. If parental choices can mean that the "compulsion" to protect a child's conscience dissipates, then the safest place for a child's conscience is the old-fashioned public school.

Wherever it occurs, a public education teaches two complementary values that our legal culture has considered essential to a democratic society: the self-directed value of autonomy, the other-directed value of tolerance. In this regard, while some parental requests to opt out of educational requirements make more modest demands than others, they all portend diminished educational opportunity for the child. This loss demands a direct and candid treatment of the constitutional challenges posed by such requests. We might begin with these principles:

- There is no fundamental parental or group right that would require a showing of harm to justify state regulation of private educational choices.
- The educational interests of parent and child are not identical. The child has an independent interest (one that the *Meyer* Court acted to protect) in securing "the opportunit[y] . . . to acquire knowledge."[112]

- The state has a compelling interest in "inculcating fundamental values necessary to the maintenance of a democratic
  political system."[113] To this end, all schools, public and
  private, should be subject to a common core curriculum
  that eschews the minimalism necessary, though probably not
  sufficient, to accommodate the authoritarian parent.[114] (The
  requirement that private schooling satisfy the state's universal
  educational requirements raises the possibility that public
  schools should not enjoy a monopoly on state funding.)[115]
- The state does not have a monopoly on educational authority.
  Parents and private schools, under *Meyer*, may supplement
  the state-mandated curriculum as they choose (though, under
  Pierce, private schools are not free to teach material "which is
  manifestly inimical to the public welfare").[116]
- Mere exposure to diverse curricular materials *will* "burden"
  students' moral principles and religious beliefs, and some
  more so than others. The Old Order Amish do not have a
  monopoly on moral and religious sensitivity. This burdening
  cannot be disregarded. The classroom must be a model of
  respect and reciprocity.
- Parents should not be allowed to opt out of state-mandated
  curricular requirements. We can disagree about what these
  mandated courses and programs should be, and we can
  fight about them—and fight fiercely—but they are required,
  presumably, because the state believes that children—all
  children—need to know this material. If so, the child's
  interests should not be conflated with those of the parent.
  On the other hand, if some children do not need to know
  this material, then such courses should be optional across the
  board.[117]
- Any number of institutional forms "are all potentially consistent with the demands of a common education."[118] What is
  not consistent with these demands, as Rob Reich has said, are
  "schools that would refuse to expose children to and engage

164

them with value diversity. . . . To allow this would indeed
establish a kind of parental despotism over children."[119]

Children who are cut off from an understanding of, or at least an introduction to, foreign ideas and values, cultures and traditions, suffer more
than an intellectual loss. Understanding what is other is an exercise of heart
and soul as well as mind; in Callan's phrase, it requires "the enlargement of
the imagination," the experience "of entering imaginatively into ways of life
that are strange, even repugnant, and some developed ability to respond to
them with interpretive charity."[120] This is why, according to Nord, a liberal
education must nurture "passions and imagination as well as thinking," the
faculties that allow children "to feel the intellectual and emotional power"
of alternative ways of life. This is not an elective subject, an option to be
selected after the child has learned basic reasoning skills. "[I]t is only when
we can feel the intellectual and emotional power of alternative cultures
and traditions that we are justified in rejecting them," Nord writes. "If they
remain lifeless and uninviting this is most likely because we do not understand them, because we have not gotten inside them so that we can feel
their power as their adherents do."[121] A public education requires a willingness to entertain, if only for the sake of argument—and, we might also
hope, for the sake of adventure—ideas that go against the familial grain. But
"getting inside difference" does not presuppose the child's rejection of his or
her primary culture. It presupposes an engagement with the unfamiliar that
is both sympathetic and critical.[122] In this sense, it is a process at the core of
identity formation. Kept out of a conversation that their birthright entitles
them to join, cloistered children are cut off from themselves, bereft of self-
consciousness and awareness of their cultural place.

To think for themselves, children must know how others think; to take
their place as members of a liberal democracy, they must learn to make
room for the places that other members take. The Supreme Court has said,
a bit hyperbolically perhaps, that "'[t]eachers and students must always remain free to inquire, to study and to evaluate, to gain new maturity and understanding; otherwise our civilization will stagnate and die.'"[123] These are
the predicates of our constitutional freedoms: an age-old republican distrust

of authoritarian ideologies (parental and political), a still-revolutionary skepticism toward final and complete truths. Constitutionally speaking, we are all students and teachers.

Rights, Responsibilities, and Religion: The Parent as Spiritual Trustee

Spiritual Custody: Parental Rights and Parental Wrongs

Both Mormons, Stanley and Tracey Shepp had divorced, according to Tracey's testimony, primarily because they disagreed about polygamy.[124] A fundamentalist Mormon, Stanley Shepp believed in polygamy as a matter of religious conscience.[125] He may have stated this as clearly, and certainly as succinctly, as one could when he told his thirteen-year-old stepdaughter that if she did not agree with his religious views—indeed, if she did not practice polygamy—she was going to hell.[126] Following separation, Shepp petitioned for shared custody of his daughter Kaylynne, who had been living with her mother and her stepsisters from the mother's previous marriages. In its final order, the trial court awarded legal custody of Kaylynne to both parents and directed that the child be raised in the nonfundamentalist Mormon faith. It also prohibited Shepp from teaching her about polygamy. The court did not find, however, that Shepp's conduct had subjected his daughter to a grave threat of harm.[127]

On appeal, the state Superior Court affirmed the decision of the trial court. Tracey Shepp argued to the court (1) that a parent "may pursue any course of religious indoctrination during periods of lawful custody or visitation," and (2) that "the objecting parent must establish a substantial risk of harm in absence of the restriction proposed." Relying on *Yoder*, Stanley Shepp contended that strict scrutiny required "proof of a 'substantial threat' rather than 'some probability'" of harm: "We also emphasize that while the harm involved may be *present or future* harm, the speculative possibility of mere disquietude, disorientation, or confusion arising from exposure to 'contradictory' religions would be a patently insufficient 'emotional harm' to justify encroachment by the government upon constitutional parental and religious rights of parents, even in the context of a divorce."[128]

Tracey countered that *Yoder* did not apply because the trial court's order was merely a means of enforcing a neutral and generally applicable prohibition on bigamy. Comparing the statute to the law at issue in *Smith* (prohibiting the use of peyote), she maintained that the state could prohibit conduct or speech incidental to criminal activity, even though that conduct is sanctioned by religious doctrine.[129] The fact that polygamy was a crime meant that Stanley's conduct was not protected by the First Amendment; thus, *Yoder*'s strict scrutiny standard was not required:

> The behavior Father wishes to teach his daughter about is a *crime*. It is not behavior protected by the First Amendment's Free Exercise Clause or Freedom of Speech Clause. Father is of course free to hold religious beliefs regarding polygamy, however illegal, immoral and illogical those beliefs may be. He is not free however to act on those religious beliefs. The First Amendment does not give him leave to practice or teach polygamy because it is a religious belief. . . .
>
> The Appellant claims protection from the First Amendment's Free Exercise clause to teach and indoctrinate his child with polygamy, an illegal act. The First Amendment provides no such protection. The beliefs he holds, if practiced, are a crime. . . . *Yoder* is a case about Old Order Amish objecting to Wisconsin's compulsory school-attendance statutes—a far cry from polygamy. The balancing test the court set forth in *Yoder* is an exception to the usual rule. It is aimed at promoting and protecting the unique lifestyle of the Old Order Amish. The Amish lifestyle is not illegal, nor does it promote dangerous criminal behavior such as Mormon polygamy. The rule in *Yoder* does not apply in this case.

Though Tracey protested that strict scrutiny was not the proper standard of review, she added that both prongs of the *Yoder* standard—harm to the child and significant social costs—were satisfied: "In the present case there are very real concerns for the health and safety of the child Kaylynne as well as significant social burdens if Father is permitted to teach and advocate polygamy. Kaylynne is of the age where polygamists are interested in her as a bride. This would certainly jeopardize her health and safety, as well as being a crime against society."[130]

The Superior Court applied strict scrutiny, but it upheld the trial court's prohibition. The court found that by advocating a religious practice prohibited by law, Shepp did indeed pose a grave threat to Kaylynne (and the trial court's conclusion to the contrary was both erroneous and unreasonable). The court also held that the trial court's restriction was the least restrictive means of protecting Kaylynne from indoctrination in a criminal practice. What mattered to the Superior Court was Shepp's intent to inculcate a belief in what he knew to be illegal. The court distinguished parental instruction in polygamous religious beliefs, or other forms of criminal conduct, from "insistence that [Kaylynne] engage in such conduct." For the court, Shepp's promotion of his beliefs amounted to more than mere instruction. Critical to this judgment was the testimony of his stepdaughter (whose testimony was accepted as true by the trial court): "[The father's] promotion of his beliefs to his stepdaughter involved not merely the superficial exposure of a child to the theoretical notion of criminal conduct, but constituted a vigorous attempt at moral suasion and recruitment by threats of future punishment. The child was, in fact, warned that only by committing an illicit act could she comply with the requirements of her religion."[131] By telling his stepdaughter that she would go to hell if she did not "comply with the requirements of her religion,"[132] Shepp was demanding that she practice what he preached. (The stepdaughter also testified that "Father had suggested that when she became of age, that they would perhaps be married.")[133] The fact that the act in question was a religiously mandated one made no difference to the court: "The question whether we would find similarly benign advocacy of drug abuse or child prostitution were they presented as foundational religious beliefs *is no question at all.*"[134]

But, as a matter of law, whether parental advocacy of criminal conduct *is* a question may well depend on what kind of foundational beliefs are involved. If those beliefs are religiously motivated, such advocacy is likely to pass judicial muster, even if adverse to the best interests of the child.

For the Pennsylvania Supreme Court, the critical task was to determine the level of scrutiny to apply to Stanley Shepp's claim. The court agreed that *Smith* was "critical to this issue." In fact, it conceded that the Pennsylvania statute was neutral and generally applicable and thus would override the father's claim that "such [a] law places an improper limitation on the free exercise of religion."[135] But the court applied a compelling interest test nonetheless. *Smith* did not apply because the facts presented a free exercise claim made in conjunction with a due process parenting claim—in other words, the case involved a type of the hybrid situation (i.e., religious parenting) that, even after *Smith*, is subject to strict scrutiny.[136] The "appropriate standard" was provided by *Yoder*. Under *Yoder*, only those interests of the highest order—where "it appears that parental decisions will jeopardize the health or safety of the child, or have a potential for significant social burdens"—can justify a restriction on religious parenting rights.[137] Like other family law courts before and after it, the *Shepp* court relied on this formulation to decide that "[t]he state's compelling interest to protect a child in any given case, however, is not triggered unless a court finds that a parent's speech is causing or will cause harm to a child's welfare."[138]

With interfaith marriages on the rise,[139] more and more parents bring differing religious backgrounds to their marriages—and, sadly, to the courtroom. In these spiritual custody cases, parents fight for control of the child's religious upbringing, and their attorneys fight for a favorable legal standard.

The long-standing rule in child custody cases—a rule that has been in place since American courts started hearing custody cases—is that the trial court, in furtherance of the best interests of the child, is vested with wide discretion to determine the general welfare of the child. Prior to *Yoder*, the best interests standard governed most spiritual custody cases, too. But *Yoder* provided constitutional support for a more rigorous test.[140] Today, following *Yoder*, most courts protect religious parenting rights by making substantial harm the legal standard in spiritual custody cases.[141] There may be some disagreement on the degree of harm that qualifies as substantial harm[142]—citing *Yoder* on "[t]he importance of the combined interest of parents in religious liberty and autonomy in raising one's children," the American

Law Institute's *Principles of the Law of Family Dissolution* (hereafter ALI *Principles*) prohibits courts from examining "the religious practices of a parent or the child, except to the minimum degree necessary to protect the child from *severe and almost certain harm* or to protect the child's ability to practice a religion that has been a significant part of the child's life"[143] — but whatever "substantial" may mean, "[v]ery few [courts] have actually ruled that substantial harm has been demonstrated."[144]

Once the *Shepp* court borrowed "the appropriate standard" from *Yoder* and adapted it to meet the particulars of the spiritual custody case,[145] it easily disposed of the case. For the court, "it [was] clear that the Commonwealth's interest in promoting compliance with the statute criminalizing polygamy is not an interest of the 'highest order' that would supersede the interest of a parent in speaking to a child about a deeply held aspect of his faith." "[A]dvocating religious beliefs that, if acted upon, would constitute criminal conduct" did not pose a grave threat of harm; thus, there was "insufficient basis for the court to infringe on a parent's constitutionally protected right to speak to a child about religion as he or she sees fits." The court simply ignored the second, social burden prong of the *Yoder* test. Objecting to this silence, the dissent argued that had this "distinct inquiry" been conducted, the court may well have been required "to uphold the trial court's custody order . . . because the practice of polygamy long has been identified as a 'substantial threat' to public welfare, an unsustainable burden on society, and a crime."[146]

Judicial deference in spiritual custody cases is meant to respect "the constitutional prerequisite of 'benign neutrality' towards *both* parents' religious viewpoints."[147] But to what end? Where parents have equally compelling free exercise claims, a neutral rights stance has little adjudicatory value.[148] Generally, spiritual custody courts decide to "split" the religious difference, allowing each parent to control the child's religious upbringing during separate times of custody. But this posture of neutrality makes little sense in cases where the parties are responding to the special dictates of religious conscience. The harm standard assumes that judicial neutrality serves religious liberty, yet nonintervention is bound to impinge upon the religious preferences of one or both parents.[149] To split the difference — as though the custody hearing were to determine whether the child would play tennis or soccer—is to respect neither party. Because a focus on the parent as a rights-holder offers no basis for resolving such controversies, we are left with a domestic stalemate. For some parents, the spiritual stakes are too high to be made the subject of bargaining and compromise, and it is not unusual for a parent frustrated by the courts to seek a self-help remedy, perhaps secreting off a child to religious rituals against court orders.[150]

The hands-off posture that accompanies strict scrutiny leaves children in a truly untenable position, for the law can protect them only when the risk of harm is already substantial. Worse, under a harm standard, children face the risk of injury from behavior that *would* warrant intervention in cases not in-volving religious matters. In light of the child's best interests, custody courts freely restrict parental conduct, including speech, without subjecting such measures to heightened scrutiny. Such restrictions are especially common in cases of parental alienation—cases, that is, involving the ways, sometimes subtle, often not, in which one parent may seek to turn a child against the other parent. Highly sensitive to "'the ability and disposition of each par-ent to foster a positive relationship . . . with the other parent,'"[151] custody courts will not hesitate to prohibit each parent from making disparaging remarks about the other, thus imposing a judicially mandated obligation of tolerance. The penalties for subverting this obligation, in word, action, or demeanor, can be severe. But toleration gives way to entitlement where dis-paragement is religiously motivated. The harms to the child do not change. If anything, they may be more severe where parents believe that a child's soul is at stake. What changes is the deference shown to the parents' con-stitutional claims. (Forlornly, the ALI *Principles* concludes that religiously motivated interference is a kind of harm "as to which the law is ill-equipped to save children.")[152] As one court has said, with no little indignation, it is an "outrageous price" to pay to shore up parental control of a child's religious destiny: "It is grossly unfair because the children ultimately bear it."[153]

Pamela and David Zummo were married on December 17, 1978. When they divorced ten years later, the Zummos were unable to agree on the reli-gious upbringing of their children. Pamela had been raised as a Jew, David as a Roman Catholic. Prior to their marriage, the couple had agreed that any children would be raised in the Jewish faith, and during the marriage the family "participated fully in the life of the Jewish faith and community." Before the parents separated, "the children attended no religious services outside the Jewish faith." Adam was beginning to prepare for his Bar Mitzvah; Rachel was soon to begin her formal Jewish education and training. After separation, however, David Zummo, while exercising visitation rights on alternate weekends, refused to take Adam to Hebrew Sunday School. In addition, David requested that he be allowed to take the children, on occasion, to Roman Catholic services. While David suggested that "the children would benefit from a bi-cultural upbringing and should therefore be exposed to the religion of each parent," Pamela "oppose[d] exposing the children to a second religion which would confuse and disorient them."[154]

The Court of Common Pleas entered an order that *"obligated [David] during his weekend visitations to arrange for the children's attendance at their Synagogue's Sunday School."* In addition, David was not *"permitted to take the children to religious services contrary to the Jewish faith."* The latter provision was not meant "to prevent [David] from taking the children to weddings, funerals, or family gatherings," nor "to prevent [him] from arranging for the presence of the children [at] events involving Christmas and Easter."[155] The trial court applied the best interests of the child standard, which, under state statutory law, allowed for consideration of "all factors which legitimately impact upon the child's physical, intellectual, moral and *spiritual* well-being." With this standard in mind, the court noted several factors supporting its conclusion "that restrictions upon David's right to expose his children to his religious beliefs were permissible and appropriate":

> [T]he Zummo[s] had orally agreed prior to their marriage that any children to their marriage would be raised as Jews; during the marriage the children were raised as Jews; it was in the children's best interests to preserve the stability of their religious beliefs; the father's practice of Catholicism was only sporadic while the mother's practice of Judaism had been active; Judaism and Catholicism are irreconcilable; and, exposure to both religions

might "unfairly confuse and disorient the children, and perhaps vitiate all benefits flowing from either religion."[156]

Relying heavily upon *Yoder*, the Superior Court found that consideration of religious factors as part of the custody analysis was improper. The best interests standard is not free from constitutional limitations; and, when "applied in the context of religious upbringing disputes," the court maintained, "it may . . . encroach impermissibly upon constitutionally protected religious freedoms." The trial court had allowed such encroachment, miscalculating the limitations that the Constitution places upon "the application of the *spiritual* well-being component of the best interests analysis." Specifically, the Superior Court declared, the Constitution requires that a restriction on religious parenting rights must satisfy the rigorous demands of strict scrutiny. So, Pamela Zummo would have to demonstrate that "the belief or practice of the party to be restricted actually presents a substantial threat of present or future physical or emotional harm to the particular child or children involved in absence of the proposed restriction, and that the restriction is the least intrusive means adequate to prevent the specified harm." Citing *Yoder* and *Smith*, the court derived this harm standard from the hybrid nature of the father's claim:

> The constitutionally recognized parental authority over the upbringing of children is augmented by the Free Exercise and the Establishment Clauses of the First Amendment with regard to the *religious* upbringing of children. . . . The United States Supreme Court has specifically held that parental authority in matters of religious upbringing may be encroached upon, only upon a showing of a "substantial threat" of "physical or mental harm to the child, or to the public safety, peace, order, or welfare."

Because the evidence presented by Pamela Zummo was insufficient to meet this standard, the Superior Court (1) vacated that part of the district court's order forbidding David to take his children to religious services contrary to the Jewish faith, and (2) affirmed that part of the order requiring the father to present his children at Sunday School.[157]

In the view of the Superior Court, strict scrutiny in spiritual custody cases is "in full accord" with the "developing constitutional jurisprudence" of parental rights. Summoning the rights spirit of *Meyer* and *Pierce*, the court called into question the viability of the best interests standard in spiritual custody cases: "The statist notion that the government may supercede parental authority in order to ensure bureaucratically or judicially determined 'best interests' of children has been rejected as repugnant to American traditions." The proper standard, suggested the court, ought to be the tougher measure applied in proceedings to terminate parental rights. This heightened scrutiny, the court reasoned, is more consistent with the protection extended to other important freedoms. "The custody, care, nurture, and instruction of children," the court declared, "resides first in the children's natural parents, as a constitutionally recognized fundamental right."[158]

Courts tread warily the difficult terrain of the spiritual custody dispute—and properly so. The risk of religious viewpoint discrimination is a real one. But, being overly solicitous of religious parenting rights, spiritual custody courts have replaced a flexible and fact-sensitive inquiry into the needs of individual children with a rigid parental rights standard. It may have been in the best interests of the Zummo children to be exposed to "contrary" religious traditions. Nonetheless, when the Superior Court grounded that decision on "the constitutional prerequisite of 'benign neutrality' towards *both* parents' religious viewpoints," it chose not to consider factors that would be highly relevant to the custody determination. This, it was not constitutionally required to do.

Tellingly, the child's preferences formed no part of the court's analysis. Today, as in the past, courts routinely take into consideration the wishes of a child who is sufficiently mature to express an opinion as to custody rights.[159] But the *Zummo* court gave short shrift—really, no shrift at all—to the children's religious preferences. A child's religious identity, the court stated, is defined by parents under the rules of the religion they practice, and "[o]ften such rules impose a presumed religious identity upon a child without requiring the children's consent or understanding." The court might concede a legally cognizable religious identity "when such an identity is asserted by the child itself, and then only if the child has reached sufficient maturity and intellectual development to understand the significance of such an assertion." But then again it might not:

> Moreover, even if the children had expressed a personal religious identity it is not clear that the children would have had any constitutional right to resist, or to be protected from, attempts by either parent to exercise their constitutional rights to inculcate religious beliefs in them contrary to their declared preferences prior to their legal emancipation. In *Wisconsin v. Yoder*, the majority declined to reach the issue of whether children had constitutional rights pertaining to religious education which could be asserted against parents, though the majority expressed concerns suggesting they were not predisposed to favor a claim to such rights.[160]

The court also ignored the secular effects associated with some of the religious factors considered by the district court. The trial court considered "stability and consistency in a child's religious education as an important factor in determining the best interests of the child." It is hardly controversial, the court pronounced, that "the desire to promote or maintain stability in the already tumultuous context of a divorce is generally a significant factor in custody determinations." In pursuit of rights neutrality, however, the Superior Court disavowed the suggestion "that *governmental* interests in maintaining stability in *spiritual inculcation* exist which could provide a justification to encroach upon constitutionally recognized parental authority and First Amendment Free Exercise rights of a parent to attempt to inculcate religious beliefs in their children." Here, however, the Superior Court conflated two separate matters: a subjective (and constitutionally impermissible) inquiry into the intrinsic merits of religious belief and an objective (and permissible) assessment of the effect of parental conflict on the secular well-being of the child:

> Stability in a path to damnation could not be said to be more in a child's "best interests" than an instability which offered the hope of movement toward a path to eternal salvation. Similarly, if all religions or a particular religion were merely harmful and

repressive delusion, then stability in such a delusion could not be said to be more in a child's "best interests" than instability which might pave the way to escape from the delusion. Because government cannot presume to have any knowledge as to which if any religions offer such eternal rewards or repressive delusions, and may not declare the complete absence or the universality of such eternal rewards or repressive delusions, a child's "best interests" with regard to the spiritual aspect of religion cannot be determined by any governmental authority.[161]

This is a clumsy equation of psychological and spiritual welfare. The custody question did not require the court to determine which religions offer eternal rewards and which repressive delusions. The proper analysis would consider only objective measures of harm, not the merit or worthiness of religious teachings.[162] To borrow from the law of evidence, the court did not need to decide the truth of the matter asserted.[163] As long as the court confines its investigation to the secular effects of religious belief and practice on the child, there is no reason why the best interests of the child should not prevail in spiritual custody cases, and unless the court's investigation considers these effects, it fails to give due consideration to the welfare of the child.

The *Zummo* trial court had relied on a prior decision of the Superior Court. In *Morris v. Morris*,[164] the court upheld restrictions on a father's visitation rights against his claim of religious liberty. Agreeing that *Yoder* stood for the proposition that only "interests of the highest order" might permit the state "to pierce the cloak of the familial unit," the *Morris* court reasoned that a strict scrutiny standard was applicable only when the state was "attempting to intrude on a unified, nuclear family." In matters of custody, the court stressed, "the family unit has already been dissolved, and that dissolution is accompanied by a weakening of the shield constructed against state intervention." With a somewhat archaic tone of indignation, the *Morris* court declared that "[a] parent cannot flaunt the banner of religious freedom and familial sanctity when he himself has abrogated that unity."[165] The Superior Court rejected this argument. "Parents who 'abrogate the unity of marriage,'" the court insisted, "are not to be punished for their decision to divorce." The court pointed out that intact families are not always models of unity, yet the state is not permitted to punish parents in these "healthy" marriages:

> One parent may be a Republican the other a Democrat, one may be a Capitalist the other a Communist, or one may be a Christian and the other a Jew. Parents in healthy marriages may disagree about important matters; and, despite serious, even irreconcilable, differences on important matters, the government could certainly not step in, choose sides, and impose an orthodox uniformity in such matters to protect judicially or bureaucratically determined "best interests" of the children of such parents.[166]

Typical of spiritual custody cases, the *Zummo* decision rests on the status of the parent as parent, not on the relation of parent to child. The court took its cue from the Supreme Court, which similarly had opined that a "marital couple is not an independent entity with a mind and heart of its own, but an association of two individuals each with a separate intellectual and emotional makeup."[167] An association, that is, of two individual rights-holders. When marriage dissolves, the point is, we still have two individual rights-holders, each equally entitled to direct the religious upbringing of the child.

But to state the (sometimes painfully) obvious, children change everything. When children enter the family "association," the layers of interdependence are more complicated and more consequential. In effect, the *Zummo* court insists that divorce brings with it no change with regard to parental authority. Yet the very nature of the custody decision belies that conclusion. No court can remove the "punishment" of compromise that accompanies shared and judicially supervised child custody. And where there is conflict, there is inescapably a tension between the rights of the parents and the needs of the dependent child. With its eye keenly on individual parenting rights, the *Zummo* court disregarded the relational sphere within which the parenting right arises and is exercised. Where the child needs protection from a domestic civil war (fought, at times, with all the intensity of grander religious conflicts), the rights-oriented posture of traditional liberalism is unable to settle the question. Divorced parents remain entrusted with the welfare of their children, their fiduciary duties intact; and the state still has the duty to see that parents make the best use of the authority entrusted to them. The spiritual custody court fails to discharge this responsibility when it employs a harm standard before it restricts religious parenting rights. In the words of the *Morris* court, "the very concept of 'best interests' would be but a hollow shibboleth were not parental rights to yield to the welfare of the child."[168]

Even if it were possible for a custody court to split the spiritual difference, benign neutrality toward religious viewpoints may come at too high a cost. The *Yoder* standard requires a showing of harm that leaves the child unprotected from injuries deemed sufficient to call for judicial intervention in cases involving only secular matters. One such injury results from conduct by a parent that tends to alienate a child's affections from the other parent. It is a commonplace in custody cases that each parent has "a duty to not turn a child away from the other parent by 'poisoning the well.'" Typically, custody courts hold fast to the principle that "minor children are entitled to the love and companionship of both parents insofar as this is possible and consistent with their welfare."[169] Behavior that causes alienation can be a critical factor in custody determinations "because it is so contrary to children's best interests to learn from their parents hatred, intolerance and prejudice for the other parent."[170] Under the ALI *Principles*, interference with the other parent's access to the child is one of several risk factors, along with abuse, neglect, and abandonment, that a court is required to consider in formulating a parenting plan.[171] Indeed, such interference has been said to be "'an act so inconsistent with the best interests of the children as to, per se, raise a strong probability that the [offending party] is unfit to act as custodial parent.'"[172] When awarding custody, courts may consider, under the "friendly parent" doctrine, which parent is most likely to foster the child's relationship with the other parent,[173] and alienating conduct may provide a basis for the modification of a custody arrangement (that is, it may be treated as a material change of circumstances).[174] Denial of access can take many forms, from making the child physically unavailable to "a more subtle and insidious form of interference, a form of interference which, in many respects, has the potential for greater and more permanent damage to the emotional psyche of a young child than other forms of interference; namely, the psychological poisoning of a young person's mind to turn him or her away from the [other] parent."[175]

The antidote to this brand of psychological poisoning can be harsh. Without requiring a showing of harm, relying solely on the best interests of the child, custody courts may prohibit disparaging conduct "either in words, actions, demeanor, implication or otherwise."[176] These restrictions may be phrased negatively, forbidding behavior that can be construed as uncomplimentary—for example, ordering a parent to "refrain[] from doing anything likely to undermine the [child's] relationship [with the other parent]."[177] Or courts may impose more affirmative obligations designed to build relationships of trust and tolerance. ("The courts in all custody cases make it a firm rule to insist that each spouse inculcate [in] a child love and respect for the other.")[178] Parents have been ordered "to instill in the child . . . the good and kind qualities of the other parent."[179] Not especially concerned about the genuineness of such feelings, one court ordered the mother "to affirmatively express feelings and beliefs which she does not have." The court found (with no little literary zeal) that "the cause of the blind, brainwashed, bigoted belligerence of the children toward the father grew from the soil nurtured, watered and tilled by the mother"; nonetheless, it ordered the mother "to do everything in her power to create in the minds of [the children] a loving, caring feeling toward the father . . . [and] to convince the children that it is the mother's desire that they see their father and love their father."[180] Courts may also require parents not to expose a child to derogatory comments made by third parties.[181]

Such orders may well restrict a parent from speech that is ideological in orientation—unless that speech derives from religious belief. For example, a court may order one parent to make sure that his child is not exposed to homophobic teachings (because the other parent is homosexual), without any finding that exposure to such teachings would endanger the child's physical health or significantly impair her emotional development.[182] But if these same comments were faith-based (like Stanley Shepp's advocacy of polygamy), most courts would require a showing of harm. In short, disparagement born of religious conviction is likely to get a constitutional pass from strict judicial scrutiny.

First Amendment scholar Eugene Volokh argues that court-ordered restrictions on parental speech are "generally unconstitutional."[183] Volokh's defense of parental free speech rights is a vigorous one, but even he would allow restrictions on "non-ideological speech that interferes with the children's relationship with the other parent." Such speech Volokh considers of little constitutional value. But not so with disparaging speech that is ideologically grounded. For Volokh, restrictions on disparaging or "poisoning" sentiments against the other parent have to "be tailored to allow ideological teachings that don't expressly mention the other parent, even when the ideology condemns some behavior that the other parent happens to engage in or some beliefs that he holds." This tailoring makes for some fine linguistic, as well as constitutional, distinctions:

> Many a mother who genuinely loves her husband, but disapproves of his racism, may teach her children that racism is bad, and may even feel more of a need to do so precisely because the children are especially likely to learn otherwise by looking at her husband's actions. When the children ask her if this means their father is bad, too, she can tell them that he's a good person who has some bad habits, like all of us do; and that the kids should emulate his many good traits but not his few bad ones. Likewise, a father who says, "anyone who doesn't embrace Jesus will go to Hell," "homosexuality is a sin," "racists are bad people," or "religion is superstitious folly," and whose children then ask, "Does that mean mommy will go to Hell/is a sinner/is a bad person/is stupid?," can respond with something positive: "Mommy is a good person who loves you very much, and while she's wrong about this, I'm sure she'll come to the right path eventually."

Such subtle requirements may not be easy to set forth or to enforce, especially when the family is split and each parent is not emotionally inclined to defend the other parent to the children. A flat "Don't say anything that is expressly or implicitly critical of the other parent" or "Don't express any anti-homosexual views" may seem relatively enforceable. A more nuanced "Don't make any non-ideological statements critical of the other parent, don't use the other parent as an example for any of your ideological teachings, and if the children ask you whether the other parent is bad, tell them 'no' and sound credible" may seem like a recipe for endless future debates. Nonetheless, it seems to me that on balance courts should try to narrow their injunctions as much as possible, rather than completely banning parents from teaching their moral views whenever those views might cast the other parent in a bad light.[184]

The idea that disparagement based on religion can be mitigated by such subtle linguistic requirements depreciates the special forcefulness of religious mandates. Perhaps a parent could be asked to temper moral or philosophical views that reflect unkindly on the other parent, but flatly banning discussion of religious matters (when such discussion is not in the best interests of the child) would actually be less ideologically intrusive than asking a parent to reduce deeply held beliefs to verbal nuance. Volokh is, to say the least, sanguine about human nature: "We as adults recognize that people may have traits or beliefs that we disapprove of, yet still be generally good people. Children can likewise be taught this, and often are taught this."[185] But many adults recognize no such thing. Nor are children likely to find such spiritual tempering to be credible anyway. It is small comfort for a child to learn that Mommy, who is going to Hell if she doesn't get on the right path, is a generally good person.

The same confidence in fine scholastic distinctions is seen in the ALI *Principles*. The *Principles* adopts a strict test when courts are asked to restrict a parent's religious practices, rejecting consideration of such practices "except to the minimum degree necessary to protect the child from severe and almost certain harm."[186] So it is of considerable significance that the *Principles* treats "substantial interference with the relationship between the child and the other parent" as per se severe and certain harm.[187] When a child is turned against a parent, regardless of motivation, the child's entitlement to parental love and companionship is violated. It is always damaging to the secular welfare of the child.

But the nature of religious faith makes it difficult to apply the harm exception. As the *Principles* admits, "[a] religious practice considered harmful by one parent may be considered necessary to eternal salvation by the other parent."[188] In light of this difficulty, the *Principles* seeks to distinguish the mere difference of religious belief from speech or conduct that is actually alienating. The fact that parents have conflicting religious beliefs, without more, would not warrant court intervention, as the following example from the *Principles* illustrates:

> Constance is a fundamentalist Christian. Edgar insists that religious fundamentalism is hypocritical and that religious indoctrination interferes with the moral and intellectual values he wishes for their two boys, ages four and six. His religious disagreements with Constance are what led to their separation. Each parent wants primary responsibility of the children.
>
> The court may not favor either Constance or Edgar in the allocation of custodial or decisionmaking responsibility based on the content of their religious beliefs or views about children.[189]

Here, in the absence of factual detail, religious instruction is presented as though it were mere abstract advocacy. To illustrate disparaging actions, the *Principles* draws religious indoctrination in more concrete strokes:

> Susan is a member of a small religious community of faith in which nonbelievers are shunned as irredeemable sinners. She believes that the only opportunity for salvation from eternal damnation is through the teachings and practices of her community. She wants her three daughters, ages two, four, and seven, to have the opportunity for salvation. Because the girls' father, Jerome, is not a member of the community, Susan has instructed the girls not to

speak with him and to avoid all contact with him. As a result the girls have been uncommunicative with Jerome since the parents' separation. Jerome argues that this conduct should be taken into account by the court in allocation of custodial responsibility.

Parents are entitled to raise their children in a religious community whose members live separately from others; the isolation of the girls from nonmembers in this case is insufficient to establish severe and almost certain harm to the children. Susan's actions in turning the children against Jerome, however, interfere substantially with his relationship to the children. Thus, despite the religious roots of Susan's practices, the harm is both severe and certain and thus may be taken into account.[190]

Susan's actions—presumably, instructing the children to avoid Jerome—pose a serious risk of harm to the children. By itself, the isolation of the children from their nonmember father would not be sufficient to meet the *Principles'* tough harm standard. Yet Susan's religious instruction, by itself, makes it all too clear to the children that their father should be shunned as an irredeemable sinner. To make the harm standard workable, the *Principles* must ignore the coercive nature of religious beliefs (children are caught between competing moral commands) and the coercive familial context in which such speech occurs (children are caught between competing parental commands). The fact that the other parent is not expressly mentioned is of little significance. Religious disparagement—really, one might say, the ultimate kind of alienation—need not take the form of overt hostility. If Dad says, "Anyone who doesn't embrace Jesus will go to Hell," he hardly needs to point out to the child the fact that Mom doesn't embrace Jesus. Some religious tenets make alienation inevitable. Disparagement may be couched even in the language of love, of caring for a soul in mortal danger.

In cases of religious disparagement, custody courts wait for harm, or the substantial threat of harm, to happen. Even then, court-ordered restrictions may be so protective of parental rights that there is little chance they will have much effect. *Kendall v. Kendall* is a good example.[191] The mother was an orthodox Jew. The father was a member of the Boston Church of Christ, a fundamentalist Christian faith. The trial court made the following findings that bear on the question of alienation:

> I find that the Boston Church of Christ services to which [the defendant] has taken his children have included teachings that those who do not accept the Boston Church of Christ faith are damned to go to hell where there will be "weeping and gnashing of teeth."

> I find that the oldest child, Ari, has drawn from the above teaching the conclusion that [the plaintiff] may go to hell, and that this causes him "substantial worry and upset."

> [The defendant's] behavior toward his children fosters negative and distorted images of the Jewish culture. [The defendant] insists that all individuals who do not accept his beliefs about life and existence are sinners who are destined to tortuous punishment.

> I credit the G.A.L.'s [guardian ad litem] report and testimony that Ari "may experience choosing a religion as choosing between his parents, a task that is likely to cause him significant emotional distress." In fact, the G.A.L. specifically concludes, and I credit his conclusion, that the children are now in a position where they are perilously close to being forced to choose between their parents, and to reject one.

> I credit the report of the G.A.L. that "should the children come to accept the religious beliefs that [the defendant] reports he wants them to accept, they are likely to come to view their mother negatively and as a person who will be punished for her sins . . ." resulting in a ". . . negative impact on their relationship with their mother . . . and difficulty accepting guidance and nurturance from her." I find this would be to the children's substantial detriment.[192]

Reviewing the facts, the state supreme court said that "[w]hether the harm found to exist amounts to the 'substantial harm' required to justify interference with the defendant's liberty interest is *a close question*, especially because there is considerable value in . . . 'contact with the parents' separate religious preferences.'" The *Kendall* court noted, to show how close the question was, that "the G.A.L. has not found current damage to the children so severe that it has caused them to suffer a psychotic break, or to have a 'formal psychiatric diagnosis.'" (The court did add, comfortingly, that "[t]he case law does not require the court to wait for formal psychiatric breakdown.")[193]

When nonreligious conduct poses a possible risk to a child's safety or welfare, courts intervene to protect the child—they act to ensure that the risk does not result in harm; where religious conduct is involved, however, most courts require not only evidence of substantial harm but also that the complaining parent prove a causal connection between the harm and the other parent's interfering conduct.[194] When the risk of harm to the child derives from nonreligious factors, courts may impose restrictions intended to constrain a parent's conduct; where the risk of harm has a religious origin, however, courts impose restrictions calculated to ensure a minimal burden on parental rights: "[T]he remedy should be that 'which intrudes least on the religious inclinations of either parent and should be narrowly tailor[ed] . . . so as to result in the least possible intrusion upon the constitutionally protected interest of the parent.'"[195] The *Kendall* court upheld the "least possible intrusion" placed on the father by the trial court: that he "not share his religious beliefs with the children *if those beliefs cause the children significant emotional distress or worry about their mother or about themselves.*"[196] But minimalism is not the same as clarity, and not surprisingly the Kendalls soon found themselves in court again, arguing about the meaning of the court order.[197]

Hard cases can make bad law, but the courts must deal with a parent who teaches a child, or allows a child to be taught, that the other parent is "spiritually unclean" or one of "God's enemies" or "destined for eternal damnation"; or a parent who counsels a child that for religious reasons it is allowable to lie to or behave violently toward the other parent.[198] Nonintervention amounts to little more than a way of not dealing with such cases. Or at least not until, for the child, it is too late.

Carol Peterson believed that her ex-husband, Roger, had the devil in him.[199] After Carol and Roger Peterson divorced, Carol became a member of the Good Life Pentecostal Church, which teaches that "all religions which believe in the Trinity . . . are daughters of 'the great whore.'" Subjected to this teaching, the Peterson children became "afraid that the father and other relatives were consigned to perdition and that the father follows the devil, or has the devil in him or living in his house." Roger was awarded custody of the children, and the trial court ordered Carol to "abstain from making any comments to the children with regard to her religious beliefs." On appeal, the state supreme court modified this restriction to provide that Carol "abstain from making any comment to the children which in any way contradicts, disparages, or questions the validity of the father's religion or of those with whom he or the children associate, or which in any way interferes with the children's relationship with the father." The *Peterson* court came to a conclusion that few other custody courts are willing to entertain: that alienation, though motivated or mandated by religious belief, is tantamount to harm.[200]

If it is to make the best interests of the child its paramount consideration, the spiritual custody court must be free to act in ways that *prevent* harm from occurring. The scope of its inquiry must be broad enough for a court to "consider evidence of the religious views or practices of a party . . . to the extent that such views or practices are demonstrated to bear upon the physical or emotional welfare of the child." If one parent's views or practices tend to alienate the child's affections from the other parent, this fact should not be ignored because the view or practice is religious: "To ignore such evidence would be a dereliction of the duty of courts to 'monitor the welfare of children in their jurisdiction and promote the children's best interests'"; and the evocation of the best interests standard would truly be but a "hollow shibboleth."[201]

In the most famous literary account of a custody case, it takes the wisdom of Solomon to discern that the "real" mother is the one who attends to the child's needs, willingly sacrificing her own claim to parenthood.[202] By "focus[ing] on the context of relationships rather than on isolated rights,"[203] the modern spiritual custody court can honor the principle that parental authority is contingent on the parental choice to form a caring relationship with the child. It may be that the best way to do this is not to "protect" children from contrary points of view;[204] and it is surely too much to claim that "it is beyond dispute that a young child reared into two inconsistent religious traditions will quite probably experience some deleterious physical or mental effects."[205] But it may also be the case that parental religious intolerance is anything but "a sound stimulant for a child."[206] Where this is the case, courts can and should do the work of inculcating the habits of civility and the fundamental values that are "indispensable to the practice of self-government in the community and the nation." If, as the *Prince* Court thought, the welfare of a "democratic society rests, for its continuance, upon the healthy, well-rounded growth of young people into full maturity as citizens," the welfare of young people requires that those responsible for their upbringing observe, or be made to observe, "the boundaries of socially appropriate behavior."[207]

Who Owns the Soul of the Child?: Revisiting Prince and Yoder

Its focus on the welfare of the child notwithstanding, the *Prince* Court managed to ignore the real child whose welfare was the central issue of this landmark case. No one on the Court suggested that Betty may have been too young to choose such a strong religious commitment, or that she may not have chosen her religious commitment at all. Writing for the Court, Justice Wiley Rutledge noted that "Betty believed it was her religious duty to perform this work and failure would bring condemnation 'to everlasting destruction at Armageddon.'"[208] On this point, the Court's four dissenting justices agreed with the majority: Betty went of her own desire, motivated to engage in missionary evangelism by her love of the Lord.[209] Sarah Prince's brief to the Court also stressed that Betty "desired to serve Almighty God." Her service was freely given to the Lord. In Prince's words, "[Betty] was serving Jehovah God and not her guardian, not any man, not the society or any earthly institution. The girl desired to pay her vows unto her God. Since she was thus serving Jehovah it cannot be said that she was working for any creature on earth. No man or government has authority to punish a child or another creature because the child is permitted to serve Jehovah God."[210] From this point of view, Betty's street preaching was not child labor at all.

No constitutional truism is more universally accepted than Justice Jackson's famous assertion, in *West Virginia v. Barnette*, that "no official, high or petty, can prescribe what shall be orthodox in politics, nationalism, religion, or other matters of opinion or force citizens to confess by word or act their faith therein." In *Barnette*, the Supreme Court protected schoolchildren against the action of local authorities, who, by compelling the flag salute and pledge, had "transcend[ed] constitutional limitations" on the authority of the state. The injury caused by such a compelled statement of belief was a grave one, a blow to the intellectual and moral personhood of the young children. The compulsory flag salute and pledge "require[d] affirmation of a belief and an attitude of mind." By forcing the children to utter what was not in their minds, the state had invaded "the sphere of intellect and spirit which it is the purpose of the First Amendment to our Constitution to reserve from all official control."[211]

In the catalogue of opinions not subject to official prescription, religion occupies a privileged place. The Constitution's commitment to religious freedom is built on the idea that religious principles are uniquely the dictates of conscience. Because religion is, as James Madison put it, "the duty which we owe to our Creator," it can be "directed only by reason and conviction, not by force or violence."[212] Not, that is, by the state. Even a benign expression of religious views by the state "may end in a policy to indoctrinate and coerce," calling into question the voluntariness, and thus the genuineness, of belief. "A state-created orthodoxy," the Supreme Court has said, "puts at grave risk that freedom of belief and conscience which are the sole assurance that religious faith is real, not imposed."[213]

Yet children are left legally unprotected from most forms of private religious coercion. The religious identity of children is determined without
their consent or understanding. They are made "members" of religious
groups by birthright or ceremonies of religious association. We permit parents to raise and educate their children in religiously segregated enclaves.
We permit parents to inculcate religious beliefs that effectively compel adherence. Indeed, where the religious upbringing of children is concerned,
freedom of belief can lose its customary meaning. Somehow, Betty's fear
of "everlasting destruction" showed that her evangelical desires were the
product of free choice. The Court did not pause to consider whether Betty's
religious training had left her unable to choose—freely to embrace, freely to
reject—the religious commitments of her guardian. We might ask how free
a young child can be to make religious choices when the consequences of
choosing wrongly are so stark. We might also ask what it means for the psychological welfare of a child to believe that her own conduct—or, in Betty's
view, misconduct—could bring about her everlasting destruction.

The Supreme Court did not stop to think about such things. It held
against Prince on the basis that street preaching was dangerous work for
children. But the Court chose to overlook a real risk of harm to Betty: the
threat posed by a religious regime that makes genuine choice and real faith
difficult, if not impossible. Or perhaps it should be said not that the Court
ignored this harm, but that it could not see it. The Court could not see the
possibility that Betty's obedience was the product not of choice, but of the
loss of choice, of childlike surrender to a familial authoritarianism. "For the
most part we do not see, and then define," Walter Lippmann wrote, "we
define and then see."[214] The danger to Betty of emotional maltreatment was
hidden in plain sight,[215] but the Court could not question the cultural norm
that parents have the right to form the religious beliefs of their children.

A liberal democracy rests on a model of maturation that takes as its norm
the individual's full capacity to make free and independent choices. As
Justice Stewart writes, "The Constitution guarantees . . . a society of free
choice."[216] Freedom of choice is both the presupposition and the product
of our First Amendment protections. It follows, then, that it is a primary
duty of parents to nourish this capacity. It does *not* follow that parents need

abandon the role of religious mentor and guide (not that that would be possible: nonmentoring would itself be a form of mentoring); it would hardly be practical or helpful to children to adopt some ideologically neutral model of parenting.[217] In a democracy, Galston writes, parents must be able to introduce their children "to what they regard as vital sources of meaning and value, and to hope that their children will come to share this orientation."[218] For many, the most vital source of meaning and value is their religious faith, and it should go without saying that parents may introduce their children to what they regard as spiritually true and hope their children will come to share a similar religious orientation.

Yet this simple proposition raises surprisingly tough questions about the parent-child relationship. Parents may "introduce" their children to vital sources of meaning, but what limits, if any, can be placed on this introduction? Parents may "hope" that their children will come to share their values, but how far can parents go to make this hope a reality? If Galston seems to write with some caution, there is good reason for it because, as he also observes, children have freestanding intellectual and moral claims of their own, claims that "imply enforceable rights of exit from the boundaries of community defined by their parents."[219] The care of children may reside first in the parents, but not first and last.

If children have a right to cross the boundaries set by their parents, then they must be able to exercise this right freely. They must not be disempowered from making their own intellectual and moral claims in the first place.[220] What must be protected is the child's future right to make these claims; what must be secured is the child's present opportunity to develop the capacity to make these claims.[221] Ideally, it would be part of the parent's task to safeguard the child's right to moral autonomy, but where the law deals with the transmission of religious belief, it is acceptable for parents to enforce spiritual conformity from their children, demanding (often in a loving and compassionate voice) uncritical obedience toward religious authority. It is only natural for parents to want a child to embrace their values, to believe their beliefs, and our legal system leaves parents free to transmit their religious values, as it ought; but parents abuse this freedom when they give children no real opportunity to embrace other values and to believe other beliefs. Religious freedom for the parent ought not to come at the cost of spiritual servitude for the child.[222]

The law assumes that adults consent to religious association.[223] By voluntarily uniting themselves with the spiritually like-minded, they submit to be governed by the rules of religious membership. Thus, religious authority may not be imposed on those unwilling to subject themselves to it. Once a member withdraws consent,[224] or where a religious entity has used coercive techniques to undermine a member's capacity to consent,[225] the constitutional shield that safeguards religious freedom against tort liability is broken. But it is the opposite case with children. Young children lack the full capacity to assert, or to choose not to assert, a personal religious identity. They are by their very nature captive to the will of others.[226] For this reason, the constitutional parent takes on a spiritual fiduciary duty, here as elsewhere validating the child's steps toward self-determination.

But we should not presume that all parents do so. The narcissistic parent distorts this process, using any number of emotional tools—often disguised to parent and child alike—to create the child in his or her own image.[227] This type of parental rule can take a terrible emotional toll on the child—to be fully loved, the child has no choice but to be obedient; and when parental authoritarianism has the sanction of religious authority, its emotional toll is compounded, its emotional effects more entrapping. It is one thing to disobey and displease a parent, another to disobey and displease God. When God himself demands the child's self-sacrifice, the child is bound to suffer sorely for everyday acts of self-assertion.[228] Compelled religious belief is an affront to the child's dignity, whether the source of compulsion be parent or state, but coercion is likely to be more effective, and the injury it inflicts deeper, when children are compelled to believe by those closest to them. One lesson of the parental alienation cases is that the content of religious teaching, regardless of its truth or falsity, can cause substantial harm to children. Religious teaching may destroy a child's self-esteem, or subject a child to the terror of divine retribution, or alienate a child from his or her parent.

Few disputes generate the degree of heat or the depth of hostility that accompanies religious controversy. When such controversy touches the lives of our children, it is often a struggle to see compromise as anything less than a violation of one's conscience. The religious destiny of our children matters so deeply, so personally—it matters so much—that we may fight with nothing less than religious fervor. In our homes, schools, and communities, and in our courts, we seek to control our children's religious upbringing as though we are (and many truly believe they are) fighting for the soul of the child. Sadly, if predictably, it is children who suffer from the fallout of uncompromising religious conviction. When parents educate their children in a way that does not fairly introduce them to other religious (and nonreligious) points of view, when parents disagree about and compete to control a child's religious upbringing, when children are subjected to religious indoctrination that is psychologically inappropriate—in all the ways that children can find themselves at the center of religious controversy, it is their best interests that are neglected. Children are poorly served by a legal regime that is too quick to fold before the "trump card" of religious parenting rights.

It is a remarkable "right" to control the spiritual consciousness of another.[229] It is not immune from abuse. "Nobody is born a member of any church," Locke counsels us:

> [O]therwise, the religion of parents would descend upon children, by the same right of inheritance as their temporal estates, and every one would hold his faith by the same tenure he does his lands; than which nothing could be more absurd. . . . No man by nature is bound unto any particular church or sect, but every one joins himself voluntarily to that society, in which, he believes, he has found that profession and worship which is truly acceptable unto God.[230]

In a free society, the binding power of moral commandments must depend on individual acceptance.[231] Religious teaching should make, so to speak, no permanent marks on the child; it must not foreclose the child's prospective religious freedom. To direct, rather than to control, the religious destiny of the child: This is the great and challenging task, the heart and soul of the parent's responsibilities as a spiritual trustee.

For the *Yoder* majority, mandatory secondary schooling was objectionable because it would take Amish adolescents "away from their community, physically and emotionally, during the crucial and formative adolescent period of life." In what sense, then, does the Court consider this period crucial and formative? It is during this period, the Court says, that these children "*must* acquire Amish attitudes favoring manual work and self-reliance and the specific skills needed to perform the adult role of an Amish farmer or housewife." During this period, children "*must* learn to enjoy physical labor." During this period, "the Amish child *must* also grow in his faith and his relationship to the Amish community if he is to be prepared to accept the heavy obligations imposed by adult baptism."[232] For the Amish child, apparently, the adolescent period is crucial and formative not in the sense that the child is forming his or her identity; rather, the child labors under a number of "must's," all of which are crucial if the child is to conform successfully to communal religious traditions. The *Yoder* decision turns upside down the nature of adolescence, ignoring what is really important about this stage of development—the increasing independence from adult guidance; the defining of a self by reference to new ideas and by association with like and unlike peers; the preparation for intelligent participation in the democratic process; even the adolescent's own quest for spiritual meaning—and consigns the young adult to a life of "idiosyncratic separateness."[233] It was no mean feat of legal analysis for the Court to find that the "limitations" accompanying the Amish way of life are "self-imposed."[234]

In general, the Supreme Court sees the liberty interests of the parent and child as "inextricably linked."[235] The child is not, however, without independent constitutional standing to challenge deprivations of educational opportunity.[236] Though the Supreme Court has seen the need to act "with sensitivity and flexibility to the special needs of parents and children," it is undisputed that "whatever may be their precise impact, neither the Fourteenth Amendment nor the Bill of Rights is for adults alone." It is the child's due process rights that, in part, explain why "state-operated schools may not be enclaves of totalitarianism": "Students in school as well as out of school are 'persons' under our Constitution. They are possessed of fundamental rights which the State must respect, just as they themselves must respect their obligations to the State. In our system, students may not be regarded as closed-circuit recipients of only that which the State chooses to communicate. They may not be confined to the expression of those sentiments that are officially approved."[237] With respect to some due process claims, in fact, the Court has concluded "that the child's right is virtually coextensive with that of an adult."[238] In effect, the Court has at times shifted the boundary line between childhood and adulthood when dealing with minors' constitutional claims.[239] Even *against* parents, the child is not beyond the protection of the Constitution, the due process protections from which the right to parent arises also working, in an interesting twist of constitutional fate, on behalf of the child.

The law of parent-child relations accepts as a starting point the long-standing legal presumptions (1) that "parents possess what a child lacks in maturity, experience, and capacity for judgment required for making life's difficult decisions," and (2) that "natural bonds of affection lead parents to act in the best interests of their children." The Supreme Court has had numerous opportunities to test the currency of these legal presumptions. In *Parham v. J.R.*,[240] the Court considered the constitutionality of a state mental health code provision permitting parents to admit their children to hospitals for treatment. On behalf of the children, it was argued that "the constitutional rights of the child are of such magnitude and the likelihood of parental abuse is so great that the parents' traditional interest in and responsibility for the upbringing of their child must be subordinated at least to the extent of providing a formal adversary hearing prior to a voluntary commitment." But the Court thought this argument swept too broadly:

> Simply because the decision of a parent is not agreeable to a child or because it involves risks does not automatically transfer the power to make that decision from the parents to some agency or officer of the state. The same characterizations can be made for a tonsillectomy, appendectomy, or other medical procedure. Most

children, even in adolescence, simply are not able to make sound judgments concerning many decisions, including their need for medical care or treatment. Parents can and must make those judgments. . . . We cannot assume that the result in *Meyer v. Nebraska* and *Pierce v. Society of Sisters* would have been different if the children there had announced a preference to learn only English or a preference to go to a public, rather than a church, school. The fact that a child may balk at hospitalization or complain about a parental refusal to provide cosmetic surgery does not diminish the parents' authority to decide what is best for the child.

The Court rejected the "statist notion that governmental power should supersede parental authority in *all* cases because *some* parents abuse and neglect children." Absent evidence that rebutted the traditional presumptions in favor of parental control, parents retain "a substantial, if not the dominant, role" in the commitment decision. Still, the Court did not walk away from the interests of children. It added that "the child's rights and the nature of the commitment decision are such that parents cannot always have absolute and unreviewable discretion to decide whether to have a child institutionalized." Treading the line between the interests of child and parent, the Court cautioned that "experience and reality may rebut what the law accepts as a starting point."[241]

Sometimes, experience and reality *do* rebut legal presumptions. The liberty interests of children and parents are not always compatible; there will be points of collision where the protection of children's interests has to come at the cost of parental authority. This has been the case in the area of medical decision making, where courts have most readily acknowledged circumstances requiring a reversal of traditional presumptions. In some especially sensitive medical areas, courts accept as a starting point that (1) a child *does* have the maturity, experience, and capacity for judgment required for making life's difficult decisions, and (2) the natural bonds of affection will *not* always lead parents to act in the best interests of their children. Under this mature minor doctrine, which may be a matter of judicial prescription or statutory law, unemancipated minors can get medical care without their parents' consent and even without their parents' knowledge. In many states minors may consent to treatment for substance abuse and venereal disease, including testing for HIV and sexually transmitted diseases, and to counseling for mental health problems, sexual abuse, and family planning. Minors can get birth control, including prescription contraceptives, as well as prenatal care. Information about these medical services remains confidential.[242]

It is true that there are practical concerns operating here. The worry is that parents will object to these services, thus discouraging adolescents from seeking treatment important to their health and to the welfare of society as a whole. So, to protect these interests, legislators have provided minors with what amounts to a parental bypass option. But to cast these decisions as medical, not ethical—itself a value-laden judgment—too easily dismisses the moral and religious concerns of parents. The truth is that the state has wrested from parents control over some of a young person's most intimate and difficult moral decisions.

In fact, the Supreme Court has taken a mature minor approach to the most value laden of medical decisions. The legal struggle to guarantee a woman's right to terminate a pregnancy has put the Court squarely in the business of defining the allocation of moral authority between parent and child. In *Planned Parenthood of Central Missouri v. Danforth*,[243] the Court held that the state could not authorize an absolute parental veto over the decision of a minor to terminate her pregnancy. The Court made the customary nod toward *Meyer, Pierce,* and *Yoder* but finally rejected chronological age as a constitutional yardstick by which to measure whether a minor can independently make the abortion decision: "Constitutional rights do not mature and come into being magically only when one attains the state-defined age of majority. Minors, as well as adults, are protected by the Constitution and possess constitutional rights."[244]

On this fluid doctrinal platform, the *Danforth* Court decided that "the safeguarding of the family unit and of parental authority" was not a state interest sufficiently significant to justify conditioning the minor's access to abortion on parental consent.[245] In *Bellotti v. Baird*, the Supreme Court held that a mature minor must be allowed to terminate her pregnancy without parental consent or notification. (Even a minor deemed incompetent to make the abortion decision independently must be allowed the opportunity to show that termination of pregnancy would be in her best interests, and to do so without any parental involvement.)[246] The *Bellotti* Court did its best not to challenge the core presumptions governing the relations of parent and child, noting several good reasons why the state may limit a minor's freedom to make independently "important, affirmative choices with potentially serious consequences." In the context of abortion, however, none of these reasons was reason enough to require parental notification. The Court based its decision on the uniquely "grave and indelible" nature of the abortion decision. Unlike few other personal choices, the decision to abort cannot be postponed, nor can its consequences be undone. Given what the Court described as the "profound moral and religious concerns" associated with the abortion decision, it would be unrealistic to think that some parents would not make (all too emphatically) clear their objection to the minor's decision: "[M]any parents hold strong views on the subject of abortion, and young pregnant minors, especially those living at home, are particularly vulnerable to their parents' efforts to obstruct both an abortion and their access to court. It would be unrealistic, therefore, to assume that the mere existence of a legal right to seek relief in superior court provides an effective avenue of relief for some of those who need it the most."[247] That the consequences of the abortion decision are uniquely grave and indelible would strike many as *more* reason for parents to be involved. Regardless of one's position on abortion, it is difficult not to conclude that the Supreme Court's abortion jurisprudence has changed the legal landscape of parent-child relations. If minors can make a decision as profound as whether to terminate a pregnancy, why should courts presume that parents possess what a child lacks in maturity, experience, and capacity for judgment required for making life's other difficult decisions? There are more than practical concerns at work here. There is, at bottom, a constitutional commitment to the personhood of the prospective mother.

The abortion cases take into account the fundamental "moral fact that a person belongs to himself and not others nor to society as a whole."[248] Surely, Kenneth L. Karst is correct when he asserts that "freedom of associational choice enhances the values of intimate association to a degree that would not be obtainable if choice were absent." As children mature, they will have to decide whether to identify with their parents; they will have to choose whether to maintain "a caring intimacy" with them. The decision to "choose one's parents," so to speak, is meaningful only if the maturing child is free not to make the association, or at least not to make it a close one. As Karst writes, the full value of commitment can be measured "only when there is freedom to remain uncommitted. . . . [C]oerced intimate associations are the most repugnant forms of compulsory association." The value of free choice is (again, Karst) "equally applicable to associations that are primarily ideological."[249] It hardly needs to be said that parental control over a child's religious associations lies directly at the intersection of the intimate and the ideological.

Frieda Yoder was fifteen years old when she testified that religious beliefs guided her decision to discontinue school attendance; Lillian Gobitis was not yet a teenager when the court heard her objection to compulsory patriotic rituals; and Betty Simmons was only nine years old when she testified that street preaching was for her a religious duty. The courts should be no less reluctant to hear from children who choose not to follow the religious preferences of their parents. When there are, as Justice Douglas put it, "potentially conflicting desires,"[250] it will not always be easy to determine if the child is speaking freely or speaking merely as the product of a religious or nonreligious culture, or to determine whether the child is sufficiently mature to make decisions about religious identity. But these are matters with which courts are familiar enough. The reality is that children can be coerced by not being heard as surely as they can by being forced to utter what is not in their minds. If the child belongs to itself, he or she may not be made a means by which parents perpetuate their own moral mandates or preferences.[251] Before the full moral personhood of the child, the right to parent, even when joined to a claim of religious liberty, must give way.

Galston, among others, describes parenting as a form of "expressive liberty." By expressive liberty he means "the absence of constraints . . . that make it impossible (or significantly more difficult) for the affected individuals or groups to live their lives in ways that express their deepest beliefs about what gives meaning or value to life." Not all modes of life will express a preference for the ordinary civil liberties. "Expressive liberty," Galston adds, "protects the ability of individuals and groups to live in way that others would regard as unfree."[252]

For Galston, the expressive interests of parents "are not reducible to their fiduciary duty to promote their children's interests."[253] But does the expressive liberty of parents include the right to force children to live in unfree ways? Though Galston rejects the premise that the state may structure public education to raise doubts about inherited ways of life,[254] he does agree with Callan's critique of parenting that keeps children in a state of ethical servility. "As a parent," Galston writes (quoting Callan), "I cannot rightly mold my child's character in a way that effectively preempts 'serious thought at any future date about the alternatives to my judgement.'" The child, too, has an interest in expressive liberty (in "personal sovereignty," to use Callan's term), though a prospective one, "that parents cannot rightly undermine."[255]

We would all (Galston included) agree, then, that the expressive interests of parents can be pushed too far. The question is, how far is too far?[256] Galston appears to set a tough standard when he proposes that "parents abuse their expressive liberty if . . . they deprive their children of the opportunity to exercise their own expressive liberty." But it turns out that the bar is not very high. What Galston means is that parents abuse their expressive liberty "if they turn their children into automatons." It would be abusive to seal off the outside world so that children "are not even aware of alternatives to the group's way of life." So, for Galston, *Yoder* is a correct decision. It protects the expressive liberty of Amish parents without depriving Amish children of the opportunity "to live their lives in ways that express their deepest beliefs about what gives meaning and value to life." After all, he observes, the world of the Amish is not a prison.[257]

Galston knows, of course, that parents can undermine the expressive liberty of children without turning them into automatons. The narcissistic parent may create a regime of filial obedience that makes it impossible for children fairly to consider available alternatives. "[T]he ordinary Amish adolescent," Colin M. Macleod observes, "can hardly be said to have an informed opinion about other possible life choices and for most of her life has, in effect, been subjected to the will of parents and community."[258] Galston writes that "[t]he nonexercise of a justified claim becomes questionable only when the potential claimant is subject to intimidation or is deprived of the information and self-confidence required for independent judgment."[259] But is not schooling beyond the eighth grade a prerequisite for the information and self-confidence required for independent judgment? Is not rejection from home and community a form of intimidation? Galston notes that substantial numbers of Amish children decide to leave their religious community.[260] (*Yoder*, though, was based on the premise that secondary schooling was not needed because the children were being prepared "for life in the separated agrarian community that is the keystone of the Amish faith.")[261] Yet those who do decide to leave face the prospect of being shunned—that is, they exercise a justified claim of religious liberty (their freestanding exit right) only at the cost of forsaking the only life they know, of being abandoned by home and community.[262] We ought to remind ourselves that the ritual sacrifice of children can take more than one form.

The ALI *Principles* proposes that custody courts not consider parental religious beliefs and practices unless they will cause the child severe and almost certain harm. To illustrate the point, the *Principles* provides the hypothetical case of ten-year-old Hugh. Diane, Hugh's Catholic mother, objects to the religious teachings of Hugh's father, Edward, who is a Jehovah's Witness. Edward's religious beliefs include a requirement of door-to-door "witnessing," a duty that he insists Hugh must follow during their time together. To prohibit Edward from demanding that Hugh participate in this practice, Diane offers "to prove that Hugh is confused by the inconsistencies between the two religions and that he deeply resents having to go door-to-door with [the father] when they are together." Following the harm standard, a court must reject the mother's request because it would interfere with Edward's religious practices. The *Principles* offers this explanation: "Hugh's confusion, without more, does not satisfy the high standard that harm be severe and almost certain" before it is permissible to restrict a parent's religious practices."[263]

Left unanswered, because left unraised, is the question of whether it might be harmful, in the absence of spiritual inconsistencies, to force Hugh to engage in a religious practice he deeply resents. If the state as educator demanded submission to its ideological authority, the injury would be self-evident. But we do not define the same requirement as injurious when compelled by private mentors. Quite the opposite: We applaud the obedient child—the child who, like Betty Simmons, embraces filial devotion, unaware of its true costs. And because we do not define the child's self-sacrifice as injury, we do not see it.

Nonparental Claims: The Third Party as Trustee

In 1977, Maryland's highest court gave custody of ten-year-old Melinda Dawn Sterquel to the girl's babysitter.[264] *Ross v. Hoffman* is the type of case certain to outrage supporters of traditional, biological parenthood. Yet it might give pause as well to those who call for a functional definition of parenthood, one that would make the fulfillment of parental responsibility the legal as well as the moral basis of parental authority. In recent years, a brave new world of parenthood possibilities has emerged, each premised on the substitution of caregiving for biology as the core legal criterion of parenthood status.[265] Not surprisingly, such proposals almost always come packaged with the assurance that there is a well-defined perimeter to the circle of parental candidates. No fear, in other words, that the nanny or the schoolteacher or the minister could assert rights of custody or visitation.[266] For Melinda's sake, however, the Court of Appeals of Maryland took a step further than most proponents of functional parenting are willing to go.

And the court took a step backward—a hundred years backward, in fact. For the court turned its attention, in part, to the third-party cases of the nineteenth century, which made the best interests of the child the controlling factor in custodial disputes. This policy, the *Hoffman* court observed, has deep roots in the law. It "could hardly be expressed with more clarity or emphasis" than it was in the case *In re Bort* (1881), which the court quoted at length:

We understand the law to be, when the custody of children is the question, that the best interest of the children is the paramount fact. Rights of father and mother sink into insignificance before that. Even when father and mother are living together, a court has the power, if the best interests of the child require it, to take it away from both parents, and commit the custody to a third person. In other words, a court of chancery stands as a guardian of all children, and may interfere at any time, and in any way, to protect and advance their welfare and interests.[267]

The past was legal prologue to Melinda's case in a more particular way. For guidance, the Maryland court turned to *Chapsky v. Wood* (also 1881); specifically, it relied heavily on *Chapsky's* seminal statement of the established ties doctrine.[268] In *Chapsky*, it will be remembered, a father sought to reclaim custody of the child he had left in the care of his wife's sister (see chap. 2). There was "no testimony showing that the father [was] what might be called an unfit person, that his life has not been a moral one"; indeed, there was "more wealth on the side of the father." Yet the court, finding it impossible to "believe it wise or prudent to take this child away from its present home," granted custody to the aunt. The "controlling consideration" for the court was the established affection between the child and her foster mother:

[T]he child has had, and has to-day, all that a mother's love and care can give. The affection which a mother may have and does have, springing from the fact that a child is her offspring, is an affection which perhaps no other one can really possess; but so far as it is possible, springing from years of patient care of a little, helpless babe, from association, and as an outgrowth from those little cares and motherly attentions bestowed upon it, an affection for the child is seen in [the child's aunt] that can be found nowhere else. *And it is apparent, that so far as a mother's love can be equaled, its foster-mother has that love, and will continue to have it.*[269]

The *Chapsky* court relied on legal propositions that were, according to Judge David Brewer, "not subject to much doubt." While the father is the "natural guardian" of the child, the child is not in any sense the father's property ("not in any sense like a horse or any other chattel"), and the father's right to custody of the child is "not like the right of property, an absolute and uncontrollable right." The fourth proposition—the controlling consideration of established ties—the *Hoffman* court quoted in its entirety:

> [Yet when] the gift has been once made and the child has been left for years in the care and custody of others, who have discharged all the obligations of support and care which naturally rest upon the parent, then, whether the courts will enforce the father's right to the custody of the child, will depend mainly upon the question whether such custody will promote the welfare and interest of such child. . . . [W]hen new ties have been formed and a certain current given to the child's life and thought, much attention should be paid to the probabilities of a benefit to the child from the change. It is an obvious fact, that ties of blood weaken, and ties of companionship strengthen, by lapse of time; and the prosperity and welfare of the child depend on the number and strength of these ties, as well as on the ability to do all which the promptings of these ties compel.

The fifth proposition was that reclamation cases require a balancing of interests: "The right of the father must be considered" but so must "the right of the one who has filled the parental place for years." Though it might not be "technically correct" to speak of the third-party caregiver as a rights-holder, the *Chapsky* court insisted that it was "but fair and proper that [the aunt's] previous faithfulness, and the interest and affection which these labors have created in them, should be respected."[270] (One nineteenth-century court put aside technical correctness with less reservation, declaring that the child's aunt and uncle, "[having] performed a parent's duties for nine years, . . . are entitled to a parent's rights.")[271] Above all, the welfare of the child remains the court's paramount consideration.[272]

The Maryland Court of Appeals tested these propositions in a tough case. Under financial necessity, Karen Ross placed her child Melinda, then three months old, in the care of Mrs. John Hoffman, who was not a blood relation to the child. At first, Melinda stayed with Hoffman only at night, while Karen was working on a night shift. However, the demands on Karen took their toll on both mother and child, and Melinda began to stay with her babysitter both day and night throughout the working week. Karen would take the child on weekends and her days off. It would not be long, though, before Melinda began to reside with Hoffman on a full-time basis: "After about a month, the mother stopped taking the child even on weekends, and Melinda actually resided with the Hoffmans full time. Although Mrs. Ross's working shifts varied between 1967 and 1971, the custodial arrangement apparently did not." Melinda remained with Hoffman for more than eight years. During this time, Karen's visits and her support of Melinda were sporadic. As Hoffman testified, "Over the whole eight years I remember one week out of that whole eight years that (Mrs. Ross) had her for a week, and then maybe a different occasion, maybe over that period of time, maybe once or twice, you know, overnight visits when she took her to her grandparents." The emotional effect of this arrangement, according to a medical doctor whose qualifications were stipulated by both parties, was that Melinda "viewed 'her primary source of nurturents [sic] as coming from Mrs. Hoffman. . . . The child's tie (was) psychologically united with Mrs. Hoffman, so that the biological tie (was not) a primary concern.'"[273]

The lower court found that the babysitter was "psychologically the parent." In the words of the chancellor, "it is a little late to make any serious uprooting of this child from Mrs. Hoffman." Upon review, the Court of Appeals relied on long-standing trust principles. The right of a parent to custody of the child was not to be "enforced inexorably, contrary to the best interest of the child, on the theory of an absolute legal right." It is to be presumed that the child's best interest is subserved by granting custody to the biological parent, but that presumption can be overcome and custody denied "if (a) the parent is unfit to have custody, or (b) if there are such exceptional circumstances as make such custody detrimental to the best interest of the child."[274] On the facts before it, the court found the existence of such circumstances in the details of Melinda's custodial arrangement.[275] Strikingly, though, while the facts of *Ross v. Hoffman* may have been "exceptional," the doctrine relied on by the court—the doctrine of established ties—might well apply to more ordinary situations. The child may be so long in the custody of the nonparent, the court observed, "that, *even though there has been no abandonment or persistent neglect by the parent*, the psychological trauma of removal is grave enough to be detrimental to the best interest of the child."[276]

It is not surprising that a case like *Chapsky v. Wood* should have a modern legacy, for the claims of third parties have been a perennial feature of the custody law landscape, and no more so than today. Though biology is hardly a dead letter in custodial determinations,[277] modern courts routinely face a confounding welter of custody and visitation candidates whose claims are not based on biological parenthood.[278] It would be hard to disagree that "social and legal conceptions of what it means to be a 'parent' are now in play as never before."[279] To add to the legal bewilderment, each of the claimants speaks the language of rights, seeking as they do to capture familiar parental entitlements, however novel the arguments for parental status they advance. So, not only does this contest of custodial rights probe the boundaries of parenthood, more generally it tests the limits of rights discourse. Like spiritual custody disputes, these cases pit individual rights claimants against each other. The law treats these parties—it tries to, at least—as though they were private actors, staking out rights territory against the state, when, in truth, their claims (in Justice Stevens's words) "do not present a bipolar struggle between the parents and the State." This privileging of the isolated, private actor allows—in fact, it promotes—a constitutionally unnecessary competition for the child. The best interests of the child are not served by granting rights to more and more parental claimants or by creating new varieties of constitutionally protected parenthood.

The parent's task, the Supreme Court reminds us, is to prepare the child for "additional obligations." In this sense, the child is a public trust. Whatever the scope of these obligations, surely they extend to a network of relationships outside the nuclear family. The extended family, according to the Court, "has roots equally venerable and equally deserving of constitutional recognition."[280] But the extended family is hardly the extent of it. Unless children are to be sheltered from the world, third parties well beyond the family will have an interest in them. Under a trust model of parenthood, the child is, from birth, "a member of the human family."[281] Relatedness begins with parents, to whom the state delegates authority over its children. But "[c]hildren are not born for the benefit of the parents alone."[282] How the interests of child, family, and state are best balanced ought to be "a question, not of constitutional power for the courts, but of expediency and propriety, which it is the sole province of the legislature to determine."[283] Yet with each newfound right, we take a step toward removing this question from the arena of social deliberation and a step toward removing our children from their rightful place in the human family. The teacher, the librarian, the religious mentor—these, too, have their role to play in the child's upbringing. And, perhaps, so might the babysitter.

Modern third-party law has been shaped by cases with a solid historical pedigree: the claims of grandparents for visitation and, on occasion, custody rights. In the 1960s, state statutes began to grant some third parties standing to seek visitation rights; by 1988, every state had such legislation.[284] The individual statutes varied with regard to several issues: who may petition, when a person may petition, and what standard should be applied by the court in determining whether to grant visitation. Most states permitted only grandparents to petition, but some granted standing to non-grandparents, including great-grandparents, siblings, relatives, or any person who maintained a parent-child type of relationship with the child.[285] While a few states allowed courts to hear visitation petitions where the nuclear family was intact,[286] most states required some specific family disruption, such as divorce or the death of a parent, to trigger standing to sue.[287] Significantly, no state adopted a harm measure as the legal standard for third-party visitation cases. Forty-one states explicitly used the best interests of the child standard. Others used somewhat looser language ("at the discretion of the court," "as the court shall determine"), and a few state statutes did not articulate a legal standard.[288]

Until the mid-1990s, grandparent visitation statutes were likely to survive constitutional challenges.[289] But the constitutional tide, if it did not turn, showed some signs of receding by 1993.[290] In that year, the Supreme Court of Tennessee decided *Hawk v. Hawk*,[291] which held that the state's grandparent visitation statute, as applied to a married couple whose fitness was unchallenged, violated the state constitution. Rejecting "a sentimental reflection on the 'special bond' between grandparent and grandchild," the court read *Meyer, Pierce,* and *Yoder* to set forth a fundamental right to parent: "[T]he right to rear one's children is so firmly rooted in our culture that the United States Supreme Court has held it to be a fundamental liberty interest protected by the Fourteenth Amendment to the United States Constitution." Of great weight to the *Hawk* court was the fact that, in the Supreme Court's seminal parenting decisions, the activities restricted by the state were not deemed inherently harmful to children. (The court: "The federal cases that support the constitutional right to rear one's child and the right to family privacy also indicate that the state's power to interfere in the parent-child relationship is subject to a finding of harm to the child.")[292] Yet, as we have seen, neither *Meyer* nor *Pierce* used a strict scrutiny standard. In both cases, the Court ruled that the state statutes at issue bore no rational relation to their stated end. And *Yoder* stated quite plainly that "where nothing more than the general interest of the parent in the nurture and education of his children is involved," the state acts constitutionally when it acts reasonably (at least with regard to educational regulation). *Yoder* did set forth a harm standard where religious parenting rights are involved, but it did so only on a showing that compulsory secondary school attendance threatened a religious community's entire way of life—a showing, the Court advised, that "few other religious groups or sects could make."

Nonetheless, the *Hawk* court concluded that "without a substantial danger of harm to the child, a court may not constitutionally impose its own subjective notions of the 'best interests of the child' when an intact, nuclear family with fit, married parents is involved."[293] (The severity of this substantial harm test is hard to pin down. For some courts, strict scrutiny means that the threat of harm must be substantial; for others, the harm itself must be. The *Hawk* court spoke both of "substantial harm that threatens a child's welfare" and "a substantial danger of harm to the child."[294] For other courts, the third party has to show parental unfitness.)[295] Likewise, two years later, the Georgia Supreme Court held that, under the federal Constitution, "even assuming grandparent visitation promotes the health and welfare of the child, the state may only impose that visitation over the parents' objections on a showing that failing to do so would be harmful to the child."[296] And other jurisdictions followed suit.[297] With courts divided on the question, it was left to the Supreme Court to sort things out.

The Supreme Court had already entered the third-party fray, both indirectly (in *Moore v. City of East Cleveland*) and directly (in *Smith v. Organization of Foster Families for Equality and Reform* [hereafter OFFER]) — and did so in the same year, 1977. In *Moore*,[298] the Court addressed the question of what, for constitutional purposes, a family is, and endorsed a broad definition. Specifically, *Moore* tested the constitutionality of East Cleveland's housing ordinance, which limited occupancy of a dwelling unit to members of a single family. The definitional section of the ordinance "recognize[d] as a 'family' only a few categories of related individuals."[299] The family of Inez Moore — Moore lived with her son and two grandsons, who were first cousins — fit none of these groups. When Moore failed to comply with the ordinance, the city filed a criminal charge against her.

In a preemptive due process strike, the city argued that *Meyer* and *Pierce* were on its side — or, at any rate, not against it. The city contended that neither case "gives grandmothers any fundamental rights with respect to grandsons." From the city's point of view, "any constitutional right to live together as a family extends only to the nuclear family." This reading of the Due Process Clause prompted a discussion of the Court's rationale for according constitutional shelter to certain unenumerated rights. Justice Lewis Powell, writing for the Court, rejected the city's arbitrary line drawing, stressing that appropriate limits on due process come from "careful 'respect for the teachings of history [and] a solid recognition of the basic values that underlie our society.'" While history counsels caution, Powell wrote, lest judges "'felt free to roam where unguided speculation might take them,'" it is history that safely guides the Court through turbid due process waters: "[T]he Constitution protects the sanctity of the family precisely because the institution of the family is deeply rooted in this Nation's history and tradition." Then, Powell took a spacious view of our family law tradition: "Ours is by no means a tradition limited to respect for the bonds uniting the members of the nuclear family. The tradition of uncles, aunts, cousins, and especially grandparents sharing a household along with parents and children has roots equally venerable and equally deserving of constitutional recognition." The liberty protected by the Court's due process parenting precedents was not limited to *parental* authority. The Due Process Clause, Powell declared, speaks broadly of "*family* authority as against the State."[300]

The content of due process, Powell maintained (quoting Justice John Harlan II), cannot be "'reduced to any formula, its content cannot be determined by reference to any code.'" Due process is a balancing act: "'The best that can be said is that through the course of this Court's decisions it has represented the balance which our Nation, built upon postulates of respect for the liberty of the individual, has struck between that liberty and the demands of organized society.'" This balance is not fixed: "'[T]radition is a living thing. A decision of this Court which radically departs from it could not long survive, while a decision which builds on what has survived is likely to be sound.'"[301] In dissent, Justice White argued that, apparently, history had not counseled caution strongly enough. For White, Powell's "deeply rooted" gloss on the Due Process Clause "suggest[ed] a far too expansive charter for this Court." He protested, "What the deeply rooted traditions of the country are is arguable, which of them deserve the protection of the Due Process Clause is even more debatable. The suggested view would broaden enormously the horizons of the Clause."[302]

Yet not enormously enough to offer protection to foster families. In *OFFER*,[303] the legal issue before the Court concerned the procedures by which the state removed children from foster homes. But the foundational question was whether the Due Process Clause provided foster parents the same rights granted to natural parents. "[I]s the relation of foster parent to foster child," the Court asked, "sufficiently akin to the concept of 'family' recognized in our precedents to merit similar protection?"[304]

The foster parents answered, obviously enough, in the affirmative. They argued that foster parents enjoyed a "right to familial privacy" that should protect the foster family against disruption of established ties. For constitutional purposes, the "psychological family" is a true family, "entitled to the same constitutional deference as that long granted to the more traditional biological family."[305]

Justice Stewart, in a concurring opinion, had little patience with the question. Rather than "tiptoeing around," he complained, the Court should just "squarely hold" that the interests asserted by the foster parents are not of the type protected by the Fourteenth Amendment. With less than a supreme effort at tact, he rejected the notion that "'third-party custodians may acquire some sort of squatter's rights in another's child.'"[306] Writing for the Court, Justice Brennan took a more deliberative and delicate approach. He described the interest in family privacy as having "its source . . . in intrinsic human rights."[307] Brennan proceeded from the premise, set out in *Moore*, that the scope of due process rights is not limited to natural parents; the protection of the Fourteenth Amendment extends to "a larger conception of the family." Thus, Brennan was obliged to distinguish the foster family from the biological family. This he did by focusing on the naturalness of the "natural family," which, according to Brennan, has its origins "entirely apart from the power of the State." The same could not be said of the foster family, which has its source "in state law and contractual arrangements." While "emotional ties may develop between foster parent and foster child," what mattered to the Court was that these ties "have their origins in an arrangement in which the State has been a partner from the outset."[308]

With regard to the assertion that the "natural" family has its origins "entirely apart from the power of the State," one might object that "the state is always implicated in the formation and functioning of families."[309] Certainly the family, whatever its source, has never been considered beyond state regulation.[310] Putting this question aside, the meaning of "family" as a matter of constitutional law remains at best uncertain. In *Moore*, the Court took a liberal position, looking to history and tradition as a guide. In *OFFER*, the Court shut the door on further due process expansion. The Court allowed that "a deeply loving and interdependent relationship between an adult and a child in his or her care may exist even in the absence of blood relationship," but it provided no guidance with regard to due process claims based on a latter-day theory of established ties.[311] In *Moore*, Brennan seconded the Court's due process historicism, noting the prominence of nonnuclear households "since our beginning as a Nation."[312] Why not adopt a similar due process posture in *OFFER*? Perhaps Brennan turned to a natural rights rationale because history was not an entirely safe guide. After all, a strong case could be made that the foster family (or some version of it), like the nonnuclear family, has a deep, if at times troubling, tradition in American law and culture.

The Court's reliance on family authority (in *Moore*) and intrinsic rights (in *OFFER*) obscures the tensions created by a rights-based approach to domestic conflicts. First, it is too easy to lose sight of individual interests, especially those of the child, in the forest of family authority. (It is hardly the case that the "[t]he government allows *families* to inculcate their own values by choosing private schools.")[313] Second, the uncontoured character of a due process jurisprudence based on "intrinsic human rights" inevitably forces upon us the question, What happens when rights—possibly, fundamental rights—collide? Who gets the benefit of strict scrutiny? For that matter, what happens when different understandings of the same right collide? In *OFFER*, both sides argued on the basis of children's rights: on one side, the right to be reared by a biological parent; on the other side, the child's right to "maintain[] the emotional and psychological relationship with caretaking adults who give the child his or her sense of security and identity."[314] Do our history and traditions not support both rights? Which is the intrinsic human right?

Perhaps, when personal rights collide, they cease being fundamental. David Meyer argues that "[t]he presence of preexisting family discord lowers the justificatory burden for state intervention." Because at least one party has "invited the state's role as mediator," the intrusiveness of the state's action is lessened.[315] This was the position of the court, we have seen, in the spiritual custody case *Morris v. Morris*.[316] But it is not clear why, as a matter of constitutional law, the dissolution of the family "is accompanied by a weakening of the shield constructed against state intervention." It may satisfy one's sense of moral outrage to declare that "[a] parent cannot flaunt the banner of religious freedom and familial sanctity when he himself has abrogated that unity,"[317] but is it not troubling that one party to the marriage can veto the constitutional rights of his or her spouse?

What we learn from history and tradition is that family is a fluid concept. One group may not follow the family pattern set by others. ("The Constitution cannot be interpreted . . . to tolerate the imposition by government upon the rest of us of white suburbia's preference in patterns of family life." This is Brennan, concurring in *Moore*.)[318] One era may find the welfare reforms of the past to be offensive as a matter of law or policy. ("From the standpoint of natural parents, . . . foster care has been condemned as a class-based intrusion into the family." Brennan again, in OFFER.)[319] Yet a jurisprudence of rights deals in absolutes. Whether parents are granted the right to deny access to third parties or third parties are granted rights despite parental opposition, the law takes a categorical stance that can only hamper the judicial discretion needed to address the existential intricacies of family conflict.

Missing from this talk of rights is any reference to the moral duty and the parens patriae authority of the state to take care of its children. In OFFER, it was argued that "[i]n all but a few cases the 'gain' derived from a child's return to the natural parents more than offsets any 'loss' resulting from the removal from a foster home."[320] Perhaps. But the state has an interest in the few as well as the many. A jurisprudence of rights protects us, as it should, as individual actors against a state that seeks to limit what is ours. But it is a weak base on which to erect a law of parent-child relations. Brennan may be right that the marital couple is "an association of . . . individuals each with a separate intellectual and emotional makeup," but Douglas is right, too: A marital couple is also "an independent entity with a mind and heart of its own." Marriage is a "coming together" of separate individuals, their own and not their own.[321] So it is with parent and child. The parent has chosen to place limits on his or her separateness—the child will gain independence only if adults are willing to surrender theirs. The parent has chosen to place limits on his or her claims of ownership—the child will not gain independence unless adults are willing to forego their "possessory" interests. If there is a liberty interest to protect here, it is the one protected by the traditional trust model of parenting: the perfect right of the child not to be made the object of someone else's rights claims.

With *Moore* and *OFFER* as legal guideposts, the Supreme Court turned its attention to the custody conflict arising from the competing claims of parent and grandparent. What *Troxel* did not do—and, it turns out, this is the most important thing one can say of the case—was to hold that the right to parent is fundamental. Nonetheless, as in *Meyer* and *Pierce*, the rhetoric of the case easily trumped its result. Taking their cue from O'Connor's easy ways with the word "fundamental," lower courts would, with increasing frequency, subject state statutes to strict scrutiny.[322] Using a favored trope, the Iowa Supreme Court, echoing *Hawk*, declared that it would no longer uphold a statute that "effectively substitutes sentimentality for constitutionality."[323]

Only months after the *Troxel* decision, the Supreme Court of Illinois, in *Lulay v. Lulay*, ruled that the state's grandparent visitation statute "impinges upon the fundamental constitutional right of parents to make decisions regarding the upbringing of their children." The court surveyed a familiar case law lineage (*Meyer, Pierce, Yoder*—and, now, *Troxel*) and concluded that the statute "usurp[ed] the decisionmaking function of parents with respect to the relationships that their children will have":

> Encompassed within the well-established fundamental right of parents to raise their children is the right to determine with whom their children should associate. It is the role of parents to nurture their children and to influence and shape their children's character. . . . [The visitation statute] allows the state to usurp the decisionmaking function of parents with respect to the relationships that their children will have. This decisionmaking function lies at the core of parents' liberty interest in the care, custody, and control of their children. To hold that [the statute] is not a significant interference with the fundamental right of parents to raise their children would be to effectively *obliterate* that fundamental right.

The grandparents argued that the state had a compelling interest "as parens patriae, to protect children whose lives have been disrupted through certain triggering events such as the divorce of the parents." But to no avail.[324]

Lulay involved the parents' joint decision to deny grandparent visitation. The next year, the Illinois Supreme Court struck down part of a state statute permitting visitation over the objection of a fit parent in cases where the child's other parent is deceased. Rita and Brent Langman maintained a close relationship with their grandchildren, seeing the children two or three times a month. After the death of their son, Rhett, they continued this relationship. When disagreements between the Langmans and their daughter-in-law arose, the trial court ordered visitation. Taking the child's best interests as its standard, the trial court stressed the need for continuity of family affection. The "surviving family," the court concluded, was "the only connection the children can have with those who had an intimate and close family relationship."[325]

Such sentimental reflections were not to carry the day. The appellate court decided that the statute "unconstitutionally infringed on [the mother's] fundamental right to make decisions concerning the care, custody, and control of her children." The state supreme court agreed. The reasoning of the trial court, the supreme court insisted, "overlooks the clear constitutional directive that state interference should only occur when the health, safety, or welfare of a child is at risk." It was simply not a compelling interest of the state "to protect and maintain the children's family heritage," however deeply rooted.[326]

In the post-*Troxel* era, custody courts have been kept busy with claims based on nontraditional ties. New reproductive technologies, for instance, breed novel parental candidates.[327] As do new family arrangements. These custody claimants might well agree with parentalist principles—they, too, might want any state-mandated restrictions on parental rights to be subject to strict judicial review; but what they want first is a declaration of their own legal standing as a constitutionally protected parent.

One modern family type, lesbian coparenting, has with some frequency tested the courts' readiness to embrace functional definitions of parenthood.[328] The story behind the litigation is familiar enough: A former partner petitions for parenting time over the objections of a fit legal parent. (Though marriage equality for lesbians and gay men will make obsolete some types of third-party cases, the principles of psychological parenthood on which such cases rest will continue to keep custody courts busy.) Typical of such cases is *In re E.L.M.C.*, decided in 2004 by the Colorado Court of Appeals.[329] At the outset of its opinion, the court remarked, in a fine stroke of understatement, that "[t]his case illustrates the evolving nature of parenthood."[330] One might with equal safety add that it also illustrates the doctrinal straits that courts must navigate as they try to sort out functional parenting claims.

Before their custody dispute, Cheryl Ann Clark and Elsey Maxwell McLeod had lived together for eleven years in what the court described as "a committed relationship." They had a commitment ceremony; they owned a home in joint tenancy—and they decided to adopt a child. Because China, where they went to adopt, did not permit adoption by same-sex couples, the legal papers were made out in Clark's name alone. When Colorado recognized the adoption, the couple sent to friends an "arrival announcement" with the celebratory note that the child "now lives with two adoring moms." The couple filed a joint "Petition for Custody," writing, "Co-Petitioners have lived together for the past six and one-half years as a couple. They had a commitment ceremony on July 31, 1993. They carefully discussed having a family together. Clark's plans to adopt [E.L.M.C.] included an intention to have [E.L.M.C.] raised by Clark and McLeod as one family with two parents." In support of their custody petition, Clark and McLeod submitted a brief that read: "[E.L.M.C.] considers each of the Co-Petitioners to be a parent; she refers to McLeod as 'mommy' and Clark as 'momma.' She looks to both Co-Petitioners for love, affection and nurturance. Co-Petitioners have shared the financial cost of supporting [E.L.M.C.] and they share all major decisions involving [E.L.M.C.'s] life, including provisions of daycare during the times that Co-Petitioners must both work."

The district court awarded joint custody, and Clark changed the child's name to include McLeod's, so as "to acknowledge an important family member instrumental to [the child's] adoption from China." McLeod was identified as a "mother" on the pediatrician's information sheet, which

Clark signed, and both women were listed as mothers of the child in the school directory. According to the child's nanny, Clark and McLeod equally parented the child.

When their relationship ended, Clark and McLeod were unable to agree on the apportionment of parental responsibilities. Eventually, Clark sought to terminate all of McLeod's parenting time; on her part, McLeod petitioned for a "roughly equal" allotment, though she did not dispute that Clark was a fit parent. The district court awarded joint parenting responsibilities.[331]

On appeal, Clark relied on *Troxel*, seeking the safe harbor of strict scrutiny. She argued that the court could no longer apply the best interests of the child standard in custody disputes between a fit legal parent and a third party. This is precisely what the Colorado Supreme Court had done in the pre-*Troxel* custody case *In re Custody of C.C.R.S.* (1995),[332] which pitted a biological mother against potential adoptive parents. The *C.C.R.S.* court gave priority "to resolv[ing] the dispute in a way that minimizes the detriment to the child." Though the court recognized the "presumption that the biological parent has a first and prior right to custody," it concluded that unfitness of the natural parent need not be established to award custody to nonparents;[333] and, applying the best interests of the child standard, the court upheld the lower court's judgment granting custody to the prospective adoptive parents. It was on this pre-*Troxel* precedent that McLeod rested her hopes.

The *E.L.M.C.* court thought that strict scrutiny was consistent with *Troxel*'s description of the right to parent as a fundamental liberty interest.[334] McLeod would have to show that the state had a compelling reason to permit state interference with Clark's parental rights. Harm to the child, actual or threatened, would be enough. (However, the court rejected Clark's contention that strict scrutiny required a showing of unfitness before parental responsibilities could be allocated to a third party.) But would a refusal to apportion parental responsibilities to McLeod harm the child? The court found the answer to this question in the idea of psychological parenthood.

Psychological parenthood is the established ties doctrine of the nineteenth century writ anew. It is not difficult to state the general contours of the doctrine. In the words of the *E.L.M.C.* court, the psychological parent and child form "a relationship with deep emotional bonds such that the child recognizes the person, independent of the legal form of the relationship, as a parent from whom they receive daily guidance and nurturance."[335] Some form of equitable parenthood has a long standing in the law, allowing courts to consider the claims of nontraditional petitioners for parental status. For some courts, the equitable parent looked, objectively speaking, like a legal parent, by virtue of having lived with and cared for the child,[336] or by having stood in the place of the parent.[337] For other courts, psychological parenthood meant more than the assumption of parental status and obligations. Their decisions might turn on subjective considerations of emotional attachment, with courts asking if the third party not only looked like a parent but, so to speak, "felt" like a parent (to the court, to the child).[338]

Some courts sought to delimit the universe of parental candidacy by creating multipronged tests that addressed the multiple functions, material and emotional, of parenthood. Typical of such efforts is the test established by the Wisconsin Supreme Court. In addition to some triggering event, the petitioner must "demonstrate the existence of [a] parent-like relationship with the child." This requires proof of four elements:

> (1) that the biological or adoptive parent consented to, and fostered, the petitioner's formation and establishment of a parent-like relationship with the child; (2) that the petitioner and the child lived together in the same household; (3) that the petitioner assumed obligations of parenthood by taking significant responsibility for the child's care, education and development, including contributing towards the child's support, without expectation of financial compensation; and (4) that the petitioner has been in a parental role for a length of time sufficient to have established with the child a bonded, dependent relationship parental in nature.

The first factor protects the rights of the third-party claimant by estopping the legal parent from "erasing a relationship between her partner and her child which she voluntarily and actively fostered." The other factors protect the rights of the legal parent by forestalling claims from a familiar litany of "unreasonable" candidates: "mere neighbors, caretakers, babysitters, nannies, au pairs, nonparental relatives, and family friends." These criteria "indicate that a given person's eligibility for 'psychological parenthood' with respect to an unrelated child will be strictly limited to those adults who have served *literally* as one of the child's de facto parents."[339] In effect, the test enforces a quasi-contract agreement to coparent.

One of the more systematic efforts to define functional parenthood has been undertaken by the American Law Institute, which discarded traditional legal boundaries of parenthood in its most recent edition of the ALI *Principles*.[340] Chapter 2 of the *Principles* sets out three classes of parents who are entitled to begin an action for custodial or decision-making responsibility:

1. A *legal parent* is an individual who is defined as a parent under state law. Typically, legal status is extended to biological and adoptive parents.[341]

2. A *parent by estoppel* is an individual who has lived with the child for at least two years, acted with a reasonable, good-faith belief that he was the child's biological father, and fully accepted parental responsibilities.[342] A parent by estoppel may also be an individual who is a co-parent by agreement with the legal parents.[343]

3. A *de facto* parent is an individual who for at least two years has lived with the child and regularly performed caretaking functions, for reasons primarily other than financial compensation, with the agreement of the legal parent or as a result of the failure or inability of the legal parent to perform caretaking functions.[344]

The functional criteria of parenthood adopted by the *Principles* illustrate nicely the competing pressures faced by courts as they continue to adjudicate third-party claims. On the one hand, there is a radicalism to the designation of third-party caregivers as parents. "These new parents," Meyer points out, "would add to, rather than substitute for, any existing parents, so that a child might have at once three, four, or even more parents sharing in his or her upbringing." For Meyer, "adding new parents" is constitutionally less offensive than "simply reassigning parent status and displacing the old." "Whereas a wholesale reassignment of exclusive parent status ordinarily extinguishes the former parent's family status," he suggests, "the addition of new parents only dilutes the prerogatives of existing parents."[345] But no doubt many parents would consider dilution, with its repudiation of exclusive parenthood, to be an equally significant incursion, legally and psychologically, on the prerogatives of the parent, and more detrimental to the welfare of the child.[346] To whom does the child now belong?

On the other hand, the *Principles* seeks to bring a new certainty to the boundaries of functional parenthood. To begin with, the *Principles* does not cover disputes between parties arising in the context of an intact family: "Ordinarily, state intrusion into the intact one- or two-parent family is justified only under the state's law relating to child abuse and neglect, adoption, and guardianship."[347] Obviously, this raises a high wall of separation against third-party claimants. We are far removed from the *Chapsky* court's assertion of power to remove children from both parents "[e]ven when father and mother are living together . . . and [to] commit the custody to a third person." And once some fracture of the family has occurred, the ALI's boundary lines are built on "objective requirements," placing a categorical stop on the slippery slope of parenthood possibilities. These requirements are meant to restrict the designation of functional parenthood "to the most appropriate cases."[348] Here, they say, and no further. Nor is the ALI's approach a purely functional one. It rests, rather, on "a combination of the parental functions performed and the expectations of the parties."[349] In other words, under the *Principles*, the status of functional parent may be hostage to the legal parent's agreement to coparent.[350] This quasi-contract approach allows legal parents to keep third-party relationships from being established in the first place. (The *Principles* offers the specific reassurance that "[a]greement is not established by the mere delegation of babysitting duties.")[351] In all of this, the *Principles* takes, as Barbara Bennett Woodhouse argues, a decidedly "adult-centric" approach to family conflict, focusing more on equity between adults than on the best interests of the child.[352]

In deciding the custodial fate of E.L.M.C., the Colorado Court of Appeals took a less secure approach to legal parenthood, venturing, as did the custody courts of the nineteenth century, into the domain of the child's psychological needs and welfare. The court's foremost concern was not fairness between adults, but the emotional attachment between adults and the child. Not that the court ignored objective considerations. It cited approvingly definitions of psychological parenthood that served "to restrict the class of nonparents who may seek parental rights." But the court directed its heightened scrutiny less to the matters of agreement between adult parties or the assumption of parental status and duties, and more to "the risk of emotional harm to the child should [the third-party] relationship be significantly curtailed or terminated." It defined psychological parenthood by the results of its curtailment: The cutting of the bond, that is, "creates an inherent risk of harm to a young child's emotional well-being." Thus, proof of psychological parenthood and proof of threatened emotional harm "are two sides of the same coin." On both sides of the coin McLeod satisfied the court. The evidence "both rebutted the *Troxel* presumption in favor of Clark and constituted a compelling state interest justifying court modification of her parenting plan."[353]

The Court of Appeals upheld the trial court's award of joint parental responsibilities. It did so, in its words, "without violence to Clark's constitutional rights." Like *Troxel*, the court's decision left considerable work undone. In particular, it left "for another day" the question of whether, in the absence of emotional harm, it *would* work violence to a legal parent's constitutional rights if the court ordered shared parenting with a third party. The question assumes, of course, that after *Troxel* strict scrutiny applies. But in *Troxel* the Supreme Court did not reject the best interests standard; rather, it objected to the fact that the Washington State visitation statute "place[d] the best-interest determination solely in the hands of the judge."[354]

The best interests standard does not have to be without bite. In fact, the best interests standard has more bite than its critics concede. The term "best interests" does not mean—or, it should not be taken to mean—that, as a matter of a judge's mere personal preference, a good parent will be trumped by a "better" parent;[355] it will not allow for "a redistribution of the entire minor population among the worthier members of the community."[356] The standard can be abused, but it does the job of directing courts to focus on what is right for the child—a specific child, living under a specific set of circumstances—not on what the categorical rights of the parents are. In their grandparent visitation statutes, or through judicial construction of these laws, states have found ways to serve due process that are far less drastic than a requirement of harm.[357] "Plus" factors, which help ensure that judges will not merely substitute their own ideas of good parenting for those of the legal parent, include the following:

1. **The burden of proof**
   A number of states require that a third party seeking visitation "must prove, by clear and convincing evidence, that the requested visitation is in the best interest of the child."[358] (The Supreme Court "has mandated an intermediate standard of proof—'clear and convincing evidence'—when the individual interests at stake in a state proceeding are both 'particularly important' and 'more substantial than mere loss of money.'")[359]

2. **Best interests plus**
   Some states require, in addition to a showing that visitation would be in the child's best interests, an affirmative determination that such visitation "would not substantially interfere with the parent-child relationship."[360] Other states require a determination that the grandparent has established, or has attempted to establish, a relationship with the child.[361] And a few states require both showings.[362]

3. **Enumerated factors**
   By delineating an array of specific factors for judicial consideration, states provide direction to the judge's inquiry in order to enforce the parental presumption.[363]

None of these measures can entirely check judicial discretion, but neither can the harm standard. Harm, too, is not without its subjectiveness. The only way that a harm requirement works as a truly determinate standard is to require a degree of severity that by any measure amounts to actual child abuse. Even if it be true that "[w]hile there is no consensus about what is best for a child, there is much consensus about what is very bad,"[364] neither due process nor sound policy requires that the state refrain from reasonable regulation of the family until things are very bad for the child.

These "plus" measures ensure that special weight is given to a parent's visitation preferences. Following them, a court could no longer "enforc[e] on a child its own special and partisan conception of the way of life that is truly best for it."[365] Thankfully, a father could not be denied custody based solely upon his Bohemian credentials. (This was the judgment of the Iowa Supreme Court in the infamous case *Painter v. Bannister* (1966). The court was not inclined to send young Mark Painter to a household that would be "unstable, unconventional, arty, Bohemian, and probably intellectually stimulating.")[366] Equally important, these measures do not dilute judicial safeguards against *parental* discretion. They assume, that is, that a parent has no fundamental right to enforce on a child a special and partisan way of life by secluding the child from third parties.

Those who lament "[t]he individualistic themes" of modern family law might find some solace, curiously, in the idea that, as a matter of constitutional right, children do not belong to their parents.[367] Constitutional parenthood embraces the common law principle of sociability, acknowledging that the family stands as the primary mediating institution between children and the communities (the "additional obligations") that surround them. The constitutional parent takes seriously the fiduciary task of mediation. From families, our children are passed on to third parties, in countless social forms (private and public), in diverse measures of affinity. These connections help to bring the child to a genuine autonomy. Martha Minow is one of many who celebrates a conception of the self "as interdependent: needing others, and needing to be needed." It is this alternate conception of the self, Minow maintains, that constitutes the "I." And it is this self that calls for a conception of law embodying the idea that "belonging is essential to becoming."[368]

The state can make it possible for children to be part of the relational world to which they belong: the world of family, friends, classmates, teachers.[369] We may choose to create a parental presumption against third parties—or, for that matter, a harm standard—because we believe this to be in the child's best interests, but there is no constitutional requirement to do so. It would be just as constitutionally sound to create a third-party presumption: that contact with third parties is in the child's best interests, even in the case of fit parents. Sounder, perhaps. Such a presumption is more consistent with the (perhaps surprising) fact that the law has treated the parent as the child's trustee; it is more reflective of the (always surprising) fact that relatedness is the precondition of autonomy. If the parent, after years of sacrifice, must finally relinquish the child to the world, the law best supports this bittersweet task, not by manufacturing rights, but by building relationships.

The World All Before Them

A parent has no more right to control or dictate a
child's marriage than the child's religious tenets or his dreams.
— "The Contract of Marriage," Albany Law Journal (1874)

Throughout his history of marital law in America, Hendrik Hartog allows us to understand, feelingly, what it meant to be a wife in the nineteenth century. To illustrate what was considered a "good wifely identity," Hartog describes how the theater critic Henry Hudson, writing in 1848, viewed Shakespeare's Desdemona. For Hudson, Desdemona "was the pure embodiment of married womanhood. . . . [T]he foundation of her goodness derived from her total and absolute obedience." This vision of wifely goodness, Hartog explains, was in no small part a construction of the legal strictures that denied wives their own legal identity. Yet Desdemona is the law's creation in a more subtle, if equally disheartening, way. Within the portrait of Desdemona as Othello's wife lurks the picture of Desdemona as, first, Brabantio's daughter.[1]

By his own estimation, Othello is a man who loved too well. The tragedy of the play, we assume, belongs to him. But if we are prepared to look at what Shakespeare shows us, we must ask what there is to admire or pity. Othello murders his wife for the same reasons, both banal and shocking, that other men abuse their wives. There *is* a real tragedy in the play, however. It is in the awful display of a woman who, as Hudson writes approvingly, is "submissive even unto death where she owes allegiance."[2]

The play begins with Roderigo and Iago taunting Desdemona's father, Brabantio, with allegations of her sexual activity. When Brabantio appeals to the Venetian Senate for justice, he recalls for them what Desdemona was like as a child. His portrait of Desdemona as a young maiden is meant to show that Othello has won her by witchcraft and thus to confirm a father's image of his daughter's purity, now violated. Brabantio remembers

> A maiden never bold;
> Of spirit so still and quiet that her motion
> Blushed at herself.[3]

"Her motion blushed at herself" is an awkward construction, and the meaning is not certain; but Shakespeare seems to be suggesting something like, "She was so modest that her natural impulses blushed at themselves." The picture is clear even if (in sometimes Shakespearian fashion) the meaning is inexact. Brabantio's daughter was a "perfect" child, not bold of spirit. After she elopes, Brabantio says that Desdemona is dead to him. But is it not fair to ask what she was to him when she was alive? Desdemona's attraction to the Moor makes sense as a form of rebellion—and obedience. Her marriage to Othello re-creates the parent-child relationship with which she is familiar. When she is brought before the Senate, her father asks, "Do you perceive in all this company / Where most you owe obedience?"[4] Her answer suggests that her rebellion is really no rebellion at all; it merely transfers the obligation to obey from father to husband:

> My noble father,
> I do perceive here a divided duty;
> To you I am bound for life and education,
> My life and education do learn me
> How to respect you, you are the lord of all my duty.
> I am hitherto your daughter; but here's my husband;
> And so much duty as my mother show'd
> To you preferring you before her father,

So much I challenge, that I may profess,
Due to the Moor my lord.[5]

For Desdemona, a woman's task, and her personal destiny, is to transform herself from perfect child to perfect wife. Her last words—"Commend me to my kind lord"—give us every reason to believe that she was successful.[6]

The obedient child Desdemona is as much a creation of the law as the subservient adult Desdemona. The law represents what we think it means to love and to take care of our children. It can teach us selfishness and the assertion of control. From Shakespeare's fictional Theseus, speaking as the law's representative:

What say you, Hermia? be advised fair maid:
To you your father should be as a god;
One that composed your beauties, yea, and one
To whom you are but as a form in wax
By him imprinted and within his power
To leave the figure or disfigure it.[7]

—to the attorneys William Guthrie and Bernard Hershkopf, in *Pierce*, arguing against mandatory public schooling:

Children are, in the end, what men and women live for. Through them parents realize, as it were, immortality. To the parent the child represents the sum of all his hopes. One's defeated aspirations, his children may achieve; his unfulfilled ambitions, they may realize. All that we missed, lost, failed of, our children may have, do, accomplish, in fullest measure.[8]

—to a modern instance, from a recent political candidate:

Oh, I understand why [President Obama] wants you to go to college. He wants to remake you in his image. I want to create jobs so people can remake their children into their image, not his.[9]

there is abundant, and melancholy, testimony to the endurance of a narcissism that would (in the guise of caring? in the name of love?) use the personal freedoms of parenthood to deny personal freedom to future generations. A liberal democracy cannot prosper, nor its children flourish, with too many parents like this.

Or, the law can help us learn how, as parents, to practice sacrifice, to surrender control. Our primal creation myth tells us that children are not born to be obedient. For most of us, our own parenting experience confirms the ancient truth that children will not be made in anyone else's image. Not easily, at any rate. It should be our joy that children become someone else, though it be a joy tinged with elegiac tones.

Thankfully, we are not mere products of the law. We create the law that creates us, though we do need to be reminded of this fact. Blackstone describes the law of coverture as a rule having no foundation in nature, as a "right" fashioned by men for the purposes of civil society. Yet, with the passage of time, the rule becomes hardened law, received and unchanging. It was always thus.

The history of parent-child relations holds two important lessons for us. First, it was not always thus. The right to parent free of state interference is not deeply rooted in our legal tradition. Long before the *Lochner* era, the law rewarded the parent who is selfless enough to assume responsibilities rather than to assert rights. The historical record is important because our due process jurisprudence looks to tradition as the measure of whether a right is to be considered fundamental. In this regard, the past plays a direct role in constitutional lawmaking.

Second, it does not have to be thus. The historical record is important because it encourages us to think about the law normatively—not what it is, but what it should be. In this regard, the past plays an indirect role in lawmaking generally. The trust principles that are deeply rooted in our legal culture remain a rich deposit of social values that can inform the normative inquiry. They are values that bespeak a belief in a liberty not reducible to rights, a freedom in which we are duty-bound one to another. If we have substituted constitutionality for sentimentality, we are not the more free for it; and children are not the more secure when we forget—it is as true today as it was in 1836—that from birth they are members of the human family. History does not dictate what the future of parent-child relations should look like, but it can remind us that that future is unwritten.

Chapter 1. Sacred Trust or Sacred Right?

Epigraph. John Milton, *Paradise Lost*, in *John Milton: Complete Poems and Major Prose*, ed. Merritt Y. Hughes (Indianapolis: Odyssey Press, 1957) (1667) 469 (XII, 645–49).

1. The Etna, 8 F. Cas. 803, 804 (D. Me. 1838).
2. 8 F. Cas. at 804.
3. 8 F. Cas. at 806; see also 8 F. Cas. at 804. 8 F. Cas. at 804. 8 F. Cas. at 807.
4. Cf. Joel Prentiss Bishop, *Commentaries on the Law of Marriage and Divorce* (Boston: Little, Brown, 1852) 515 (§ 632) ("At common law the father is, in some sense, the guardian of his children, though in precisely what sense, the books do not seem perfectly to agree.") (footnote omitted). In referring to a right to parent, I do not mean the right to bear or beget a child. See Eisenstadt v. Baird, 405 U.S. 438, 453 (1972) (recognizing "the right of the individual, married or single, to be free from unwarranted governmental intrusion into matters so fundamentally affecting a person as the decision whether to bear or beget a child").
5. United States v. Bainbridge, 24 F. Cas. 946, 949 (C.C.D. Mass. 1816) (emphasis added). Christopher G. Tiedeman, *A Treatise on the Limitations of Police Power in the United States* (St. Louis: F. H. Thomas Law, 1886) 554; see also Tiedeman, *The Limitations of Police Power*, 552: "By the abolition of the family relation as a political institution, the child, whatever may be his age, acquires the same claim to liberty of action as the adult, viz.: the right to the largest liberty that is consistent with the enjoyment of a like liberty on the part of others; and he is only subject to restraint, so far as such restraint is necessary for the promotion of the general welfare or beneficial as a means of protection to himself. *The parent has no natural vested right to the control of his child*" (emphasis added).

6. Lewis Hochheimer, *The Law Relating to the Custody of Infants*, 3d ed. (Baltimore: Harold Scrimger, 1899) 22 (§ 22).

7. Uniformity is hardly to be expected from "[t]he American federal system in which each state had jurisdiction over domestic relations," a system which "produced a range of custody and other family laws." Michael Grossberg, Comment, "Who Determines Children's Best Interests?" *L. & Hist. Rev.* 17 (1999): 309, 313–14.

8. Hochheimer, *The Custody of Infants* (1899) 22–23 (§ 22); cf., e.g., Rollin C. Hurd, *A Treatise on the Right of Personal Liberty and on the Writ of Habeas Corpus*, 2d ed. (Albany: W. C. Little, 1876) 461 ("In controversies between parents for the custody of their legitimate children, the right of the father is held to be paramount to that of the mother; but the welfare of the child and not the technical legal right is the criterion by which to determine to whom the custody of the child shall be awarded"); James Schouler, *A Treatise on the Law of the Domestic Relations*, 2d ed. (Boston: Little, Brown, 1874) 365 (§ 339) ("The cardinal principle relative to such matters is to regard the benefit of the infant; to make the welfare of the children paramount to the claims of either parent. . . . [J]udicial precedents, judicial *dicta*, and legislative enactments all lead to one and the same irresistible conclusion. The primary object of the American decisions is then to secure the welfare of the child, and not the special claims of one or the other parent") (footnote omitted); English v. English, 32 N.J. Eq. 738, 742–43 (N.J. Err. & App. 1880) ("In considering the grounds which should have weight in deciding controversies of this character, while the rights of parents will not be disregarded or their interests overlooked, the court will not be controlled in its decision by the strict rights of either party, but will determine the question of custody mainly upon considerations of advantage to the infant; the cardinal rule of action governing the court being regard to the benefits of the minor, holding its welfare superior to the claims of either parent"); cf. also "Developments in the Law: The Constitution and the Family," *Harv. L. Rev.* 93 (1980): 1156, 1223 ("[Nineteenth-century custody courts] often held that the presumption of parental custody was based upon the extent to which the parent successfully served the *state*'s interest in promoting the child's welfare, rather than upon any inherent right of the parent. Most late nineteenth century courts thus acknowledged that the *child*'s welfare, not the parent's legal right, was the determinative factor in private custody decisions under the parens patriae power") (footnotes omitted).

9. James Kent, 2 *Commentaries on American Law*, ed. O. W. Holmes Jr., 12th ed. (Boston: Little, Brown, 1873) 252 (emphasis added). Kent, 2 *Commentaries*, 227. Joseph Story, 2 *Commentaries on Equity Jurisprudence* (Boston: Hilliard, Gray, 1836) 574–76 (§§ 1341–43) ("For, though in general parents are entrusted with the custody of the persons and the education of their children; yet this is done upon the natural presumption, that the children will be properly taken care of, and brought up with a due education in literature, and morals, and religion; and

that they will be treated with kindness and affection. But whenever this presumption is removed . . . in every such case, the Court of Chancery will interfere, and deprive him of the custody of his children, and appoint a suitable person to act as guardian, and to take care of them, and to superintend their education"); see also Story, 2 *Equity Jurisprudence*, 577 (§ 1345) ("Why is not the conduct of the father to be considered a trust, as well as the conduct of the person appointed as guardian?"). Hochheimer, *The Law Relating to the Custody of Infants* (Baltimore: John Murphy, 1887) 42 (§ 10) ("[T]he general drift of opinion [in the American cases] is in the direction of treating the idea of trust as the controlling principle in all controversies in relation to such custody. As the trust which is implied in the guardianship of an infant calls into requisition the exercise of moral qualities, the tenderest and most sacred impulses of our nature, — love, affection, self-sacrifice — and as there is no fixed standard by which the quality of these can be gauged or their operation determined, it follows, in the very nature of things, that any system of fixed, inflexible rules to be applied in the disposing of infants would lead to gross injustice and incalculable evil"). Hochheimer, *The Custody of Infants* (1899), 4 (§ 4). Tiedeman, *The Limitations of Police Power*, 552–53; cf. Ernst Freund, *The Police Power: Public Policy and Constitutional Rights* (Chicago: Callaghan, 1904) 248 (§ 260) ("Our constitutions are silent upon family rights and relations, and we should have to regard the parental power not only as a natural right, but as a natural right above the power of the state, to declare its legislative restraint to be unconstitutional. . . . There is indeed a tendency to treat this right altogether as a power in trust, which may not only be checked in the case of manifest abuse, but the exercise of which may be directed by such rules as the legislature may establish as best calculated to promote the welfare of the child").

10. See, e.g., People ex rel. Brooks v. Brooks, 35 Barb. 85, 87 (N.Y. 1861). For a discussion of the American cases, see Hurd, *Habeas Corpus*, 472–521. On the right of guardianship as a trust in early English cases, see Kerry O'Halloran, *The Welfare of the Child: The Principle and the Law* (Brookfield, Vermont: Ashgate, 1999) 7–35; Sarah Abramowicz, Note, "English Child Custody Law, 1660–1839: The Origins of Judicial Intervention in Paternal Custody," *Colum. L. Rev.* 99 (1999): 1344, 1353–55; cf. Eyre v. Shaftesbury, 24 Eng. Rep. 659, 660 (Ch. 1722) ("The father by the statute has a right to dispose of the guardianship of his child until twenty-one, and having done so here, it will be binding, unless some misbehaviour be shewn in the guardian, in which case it being a matter of trust, this court has a superintendency over it") (citation omitted).

11. Brooks v. Brooks, 35 Barb. at 87–88; cf., e.g., Lippincott v. Lippincott, 128 A. 254, 255 (N.J. Err. & App. 1925) ("Manifestly, the touchstone of our jurisprudence in matters dealing with the custody and control of infants is the welfare and happiness of the infant, and not the filial affections naturally arising from parental or family relationship. Thus, it has been quite generally held that even the natural

right of the father to the custody of his child cannot be treated as an absolute property right, but rather as a trust reposed in the father by the state, as parens patriae
for the welfare of the infant") (citations omitted).

12. The Etna, 8 F. Cas. at 804.

13. William Blackstone, 1 *Commentaries on the Laws of England* (Oxford: Clarendon
Press, 1765) 435; cf. Francis Hutcheson, *A System of Moral Philosophy* (1755) 192
("This grand end of the parental power shows that it includes few of those rights
contained in the *patria potestas* of the Romans. The child is a rational agent, with
rights valid against the parents; though they are the natural tutors or curators, and
have a right to direct the actions, and manage the goods of the child, for its benefit,
during its want of proper knowledge"). John Locke, *Two Treatises of Government*,
ed. Peter Laslett (New York: Cambridge University Press, 1960) II, VI, § 68.

14. See Steven G. Calabresi and Sarah E. Agudo, "Individual Rights Under State
Constitutions When the Fourteenth Amendment Was Ratified in 1868: What
Rights Are Deeply Rooted in American History and Tradition?" *Tex. L. Rev.* 87
(2008): 7, 108–11. In 1868, thirty-six out of thirty-seven states made the provision of
public education a constitutional duty. Calabresi and Agudo conclude that "[a]
right to a public-school education is thus arguably deeply rooted in American
history and tradition and is implicit in the concept of ordered liberty." "Individual
Rights Under State Constitutions," 108; see also Allen W. Hubsch, "The Emerging
Right to Education Under State Constitutional Law," *Temple L. Rev.* 65 (1992):
1325. On state constitutions and positive rights, see Burt Neuborne, "Foreword:
State Constitutions and the Evolution of Positive Rights," *Rutgers L.J.* 20 (1989):
881; cf. Jonathan Feldman, "Separation of Powers and Judicial Review of Positive Rights Claims: The Role of State Courts in an Era of Positive Government,"
Rutgers L.J. 24 (1993): 1057. States have also protected unenumerated rights under
various constitutional provisions, see Calabresi and Agudo, "Individual Rights Under State Constitutions," 88–89; cf. Suzanna Sherry, "Natural Law in the States,"
U. Cin. L. Rev. 61 (1992): 171, including a fundamental right to parent, see, e.g., In
re J.P., 648 P.2d 1364 (Utah 1982).

15. Hochheimer, *The Custody of Infants* (1899), 22 (§ 22) (footnote omitted); cf.
Bishop, *Commentaries*, 526 (§ 643) ("[T]he children, though younger in years,
have themselves an interest even more sacred than their parents, and more deserving of protection. Indeed, no parent has properly an *interest* in the mere *custody* of
a child").

16. Hochheimer, *The Custody of Infants* (1887), 41 (§ 10).

17. Martha Fineman, "Dominant Discourse, Professional Language, and Legal
Change in Child Custody Decisionmaking," *Harv. L. Rev.* 101 (1988): 727, 737;
cf., e.g., Elizabeth S. Scott and Robert E. Scott, "Parents as Fiduciaries," *Va. L.
Rev.* 81 (1995): 2401, 2406 ("Before the twentieth century, the combined status of
biological parenthood and marriage signified a legal authority [over children] of

almost limitless scope"); Janet L. Dolgin, "Just a Gene: Judicial Assumptions About Parenthood," *UCLA L. Rev.* 40 (1993): 637 n.29 (Before the Industrial Revolution, "under common law, fathers had an absolute right to the custody of their children. The common law view [of paternal rights] represented a modification of Roman law under which children were fully defined as paternal property") (citation omitted).

18. See, e.g., State v. Clottu, 33 Ind. 409, 411 (1870) ("The duties and authority pertaining to the relation of parent and child have their foundations in nature, it is true. Nevertheless, all civilized governments have regarded this relation as falling within the legitimate scope of legislative control. Except in countries which lie in barbarism, the authority of the parent over the child is nowhere left absolutely without municipal definition and regulation"); People ex rel. Barry v. Mercein, 3 Hill 399 (N.Y. Sup. 1842) ("Those countries in which the father has a general power to dispose of his children, have always been considered barbarous. Our own law never has allowed the exercise of such power except for some specific and temporary purpose, such as apprenticeship during the father's life, or guardianship after his death"); cf. Joel Prentiss Bishop, 2 *New Commentaries on Marriage, Divorce, and Separation* (Chicago: T. H. Flood, 1891) 454 (§ 1163) ("Under laws which have prevailed in some ages and countries, rendering the child a sort of chattel in the hands of its father, who could sell or kill it, the paternal right to its custody was necessarily inflexible. But this old barbarity has gradually given way until the modern civilization concedes to the child the same attributes which it acknowledges in the father") (footnote omitted).

19. Story, 2 *Equity Jurisprudence*, 578 (§ 1347).

20. In discussing American case law, I use "common law" to refer to judge-made law, whether formally derived at law or in equity. On the early embrace of equitable principles by American courts of law, see, for example, Hurd, *Habeas Corpus*, 465 ("[T]he equitable doctrine maintained in [*Rex v. Delaval*, 3 Burr. 1434, 1436 (K.B. 1763)] has been commonly practiced in this country and may now be considered as thoroughly incorporated in the American common law"); Kent, 2 *Commentaries*, 231 ("The father may obtain the custody of his children by the writ of *habeas corpus*, when they are improperly detained from him; but the courts, both of law and equity, will investigate the circumstances, and act according to sound discretion") (footnote omitted); cf. People ex rel. Barry v. Mercein, 8 Paige Ch. 47, 55–56 (N.Y. Ch. 1839) ("[T]he power of the chancellor to issue a habeas corpus is not derived solely from the statute, but is also an inherent power in the court, derived from the common law. . . . The court of chancery, upon such writ [of habeas corpus], will exercise its discretion, in disposing of the custody of the infant, upon the same principles which regulate the exercise of a similar discretion by other courts and officers who are authorized to allow the writ in similar cases"); cf. Stanley N. Katz, "The Politics of Law in Colonial America: Controversies over Chancery

Courts and Equity Law in the Eighteenth Century," in *Law in American History*, eds. Donald Fleming and Bernard Bailyn (Boston: Little, Brown, 1971) 257. Katz charts the emergence of a "distinctively colonial equity law." Where separate colonial chancery courts were not established, "equity law and procedure were amalgamated into the courts of the common law or also, as in New England, into the legislatures." Katz, "The Politics of Law in Colonial America," 263.

It is not always clear what time period is meant by reference to "common law" or "early common law." For instance, R. Collin Mangrum begins his discussion of child custody cases by describing the "near absolute power of the father over his children" at "early common law." He refers to feudalism and the patriarchal orientation of Christianity as firmly establishing property-oriented custody principles. He cites Blackstone to show that paternal power "was akin to the Roman rule of *patria potestas*." Yet he also notes that Blackstone himself depicted the common law as "much more moderate" than the Roman code, and Mangrum goes on to discuss how eighteenth-century equitable modifications mitigated "the harshness of the common law rule." So what common law did the American colonies receive? Mangrum notes that "[t]he feudal structure out of which the property-oriented rule of paternal preference arose was never part of our tradition. The English common law was 'received' by the newly-formed states after the Revolution only insofar as it fit the circumstances of the respective states." See Mangrum, "Exclusive Reliance on Best Interest May Be Unconstitutional: Religion as a Factor in Child Custody Cases," *Creighton L. Rev.* 15 (1981): 25, 31–44.

On local custom and the adaptability of American common law, see Ellen Holmes Pearson, *Remaking Custom: Law and Identity in the Early American Republic* (Charlottesville: University of Virginia Press, 2011) 11–30.

21. Blackstone, 1 *Commentaries*, 440–41; cf. Kent, 2 *Commentaries*, 231 ("The father . . . has the benefit of his children's labor while they live with him, and are maintained by him; and this is no more than he is entitled to from his apprentices or servants") (footnote omitted).

22. Kent, 2 *Commentaries*, 231; see also Hochheimer, *The Custody of Infants* (1899), 54–59 (§§ 44–46).

23. In re Gregg, 5 New York Legal Observer 265, 267 (N.Y. Super. 1847).

24. Legate v. Legate, 28 S.W. 281, 282 (Tex. 1894).

25. Kent, 2 *Commentaries*, 225–26; cf. Kelley v. Davis, 6 Am. Rep. 499, 502 (N.H. 1870) ("[T]he common law considered moral duties of this nature as better left in their performance to the impulses of nature") (internal quotation marks omitted).

26. See, e.g., Hochheimer, *The Custody of Infants* (1899), 36–40 (§§ 34–38).

27. In re Gregg, 5 New York Legal Observer at 267. Mercein v. People ex rel. Barry, 25 Wend. 64, 103 (N.Y. 1840). United States v. Green, 25 F. Cas. 30, 32 (C.C.R.I. 1824). Ex parte Crouse, 4 Whart. 9, 11 (Pa. 1839); cf. In re Ferrier's Petition, 103 Ill.

367, 372 (1882) ("[The court's] jurisdiction extends to the care and person of the infant, so far as is necessary for his protection and education, and upon this ground that court interferes with the ordinary rights of parents in regard to the custody and care of their children") (emphasis added).

28. Legate v. Legate, 28 S.W. at 282.

29. See, e.g., Swoap v. Superior Court, 516 P.2d 840, 849 (Cal. 1973) ("It is thus abundantly clear that a long tradition of law, not to mention a measureless history of societal customs, has singled out adult children to bear the burden of supporting their poor parents").

30. Gerald Gunther, "Foreword: In Search of Evolving Doctrine on a Changing Court: A Model for a Newer Equal Protection," *Harv. L. Rev.* 86 (1972) 1, 8 (internal quotation marks omitted). But see Adarand Constructors, Inc. v. Pena, 515 U.S. 200, 237 (1995) ("[W]e wish to dispel the notion that strict scrutiny is 'strict in theory, but fatal in fact.'"); see also Adam Winkler, "Fatal in Theory and Strict in Fact: An Empirical Analysis of Strict Scrutiny in the Federal Courts," *Vand. L. Rev.* 59 (2006): 793.

31. See Slaughter-House Cases, 83 U.S. 36, 80 (1872) (The protection of due process "has been in the Constitution since the adoption of the fifth amendment, as a restraint upon the Federal power. It is also to be found in some form of expression in the constitutions of nearly all the States, as a restraint upon the power of the States. This law then, has practically been the same as it now is during the existence of the government, except so far as the present amendment may place the restraining power over the States in this matter in the hands of the Federal government"); see also Calabresi and Agudo, "Individual Rights Under State Constitutions," 66 (noting that, in 1868, thirty out of thirty-seven states "had clauses in their state constitutions that explicitly prohibited the deprivation of life, liberty, or property without due process of law or by the law of the land").

32. Michael H. v. Gerald D., 491 U.S. 110, 122 (1989) (quoting Snyder v. Massachusetts, 291 U.S. 97, 105 [1934]); see also Griswold v. Connecticut, 381 U.S. 479, 501 (1965) (Harlan, J., concurring in the judgment) ("Judicial self-restraint will . . . be achieved in this area, as in other constitutional areas, only by continual insistence upon respect for the teachings of history, solid recognition of the basic values that underlie our society, and wise appreciation of the great roles that the doctrines of federalism and separation of powers have played in establishing and preserving American freedoms"). Palko v. Connecticut, 302 U.S. 319, 325 (1937).

33. Troxel v. Granville, 530 U.S. 57, 65, 66 (2000).

34. The work of David D. Meyer is especially helpful on this point. Meyer argues that, "notwithstanding the [Court's] broad language exalting the 'fundamental' nature of family privacy rights, the Court in truth has applied something less than strict scrutiny in their defense." "What Constitutional Law Can Learn from the

ALI *Principles of Family Dissolution,"* *BYU L. Rev.* 2001 (2001): 1075, 1090; see also David D. Meyer, "The Paradox of Family Privacy," *Vand. L. Rev.* 53 (2000): 527, 536–47 (reviewing cases); Lee E. Teitelbaum, "Family History and Family Law," *Wis. L. Rev.* 1985 (1985): 1135, 1157 ("What is most striking about these cases [where the Court has drawn a line against state regulation of parent-child relations], however, is not the strong language they employ in support of values of pluralism and deference to parental authority but the narrowness of the exceptions they recognize to state authority in respect of education"); cf. James E. Fleming and Linda C. McClain, *Ordered Liberty: Rights, Responsibilities, and Virtues* (Cambridge: Harvard University Press, 2013) 237–72 (arguing that the Supreme Court's due process jurisprudence has not relied on strict scrutiny of fundamental rights). The exceptionalism of family law—specifically, its (sometimes) exemption from strict scrutiny—is also evident in the equal protection context. See, e.g., David D. Meyer, "*Palmore* Comes of Age: The Place of Race in the Placement of Children," *U. Fla. J.L. & Pub Pol'y* 18 (2007): 183; Elizabeth Bartholet, "Where Do Black Children Belong?: The Politics of Race Matching in Adoption," *U. Pa. L. Rev.* 139 (1991): 1163.

35. Troxel v. Granville, 530 U.S. at 92 (Scalia, J., dissenting) ("Only three holdings of this Court rest in whole or in part upon a substantive constitutional right of parents to direct the upbringing of their children—two of them from an era rich in substantive due process holdings that have since been repudiated") (footnote omitted).

36. For example, as Paula Abrams has pointed out, the parent petitioners in *Bolling v. Sharpe,* 347 U.S. 497 (1954)—this is the companion case to *Brown v. Board of Education,* 347 U.S. 483 (1954)—asked the Court to hold that segregated public schooling violates the fundamental due process right of parents to direct the education of their children. See *Cross Purposes: Pierce v. Society of Sisters and the Struggle over Compulsory Public Education* (Ann Arbor: University of Michigan Press, 2009) 217. Relying on *Meyer v. Nebraska,* 262 U.S. 390 (1923), *Pierce v. Society of Sisters of the Holy Names of Jesus and Mary,* 268 U.S. 510 (1925), and *Farrington v. Tokushige,* 273 U.S. 284 (1927), the parents claimed that "[t]his Court has recognized that this right includes liberty of choice of parents and their children in the selection of the type of education which *parents* and *their children* think important." Brief of Petitioners on Reargument, Spottswood Thomas Bolling, et al., at 51, Bolling v. Sharpe, 347 U.S. 497 (1954).

37. Meyer v. Nebraska, 262 U.S. 390 (1923). Pierce v. Society of the Sisters of the Holy Names of Jesus and Mary, 268 U.S. 510 (1925). In *Pierce,* the appellee Society of Sisters did address parental rights, see Brief of Appellee, in *Oregon School Cases: Complete Record* (Baltimore: Belvedere Press, 1925) 321–330, and before the Court attorney William Guthrie briefly argued the position "that the right of parents to

send their children to private schools of their own choice is a fundamental, natural and sacred right," Transcript of Oral Argument, in *Oregon School Cases*, 653.

38. Meyer, 262 U.S. at 402; cf. Runyon v. McCrary, 427 U.S. 160, 178 (1976); Wisconsin v. Yoder, 406 U.S. 205, 234–35 (1972); Bd. of Educ. v. Allen, 392 U.S. 236, 247 (1968).

39. Poe v. Ullman, 367 U.S. 497, 543 (1961) (Harlan, J., dissenting).

40. Justice Thomas's dissent in *Brown v. Entertainment Merchants Association*, 131 S.Ct. 2729, 2758–59 (2011), suggests, unintentionally one presumes, that traditionally the state could go very far indeed: "In the decades leading up to and following the Revolution, the conception of the child's mind evolved but the duty and authority of parents remained. Indeed, society paid closer attention to potential influences on children than before. By weakening earlier forms of patriarchal authority, the Revolution enhanced the importance of childrearing and education in ensuring social stability. Teachers and schools came under scrutiny, and children's reading material was carefully supervised. *Laws reflected these concerns and often supported parental authority with the coercive power of the state*" (emphasis added) (citation and internal quotation marks omitted). Thomas cites Benjamin Rush, among other authorities, to support the contention that, at the time of the founding generation, parents had total control over their children's lives. It would be more accurate to say that what Rush supported was total *state* control over the lives of its future citizens. See Benjamin Rush, "Thoughts upon the Mode of Education Proper in a Republic," in *Essays on Education in the Early Republic*, ed. Frederick Rudolph (Cambridge: Harvard University Press, 1965) 11 ("From the observations that have been made it is plain, that I consider it possible to convert men into republican machines. This must be done if we expect them to perform their parts properly, in the great machine of the government of the state"); see also Rush, "Thoughts upon the Mode of Education," 14 ("Let our pupil be taught that he does not belong to himself, but that he is public property. Let him be taught to love his family, but let him be taught at the same time that he must forsake and even forget them when the welfare of his country requires it"). Among other measures meant to produce republican uniformity of character, Rush urged the creation of a federal university "where the youth of all the states may be melted (as it were) into one mass of citizens." 1 *Letters of Benjamin Rush*, ed. Lyman H. Butterfield (Princeton: Princeton University Press, 1951) 388.

41. Meyer v. State, 187 N.W. 100, 104 (Neb. 1922) (Letton, J., dissenting); cf. Berea College v. Kentucky, 211 U.S. 45, 67 (1908) (Harlan, J., dissenting) ("The capacity to impart instruction to others is given by the Almighty for beneficent purposes and its use may not be forbidden or interfered with by Government—certainly not, unless such instruction is, in its nature, harmful to the public morals or imperils the public safety").

42. Pierce, 268 U.S. at 534.

43. Yoder, 406 U.S. at 213; cf. State v. Counort, 124 P. 910, 911–12 (Wash. 1912) (rejecting homeschooling claim) ("We do not think that the giving of instruction by a
parent to a child, conceding the competency of the parent to fully instruct the
child in all that is taught in the public schools, is within the meaning of the law 'to
attend a private school.' Such a requirement means more than home instruction.
It means the same character of school as the public school, a regular, organized
and existing institution, making a business of instructing children of school age in
the required studies and for the full time required by the laws of this state").

44. See, e.g., Kenneth B. O'Brien Jr., "Education, Americanization, and the Supreme
Court: The 1920's," *American Quarterly* 13 (1961): 161, 171 ("It is difficult to overesti-
mate the import [of these cases]"); see also, e.g., Stephen Arons, "The Separation
of School and State: *Pierce* Reconsidered," *Harv. Educ. Rev.* 46 (1976): 76; cf.
Stephen L. Carter, "Parents, Religion, and Schools: Reflections on *Pierce*, 70 Years
Later," *Seton Hall L. Rev.* 27 (1997): 1194.

    Even Pope Pius XI lavished praise on *Pierce*, writing in a 1929 encyclical letter
on education: "This incontestable right of the family has at various times been
recognized by nations anxious to respect the natural law in their civil enactments.
Thus, to give one recent example, the Supreme Court of the United States of
America, in a decision on an important controversy, declared that it is not in
the competence of the State to fix any uniform standard of education by forcing
children to receive instruction exclusively in public schools, and it bases its decision on the natural law: the child is not the mere creature of the State; those who
nurture him and direct his destiny have the right coupled with the high duty, to
educate him and prepare him for the fulfillment of his obligations." *Divini Illius
Magistri* ("On the Christian Education of Youth") (Dec. 31, 1929), 37, at http://
www.vatican.va/holy_father/pius_xi/encyclicals/documents/hf_p-xi_enc_31121929
_divini-illiusmagistri_en.html, cited in David R. Upham, "*Pierce v. Society of Sisters*, Natural Law, and the Pope's Extraordinary—But Undeserved—Praise of the
American Republic" [Draft], 4, at http://papers.ssrn.com/sol3/papers.cfm?abstract
_id=2018396; see also Christopher Wolfe, "The Supreme Court and Catholic
Social Thought," *Am. J. Juris.* 29 (1984): 45, 50–51.

45. Yoder, 406 U.S. at 239 (White, J., concurring).

46. Consider the dissenting opinion of Judge (and later Supreme Court Justice)
Peckham, who would author *Lochner*, in *People v. Budd*, 117 N.Y. 1, 47–48 (1889)
(Peckham, J., dissenting): "I have spoken thus somewhat at length upon this
subject . . . for the purpose of showing that, because the rule [regarding common
carriers] is correctly stated in those cases, no reason exists in such fact for the
extension of the principle of that rule to other cases, and, by doing so, go back to
the seventeenth or eighteenth century ideas of paternal government, and thereby

wholly ignore the later and, as I firmly believe, the more correct ideas which an increase of civilization and a fuller knowledge of the fundamental laws of political economy, and a truer conception of the proper functions of government have given us at the present day. Rights which we would now regard as secured to us by our bill of rights against all assaults, from whatever quarter, were in those days regarded as the proper subjects of legislative interference and suppression. The fact that certain rules of the common law have come down to us unimpaired, although based upon a view of the relations of government to the people which obtained in the seventeenth century, should certainly furnish no reason for extending those rules to cases which, but for such extension, would be regarded as clearly within the protection of the constitutional limitations contained in our bill of rights."

47. Both liberals and conservatives have sought to distance *Meyer* and *Pierce* from *Lochner* (or, at least, from what David E. Bernstein calls the "mythical, evil *Lochner*" of modern constitutional law). See *Rehabilitating* Lochner: *Defending Individual Rights Against Progressive Reform* (Chicago: University of Chicago Press, 2011) 108–24. As Bernstein argues, this distancing is more strategically prudent than historically sound. "Justice Peckham's enunciation of an expansive liberty-protective interpretation of the [Due Process Clause] in *Lochner* (and *Allgeyer*) begot Justice McReynolds' even more expansive opinion in *Meyer*, which continues to serve as the constitutional foundation of various Fourteenth Amendment rights protected by the Supreme Court." Bernstein, *Rehabilitating* Lochner, 124.

48. Employment Div., Dept. of Human Res. of Oregon v. Smith, 494 U.S. 872 (1990).

49. Yoder, 406 U.S. at 233 (1972).

50. Smith, 494 U.S. at 881. Yoder, 406 U.S. at 234.

51. Smith, 494 U.S. at 879 (quoting Reynolds v. United States, 98 U.S. 145, 166–67 [1878]).

52. The *Yoder* Court suggested that its holding might be limited to "a free exercise claim of the nature revealed by this record." See 406 U.S. at 233.

53. Stephen Gilles, "On Educating Children: A Parentalist Manifesto," *U. Chi. L. Rev.* 63 (1996): 937.

54. See Santosky v. Kramer, 455 U.S. 745 (1982).

55. Meyer, "Paradox of Family Privacy," 527.

56. 530 U.S. 57 (2000).

57. Brown v. Hot, Sexy and Safer Prods., 68 F.3d 525, 533 (1st Cir. 1995).

58. Cf. Bertrand Fry, "Breeding Constitutional Doctrine: The Provenance and Progeny of the 'Hybrid Situation' in Current Free Exercise Jurisprudence," *Tex. L. Rev.* 71 (1993): 833, 62 ("About the lack of coherent protection there can be no doubt. In different areas of law, the hybrid situation doctrine generates different effects").

59. Cf. John P. Forren, "Revisiting Four Popular Myths about the Peyote Case," *U. Pa. J. Const. L.* 8 (2006): 209, 219 ("*Smith* left lower court judges . . . with extraordinary amounts of doctrinal leeway to decide precisely what controlling First Amendment precedents now required them to do").

60. See http://www.parentalrights.org/index.asp?Type=B_BASIC&SEC={DE675888-E60A-4219-8A5E-000083244D13}&DE=. The justification of the amendment rests on twin pillars of concern for the uncertain status of parental rights. First, supporters worry that the federal courts have been less than strident in their defense of the right to parent. Second, supporters worry about erosion of parental authority should the United States ratify the United Nations Convention on the Rights of the Child. The amendment reads in its entirety: "Section 1: The liberty of parents to direct the upbringing and education of their children is a fundamental right. Section 2: Neither the United States nor any State shall infringe upon this right without demonstrating that its governmental interest as applied to the person is of the highest order and not otherwise served. Section 3: No treaty may be adopted nor shall any source of international law be employed to supersede, modify, interpret, or apply to the rights guaranteed by this article."

Since 1990, critics of *Smith* have also sought a statutory return to the heightened review of free exercise claims. In 1993, Congress passed the Religious Freedom Restoration Act (RFRA), which reinstated *Yoder's* strict scrutiny standard for any federal or state action that "substantially burden[s] a person's exercise of religion even if that burden results from a rule of general applicability." See 42 U.S.C. § 2000bb-1(b) (1993) ("Government may substantially burden a person's exercise of religion only if it demonstrates that application of the burden to the person—(1) is in furtherance of a compelling governmental interest; and (2) is the least restrictive means of furthering that compelling governmental interest"). The federal RFRA was overturned insofar as it applied to the states. See City of Boerne v. Flores, 521 U.S. 507 (1997). But cf. Gonzales v. O Centro Espírita Beneficente União do Vegetal, 546 U.S. 418 (2006) (upholding under RFRA decision enjoining federal government from enforcing Controlled Substances Act to ban use of hoasca, a tea with hallucinogenic properties, in religious ceremonies). The downfall of RFRA as applied to the states led to the passage of the Religious Land Use and Institutionalized Persons Act (RLUIPA), Pub. L. No. 106–274, 114 Stat. 803 (2000) (codified at 42 U.S.C. §§ 2000cc [2000] (applying strict scrutiny to prisoner rights and discriminatory land use claims). A number of states have passed RFRAs of their own. See Christopher C. Lund, "Religious Liberty After *Gonzales*: A Look at State RFRAs," *S.D. L. Rev.* 55 (2010): 466, 466–67 n.7 & 477 n.67 (citing and describing state statutes). The successful assertion of fundamental rights under state RFRA regimes has been modest at best. Lund, 479–96. It should also be noted that some states interpret their state constitutions to be more protective of religious liberty than the federal constitution. Lund, "Religious Liberty After *Gonzales*," 478.

61. Meyer, "What Constitutional Law Can Learn from the ALI *Principles*," 1090. Troxel v. Granville, 530 U.S. at 86 (Stevens, J., dissenting).
62. Cf. generally James G. Dwyer, *The Relationship Rights of Children* (New York: Cambridge University Press, 2006); Dwyer, "Parents' Religion and Children's Welfare: Debunking the Doctrine of Parents' Rights," *Calif. L. Rev.* 82 (1994): 1371.
63. Cf. Troxel v. Granville, 530 U.S. at 88 (Stevens, J., dissenting) ("A parent's rights with respect to her child have thus never been regarded as absolute, but rather are limited by the existence of an actual, developed relationship with a child, and are tied to the presence or absence of some embodiment of family. These limitations have arisen, not simply out of the definition of parenthood itself, but because of this Court's assumption that a parent's interests in a child must be balanced against the State's long-recognized interests as *parens patriae* and, critically, the child's own complementary interest in preserving relationships that serve her welfare and protection") (citations omitted).
64. Martha Minow, *Making All the Difference: Inclusion, Exclusion, and American Law* (Ithaca: Cornell University Press, 1990) 293; see also *Making All the Difference*, 383 ("Especially in struggles to secure greater respect for those . . . who remained dependent after others had secured rights for autonomous action, rights provide a rhetoric for naming and scrutinizing both private and public power"). Indeed, as Minow observes, asserting rights is one way that people can "signal and strengthen their relation to a community." *Making All the Difference*, 294.
65. From fiduciary principles one might argue in favor of strong deference to parental choices. See, e.g., Elizabeth S. Scott and Robert E. Scott, "Parents as Fiduciaries," *Va. L. Rev.* (1995): 2401.
66. Cf., e.g., Mary Ann Glendon, *Rights Talk: The Impoverishment of Political Discourse* (New York: Free Press, 1991) 110; Moore v. City of East Cleveland, Ohio, 431 U.S. 494, 544 (1997) (White, J., dissenting). On the rise and fall of the rights critique generated by Critical Legal Studies, see Robin West, *Normative Jurisprudence: An Introduction* (New York: Cambridge University Press, 2011) 107–76.

    Soon after the Supreme Court's decision in *Pierce*, future justice Felix Frankfurter issued a similar warning about the illiberal use of due process in the service of liberalism: "For ourselves, we regard the cost of this power of the Supreme Court on the whole as greater than its gains. After all, the hysteria and chauvinism that forbade the teaching of German in Nebraska schools may subside, and with its subsidence bring repeal of the silly measure; the narrow margin by which the Oregon law was carried in 1922 may, with invigorated effort on the part of the liberal forces, result in its repeal, at least by a narrow margin. But when the Supreme Court strikes down legislation directed against trade unions, or enshrines the labor injunction into the Constitution, or denies to women in industry the meagre protection of minimum wage legislation, we are faced with action more far-reaching, because ever so much more durable and authoritative than even the most mischievous of repealable state legislation. . . . And here is ample warning to the liberal forces that the real battles of liberalism are not won in the Supreme Court. To a large extent the Supreme Court, under the guise of constitutional interpretation of words whose contents are derived from the disposition of the Justices, is the reflector of that impalpable but controlling thing, the general drift of public opinion. Only a persistent, positive translation of the liberal faith into the thoughts and acts of the community is the real reliance against the unabated temptation to straitjacket the human mind." See Felix Frankfurter, "Can the Supreme Court Guarantee Toleration?," *New Republic*, June 17, 1925, 85, 86–87.

67. Compare Frank I. Michelman on the role that a counter-ideology can play in constitutional law and theory. "The Supreme Court, 1985 Term—Foreword: Traces of Self-Government," *Harv. L. Rev.* 100 (1986) 4, 17–18: "The role is that of a counter-ideology, a normative political vision to set against the vision believed to have predominated in the thought of the framers and in the Constitution they framed. Such a visionary 'opposite,' if reasonably clear and coherent, may serve a number of heuristic and argumentative functions important to constitutional lawyers. Viewed as a rejected alternative, the 'opposite' can be used to clarify the assumptions and aims of the prevailing scheme. Viewed as a partially accepted or surviving competitor, it offers lawyers both a framework for interpretive debate and a premise for 'deviationist doctrine.' We can dispute constitutional issues, and innovate doctrinal futures, by debating the extent to which the 'opposite' survived and entered into the Constitution as a detectable, significant influence, fairly invocable in the work of interpretation."

68. Lehr v. Robertson, 463 U.S. 248, 257 (1983); see also Caban v. Mohammed, 441 U.S. 380 (1979); Quilloin v. Walcott, 434 U.S. 246 (1978); Stanley v. Illinois, 405 U.S. 645 (1972); cf. Moore v. City of East Cleveland, 431 U.S. 494, 504–05 (1977).

69. Locke, *Two Treatises*, II, VI, § 54.

70. See generally David A. J. Richards, "The Individual, the Family, and the Constitution: A Jurisprudential Perspective," *N.Y.U. L. Rev.* 55 (1980): 1. Richards argues that "the hermeneutics of constitutional interpretation must explicate background concepts of liberal political theory because the meaning of constitutional rights is best explained in light of the theoretical perspective of the Founders and a reasonable elaboration of that perspective in contemporary circumstances." Richards, 7 n.46.

71. Kenneth Maddock, *The Australian Aborigines: A Portrait of Their Society* (Ringwood: Penguin, 1972) 193–94.

72. Caban v. Mohammed, 441 U.S. at 397 (Stewart, J., dissenting).

73. Jennifer Nedelsky, "Reconceiving Autonomy: Sources, Thoughts and Possibilities," *Yale J.L. & Feminism* 1 (1989): 7, 12; see also Elizabeth Bartholet, *Nobody's Children: Abuse and Neglect, Foster Drift, and the Adoption Alternative* (Boston: Beacon Press, 1999) 3 ("Children will be able to thrive in our society only if we

begin to think of children born to other people, and to other racial groups, and to poor people, and to people who live elsewhere, as in some sense 'ours.'").

74. William Shakespeare, *A Midsummer Night's Dream*, IV.1.190–91. All references to Shakespeare are to *The Complete Works of Shakespeare*, ed. David Bevington (New York: Longman, 1997). The midsummer night's forest journey is a passage away from possessive pronouns. Consider the language of Egeus, Hermia's father, who, at the start of the play, seeks to dispose of his daughter as he sees fit: "Scornful Lysander! True, he hath my love, / And what is mine my love shall render him. / And she is mine, and all my right of her / I do estate unto Demetrius." I.1.95–98; cf. Nedelsky, "Reconceiving Autonomy," 12 (The possessive pronoun evokes "the isolated, distancing symbol of property").

75. Locke, *Two Treatises*, II, VI, § 149. Does the state's authority to act for certain ends imply a duty to do so? Not as a matter of constitutional law doctrine. See DeShaney v. Winnebago Cnty. Dept. of Soc. Servs., 489 U.S. 189 (1989). But cf. Robin West, "Unenumerated Duties," *U. Pa. J. Const. L.* 9 (2006): 221.

76. Cf. generally, e.g., Suzanna Sherry, "Responsible Republicanism: Educating for Citizenship," *U. Chi. L. Rev.* 62 (1995): 131; Stanley Ingber, "Socialization, Indoctrination, or the 'Pall of Orthodoxy': Value Training in the Public Schools," *U. Ill. L. Rev.* 1987 (1987): 15.

77. Pierce, 268 U.S. at 535.

78. Barbara Bennett Woodhouse, "Who Owns the Child?: *Meyer* and *Pierce* and the Child as Property," *Wm. & Mary L. Rev.* 33 (1992): 995, 1001.

79. Bd. of Educ., Island Trees Union Free Sch. Dist. No 26 v. Pico, 457 U.S. 853, 867 (1982); see also Griswold v. Connecticut, 381 U.S. at 482 ("[T]he State may not, consistently with the spirit of the First Amendment, contract the spectrum of available knowledge").

80. West Virginia Bd. of Educ. v. Barnette, 319 U.S. 624, 637 (1943). Harry Brighouse, "School Vouchers, Separation of Church and State, and Personal Autonomy," in *Moral and Political Education*, eds. Stephen Macedo and Yael Tamir (New York: New York University Press, 2002) 244, 247.

81. See Bruce A. Ackerman, *Social Justice in the Liberal State* (New Haven: Yale University Press, 1980) 159 ("The entire educational system will, if you like, resemble a great sphere. Children land upon the sphere at different points, depending on their primary culture; the task is to help them explore the globe in a way that permits them to glimpse the deeper meanings of the dramas passing on around them. At the end of the journey, however, the now mature citizen has every right to locate himself at the very point from which he began — just as he may also strike out to discover an unoccupied portion of the sphere").

82. See Joel Feinberg, "The Child's Right to an Open Future," in *Whose Child?: Children's Rights, Parental Authority, and State Power*, eds. William Aiken and Hugh LaFollette (Totowa: Adams & Co., 1980) 124–53.

83. Keyishian v. Bd. of Regents of Univ. of State of N.Y., 385 U.S. 589, 603 (1967).
84. Cf. Stanley Ingber, Comment, "Religious Children and the Inevitable Compulsion of Public Schools," *Case W. Res. L. Rev.* 43 (1993): 773, 778–79 ("A value-free curriculum is clearly impossible. . . . [S]chools simply cannot attain value-neutral or balanced education. With only limited resources and time, they cannot possibly provide curricula that encompass the world's enormous mass of information and perspectives. Furthermore, subtle characteristics such as style and emphasis may undermine any substantive success in achieving balanced presentations. Even if these practical difficulties could be overcome, an insurmountable conceptual problem remains: Value neutrality itself has a value bias favoring the liberal philosophy embodied by the scientific method of inquiry") (footnote omitted).
85. Thomas Jefferson, "The Statute of Virginia for Religious Freedom" (1786), in *The Virginia Statute for Religious Freedom: Its Evolution and Consequences in American History*, eds. Merrill D. Peterson and Robert C. Vaughan (New York: Cambridge University Press, 1988) xvii.
86. The phrase "omnivorous peer-culture" belongs to Richard Hofstadter. See *Anti-Intellectualism in American Life* (New York: Alfred A. Knopf, 1963) 383.
87. Cf. Stephen Macedo, "The Constitution, Civic Virtue, and Civil Society: Social Capital as Substantive Morality," *Fordham L. Rev.* 69 (2001): 1573, 1593 ("The patterns of social life that support liberal democratic forms of civil flourishing embody definite rankings of competing human goods, which will be associated with some versions of religious truth and not others. In this sense, the project of promoting a healthy liberal democratic civil society is inevitably a deeply judgmental and non-neutral project"); William Galston, "Two Concepts of Liberalism," *Ethics* 105 (1995): 516, 526 ("[A]ny liberal argument that invokes autonomy as a general rule of public action in effect takes sides in the ongoing struggle between reason and faith, reflection and tradition. Autonomy-based arguments are bound to marginalize those individuals and groups who cannot conscientiously embrace [the principles of liberal autonomy]").
88. See Katherine Rosman, "Religion's Generation Gap," *Wall Street Journal* (March 2, 2007), at http://online.wsj.com/article/SB117280201669024334.html.
89. T. S. Eliot, "Little Gidding," in *Collected Poems 1909–1962* (Boston: Harcourt, Brace, 1963) 208: "We shall not cease from exploration / And the end of all our exploring / Will be to arrive where we started / And know the place for the first time."
90. William A. Galston, *Liberal Pluralism: The Implications of Values Pluralism for Political Theory and Practice* (New York: Cambridge University Press, 2002) 105.
91. Troxel v. Granville, 530 U.S. at 89 (Stevens, J., dissenting) (footnote omitted).
92. Cf. Dwyer, "Parents' Religion and Children's Welfare: Debunking the Doctrine of Parents' Rights," 1389 ("[L]ower courts have continued to advance an interpretation of free exercise rights that effectively treats children as non-consenting

instruments or means to the achievement of other persons' ends, rather than as persons in their own right, with interests of their own that are deserving of equal respect").

93. Cf. Ira C. Lupu, "Home Education, Religious Liberty, and the Separation of Powers," *B.U. L. Rev.* 67 (1987): 971, 976–77 ("The legal tradition of authorizing parents to speak for their offspring need not become a device by which children are made to disappear. Children, not fully competent to make decisions because of insufficient awareness of the decisions' long-term consequences, are normally subject to parental control. Parents are presumptively trustworthy decisionmakers for their children because parents generally feel affection for their young and are knowledgeable about their interests. Custodial power of this sort is never absolute, however, for it is based on a theory of fiduciary obligation. If the custodian mistreats his ward, public or private remedies designed to protect the child may be available"); cf. also S. Brennan and R. Noggle, "The Moral Status of Children: Children's Rights, Parents' Rights, and Family Justice," *Social Theory and Practice* 23 (1997): 1; Richard Arneson and Ian Shapiro, "Democratic Autonomy and Religious Freedom: A Critique of *Wisconsin v. Yoder*," in *Democracy's Place* (Ithaca: Cornell University Press, 1996) 137; Elizabeth S. Scott and Robert E. Scott, "Parents as Fiduciaries," *Va. L. Rev.* 81 (1995): 2401; Barbara Bennett Woodhouse, "'Out of Children's Needs, Children's Rights': The Child's Voice in Defining the Family," *BYU J. Pub. L.* 8 (1994): 321, and "Hatching the Egg: A Child-Centered Perspective on Parents' Rights," *Cardozo L. Rev.* 14 (1993): 1747; Jeffrey Blustein, *Parents and Children: The Ethics of the Family* (New York: Oxford University Press, 1982) 104–14. But see Thomas H. Murray, *The Worth of a Child* (Berkeley: University of California Press, 1996) 61 ("[P]arenthood as stewardship still has its shortcomings as a model for parent-child relations. As a description of a relationship, it connotes disinterestedness, selflessness, a sort of benign but emotionally distant concern for the welfare of the child. This fits poorly with the intensity, love, and intimacy we prize between parents and children"); cf. Martin Guggenheim, *What's Wrong with Children's Rights* (Cambridge: Harvard University Press, 2005) 37–38 ("Security is also furthered because children grow up in an environment in which their parents know their decisions will not be subject to close scrutiny. Parents are encouraged to care for their children by receiving maximum discretion to carry out their responsibilities free from the worry that their behavior will be monitored and second-guessed by a third party").

94. Cf. Arneson and Shapiro, "Democratic Autonomy and Religious Freedom," 138 ("[C]hildren are in no sense the property of their parents. Although most people will find the claim thus stated unexceptionable, and few would go so far as to describe their children as their property, many of the convictions to which people find themselves drawn in thinking about the authority of parents over children

nevertheless reflect the archaic idea that the child is the chattel of the parent ((which once went hand in hand with the patriarchal idea that the wife is the chattel of the husband))"). But see Galston, *Liberal Pluralism*, 103 ("Everyone can agree that children are not the 'property' of their parents. Still, when I say that this child is 'mine,' I am both acknowledging responsibilities and asserting authority beyond what I owe or claim vis-à-vis children in general. As parent, I am more than the child's caretaker or teacher, and I am not simply a representative of the state delegated to prepare the child for citizenship"); Jeffrey Blustein, *Care and Commitment: Taking the Personal Point of View* (New York: Oxford University Press, 1991) 178 ("What matters to many parents is not just that they have a son or daughter—someone on whom they can shower affection, or who will support them in their old age, or who will extend the blood line or carry on the family name, and the like—but crucially that this child is *theirs*, in the sense that he or she is the product of their commitment to and concern for one another").

95. Transcript of Oral Argument at 8, Meyer v. Nebraska, 262 U.S. 390 (1923).

96. C. Fried, "Correspondence," *Phil. & Pub. Aff.* 6 (1977): 288–89, quoted in Thornburgh v. American College of Obstetricians and Gynecologists, 476 U.S. 747, 778 n.5 (1986) (Stevens, J., concurring).

97. Milton, *Paradise Lost*, in *Complete Poems and Major Prose* 467 (XII, 587).

98. John Milton, "Areopagitica," in *Complete Poems and Major Prose*, 727–28.

Chapter 2. Parenting as a Sacred Trust

Epigraph. "Children's Rights," *Scribner's Magazine* 12 (1892): 242. The educator Kate Wiggin, the author of *Kindergarten Principles and Practice* (1896) and several books on the work of the German educational theorist Friedrich Fröbel, is best known today for her classic children's book *Rebecca of Sunnybrook Farm* (1903).

1. John Locke, *Two Treatises of Government*, ed. Peter Laslett (New York: Cambridge University Press, 1960) (1689) II, VI, § 52.

2. II, VI, § 52. That power in the family was not located solely in the father is a point to which Locke returns on several occasions. Against Sir Robert Filmer's biblically based argument for the natural authority of the father—see generally Robert Filmer, *Patriarcha and Other Writings*, ed. Johann P. Sommerville (Cambridge: Cambridge University Press, 1991) (London: Richard Chiswell, 1680)—Locke observes that whatever grant of dominion God gave Adam was given to Eve as well. The grant "was not made in particular to *Adam*, . . . it being made to more than one, for it was spoken in the Plural Number, God blessed *them*, and said unto *them*, Have Dominion." I, III, § 29. Locke also undermines Filmer's reading of scripture—and, as Melissa A. Butler notes, "one of patriarchy's longest traditions"—by pointing out that God commanded children to honor both mother

and father. See Melissa A. Butler, "Early Liberal Roots of Feminism: John Locke and the Attack on Patriarchy," *Am. Pol. Sci. Rev.* 72 (1978): 135, 143.

3. See Filmer, *Patriarcha*, passim.

4. Locke, *Two Treatises*, I, VI, § 52. I, VII, § 70.

5. II, VI, § 53.

6. I, VI, § 52. I, VI, § 53.

7. II, VI, 54. I, VI, § 52. II, VI, § 55. II, VI, § 58.

8. II, VI, § 55.

9. I, VI, § 54. II, VI, § 56. By the same reasoning, children are born to a state of spiritual equality. See *A Letter Concerning Toleration* (J. Brook, 1796) (1689) 14–15.

10. Locke was not alone in making education, not generation, the source of parental authority. See [James Tyrrell], *Patriarcha non Monarcha, The Patriarch Unmonarch'd: Being Observations on A late Treatise and divers other Miscellanies, Published under the Name of Sir Robert Filmer Baronet* (London: Richard Janeway, 1681) 16–17 ("From whence it is evident, that the highest Right which Parents can have in their Children, is not meerly natural, from generation; but acquir'd by their performance of that nobler part of their Duty"); see also Francis Hutcheson, 2 *A System of Moral Philosophy* (Glasgow: R. and A. Foulis; London: A. Millar and T. Longman, 1755) 192 ("Generation no more makes [children] a piece of property to their parents, than sucking makes them the property of their nurses, out of whose bodies more of the matter of a child's body is sometimes derived, than was from both parents. On this footing the proprietor of any cattle by whose milk and wool they are fed and cloathed for any number of years would still have a stronger claim"). On Locke and the priority of parental duties to parental rights, compare Jeffrey Blustein, *Parents and Children: The Ethics of the Family* (New York: Oxford University Press, 1982) 74–81, 108–12.

11. II, VI, § 58. II, VI, § 64. II, VIII, § 149. II, VI, § 67. II, VI, § 65. II, VIII, § 149. II, VI, § 65.

12. II, VI, § 55. II, VI, § 58. II, VI, § 58. II, VI, § 65. II, VI, § 59. II, VI, § 57. II, VI, § 63. II, VI, § 59; cf. Hutcheson, 2 *A System of Moral Philosophy*, 190 ("When [children] attain to mature years, and the use of reason, they must obtain that liberty which is necessary to any rational enjoyment of life. The parental affection naturally secures to them this emancipation, as the reason God has given them intitles them to it").

13. II, VI, § 74. II, VI, § 74. II, VI, § 76. II, VI, § 66. II, VI, § 69.

14. II, VI, § 66. Similarly, Samuel von Pufendorf suggested that parental authority "rests upon the tacit consent also of the offspring." This is, needless to say, a presumed consent, but rightly presumed because "if an infant had had the use of reason at the time of its birth, and had seen that it could not save its life without the parents' care and the authority therewith connected, it would gladly have

consented to it, and would in turn have made an agreement with them for a suitable bringing-up." The parents' authority, Pufendorf stresses, "is established when they take up the child and nurture it, and undertake to form it, to the best of their ability, into a fit member of human society." It is the nurturing task that provides the proper measure of parental authority. *On the Duty of Man and Citizen According to the Natural Law* (1672?; 1682 ed.), trans. Frank Gardner Moore (New York: Oxford University Press, 1927) 108. Parents have "only so much authority . . . as suffices for this purpose." *On the Duty of Man and Citizen*, 98.

15. II, VI, § 66. II, VI, § 66. II, VI, § 58. II, VIII, § 95.

16. I, VI, § 50.

17. Gordon J. Schochet, *The Authoritarian Family and Political Attitudes in 17th-Century England: Patriarchalism in Political Thought* (New Brunswick, N.J.: Transaction Books, 1988) 65. Cf. generally Butler, "Early Liberal Roots of Feminism," 135–50. Butler explains why Filmer's linkage of patriarchal and political power had such force: "The patriarchal family experience was universal. The family in the seventeenth century was a primary group in every sense of the term. Life was lived on a small scale and the family was at its center. The family patriarch was a universally-acknowledged authority figure with immense power. By linking the authority of the king with the authority of the father, a theorist could immediately clarify the nature of a subject's political obligations. Moreover, monarchical power grounded in patriarchal power took on the legitimacy of that least-challengeable social institution, the family. . . . Finally, the linkage of paternal and monarchical power provided a means for transcending any residual or intermediate loyalties a subject might have." Butler, "Early Liberal Roots of Feminism," 136. In practice, patriarchy in the home was subject to "the fluidity, changes, and dynamics of family life." Linda A. Pollock, "Rethinking Patriarchy and the Family in Seventeenth-Century England," *J. Fam. Hist.* 23 (1998): 3, 4 (footnote omitted). Schochet makes the point that Filmer's "conscious and intentional articulation of the patriarchal doctrine is a clue to the existence of some disturbance in the way Stuart society understood itself—that is, in its ideology—and probably an indication that the structural bases of that society were being pressured as well." "Models of Politics and the Place of Women in Locke's Political Thought," in *Feminist Interpretations of John Locke*, eds. Nancy J. Hirschmann and Kirstie M. McClure (University Park: Pennsylvania State University Press, 2007) 137.

18. Schochet, *The Authoritarian Family*, 66.

19. But cf. Edmund Leites, "Locke's Liberal Theory of Parenthood," in *Ethnicity, Identity, and History: Essays in Memory of Werner J. Cahnman*, eds. Joseph B. Maier and Chaim I. Waxman (New Brunswick, N.J.: Transaction Books, 1983) 70–73 (rejecting the idea that for Locke the family was a microcosm of the larger social world).

20. Cf., e.g., John Millar, *The Origin of the Distinction of Ranks: Or, An Inquiry Into the Circumstances which Give Rise to Influence and Authority, in the Different Members of Society* (1771), 4th ed. (Edinburgh: William Blackwood; London: Longman, Hurst, Rees, and Orme, 1806) 138 ("To say that a king ought to enjoy absolute power because a father has enjoyed it, is to defend one system of oppression by the example of another").

21. John Locke, *Of the Conduct of the Understanding*, ed. Thomas Fowler (Oxford: Clarendon Press, 1881) (1706) 44–45 (§ 19).

22. *The Educational Writings of John Locke*, ed. James L. Axtell (Cambridge: Cambridge University Press, 1968) 58.

23. "Some Thoughts Concerning Education," in *The Educational Writings of John Locke*, ed. James L. Axtell (Cambridge: Cambridge University Press, 1968) (1693) 307 (§ 195) ("[In that] which concerns a Young Gentleman's Studies, his Tutor should remember, that his business is not so much to teach him all that is knowable, as to raise in him a love and esteem of Knowledge; and to put him in the right way of knowing and improving himself, when he has a mind to it"). "Some Thoughts Concerning Education," § 36 ("The having Desires accommodated to the Apprehensions and Relish of those several Ages, is not the Fault; but the not having them subject to the Rules and Restraints of Reason: The Difference lies not in having or not having Appetites, but in the Power to govern, and deny ourselves in them").

24. Jacqueline S. Reinier, *From Virtue to Character: American Childhood, 1775–1850* (New York: Twayne Publishers, 1996) 4; cf. "Some Thoughts Concerning Education," 140 (§ 36) ("He that is not used to submit his Will to the Reason of others, *when* he is *Young*, will scarce hearken to submit to his own Reason when he is of an Age to make use of it. And what kind of a Man such [as] one is like to prove, is easie to fore-see").

25. Locke, "Some Thoughts Concerning Education," 146 (§ 43). Locke, "Some Thoughts Concerning Education," 150 (§ 50) ("*Slavish discipline* makes a *Slavish Temper*").

26. Axtell, *Educational Writings of John Locke*, 64; see also Locke, "Some Thoughts Concerning Education," 159 (§ 66) (education should be adapted "to the Child's natural Genius and Constitution"); cf. Nathan Tarcov, *Locke's Education for Liberty* (Chicago: University of Chicago Press, 1984) 109 (noting that while Locke "recogniz[es] that the possibilities of transforming temperament are limited," he does not "reject the desirability of attempts at transformation or improvement"). Axtell, *Educational Writings of John Locke*, 52.

27. William Blackstone, 1 *Commentaries on the Laws of England* (Oxford: Clarendon Press, 1765) 440, 435.

28. Blackstone, 1 *Commentaries*, 434–42.

29. Blackstone, 1 *Commentaries*, 440; see also James Kent, 2 *Commentaries on American Law*, O. W. Holmes Jr., ed., 12th ed. (Boston: Little, Brown: 1873) 203 ("The rights of parents result from their duties"). Blackstone, 1 *Commentaries*, 440; see also Kent, 2 *Commentaries*, 228–30 (observing that the father is entitled to the value of the child's labor and services "in consequence of" parental obligations).

30. Blackstone, 1 *Commentaries*, 435.

31. Blackstone, 1 *Commentaries*, 435 ("[T]he children will have the perfect *right* of receiving maintenance from their parents"); cf. Lewis Hochheimer, *The Law Relating to the Custody of Infants*, 3d ed. (Baltimore: Harold B. Scrimger, 1899) 22 (§ 22) ("The terms 'right' and 'claim,' when used in this connection, according to their proper meaning, virtually import the right or claim of the *child* to be in that custody or charge which will subserve *its* real interests").

32. Blackstone, 1 *Commentaries*, 438.

33. Blackstone, 1 *Commentaries*, 438–39 (footnote omitted).

34. See Walter I. Trattner, *From Poor Law to Welfare State: A History of Social Welfare in America* (New York: Free Press, 1979) 1–113. On the mixed motives of reform efforts, see generally Carl F. Kaestle, *Pillars of the Republic: Common Schools and American Society 1780–1860* (New York: Hill and Wang, 1983) 75–135; Samuel Bowles and Herbert Gintis, *Schooling in Capitalist America: Educational Reform and the Contradictions of Economic Life* (New York: Basic Books, 1976); David B. Tyack, *The One Best System: A History of American Urban Education* (Cambridge: Harvard University Press, 1974); Anthony Platt, *The Child Savers: The Invention of Delinquency* (Chicago: University of Chicago Press, 1969); Michael B. Katz, *The Irony of Early School Reform: Educational Innovation in Mid-Nineteenth-Century Massachusetts* (Cambridge: Harvard University Press, 1968); cf. generally David J. Rothman, *The Discovery of the Asylum: Social Order and Disorder in the New Republic* (Boston: Little, Brown, 1971). But see generally Diane Ravitch, *The Revisionists Revisited: A Critique of the Radical Attack on the Schools* (New York: Basic Books, 1978).

35. Cf. Elizabeth Bartholet, *Nobody's Children: Abuse and Neglect, Foster Drift, and the Adoption Alternative* (Boston: Beacon Press, 1999) 5 ("I understand the concerns that lead some to equate state intervention to protect and remove children with class and race warfare. But I don't see things that way. I think it's important that those of us who understand ourselves as liberals concerned with social justice speak out, rather than being silenced by doubt and fear").

36. Blackstone, 1 *Commentaries*, 440; see also Kent, 2 *Commentaries*, 253–54 (noting that municipal law "admits only the *jus domesticœ emendationis*, or right of inflicting moderate correction, under the exercise of a sound discretion").

37. Blackstone, 1 *Commentaries*, 441.

38. Blackstone, 1 *Commentaries*, 54–55.

39. Blackstone, 1 *Commentaries*, 121, 121, 125, 125, 121, 122.

40. Blackstone, 1 *Commentaries*, 119, 121, 125.
41. Blackstone, 1 *Commentaries*, 125–36.
42. Blackstone, 1 *Commentaries*, 54. Even absolute rights can be lost "by some act that amounts to forfeiture." Blackstone, 1 *Commentaries*, 54.
43. See Blackstone, 1 *Commentaries*, 55.
44. Blackstone, 1 *Commentaries*, 120, 55, 119, 55.
45. Hendrik Hartog, *Man and Wife in America: A History* (Cambridge: Harvard University Press, 2000) 118. On "adventitious" rights and the scope of parental authority, compare generally Millar, *Distinction of Ranks*, 109–39.
46. Roscoe Pound, "The End of Law as Developed in Juristic Thought," *Harv. L. Rev.* 30 (1917): 201, 213; see also Roscoe Pound, *The Spirit of the Common Law* (Francestown, N.H.: Marshall Jones, 1921) 1–31.
47. Pound, "The End of Law," 203–4. See Roscoe Pound, "Law in Books and Law in Action," *Am. L. Rev.* 44 (1910): 12. For a recent study of Pound's historical and sociological jurisprudence, see David M. Rabban, *Law's History: American Legal Thought and the Transatlantic Turn to History* (Cambridge: Cambridge University Press, 2013) 423–71.
48. Pound, "The End of Law," 218 ("In the nineteenth century the feudal contribution to the common law was in disfavor. Jurists thought of individuals and contracts rather than of groups and relations. The conception of the abstract individual ruled in legal philosophy"). See generally Michael J. Sandel, *Democracy's Discontent: America in Search of a Public Philosophy* (Cambridge: Harvard University Press, 1996).
49. Pound, "The End of Law," 217.
50. Consider Pound on the law of agency: "In our law, . . . the central idea is rather relation. Thus, in case of agency the civilian thinks of an act, a manifestation of the will, whereby one person confers a power of representation upon another and of a legal giving effect to the will of him who confers it. Accordingly he talks of a contract of mandate or of a legal transaction of substitution. The common-law lawyer, on the other hand, thinks of the relation of principal and agent and of powers, rights, duties and liabilities, not as willed by the parties, but as incident to and involved in the relation. He, therefore, speaks of the relation of principal and agent." "The End of Law," 212 (footnotes omitted).
51. Pound, "Individual Interests in the Domestic Relations," *Mich. L. Rev.* 14 (1916): 177, 182. Pound, *Spirit of the Common Law*, 189.
52. William J. Novak, *The People's Welfare: Law and Regulation in Nineteenth-Century America* (Chapel Hill: University of North Carolina Press, 1996) 24, 26. See also generally Barry Alan Shain, *The Myth of American Individualism: The Protestant Origins of American Political Thought* (Princeton: Princeton University Press, 1994).

53. Rutgers v. Washington (1784), in *Select Cases of the Mayor's Court of New York City, 1674–1784*, ed. Richard B. Morris (Washington, D.C.: American Historical Association, 1935) 312, cited in Novak, *The People's Welfare*, 28–29.

54. Aaron Garrett, "Francis Hutcheson and the Origin of Animal Rights," *J. Hist. of Phil.* 45 (2007): 243, 249.

55. See generally Garry Wills, *Inventing America: Jefferson's Declaration of Independence* (New York: Doubleday, 1978) esp. 168–255. But see Gordon S. Wood, "'Influence' in History," in *The Purpose of the Past: Reflections on the Uses of History* (New York: Penguin Press, 2008) 17–29 (reviewing Garry Wills, *Explaining America: The Federalist* [New York: Doubleday, 1981]).

56. Garrett, "Francis Hutcheson," 257. Mark Hopkins, *Lectures on Moral Science* 256 (New York: Sheldon, 1876) 256, cited in Novak, *The People's Welfare*, 33. For a recent effort to link rights and responsibilities, see generally James E. Fleming and Linda C. McClain, *Ordered Liberty: Rights, Responsibilities, and Virtues* (Cambridge: Harvard University Press, 2013).

57. Novak, *The People's Welfare*, 33; see generally 19–50. On "The Bonds of Affection" in early American history, see Melvin Yazawa, *From Colonies to Commonwealth: Familial Ideology and the Beginnings of the American Republic* (Baltimore: Johns Hopkins University Press, 1985) 9–18; on "The Missing Dimension of Sociality" in modern law, see Mary Ann Glendon, *Rights Talk: The Impoverishment of Political Discourse* (New York: Free Press, 1991) 109–44.

58. Nathaniel Chipman, *Sketches of the Principles of Government* (Rutland, Vt.: J. Lyon, 1793) 34, cited in Novak, *The People's Welfare*, 34; see also Chipman, *Sketches*, 111–12 ("[Rights] arise in society and are relative to it. Antecedently to that state, they could only exist potentially. The rights of all have a reciprocal relation to the rights of each, and can never be rightly apprehended, distinct from that relation").

59. Michael Sandel, *Liberalism and the Limits of Justice* (Cambridge: Cambridge University Press, 1982) 133.

60. Novak, *The People's Welfare*, 34, 36, 38.

61. Pound, "The End of Law," 221.

62. Milton C. Regan Jr., *Family Law and the Pursuit of Intimacy* (New York: New York University Press, 1993) 122. Robin West, "Gay Marriage and Liberal Constitutionalism: Two Mistakes," in *Debating Democracy's Discontent: Essays on American Politics, Law, and Public Philosophy*, eds. Anita L. Allen and Milton C. Regan Jr. (New York: Oxford University Press, 1998) 260, 269.

63. Hochheimer, *The Custody of Infants* (1899), 23 (§ 22); see also 23 (§ 22) ("The English courts, at one period, adopted a system of deciding questions of custody according to certain fixed, general rules, irrespective of the true merits of specific cases. The result was a line of adjudications shocking to the moral sense"); 37–39 (§ 36) (listing "deplorable" cases).

64. Joel Prentiss Bishop, 2 *New Commentaries on Marriage, Divorce, and Separation* (Chicago: T. H. Flood, 1891) 454–55 (§ 1163) ("[T]his old barbarity [that treated the child as chattel] has gradually given way until the modern civilization concedes to the child the same human attributes which it acknowledges in the father. In the early periods of our common law in England, this consummation had not been fully reached; so that judicial precedents from those periods are not altogether authorities for the present. Yet the precedents have been improving from age to age. And the jurisprudence on this subject has travelled in most of our States more rapidly toward the light than in England") (footnote omitted); cf. Norma Basch, *Framing American Divorce: From the Revolutionary Generation to the Victorians* (Berkeley: University of California Press, 1999) 24 ("From both a substantive and procedural perspective, divorce law in the early republic was light years beyond its English equivalent").

65. Dixon v. Dixon, 2 Pa. C.C. 125 (Pa. Com. Pl. 1886).

66. See Yazawa, *From Colonies to Commonwealth*, 87–110 and passim; see also Jay Fliegelman, *Prodigals and Pilgrims: The American Revolution Against Patriarchal Authority, 1750–1800* (New York: Cambridge University Press, 1982) 9–35 and passim; Edwin G. Burrows and Michael Wallace, "The American Revolution: The Ideology and Psychology of National Liberation," *Perspectives in American History* 6 (1972): 167–306. Perhaps no other American voice so neatly summed up the young country's plaintive striving for independence as did Thomas Paine's cri de adolescent coeur: "Is it in the interest of a man to be a boy all his life?" On Paine, see Burrows and Wallace, 213–15.

67. Peter Charles Hoffer, *The Law's Conscience: Equitable Constitutionalism in America* (Chapel Hill: University of North Carolina Press, 1990) 72–73.

68. See, e.g., Richard Godbeer, *Sexual Revolution in Early America* (Baltimore: Johns Hopkins University Press, 2002) 334 (In the latter part of the eighteenth century, young people "exemplif[ied] a gradual but fundamental shift that was taking place in American society. Less constrained than their parents and grandparents by ties of family, neighborhood, dependency, and deference, they operated as free individuals and asserted their right to do so; these young adults enacted the principles of independence and freedom that patriot leaders enshrined in their revolutionary declarations"); Yazawa, *From Colonies to Commonwealth*, 198 ("It was impossible to confine the impact of the republican paradigm strictly to the sphere of civil relations. The school and the family had to accommodate the leveling forces set in motion by the Revolutionary experiment in politics. In the course of the nineteenth century, as classical republicanism was engulfed by egalitarian nationalism, the 'republic' itself became symbolically important as the standard by which to measure all forms of social interaction. The republican paradigm eventually came to exert from above the kind of influence that the familial paradigm had once exerted from below") (footnote omitted); cf. Basch, *Framing American Divorce*, 21

("[T]he impress of the Revolution [on American divorce law] was unmistakable. No sooner, it seems, did Americans create a rationale for dissolving the bonds of empire than they set about creating rules dissolving the bonds of matrimony").

69. James Henretta, *The Evolution of American Society, 1700–1815: An Interdisciplinary Analysis* (Lexington, Mass.: D. C. Heath, 1973) 30. On the emergence of the "republican" or "democratic" family, see Steven Mintz and Susan Kellogg, *Domestic Revolutions: A Social History of American Family Life* (New York: Free Press, 1988) 43–65; Michael Grossberg, *Governing the Hearth: Law and the Family in Nineteenth-Century America* (Chapel Hill: University of North Carolina Press, 1985) 3–30; Fliegelman, *Prodigals and Pilgrims*, 9–12; see also Gordon S. Wood, *The Radicalism of the American Revolution* (New York: Alfred A. Knopf, 1992) 145–68. For a brief survey of the historiography of childhood, see Hugh Cunningham, *Children and Childhood in Western Society since 1500* (Great Britain: Pearson Education, 2005) 3–15. See also generally Lawrence Stone, *The Family, Sex and Marriage in England 1500–1800* (New York: Harper and Row, 1977) 405–80; Philippe Ariès, *Centuries of Childhood: A Social History of Family Life* (New York: Alfred A. Knopf, 1962). But see generally Linda A. Pollock, *Forgotten Children: Parent-Child Relations from 1500 to 1900* (Cambridge: Cambridge University Press, 1983) (disputing thesis that postmedieval world witnessed a dramatic transformation in child-rearing practices).

70. Grossberg, *Governing the Hearth*, 234; cf. Wood, *Radicalism of the American Revolution*, 148 ("Although the family remained hierarchical, the mutual relationships of its nuclear members became more complicated. Sons were no longer seen simply as the representative of the stem line of the family, and after mid-century fathers were less apt to name a son after themselves. The individual desires now seemed to outweigh traditional concerns with family lineage") (footnote omitted).

71. Mary Ann Mason, *From Father's Property to Children's Rights: A History of Child Custody in the United States* (New York: Columbia University Press, 1994) 50.

72. Mintz and Kellogg, *Domestic Revolutions*, 47 (footnote omitted).

73. Mintz and Kellogg, *Domestic Revolutions*, 47.

74. Wood, *Radicalism of the American Revolution*, 148. On "enlightened paternalism," see Wood, 145–68. Jay Fliegelman reads popular eighteenth-century educational guidebooks as making the point that parents "thwart the development of their children's reason by insisting that they accept without examination or inquiry all doctrines taught them." *Prodigals and Pilgrims*, 14.

75. Philip Greven has shown how parental authoritarianism and social reclusion went hand in hand in American evangelical households of the seventeenth and eighteenth centuries: "Ideally, evangelical families consisted only of parents and children. . . . Within relatively isolated and self-contained households, the focus of authority and the source of love were united in the parents, who dominated the

household and determined the principles and practices that were to shape the temperaments of their offspring. Within the confines of the nuclear family, children found no alternatives, no defenses, no mitigation, no escape from the assertion of power and the rigorous repressiveness of their parents." Philip Greven, *The Protestant Temperament: Patterns of Child-Rearing, Religious Experience, and the Self in Early America* (New York: Alfred A. Knopf, 1977) 25; see also Greven, 28 ("Growing up in such households ensured that children would know from experience that parental power and authority were absolute and unquestionable").

76. Grossberg, *Governing the Hearth*, 236.

77. David Hoffman, *Legal Outlines* (Baltimore, 1836) 156.

78. See Mintz and Kellogg, *Domestic Revolutions*, 45; Fliegelman, *Prodigals and Pilgrims*, 4. On the influence of Locke on American educational theory and practice, see Holly Brewer, *By Birth or Consent: Children, Law, and the Anglo-American Revolution in Authority* (Chapel Hill: University of North Carolina Press, 2005) 108–28; Fliegelman, *Prodigals and Pilgrims*, 12–16; Wood, *Radicalism of the American Revolution*, 149–52.

79. Fliegelman, *Prodigals and Pilgrims*, 13.

80. John Milton, "Areopagitica," in *The Prose of John Milton*, ed. J. Max Patrick (New York: New York University Press, 1968) (1644) 287; cf. Locke, "Some Thoughts Concerning Education," § 45 ("He that has not a Mastery over his Inclinations, he that knows not how to *resist* the importunity of *present Pleasure or Pain*, for the sake of what Reason tells him is fit to be done, wants the true Principle of Vertue and Industry, and is in Danger never to be good for any thing").

81. See Matthew 10: 24–30.

82. Fliegelman, *Prodigals and Pilgrims*, 19 (discussing Isaac Watts's pedagogical treatise *Improvement of the Mind* [1747]).

83. Wood, *Radicalism of the American Revolution*, 148–49 (footnote omitted); cf. Henretta, *The Evolution of American Society*, 30 ("[F]athers had begun to consider their role not as that of patriarchs . . . , but rather as that of benefactors responsible for the future well-being and prosperity of their offspring").

84. Fliegelman, *Prodigals and Pilgrims*, 20 (discussing Watts's *Improvement of the Mind*), 14, 20 (discussing Watts).

85. Benjamin Rush, "Thoughts upon the Mode of Education Proper in a Republic" (1786), in *Essays on Education in the Early Republic*, ed. Frederick Rudolph (Cambridge: Harvard University Press, 1965) 11.

86. Mintz and Kellogg, *Domestic Revolutions*, 47. Fliegelman, *Prodigals and Pilgrims*, 14. Reinier, *From Virtue to Character*, 19.

87. Samuel Harrison Smith, "Remarks on Education: Illustrating the Close Connection Between Virtue and Wisdom" (1798), in *Essays on Education in the Early Republic*, ed. Frederick Rudolph (Cambridge: Harvard University Press, 1965) 210.

In 1797 the prize was awarded jointly to Smith and Samuel Knox. Compare Robert Coram, "Political Inquiries: to Which is Added, a Plan for the General Establishment of Schools throughout the United States" (1791), in *Essays on Education in the Early Republic*, ed. Frederick Rudolph (Cambridge: Harvard University Press, 1965) 113 ("Education should not be left to the caprice or negligence of parents"); cf. also Kaestle, *Pillars of the Republic*, 158 ("[Nineteenth-century] [s]chool reformers argued the precedence of state responsibility over traditional parental responsibility for education. Hiram Barney, Ohio's school commissioner in 1854, wrote that 'for educational purposes, the State may with propriety be regarded as one great School District, and the population as constituting but one family, charged with the parental duty of educating all its youth'").

88. Smith, *Remarks on Education*, 190. Smith would make it "punishable by law in a parent to neglect offering his child to the preceptor for education." *Remarks*, 210; cf. Michael Grossberg, "Changing Conceptions of Child Welfare in the United States, 1820–1935," in *A Century of Juvenile Justice*, ed. Margaret K. Rosenheim et al. (Chicago: University of Chicago Press, 2002) 14–15.

89. Yazawa, *From Colonies to Commonwealth*, 183. For an introduction to American constitutionalism, the republican tradition, and the "republican revival" in legal scholarship, see Frank I. Michelman, "The Supreme Court, 1985 Term—Foreword: Traces of Self-Government," *Harv. L. Rev.* 100 (1986): 4; cf. Richard H. Fallon Jr., "What Is Republicanism, and Is It Worth Reviving?" *Harv. L. Rev.* 102 (1989): 1695.

90. Rush, "Thoughts upon the Mode of Education Proper in a Republic," 14. For Rush, we remain public property until the end of our days. In 1788 he advised John Dickinson that "[e]ven our old age is not our own property. All its fruits of wisdom and experience belong to the public." 1 *Letters of Benjamin Rush*, ed. L. H. Butterfield (Princeton: Princeton University Press, 1951) 478.

91. George Washington, "Eighth Annual Message to Congress," December 7, 1796, quoted in David Tyack, Thomas James, and Aaron Benavot, *Law and the Shaping of Public Education, 1785–1954* (Madison: University of Wisconsin Press, 1987) 163. On early efforts to create national educational uniformity, see, for example, Yazawa, *From Colonies to Commonwealth*, 141–81; David Tyack, "Forming the National Character: Paradox in the Educational Thought of the Revolutionary Generation," *Harv. Educ. Rev.* 36 (1966): 29, 29–37.

92. Lawrence Cremin, *American Education: The Colonial Experience, 1607–1783* (New York: Harper and Row, 1970) 193, 124, 124, 181–82, 196–201; cf. Kent, 2 *Commentaries*, 238 n.(g).

93. Tapping Reeve, *Law of Baron and Femme* (New Haven: Oliver Steele, 1816) 287.

94. Kent, 2 *Commentaries*, 233; cf. Reeve, *Law of Baron and Femme*, 287 ("[I]f the parents will not teach their children in such manner, the selectmen of the town

are enjoined to take their children from their parents, and bind them out to proper masters, where they will be educated to some useful employment, and will be taught to read and write, and the rules of arithmetic, so far as is necessary to transact ordinary business").

95. Cf. S. M. Heslet, "Compulsory Education," *Illinois Teacher* 14 (March 1868): 86, 87 ("The man that will not feed and clothe his children is compelled to surrender them, that they may be fed and clothed at public expense. . . . Should not he, then, who starves the minds of his children be compelled to send them where mental food is furnished free of charge?").

96. The Massachusetts School Act of 1647, popularly known as the Old Deluder Satan Law, equated educational neglect with a satanic project "to keep men from a knowledge of the Scriptures." On the colonial school as a forum for moral and religious education, see generally, for example, Cremin, *American Education*, 167–95, 271–412. Cf. generally David Tyack, "The Kingdom of God and the Common School: Protestant Ministers and the Educational Awakening in the West," *Harv. Educ. Rev.* 36 (1966): 447.

97. Reeve, *Law of Baron and Femme*, 286. Compare the Protestant outlook of Horace Mann: "[O]ur system earnestly inculcates all Christian morals; it founds its morals on the basis of religion; it welcomes the religion of the Bible; and, in receiving the Bible, it allows it to do what it is allowed to do in no other system, — to speak for itself. But here it stops, not because it claims to have compassed all truth, but because it disclaims to act as an umpire between hostile religious opinions." *Church and State in the Modern Age: A Documentary History*, ed. J. F. Maclear (New York: Oxford University Press, 1995) 208 (quoting Twelfth Annual Report of the Massachusetts Board of Education [1848] 116–17).

98. Cremin, *American Education*, 394 ("[T]he key that opened the path to salvation also opened the door to opportunity, and the coincidence could not have been lost on ambitious youngsters"); cf. Cremin, *American Education*, 192 ("[S]chools inevitably liberated at the same time that they socialized, and many a colonial youngster was doubtless freed from the social and intellectual constraints of a particular household, church, or neighborhood by attending a nearby school, which opened doors to new ideas, new occupations, and new life styles").

99. Reeve, *Law of Baron and Femme*, 287.

100. Thomas Jefferson, "The Statute of Virginia for Religious Freedom," in *The Virginia Statute for Religious Freedom: Its Evolution and Consequences for American History*, xvii. It has been noted that Jefferson's vision of civil liberties had its dark side. See generally, e.g., Leonard W. Levy, *Jefferson and Civil Liberties: The Darker Side* (Cambridge: Harvard University Press, 1963); Tyack, "Forming the National Character: Paradox in the Educational Thought of the Revolutionary Generation," 29, 37–40.

101. Jefferson, "The Statute of Virginia for Religious Freedom," xvii.
102. Jefferson, "The Statute of Virginia for Religious Freedom," xvii.
103. Jefferson, "The Statute of Virginia for Religious Freedom," xvii; cf. William E. Nelson, *Americanization of the Common Law: The Impact of Legal Change on Massachusetts Society, 1760–1830* (Athens: University of Georgia Press, 1975) 115 ("By the 1820s, if not earlier, it was clear to most that the age of moral certainty had passed and that truth could no longer be seen as a unitary set of values formulated by God and readily ascertainable by man. Men now viewed truth and morality as human values that might vary over time and place and believed that nothing existed that could 'not be plausibly argued with . . . much semblance of truth'") (quoting Caleb Cushing, *The Right of Universalists to Testify in a Court of Justice Vindicated* [1828] 26) (footnote omitted).
104. United States v. Bainbridge, 24 Fed. Cas. 946, 949 (D. Mass. 1816). Justice Story again asserted the contingent nature of custodial authority in *United States v. Green*, 26 F. Cas. 30, 31–32 (C.C.R.I. 1824) ("As to the question of the right of the father to have the custody of his infant child, in a general sense it is true. But this is not on account of any absolute right of the father, but for the benefit of the infant, the law presuming it to be for his interest to be under the nurture and care of his natural protector, both for maintenance and education. When, therefore, the court is asked to lend its aid to put the infant into the custody of the father, and to withdraw him from other persons, it will look into all the circumstances, and ascertain whether it will be for the real, permanent interests of the infant; and if the infant be of sufficient discretion, it will also consult its personal wishes. It will free it from all undue restraint, and endeavour, as far as possible, to administer a conscientious, parental duty with reference to its welfare. It is an entire mistake to suppose the court is at all events bound to deliver over the infant to his father, or that the latter has an absolute vested right in the custody").
105. See 2 U.S. 197, 197–99 (Pa. 1793). On the early development of apprenticeship law, see Grossberg, *Governing the Hearth*, 259–68.
106. 24 Fed. Cas. at 949–50.
107. Grossberg, *Governing the Hearth*, 239. "Custody rulings increasingly devalued paternally oriented property-based standards," writes Grossberg, "emphasizing instead maternally biased considerations of child nature." *Governing the Hearth*, 238. On judicial deference to the cult of motherhood, see Mason, *From Father's Property to Children's Rights*, 50–54. By the end of the nineteenth century, it would not be unusual for courts to declare that "[t]he mother is the natural guardian, and, under the general rule, is entitled to the custody of her child." In re Snook, 38 P. 272 (Kan. 1894); cf. Peter Bardaglio, *Reconstructing the Household: Families, Sex, and the Law in the Nineteenth-Century South* (Chapel Hill: University of North Carolina Press, 1995) 138 ("By the end of the nineteenth century, . . . most

southern appellate courts no longer assumed that the father had a paramount right to his child. Instead, the courts generally concurred that the mother was best fitted to have responsibility for child rearing, and therefore in determining custody they gave her preference").

108. State ex rel. Paine v. Paine, 23 Tenn. 523, 536 (1843).

109. See 23 Tenn. at 534–35.

110. See Hartog, *Man and Wife in America*, 212.

111. Paine v. Paine, 23 Tenn. at 533–34.

112. Grossberg, *Governing the Hearth*, 248.

113. 2 Root 461, 461–62 (Conn. Sup. Ct. 1796).

114. See, e.g., Kent, 2 *Commentaries*, 231 ("The father may obtain the custody of his children by the writ of *habeas corpus*, when they are improperly detained from him; but the courts, both of law and equity, will investigate the circumstances according to sound discretion") (footnote omitted). Hurd notes that "[t]he powers of a judge or court of law are the same as those of a chancellor or court of equity under the writ. It has sometimes been supposed that a chancellor or a court of equity possessed ampler powers under the writ of habeas corpus, than a judge or court of law could exercise. But this is a mistake. The jurisdiction in such cases and the powers under the writ are exactly the same." Rollin C. Hurd, *A Treatise on the Right of Personal Liberty and on the Writ of Habeas Corpus*, 2d ed. (Albany: W. C. Little, 1876) 455 (internal quotation marks and citation omitted). In a habeas action involving the custody of a child, as Hurd points out, the chief aim of a court of law, technically, is to relieve the child from improper restraint: "[The court of law] acts upon the present actual condition of the parties and for the present. It does not undertake what their *future* relations shall be. It takes care that the infant shall not leave the court under injurious custody, and *expects* that the custody to which it is committed will continue while the circumstances shown in evidence remain unaltered, but it does not *command* that it shall thus continue." Hurd, 458. In practice, however, courts of law did make orders, as Hurd acknowledges, "of a somewhat more mandatory and prospective nature." Hurd, 459. Consider the complaint of founding father John Dickinson that "it would be much properer to say every court [in Pennsylvania] is a court of equity, for both judges and juries think it hard to deny a man that relief which he can obtain no where else, and without reflecting that equity never intermeddles but where law denies *all manner* of assistance, every judgment, every verdict is a confused mixture of private passions and popular error, and every court assumes the power of legislation." Gordon S. Wood, *The Creation of the American Republic, 1776–1787* (New York: W. W. Norton, 1969) 298 (footnote omitted). Wood notes the irony that accompanied American ambivalence toward equity: "[T]he same legal complexities that were responsible for the much resented abuses of magisterial will were also responsible for the

colonists' central concern for reason and equity in their law." Wood, *The Creation of the American Republic*, 298. For an overview of the emergence of equity law in America, see Stanley N. Katz, "The Politics of Law in Colonial America: Controversies over Chancery Courts and Equity Law in the Eighteenth Century," in *Law in American History*, eds. Donald Fleming and Bernard Bailyn (Boston: Little, Brown, 1971) 257. Katz points out that American opposition to equity law was directed more toward the operation of the chancery courts than to equitable legal principles themselves. See Katz, "Politics of Law," 282–83. See generally Hoffer, *The Law's Conscience*, 47–106.

115. 3 Burr. 1434, 1436–37 (K.B. 1763). On the infant discretion rule, see, for example, Grossberg, *Governing the Hearth*, 388 n.56 (1985) (citing cases where children's wishes became the decisive factor in a final custody decision).

116. See William S. Church, *A Treatise on the Writ of Habeas Corpus*, 2d ed. (San Francisco: Bancroft-Whitney, 1893) 718–19 (§ 445) ("[O]ne rule generally prevails throughout the United States and that is substantially the one laid down by Lord Mansfield in *Rex v. Delaval*. . . . That the order of the court is discretionary will be found in nearly all of the cases"); Hurd, *Habeas Corpus*, 465 ("[T]he equitable doctrine maintained in [*Rex v. Delaval*] has been commonly practiced in this country and may now be considered as thoroughly incorporated in the American common law"). Mary Ann Mason writes that "[t]he tradition of judicial discretion became so firmly imbedded that many judges often gave no more than lip service to precedent, or even to legislation in their own state, but instead sought to probe tangled fact situations to discover the best interests of the individual child." *From Father's Property to Children's Rights*, 59 (footnote omitted); cf., e.g., Commonwealth v. Addicks, 5 Binn. 520, 520 (Pa. 1815); State v. Smith, 6 Greenl. 462, 468 (Me. 1830); Mercein v. People ex rel. Barry, 25 Wend. 64, 105 (N.Y. 1840); Corrie v. Corrie, 4 N.W. 213, 214 (Mich. 1880).

117. Paine v. Paine, 23 Tenn. at 535. Where courts "had asserted their inability to resolve any custody disputes by habeas corpus, legislatures enacted measures that authorized use of the writ of habeas corpus in custody battles between husband and wife and specifically empowered the court to award custody according to the welfare of the child." Dallin H. Oaks, "Habeas Corpus in the States—1776–1865," *U. Chi. L. Rev.* 32 (1965): 243, 273 (footnotes omitted).

118. Danaya C. Wright, "The Crisis of Child Custody: A History of the Birth of Family Law in England," *Colum. J. Gender & L.* 11 (2002): 175, 183. Cf. generally Sarah Abramowicz, Note, "English Child Custody Law, 1660–1839: The Origins of Judicial Intervention in Paternal Custody," *Colum. L. Rev.* 99 (1999): 1344.

119. De Manneville v. De Manneville, 32 Eng. Rep. 762, 763 (Ch. 1804). Though Lord Eldon "approv[ed] the general rule that fathers have custodial rights to their children," nonetheless he "acknowledged that certain actions on the part of the father

would justify judicial interference with his custodial rights." Wright, "The Crisis of Child Custody," 191–92. James Kent reads the *De Manneville* case as stating that "the jurisdiction of the Court of Chancery to control the right of the father *prima facie* to the person of the child was unquestionably established." Kent, 2 *Commentaries*, 221.

120. Wright, "The Crisis of Child Custody," 190 (note omitted). Wright's conclusions have not gone unchallenged. See Eileen Spring, Comment, "Child Custody and the Decline of Women's Rights," *L. & Hist. Rev.* 17 (1999): 315; cf. Michael Grossberg, Comment, "Who Determines Children's Best Interests?" *L. & Hist. Rev.* 17 (1999): 309 (calling into question whether the trajectory of change in custody law was as linear as Wright suggests).

121. Jamil S. Zainaldin, "The Emergence of a Modern American Family Law: Child Custody, Adoption, and the Courts," *Nw. U. L. Rev.* 73 (1979): 1038, 1063. Zainaldin notes how "English courts backed away from Lord Mansfield's judicial discretion position." But this reaction was not merely a return to the pre-Mansfield doctrinal status quo: "The nineteenth-century English judges adopted a patriarchal paradigm of family relations and applied it to the law with such force and vigor that it had the effect of creating new paternal rights, the existence of which had only been vaguely hinted at by previous judges."

122. Mercein, 25 Wend. at 93.

123. 25 Wend. at 106 (opinion of Alonzo C. Paige). But see Ahrenfeldt v. Ahrenfeldt, 1 Hoff. Ch. 497, 499, 501 (N.Y. Ch. 1840) ("The decisions . . . prove the rule to be clearly settled in England, that with perhaps the exception of very early infancy, there is no equality of right between father and mother; but the claim of the former is paramount. They prove that he will always be aided in its assertion; unless his conduct is such, as that it would endanger the bodily or moral welfare of the child. . . . It is very clear however, that upon a habeas corpus our court has paid much less respect to the authority of a father than is done in England. . . . Carefully considering [prior] decisions, I cannot but conclude that the doctrine of the common law has not been overthrown, although it has been weakened in the United States; that still upon a question of guardianship, with the exception of very tender infancy, a positive unfitness in the father must be shown before children can be withheld or withdrawn from his charge").

124. Hartog, *Man and Wife in America*, 119 ("[T]he English legal doctrine that granted husbands complete custodial control over their children, . . . a doctrinal structure that reformers characterized as the embodiment of archaic and barbarous patriarchy, was actually a recent invention").

125. Prather v. Prather, 4 Desau. 33, 38, 44 (S.C. App. 1809).

126. 1 P.A. Browne 143, 144–45 (Pa. Ct. Com. Pl. 1810).

127. 8 Johns. 328, 332 (N.Y. 1811).

128. Commonwealth v. Addicks, 2 Serg. & Rawle 174 (Pa. 1815).

129. See 5 Binn. 520 (Pa. 1813).

130. 2 Serg. & Rawle at 176–77.

131. Report of the D'Hauteville Case (Philadelphia, 1840) 289–91. See generally Michael Grossberg, *A Judgment for Solomon: The d'Hauteville Case and Legal Experience in Antebellum America* (Cambridge: Cambridge University Press, 1996).

132. Report of the D'Hauteville Case, 290 (citing People v. Nickerson, 19 Wend. 16, 19 [N.Y. Sup. 1837]). Michael Grossberg calls attention to an anonymous article published in protest of the *d'Hauteville* decision. See *Governing the Hearth*, 241–42. With unintentional prescience, the outraged author (self-described as "not [one] of those who entertain constant fears of judicial encroachments on private rights") objected that the decision was "nothing less than an assumption of power by a court to determine in regard to the domestic arrangements of a man's family. . . . This is certainly a most singular interference with domestic rights. If a court may upon the process of habeas corpus, sued out by a wife, control the wishes of a father on account of the age and health of his children, what is to prevent their interference as against both parents?" See [Peleg W. Chandler], *Review of the D'Hauteville Case* (Boston: Weeks, Jordan, 1841) 41; see also *Review*, 29–34 (reviewing American cases).

133. In re Waldron, 13 Johns. 418, 418–19 (N.Y. Sup. 1816).

134. Grossberg, *Governing the Hearth*, 234, 237.

135. Bardaglio, *Reconstructing the Household*, 137, 165. Bardaglio observes how "the law deemphasized the rights of biological parents and began to assess custodial qualifications on the basis of ability to fulfill certain duties." This assumption of authority amounted to a "systematic attempt to link women and children directly with the state." *Reconstructing the Household*, 137.

136. Hochheimer, *The Custody of Infants* (1899), 2 (§ 2) (footnote omitted); see also Mercein, 25 Wend. at 103 ("The moment a child is born, it owes allegiance to the government of the country of its birth, and is entitled to the protection of that government"); Bishop, 2 *New Commentaries on Marriage, Divorce, and Separation*, 452 (§ 1160) ("[T]he child has its own independent rights, the chief whereof is the promotion of its well-being") (footnote omitted). Michael Grossberg writes that "[p]erhaps the most enduring product of the distinctive domestic-relations law hammered out in nineteenth-century America was the legal concept of the family as a collection of separate legal individuals rather than an organic part of the body politic. This occurred at the expense of traditional notions of parental sovereignty and household legal unity." *Governing the Hearth*, 304.

137. Hochheimer, *The Custody of Infants* (1899), 2 (§ 2).

138. Bishop, 2 *New Commentaries on Marriage, Divorce, and Separation*, 448 (§ 1151) (footnote omitted).

139. Hochheimer, *The Custody of Infants* (1899), 22 (§ 22).
140. Bishop, 2 *New Commentaries on Marriage, Divorce, and Separation*, 452–53 (§ 1160) (footnote omitted).
141. Bishop, *Commentaries on the Law of Marriage and Divorce* (Boston: Little, Brown, 1852) 526 (§ 643).
142. Wilson v. Mitchell, 111 P. 21, 25 (Colo. 1910).
143. See, e.g., Allison v. Bryan, 97 P. 282, 286 (Okla. 1908) ("A child is primarily a ward of the state. The sovereign has the inherent power to legislate for its welfare, and to place it with either parent at will, or take it from both parents and to place it elsewhere"). On the state's parens patriae authority, see, for example, Lawrence Custer, "The Origins of the Doctrine of Parens Patriae," *Emory L.J.* 27 (1978): 195; George B. Curtis, "The Checkered Career of Parens Patriae: The State as Parent or Tyrant?" *DePaul L. Rev.* 25 (1976): 895; Douglas Rendleman, "Parens Patriae: From Chancery to the Juvenile Court," *S.C. L. Rev.* 23 (1971): 205; Neil Howard Cogan, "Juvenile Law, Before and After the Entrance of 'Parens Patriae,'" *S.C. L. Rev.* 22 (1970): 147; see also John Seymour, "Parens Patriae and Wardship Powers: Their Nature and Origins," *Oxford J. Legal Stud.* 14 (1994): 159, 159–62, 178–87.
144. In re Lippincott v. Lippincott, 124 A. 532, 533 (N.J. Ch. 1924).
145. State v. Bailey, 61 N.E. 730, 731–32 (Ind. 1901); cf. State ex rel. Kelley v. Ferguson, 144 N.W. 1039, 1044 (Neb. 1914).
146. Cowles v. Cowles, 3 Gilman 435, 437 (Ill. 1846); cf. Moore v. Dozier, 57 S.E. 110, 111 (Ga. 1907); Wilson v. Mitchell, 111 P. at 25; Risting v. Sparboe, 162 N.W. 592, 594 (Iowa 1917).
147. State v. Bailey, 61 N.E. at 731–32.
148. Wilson v. Mitchell, 111 P. at 25.
149. State v. Clottu, 33 Ind. 409, 412 (1870); cf. State v. Shorey, 86 P. 881, 882 (Or. 1906).
150. See State v. Shorey, 86 P. at 882 ("Laws prohibiting the employment of adult males for more than a stated number of hours per day or week are not valid unless reasonably necessary to protect the public health, safety, morals or general welfare, because the right to labor or employ labor on such terms as may be agreed upon is a liberty or property right guaranteed to such persons by the fourteenth amendment to the Constitution of the United States, and with which the state cannot interfere. But laws regulating the right of minors to contract do not come within this principle. They are not sui juris, and can only contract to a limited extent. They are wards of the state and subject to its control. As to them the state stands in the position of parens patriae and may exercise unlimited supervision and control over their contracts, occupation, and conduct, and the liberty and right of those who assume to deal with them. This is a power which inheres in the government for its own preservation and for the protection of the life, person, health, and morals of its future citizens") (citing Lochner v. New York, 198 U.S. 45 [1905]).

151. Ernst Freund, *The Police Power: Public Policy and Constitutional Rights* (Chicago: Callaghan, 1904) 247–48 (§ 259).
152. Hochheimer, *The Custody of Infants* (1887) 13 (§ 4).
153. State v. Shorey, 86 P. at 882.
154. State v. Clottu, 33 Ind. at 412; cf. State v. Shorey, 86 P. at 882.
155. Mercein, 25 Wend. at 101; see also Hochheimer, *The Custody of Infants* (1899), 2 (§ 2) ("The only limitations upon the governmental power are those resulting from the obligation towards the infant himself").
156. McKercher v. Green, 58 P. 406, 409 (Colo. App. 1899) (citation omitted).
157. Mercein, 25 Wend. at 103.
158. Joseph Story, 2 *Equity Jurisprudence* (Boston: Hilliard, Gray, 1836) 575 (§ 1341); cf. Legate v. Legate, 28 S.W. 281, 282 (Tex. 1894).
159. The Etna, 8 F. Cas. 803, 804 (D. Me. 1838).
160. Mercein, 25 Wend. at 103.
161. Legate v. Legate, 28 S.W. at 282.
162. Hochheimer, *The Custody of Infants* (1899), 4 (§ 4) (citation and internal quotation marks omitted); cf. *The Custody of Infants* (1887), 41 (§10) ("This delegation of power is a trust, designed to secure the best interests of those for whose benefit it was created. Its continuance in the persons so designated . . . is conditioned upon the faithful performance of the trust").
163. Mercein, 25 Wend. at 103; cf. State v. Smith, 6 Greenl. at 464.
164. Hochheimer, *The Custody of Infants* (1899), 31 (§ 30) (footnote omitted).
165. See Hochheimer, *The Custody of Infants* (1899), 37 (§ 35).
166. 4 Whart. 9, 11 (Pa. 1839).
167. 4 Whart. at 11; cf. State v. Kilvington, 100 Tenn. 227 (1898); Farnham v. Pierce, 6 N.E. 830, 831 (Mass. 1886); Prescott v. State, 19 Ohio St. 184, 188 (Ohio 1869). But see Bryant v. Brown, 118 So. 184, 194 (Miss. 1928) ("It cannot be said truthfully that the Industrial Training School in this state is not a penal institute. It is as much a penal institution as the modern, well-regulated, humanely managed penitentiary. Its inmates are restrained of their liberty of action, notwithstanding the purpose of the law is to reform and educate them"). On the House of Refuge reform movement and judicial reaction, see, for example, Sanford J. Fox, "Juvenile Justice Reform: An Historical Perspective," *Stan. L. Rev.* 22 (1970): 1187, 1187–1221; for a general overview of nineteenth-century child welfare policies and programs, see Grossberg, "Changing Conceptions of Child Welfare," 3.
168. Ex parte Crouse, 4 Whart at 11; cf. Commonwealth v. Fisher, 62 A. 198 (Pa. 1905).
169. 4 Whart. at 11.
170. Mercein, 25 Wend. at 101.
171. 25 Wend. at 101 (quoting In re Waldron, 13 Johns. 418 [N.Y. Sup. 1816]). On the complicated history of the case, see Hartog, *Man and Wife in America*, 193–217;

see also Hendrik Hartog, "John Barry's Custodial Rights: Of Power, Justice, and Coverture," in *Justice and Power in Sociological Studies*, eds. Bryant G. Garth and Austin Sarat (Evanston: Northwestern University Press, 1997) 166.

172. 25 Wend. at 101.

173. The Court of Errors consisted of the president of the state senate, the senators, the chancellor, and the judges of the state supreme court. See Francis Bergan, *The History of the New York Court of Appeals, 1847–1932* (New York: Columbia University Press, 1985) 9. In *Mercein*, the chancellor did not deliver a written opinion. He stated orally that "the American cases . . . showed it to be the established law of this country that the court, or officer, were authorized to exercise a discretion, and that the father was not entitled to demand a delivery of the child to him, upon habeas corpus, as an absolute right." English law to the contrary, the chancellor said, reflected "the principles of a semi-barbarous age, when the wife was the slave of the husband, because he had the physical power to control her, and when the will of the strongest party constituted the rule of right." 25 Wend. at 93.

174. Mercein, 25 Wend. at 101–02.

175. 25 Wend. at 103.

176. 25 Wend. at 103.

177. Hartog, *Man and Wife in America*, 210–11.

178. Thomas M. Cooley, *A Treatise on the Constitutional Limitations Which Rest upon the Legislative Power of the States of the American Union* (Boston: Little, Brown, 1868) 348 (emphasis added).

179. In re Gregg, 5 New York Legal Observer 265, 267 (N.Y. Super. 1847).

180. Hartog, *Man and Wife in America*, 211, 216.

181. See Hartog, *Man and Wife in America*, 211–16 (citing cases). Hartog makes the important point that "[n]early all of these cases [i.e., cases asserting a paternal custody privilege] involved struggles for custody between a husband and a wife who had 'voluntarily' separated herself from her husband and who was not, as a result, entitled to a legal divorce." The critical question was whether the separation was justified. Hartog, *Man and Wife in America*, 212; see also Zainaldin, "The Emergence of a Modern American Family Law," 1059–68 (describing "traditionalist interlude" of the 1830s); Douglas R. Rendleman, "Parens Patriae: From Chancery to the Juvenile Court," 233 (noting that the development of governmental authority to control family affairs was not "without some setbacks"); cf. Bardaglio, *Reconstructing the Household*, 163 ("Despite the considerable inroads that surrogate parents and the state made into the custodial rights of biological parents, the older view of superior parental rights remained influential in the postwar South").

182. Hartog, *Man and Wife in America*, 217. Hartog argues that the notion of parens patriae "would not have made sense to most judges without the prior existence of private rights. Parens patriae epitomized the public values of a legitimate public

sphere, of the state's growing responsibility to assure 'the best interests of the child.' As such, it would often (depending on the judge's sensibility and the precedents he found available to him) take precedence over traditional parental (husband's) rights. It was not, however, understood as an abrogation of those rights." *Man and Wife in America*, 216–17.

183. In re Gregg, 5 New York Legal Observer at 267 (emphasis added). William Gregg's claim was defeated. Taking into account the tender age and delicate health of infant Gregg, the court gave custody of the child to its mother. 5 New York Legal Observer at 268.

184. See generally Jill Elaine Hasday, "Parenthood Divided: A Legal History of the Bifurcated Law of Parental Relations," *Geo. L.J.* 90 (2002): 299; Platt, *The Child Savers*, 135; cf. generally Jacobus tenBroek, "California's Dual System of Family Law: Its Origin, Development, and Present Status" (Part I), *Stan. L. Rev.* 16 (1964): 257. The same argument could be made against most other public welfare measures, like public health regulations. See, e.g., Novak, *The People's Welfare*, 214–17.

185. See, e.g., John E. B. Myers, *Child Protection in America: Past, Present, and Future* (New York: Oxford University Press, 2006) 11–13; cf. Lee E. Teitelbaum, "Family History and Family Law," *Wis. L. Rev.* 1985 (1985): 1135, 1157 ("Nineteenth century public concern with child-rearing, it seems, was pervasive, however much Americans may have considered the home a private refuge. It reached children who, at any time, would be considered public problems by reason of their criminal behavior, those who engaged in non-criminal but undisciplined conduct, children whose circumstances suggested that they might become deviant ((by reason of neglect or dependency)), and 'normal' children whose education was nonetheless considered a governmental as well as a family responsibility. Moreover, official concern for child development was expressed daily in custody disputes").

186. Michael Grossberg, "'A Protected Childhood': The Emergence of Child Protection in America," in *American Public Life and the Historical Imagination*, eds. Wendy Gamber, Michael Grossberg, and Hendrik Hartog (Notre Dame: University of Indiana Press, 2003) 213, 218, 220.

187. Stephanie Coontz, *The Social Origins of Private Life: A History of American Families, 1600–1900* (London: Verso, 1988) 272.

188. Reva B. Siegel, "'The Rule of Love': Wife Beating as Prerogative and Privacy," *Yale L.J.* 105 (1996): 2117, 2150–61.

189. See Siegel, "'Rule of Love,'" 2154–56; cf. Wright, "The Crisis of Child Custody," 205 ("When [Lord] Eldon put a brake on the court's interference with paternal rights in *De Manneville*, he was clearly concerned with the explosive potential of inter-spousal legal disputes, not with the well-established power of the courts to interfere in the personal exercise of familial power or in jurisdictional disputes between the benches. And in the next thirty-five years, fear of opening that domestic

can of worms resulted in a law that was so strict and patriarchal that it went against virtually every well-established value recognized by the common law").

190. 61 N.C. (Phil.) 453, 459 (1868).

191. Hasday, "Parenthood Divided," 317 n.49 ("The most interesting aspect of this appearance of privacy discourse [in *State v. Rhodes*, 61 N.C. (Phil.) 453, 456 (1868)], however, is how much of a rarity such discourse was"); cf. Hasday, "Parenthood Divided," 317 n.49 ("Some scholars have assumed that nineteenth-century common law authorities deferred to parental prerogatives of correction out of a belief in the privacy of the family. Yet such presumptions are quite ahistorical. Privacy arguments began to dominate the jurisprudence on wife beating in the late nineteenth century, as feminist agitation and cultural celebrations of companionate marriage made authoritarian rationales for nonintervention seem less and less persuasive in that context") (internal quotation marks and citation omitted).

192. See, e.g., Wilson v. Mitchell, 111 P. at 26; In re Neff, 56 P. 383, 384 (Wash. 1899).

193. See, e.g., Monk v. McDaniel, 42 S.E. 360, 363 (Ga. 1902).

194. 37 Ark. 27 (1881).

195. See Hasday, "Parenthood Divided," 312.

196. Verser, 37 Ark. at 29–31.

197. Hartog, *Man and Wife in America*, 151–52.

198. See, e.g., Hurd, *Habeas Corpus*, 535–36 ("The court prefers to exercise its own judgment in each case upon the competency of the child. It looks to the capacity, information, intelligence and judgment of the child. . . . It is notorious that children attain this capacity at different ages; some, indeed, hardly ever. A procrustean rule, then, that a child's fitness to choose should be determined by his age and not his mental capacity might save the court some trouble, but would not be likely to subserve the best interests of the child").

199. Cf. Ahrenfeldt v. Ahrenfeldt, 1 Hoff. Ch. at 502 (looking upon state custody statute as "placing the parents on an equality as to the future custody of the children, even if it does not create a presumption in favor of the wife").

200. Report of the D'Hauteville Case, 292–93 (Philadelphia 1840) ("[I]f the father's right of custody could be forfeited only by immoral conduct or character, or by his unfitness to superintend the moral and intellectual culture of his child, there has been nothing developed in the present case which could properly interpose to take away from him that right. But I cannot believe that the exceptions to such right are circumscribed in so limited a circle—the reputation of the father may be stainless as crystal, he may not be afflicted with the slightest mental, moral, or physical disqualification from superintending the general welfare of the infant . . . and yet the interest of the child may imperatively demand the denial of the father's right, and its continuance with the mother"). But see, e.g., Ahrenfeldt v. Ahrenfeldt, 1 Hoff. Ch. at 499–501; Commonwealth v. Briggs, 16 Pick. 203, 204 (Mass. 1834).

201. See Cook v. Cook, 1 Barb. Ch. 639 (N.Y. Ch. 1846).
202. Foster v. Alston, 7 Miss. (6 Howard) 406, 457 (Miss. Err. & App. 1842) (citation omitted).
203. Teitelbaum, "Family History and Family Law," 1157.
204. See, e.g., Barbara Bennett Woodhouse, "'Who Owns the Child?': *Meyer* and *Pierce* and the Child as Property," *Wm. & Mary L. Rev.* 33 (1992): 995, 1050–68.
205. Christopher G. Tiedeman, *A Treatise on the Limitations of Police Power in the United States* (St. Louis: F. H. Thomas Law Book, 1886) 554.
206. Tiedeman, *Limitations of Police Power*, v–vi.
207. Tiedeman, *Limitations of Police Power*, vi–vii.
208. Tiedeman, *Limitations of Police Power*, 1, 4.
209. Tiedeman, *Limitations of Police Power*, 551–53.
210. Tiedeman, *Limitations of Police Power*, 554.
211. *Social Statics; or, The Conditions Essential to Human Happiness* (New York: Appleton and Co., 1872), 179, 121, 192, 199–200, 194.
212. Tiedeman, *Limitations of Police Power*, 561 (quoting Philemon Bliss, *On Sovereignty* [1865] 17).
213. Tiedeman, *Limitations of Police Power*, 554, 561.
214. Tiedeman, *Limitations of Police Power*, 561–63.
215. Tiedeman, *Limitations of Police Power*, 562–63.
216. In 1918, Mississippi became the last state to pass a compulsory school attendance law. (The law was repealed in 1956.)
217. See *Quigley v. State*, 5 Ohio C.C. 638 (Ohio Cir. Ct. 1891); *State v. Bailey*, 61 N.E. 730 (Ind. 1901); *State v. Jackson*, 71 N.H. 552 (1902); *Commonwealth v. Edsall*, 13 Pa. D. 509 (Pa. Quar. Sess. 1903). On conflict between parents and teachers or school officials, see Carl F. Kaestle, *Pillars of the Republic*, 158–61; cf. Carl F. Kaestle, "Social Change, Discipline, and the Common School in Early Nineteenth-Century America," *J. Interdisciplinary Hist.* 9 (1978): 1. Parental rights claims were heard in response to "an increasing authority for teachers over children, in competition with parents." Kaestle, *Pillars of the Republic*, 159. Kaestle points out that many parent-school controversies "centered on corporal punishment." Kaestle, "Social Change, Discipline, and the Common School in Early Nineteenth-Century America," 13. For a discussion of parent-teacher conflict with regard to corporal punishment, see Michael Grossberg, "Teaching the Republican Child: Three Antebellum Stories about Law, Schooling, and the Construction of American Families," *Utah L. Rev.* 1996 (1996): 429, 443–52. Grossberg describes these debates as employing "the increasingly important political dialect of rights talk to express their clashing meanings of equal education." "Teaching the Republican Child," 437.
218. State v. Bailey, 61 N.E. at 731–32.
219. 61 N.E. at 732.

220. State v. Webber, 8 N.E. 708, 711, 712–13 (Ind. 1886).
221. Kidder v. Chellis, 59 N.H. 473, 476 (1879).
222. See Hardwick v. Bd. of Sch. Trs. of Fruitridge Sch. Dist., 205 P. 49 (Cal. Dist. Ct. App. 1921) (objection to dance classes); Kelley v. Ferguson, 144 N.W. 1039 (Neb. 1914) (objection to the study of domestic science); State ex rel. Sheibley v. Sch. Dist. No. 1 of Dixon County, 48 N.W. 393 (Neb. 1891) (objection to the study of grammar); Trustees of Schools v. People ex rel. Van Allen, 87 Ill. 303 (1877) (grammar); Morrow v. Wood, 35 Wis. 59 (1874) (geography); cf. Rulison v. Post, 79 Ill. 567 (1875) (requiring attendance at mandatory, but not optional, classes).
223. Morrow v. Wood, 35 Wis. at 66; cf. State v. Sch. Dist. No. 1 of Dixon County, 48 N.W. at 395. In these cases, Stephen Provasnik writes, "the courts articulated a virtually absolute parental (i.e., paternal) authority over a child's course of study based on the father's presupposed superior interest in the child's future and knowledge of what is best for his child's welfare." "Judicial Activism and the Origins of Parental Choice: The Court's Role in the Institutionalization of Compulsory Education in the United States, 1891–1925," *Hist. of Educ. Q.* 46 (2006): 311, 326.
224. Morrow v. Wood, 35 Wis. at 66.
225. Sch. Bd. Dist. No. 18, Garvin County v. Thompson, 103 P. 578, 578–79 (Okla. 1909).
226. 103 P. at 578–79.
227. See, e.g., State v. Sch. Dist. No. 1 of Dixon Cnty. 48 N.W. 393 (Neb. 1891); State v. Webber, 8 N.E. 708 (Ind. 1886).
228. Thompson, 103 P. at 582.
229. Cf. Rulison v. Post, 79 Ill. at 573.
230. Rulison v. Post, 79 Ill. at 573; cf. Kelley v. Ferguson, 144 N.W. at 1043 ("But in this age of agitation, such as the world has never known before, we want to be careful lest we carry the doctrine of governmental paternalism too far, for, after all is said and done, the prime factor in our scheme of government is the American home"); State v. Rhodes, 61 N.C. (Phil.) at 456 ("Our conclusion is, that family government is recognized by law as being as complete in itself as the State government is in itself, and yet subordinate to it; and that we will not interfere with or attempt to control it in favor of either husband or wife, unless in cases where permanent or malicious injury is inflicted or threatened, or the condition of the party is intolerable").
231. Thompson, 103 P. at 581.
232. Morrow v. Wood, 35 Wis. at 64.
233. State v. Clottu, 33 Ind. at 412 ("Sometimes courts have gone beyond the letter and fair implications from the letter of the written constitution of government, to find, in what is called the spirit of the instrument, inhibitions upon the exercise of legislative power; and where the act in question is obviously unwise, or to the judicial mind appears likely to result in consequences very mischievous or dangerous, the

temptation to do so is certainly strong. But this search, outside of a constitution, for constitutional objections to an act of the legislature, though it has been, on rare occasions, indulged by courts of high character, is itself of doubtful propriety. It is the written constitution which is the supreme law to which legislation must conform, and not the views of even the wisest and purest judges of what should have been written in it, but was not; nor the theories of government which may be supposed to underlie it, without any expression to warrant the assumption. . . . The remedy for merely unwise laws, then, is not by application to the courts, destitute of power to grant relief; but it is found in the ballot, in the election of a legislature to repeal or amend. Whether an act is expedient or not, whether wise or not, whether right or not, are questions proper for discussion there, and wholly inadmissible in the courts, whose duty is, not to make or disregard law, but to administer it as it is written").

234. Thompson, 103 P. at 579. Morrow v. Wood, 35 Wis. at 64. Hardwick v. Bd. of Sch. Trs. of Fruitridge Sch. Dist., 205 P. at 54.

235. State v. Sch. Dist. No. 1 of Dixon County, 48 N.W. at 395, quoted in Kelley v. Ferguson, 144 N.W. at 1042; cf. Trs. of School v. People ex rel. Van Allen, 87 Ill. 303 (1877).

236. Bd. of Educ. v. Purse, 28 S.E. 896, 900 (Ga. 1897). Though the mother had caused the disruption, under state law the wife had no legal existence of her own. Thus, her husband was responsible for her conduct.

237. See, e.g., Hardwick v. Bd. of Sch. Trs. of Fruitridge Sch. Dist., 205 P. at 51; State v. Webber, 8 N.E. at 712.

238. State v. Clottu, 33 Ind. at 412.

239. On the language prohibition statutes, see Woodhouse "'Who Owns the Child?'" 1004; see also William G. Ross, "A Judicial Janus: *Meyer v. Nebraska* in Historical Perspective," *U. Cin. L. Rev.* 57 (1988): 125, 127–64.

240. Meyer v. State, 187 N.W. 100, 102 (Neb. 1922).

241. 187 N.W. at 104 (Letton, J., dissenting).

242. 187 N.W. at 104 (Letton, J., dissenting) (emphasis added).

243. Kelley v. Ferguson, 144 N.W. at 1044 (Letton, J., concurring in the judgment).

244. 321 U.S. 158 (1944). For the background facts, see 321 U.S. at 161–64.

245. 321 U.S. at 166.

246. 321 U.S. at 164. Brief of Appellant at 12, Prince v. Massachusetts, 321 U.S. 158 (1944). James Madison, "Memorial and Remonstrance Against Religious Assessments," in *The Supreme Court on Church and State*, ed. Robert S. Alley (New York: Oxford University Press, 1988) 18.

247. Brief of Appellant at 17, Prince v. Massachusetts; cf. Smith v. Organization of Foster Families for Equality & Reform (OFFER), 431 U.S. 816, 845 (1977) (describing "natural family" as "a relationship having its origins entirely apart from the power

of the State"). Brief of Appellant at 16, Prince v. Massachusetts. Brief of Appellant at 40, Prince v. Massachusetts.

248. Brief on Behalf of the Appellee, the Commonwealth of Massachusetts, at 15, Prince v. Massachusetts. Brief of Appellee at 16, Prince v. Massachusetts (citing Blackstone) (internal quotation marks omitted). Brief of Appellee at 15, Prince v. Massachusetts. Brief of Appellee at 16, Prince v. Massachusetts (quoting In re Ferrier's Petition, 103 Ill. 367, 373 [1882]).

249. 80 N.E. 802, 805 (Mass. 1907) (citations omitted).

250. 80 N.E. at 805.

251. Brief of Appellee at 19, Prince v. Massachusetts. Brief of Appellee at 17, Prince v. Massachusetts.

252. Prince, 321 U.S. at 165–66.

253. 321 U.S. at 166.

254. 321 U.S. at 168.

255. 321 U.S. at 165. 321 U.S. at 167. 321 U.S. at 166 (citation omitted).

256. 321 U.S. at 167.

257. 321 U.S. at 164–66; cf. 321 U.S. at 165–66 ("The rights of children to exercise their religion, and of parents to give them religious training and to encourage them in the practice of religious belief, as against preponderant sentiment and assertion of state power voicing it, have had recognition here, most recently in *West Virginia State Board of Education v. Barnette*. Previously in *Pierce v. Society of Sisters*, this Court had sustained the parent's authority to provide religious with secular schooling, and the child's right to receive it, as against the state's requirement of attendance at public schools. And in *Meyer v. Nebraska*, children's rights to receive teaching in languages other than the nation's common tongue were guarded against the state's encroachment") (citations omitted).

258. See Parham v. J.R., 442 U.S. 584, 600 (1979); Wisconsin v. Yoder, 406 U.S. 205, 232 (1972); cf. Good News Club v. Milford Cent. Sch., 533 U.S. 98, 121 (2001) (Scalia, J., concurring) ("What is at play here is not coercion, but the compulsion of ideas—and the private right to exert and receive that compulsion ((or to have one's children receive it)) is protected by the Free Speech and Free Exercise Clauses").

259. Prince, 321 U.S. at 166–67.

260. 321 U.S. at 165. 321 U.S. at 168–69. 321 U.S. at 170. But see 321 U.S. at 175 (Murphy, J., dissenting).

261. 321 U.S. at 171.

262. 321 U.S. at 168; cf. Santosky v. Kramer, 455 U.S. 745, 790 (1982) (Rehnquist, J., dissenting) ("Few could doubt that the most valuable resource of a self-governing society is its population of children who will one day become adults and themselves assume the responsibility of self-governance"). 321 U.S. at 165. 321 U.S. at 170.

263. 26 F. Cas. 30, 31 (C.C.R.I. 1824); cf., e.g., In re O'Neal (Mass. 1869), reported in 3 *Am. L. Rev.* (1869): 578, 579; Kelsey v. Green, 37 A. 679, 681–82 (Conn. 1897).

264. 26 F. Cas. at 31–32.

265. See, e.g., "Relinquishment of Parent's Right of Custody of Child to Third Person," *Va. L.J.* 6 (1882): 470, 470. But see Bishop, 2 *Commentaries on the Law of Marriage and Divorce*, 456 (§ 1166) ("Yet doubtless mere poverty and want of education in a parent, however extreme, should seldom or never deprive him of his child, whatever its prospects in the offered other custody; for the following of such a principle would be an overturning of the order of society") (footnote omitted).

266. On the established ties doctrine, see, for example, Green v. Campbell, 14 S.E. 212, 214 (W. Va. 1891); Chapsky v. Wood, 26 Kan. 650, 653 (1881); Clark v. Bayer, 32 Ohio St. 299, 305–6 (Ohio 1877); In re O'Neal (Mass. 1869), reported in 3 *Am. L. Rev.* (1869): 578, 579–80; Coffee v. Black, 82 Va. 567, 569 (1866); see also, e.g., Hochheimer, *The Custody of Infants* (1899), 9–17 (§§ 13–17) (citing cases); Ransom H. Tyler, *Commentaries on the Law of Infancy* (1868) 283 (§ 187) (citing cases). On third-party cases, see Grossberg, *Governing the Hearth*, 257–59; Bardaglio, *Reconstructing the Household*, 153–57. Established ties might trump the claims of biological motherhood. See, e.g., Hoxie v. Potter, 17 A. 129, 129 (R.I. 1888); Bonnett v. Bonnett, 16 N.W. 91 (Iowa 1883); Commonwealth v. Barnet, 4 Brew. 408 (Pa. 1872).

    Established ties might even trump the ties of family altogether. See, e.g., Washaw v. Gimble, 7 S.W. 389 (Ark. 1888); People ex rel. Curley v. Porter, 23 Ill. App. 196 (1887).

267. In re Snook, 38 P. at 273 (dispute between mother and paternal grandparents) ("The controlling consideration is, what does the best interest of the child require? 'We understand the law to be, when the custody of children is the question, that the best interest of the child is the paramount fact. Rights of father and mother sink into insignificance before that'") (quoting In re Bort, 25 Kan. 308, 310 [1881]).

268. 82 Va. 433 (1886).

269. 82 Va. at 434. 82 Va. at 436. 82 Va. at 437. 82 Va. at 438.

270. 82 Va. at 438 (citing Hurd, *Habeas Corpus*, 528). 82 Va. at 438. 82 Va. at 439–40.

271. 82 Va. at 440 ("The real question in a case like this is not what are the rights of the father or the other relative to the custody of the child, or whether the right of the one be superior to that of the other, but *what are the rights of the child?* This cannot be considered as a question involving a right of property in the child. The true view is that the rights of the child are first to be considered and those rights are clearly to be protected in the enjoyment of its personal liberty, according to its own choice, if arrived at the age of discretion, and if not, to have its personal safety and

interests guarded and secured by the law, acting through the agency of those who are called on to administer it").

272. The established ties doctrine would be given a modern formulation in Joseph Goldstein, Anna Freud, and Albert J. Solnit, *Beyond the Best Interests of the Child* (New York: Free Press, 1979). A focus on continuity of affection might be enlisted to support a strict scrutiny harm standard. See *Beyond the Best Interests of the Child*, 7 ("To safeguard the right of parents to raise their children as they see fit, free of government intrusion, except in cases of neglect and abandonment, is to safeguard each child's need for continuity").

273. Richard v. Collins, 17 A. 831, 832–33 (N.J. Err. & App. 1889). The court ordered the child to remain in the home of her aunt and uncle, reasoning that "[w]hatever [the child] has known of parental love and care is from them. It would be passing strange if it had not become bound to them, and the home they gave it, with a child's affection. They have faithfully executed their trust, and are still willing and abundantly able to provide for it, and advance it in life."

274. Bently v. Terry, 59 Ga. 555, 557 (1877).

275. In re Bort, 25 Kan. at 310.

276. See, e.g., Washaw v. Gimble, 7 S.W. 389 (Ark. 1888); People ex rel. Curley v. Porter, 23 Ill. App. 196 (1887).

277. The established ties doctrine was consistent with the development of adoption as a legal device, which, as Michael Grossberg writes, was the "greatest extension" of the principle that the rightful parent is the person who assumes the relationship of parent. *Governing the Hearth*, 268; see also Bardaglio, *Reconstructing the Household*, 165–75.

278. 26 Kan. 650 (1881).

279. 26 Kan. at 652.

280. 26 Kan. at 652.

281. 26 Kan. at 652–53.

282. 26 Kan. at 653.

283. 26 Kan. at 654.

284. 26 Kan. at 654.

285. 26 Kan. at 656–57; cf. 26 Kan. at 657 ("Again and lastly, the child has had, and has to-day, all that a mother's love and care can give. The affection which a mother may have and does have, springing from the fact that a child is her offspring, is an affection which perhaps no other one can really possess; but so far as it is possible, springing from years of patient care of a little, helpless babe, from association, and as an outgrowth from those little cares and motherly attentions bestowed upon it, an affection for the child is seen in [the child's aunt] that can be found nowhere else. And it is apparent, that so far as a mother's love can be equaled, its foster-mother has that love, and will continue to have it").

286. 128 A. 254 (N.J. Err. & App. 1925).
287. For the background facts, see 128 A. at 517–19; In re Lippincott, 124 A. at 533.
288. 124 A. at 533; see also 128 A. at 255 ("No question is presented in the case as to the fitness of either set of grandparents to deal properly with the child").
289. 124 A. at 533.
290. 128 A. at 255.
291. 128 A. at 255.
292. 128 A. at 255 (citations omitted).
293. 128 A. at 255 (citing Mercein v. People ex rel. Barry, 25 Wend. 64 [N.Y. 1840]).
294. 128 A. at 255 (citing Mercein v. People ex rel. Barry, 25 Wend. 64 [N.Y. 1840]).
295. 128 A. at 256. 124 A. at 533.

Chapter 3. Parenting as a Sacred Right

Epigraph. Brief of Appellee, Pierce v. Society of Sisters of the Holy Names of Mary and Joseph, 268 U.S. 510 (1925), in *Oregon School Cases: Complete Record* (Baltimore: Belvedere Press, 1925) 275.

1. People ex rel. O'Connell v. Turner, 55 Ill. 280, 282 (1870).
2. 4 Whart. 9, 11 (Pa. 1939).
3. David S. Tanenhaus, "Policing the Child: Juvenile Justice in Chicago, 1879–1925," 32 (1997) (Ph.D. diss., Chicago) (on file with author); see also Tanenhaus, "Between Dependency and Liberty: The Conundrum of Children's Rights in the Gilded Age," *Law & Hist. Rev.* 23 (2005): 351. See also generally Tanenhaus, *Juvenile Justice in the Making* (New York: Oxford University Press, 2004). The child's due process rights were recognized by the Supreme Court in *In re Gault*, 387 U.S. 1 (1966). Writing for the Court, Justice Abe Fortas objected to "[t]he right of the state, as parens patriae, to deny to the child procedural rights available to his elders." See 387 U.S. at 17; cf. Goss v. Lopez, 419 U.S. 565 (1975); In re Winship, 397 U.S. 358 (1970).
4. Cf. Wynehamer v. People, 13 N.Y. 378 (1856), which involved a challenge to the constitutionality of a state prohibition act. The decision was an early—and, at the time, novel—instance of a "vested rights" substantive due process jurisprudence. The classic treatment of vested rights is Edward S. Corwin, *Liberty Against Government: The Rise, Flowering and Decline of a Famous Judicial Concept* (Baton Rouge: Louisiana State University Press, 1948); for a modern, but no less classic, treatment, compare Randy E. Barnett, *Restoring the Lost Constitution: The Presumption of Liberty* (Princeton: Princeton University Press, 2004).
5. Turner, 55 Ill. at 284–85.
6. 55 Ill. at 285 (internal quotation marks omitted).
7. 55 Ill. at 284.

8. See also, e.g., State ex rel. Cunningham v. Ray, 63 N.H. 406 (1885) (commitment of minor to industrial school without hearing or trial violates state constitution) (citing People v. Turner, 55 Ill. 280 [1870]).

9. 19 Am. L. Reg., 366, 372 (1871).

10. 19 Am. L. Reg., 372–73.

11. 19 Am. L. Reg., 374. In this opinion, Redfield is not alone. See, e.g., Thomas James, "Rights of Conscience and State School Systems in Nineteenth-Century America," in *Toward a Usable Past: Liberty Under State Constitutions*, eds. Paul Finkelman and Stephen E. Gottlieb (Athens: University of Georgia Press, 1991) 117. See generally Diane Ravitch, *The Great School Wars: A History of the New York City Public Schools, 1805–1973* (Baltimore: Johns Hopkins University Press, 1974) 20–158.

12. 19 Am. L. Reg., 372.

13. Tanenhaus, "Between Dependency and Liberty," 354 (footnote omitted).

14. 40 Wis. 328 (1876).

15. 40 Wis. at 341. 40 Wis. at 331. 40 Wis. at 341. 40 Wis. at 337–38. 40 Wis. at 338–39.

16. 103 Ill. 367 (1882). For background, see Tanenhaus, "Between Dependency and Liberty," 374–78. See also County of McLean v. Humphreys, 104 Ill. 379 (1882) (upholding Industrial School act). In *Prince v. Massachusetts*, the state of Massachusetts relied on *Ferrier* to argue that there are some "'restrictions imposed upon personal liberty which spring from the helpless or dependent condition of individuals in the various relations of life, among them being those of parent and child. . . . There are well recognized powers of control in each of these relations over the actions of the child . . . which may be exercised. These are legal and just restraints upon personal liberty, which the welfare of society demands, and which, where there is no abuse, entirely consist with the constitutional guarantee of liberty.'" Brief on Behalf of Appellee at 16–17, the Commonwealth of Massachusetts, Prince v. Massachusetts, 321 U.S. 158 (1944) (quoting In re Ferrier's Petition, 103 Ill. at 373).

17. In re Ferrier's Petition, 103 Ill. at 371.

18. 103 Ill. at 371–72.

19. 103 Ill. at 372–73.

20. *Ninth Biennial Report of the Superintendent of Public Instruction of the State of Illinois, 1871–1872*, 223.

21. Bateman, *Ninth Biennial Report*, 222 (quoting People ex rel. O'Connell v. Turner, 55 Ill. at 287). Bateman, *Ninth Biennial Report*, 224.

22. See Plyer v. Doe, 457 U.S. 202, 221 (1982); San Antonio Indep. Sch. Dist. v. Rodriguez, 411 U.S. 1, 35 (1973).

23. 457 U.S. at 221.

24. Redfield was well aware that *Turner* would not put an end to "compulsory legislative discipline." He writes, "The particular case [i.e., *Turner*] seems to be

measurably free from doubt. But there is a wide field of debatable ground between the dominion of punishment for crime and that of mere improved culture, in which it will be long before any very exact definitions of jurisdiction or of the distributions of service between the voluntary and compulsory fields can be satisfactorily fixed." 19 Am. L. Reg., 375.

25. See, e.g., Allison v. Bryan, 97 P. 282, 286 (Okla. 1908).

26. 262 U.S. 390 (1923); 268 U.S. 510 (1925). On the historical background of *Meyer* and *Pierce*, see generally Paula Abrams, *Cross Purposes*: Pierce v. Society of Sisters *and the Struggle over Compulsory Public Education* (Ann Arbor: University of Michigan Press, 2009); William G. Ross, *Forging New Freedoms: Nativism, Education, and the Constitution 1917–1927* (Lincoln: University of Nebraska Press, 1994); Barbara Bennett Woodhouse, "'Who Owns the Child?': *Meyer* and *Pierce* and the Child as Property," *Wm. & Mary L. Rev.* 33 (1992): 995; William G. Ross, "A Judicial Janus: *Meyer v. Nebraska* in Historical Perspective," *U. Cin. L. Rev.* 57 (1988): 125; David Tyack, Thomas James, and Aaron Benavot, *Law and the Shaping of Public Education, 1785–1954* (Madison: University of Wisconsin Press, 1987) 177–92; David B. Tyack, "The Perils of Pluralism: The Background of the *Pierce* Case," *American Hist. Rev.* 74 (1968): 74.

27. See Ravitch, *The Great School Wars*, 20–158. For a useful overview of anti-Catholic sentiment in American intellectual history, see John T. McGreevy, "Thinking on One's Own: Catholicism in the American Intellectual Imagination, 1928–1960," *Journal of American History* 84 (1997): 97.

28. Ravitch, *The Great School Wars*, 48–49 (quoting W. M. Oland Bourne, *History of the Public School Society of the City of New York* [New York: Wm. Wood, 1870] 334); see generally Ravitch, 20–158. Michael Grossberg discusses the case of Thomas Wall, who was beaten for refusing to read portions of the King James Bible, in "Teaching the Republican Child: Three Antebellum Stories About Law, Schooling, and the Construction of American Families," *Utah L. Rev.* 1996 (1996): 429, 452–58; cf., e.g., Ferriter v. Tyler, 48 Vt. 444 (1876) (upholding dismissal of student for absence due to religious observance).

29. Morrow v. Wood, 35 Wis. 59, 65 (1874).

30. Kelley v. Ferguson, 144 N.W. 1039, 1044 (Neb. 1914).

31. See Meyer, 262 U.S. at 401.

32. The invitation had been extended by the appellee Society of Sisters, see Brief of Appellee, in *Oregon School Cases: Complete Record* (Baltimore: Belvedere Press, 1925) 321–30; by the attorney William Guthrie before the Court, see Transcript of Oral Argument, in *Oregon School Cases*, 653; and by the amicus brief of William A. Williams as Amicus Curiae (on behalf of the North Pacific Union Conference of Seventh-Day Adventists), see *Oregon School Cases*, 596, 615–16.

33. David R. Upham, *"Pierce v. Society of Sisters*, Natural Law, and the Pope's Extraordinary—But Undeserved—Praise of the American Republic" [Draft], 12, at http://papers.ssrn.com/sol3/papers.cfm?abstract_id=2018396 (footnote omitted).

34. On the same day that the Supreme Court decided *Meyer*, it issued an opinion that brought to a conclusion four other language-statute cases (*Bartels v. Iowa; Bohning v. Ohio; Pohl v. Ohio;* and *Nebraska Dist. of Evangelical Lutheran Synod v. McKelvie*). See 262 U.S. 404 (1923). These cases were all decided upon the authority of *Meyer*. 262 U.S. at 409. In briefs before the lower courts, plaintiffs in error Bohning and Pohl had advanced a parental rights argument. For a survey of the litigation, see Ross, "A Judicial Janus," 135–85. Ross notes that before the Supreme Court all the appellants "gave short shrift to this [parental rights] point." Ross, 168.

35. Wisconsin v. Yoder, 406 U.S. 205, 213 (1972).

36. *Meyer*, 262 U.S. at 403. *Pierce*, 268 U.S. at 534. In the *Pierce* litigation, counsel for the parents would stress their support of state regulation, "invit[ing] the fullest inspection and regulation, and the fixing of minimum standards in the education of the young and in all forms of education." See Abrams, *Cross Purposes*, 147 (internal quotation marks and citation omitted).

37. See 262 U.S. at 400 (quoting Meyer v. State, 187 N.W. 100, 102 [Neb. 1992]); cf. Bartels v. Iowa, 262 U.S. 404, 412 (1923) (Holmes, J., dissenting) ("It is with hesitation and unwillingness that I differ from my brethren with regard to a law like this but I cannot bring my mind to believe that in some circumstances, and circumstances existing it is said in Nebraska, the statute might not be regarded as a reasonable or even necessary method of reaching the desired result").

38. *Meyer*, 262 U.S. at 403.

39. See Ross, *Nativism, Education, and the Constitution*, 130.

40. Meyer v. State, 187 N.W. at 104 (Letton, J., dissenting); cf. Berea College v. Commonwealth of Kentucky, 211 U.S. 45, 67 (1908) (Harlan, J., dissenting) ("The capacity to impart instruction to others is given by the Almighty for beneficent purposes; and its use may not be forbidden or interfered with by government—certainly not, unless such instruction is, in its nature, harmful to the public morals or imperils the public safety").

41. Transcript of Oral Argument at 11, Meyer v. Nebraska, 262 U.S. 390 (1923).

42. "The only reference to parental rights in the entire opinion consists of one sentence noting that the ban on languages had the effect of interfering with 'the calling of modern language teachers, with the opportunities of pupils to acquire knowledge, and with the power of parents to control the education of their own.'" People v. Bennett, 501 N.W.2d 106, 113 (Mich. 1993) (quoting Meyer, 262 U.S. at 401).

43. *Meyer*, 262 U.S. at 401. In *Pierce*, as James G. Dwyer notes, "attorneys thought to assert a right of parents, precisely because *Meyer* had announced such a right two

years earlier. And Justice McReynolds could cite his own dictum in *Meyer* as doctrinal support for the existence of this unenumerated constitutional right." *Family Law: Theoretical, Comparative, and Social Science Perspectives* (New York: Wolters Kluwer, 2012) 497.

44. Transcript of Oral Argument at 11, Meyer v. Nebraska.

45. See, e.g., Railroad Commission Cases, 116 U.S. 307, 331 (1886) ("[I]t is not to be inferred that this power of limitation or regulation is itself without limit. This power to regulate is not a power to destroy, and limitation is not the equivalent of confiscation").

46. Meyer, 262 U.S. at 403. The state statute had stipulated that "an emergency exists." 262 U.S. at 397. But the Court rejected the legislature's conclusion: "No emergency has arisen which renders knowledge by a child of some language other than English so clearly harmful as to justify its inhibition with the consequent infringement of rights long freely enjoyed." 262 U.S. at 403.

47. See Transcript of Oral Argument at 7, Meyer v. Nebraska: "My theory of the State's control of education under the police power is this: That the State has a right to prescribe a minimum of education for the children within the United States, or within the State. It has the right, clearly, within the police power to require the children to have sufficient education to properly discharge their duties as citizens. But when that minimum is reached, the State has no police power above that. It is entirely a matter of option with the student, the teacher and the parent what the school shall teach the child above that. . . . The State has a right to prescribe minimums, but when we meet those minimums, its police power stops.

"Take, for example, the question suggested by Mr. Justice McReynolds: If the State has, as suggested by him, the power to require all children to attend the public schools, that means that private schools must close. If it has a right to pass that kind of a compulsory school law, it can close up the private institutions, because there is no need of them, then everybody must attend the public schools."

As Paula Abrams notes, "Meyer's brief conceded the authority of the state to compel public school attendance." *Cross Purposes*, 120. Meyer's brief did suggest "[t]hat a law requiring that all persons within a certain age should be required to attend the public schools for a certain period . . . would be a valid exercise of the police power." Brief of Plaintiff in Error at 14–15, Meyer v. Nebraska, 262 U.S. 390 (1923). But its argument echoed Mullen's point that the state, while it could set minimum educational standards, could not "limit[] the field of human knowledge": "[T]he relation of a law, fixing a minimum of education, to the common good is readily perceived, but how one fixing a maximum—limiting the field of human knowledge—can serve the public welfare or add substantially to the security of life, liberty or the pursuit of happiness is inconceivable." Brief of Plaintiff in Error at 15.

48. Brief of Defendant (State of Nebraska) at 12–13, Meyer v. Nebraska, 262 U.S. 390 (1923).

49. Brief of Defendant (State of Nebraska) at 14–15.

50. See Exodus 5.

51. Transcript of Oral Argument at 11, Meyer v. Nebraska.

52. Meyer, 262 U.S. at 403. See Pierce, 268 U.S. at 534.

53. Meyer, 262 U.S. at 403.

54. Brief for William D. Guthrie & Bernard Hershkopf as Amici Curiae Supporting Plaintiff in Error [Petitioner] at 3, Meyer v. Nebraska, 262 U.S. 390 (1923). For background on Guthrie, see Abrams, Cross Purposes, 112–17; Woodhouse, "Who Owns the Child?" 1070–80.

55. Brief for Guthrie & Hershkopf as Amici Curiae at 3 (citation omitted); cf. Budd v. New York, 143 U.S. 517, 551 (1892) (Brewer, J., dissenting) ("The paternal theory of government is to me odious. The utmost possible liberty to the individual, and the fullest possible protection to him and his property, is both the limitation and duty of government. If it may regulate the price of one service, which is not a public service, or the compensation for the use of one kind of property which is not devoted to a public use, why may it not with equal reason regulate the price of all service, and the compensation to be paid for the use of all property? And if so, 'Looking Backward' is nearer than a dream").

56. Transcript of Oral Argument at 10, Meyer v. Nebraska.

57. Brief of Appellant at 46, Pierce v. Society of the Sisters of the Names of Jesus and Mary, 268 U.S. 510 (1925) (No. 583); cf. Brief of Appellant at 46 ("At present, the vast majority of the private schools in the country are conducted by members of some particular religious belief. They may be followed, however, by those organized and controlled by believers in certain economic doctrines entirely destructive of the fundamentals of our government. Can it be contended that there is no way in which a State can prevent the entire education of a considerable portion of its future citizens being controlled and conducted by bolshevists, syndicalists and communists?").

58. Meyer, 262 U.S. at 401–2.

59. Pierce, 268 U.S. at 534–35.

60. Yoder, 406 U.S. at 233.

61. Richard W. Garnett, "Taking Pierce Seriously: The Family, Religious Education, and Harm to Children," Notre Dame L. Rev. 76 (2000): 109, 143.

62. See Meyer, 262 U.S. at 399; see Pierce, 268 U.S. at 535.

63. See David D. Meyer, "What Constitutional Law Can Learn from the ALI Principles of Family Dissolution," BYU L. Rev. 2001 (2001): 1075, 1090; Meyer, "The Paradox of Family Privacy," Vand. L. Rev. 53 (2000): 527, 546; cf. Francis Barry

McCarthy, "The Confused Constitutional Status and Meaning of Parental Rights," *Ga. L. Rev.* 22 (1988): 975, 992.

64. Slaughter-House Cases, 83 U.S. 36, 78 (1872).

65. People ex rel. Annan v. Walsh, 22 N.E. 682, 686 (N.Y. 1899) (Peckham, J., dissenting).

66. Blackstone, 1 *Commentaries on the Laws of England* (Oxford: Clarendon Press, 1765) 130.

67. Meyer, 262 U.S. at 399 ("While this court has not attempted to define with exactness the liberty thus guaranteed, the term has received much consideration and some of the included things have been definitely stated. Without doubt, it denotes not merely freedom from bodily restraint but also the right of the individual to contract, to engage in any of the common occupations of life, to acquire useful knowledge, to marry, establish a home and bring up children, to worship God according to the dictates of his own conscience, and generally to enjoy those privileges long recognized at common law as essential to the orderly pursuit of happiness by free men"). Compare Felix Frankfurter, "Can the Supreme Court Guarantee Toleration?" *New Republic*, June 17, 1925, 85. The future Supreme Court justice wrote that the *Pierce* decision "did immediate service on behalf of the essential spirit of liberalism." But he worried about the cost to liberalism occasioned by "judicial nullification of anti-liberal legislation." The Oregon case "is only one in a series which has been spun profusely out of the fateful words of the Fourteenth Amendment. 'No state shall . . . deprive any person of life, liberty or property without due process of law' are the vague words which hold the power of life and death over State action. These words mean what the shifting personnel of the United States Supreme Court from time to time makes them mean. The inclination of a single Justice, the tip of his mind—or his fears—determines the opportunity of a much-needed social experiment to survive, or frustrates, at least for a long time, intelligent attempt to deal with a social evil. . . . In rejoicing over the Nebraska and the Oregon cases, we must not forget that a heavy price has to be paid for these occasional services to liberalism." Frankfurter, "Can the Supreme Court Guarantee Toleration?" 86.

68. Michael P. Farris, "Parental Rights: Why Now Is the Time to Act," March/April 2006 *The Home School Court Report* 7, 9 (March/April 2006), at parentalrights. org, http://www.parentalrights.org/index.asp?Type=B_BASIC&SEC={B70D1F5 F-97FF-499A-A123–16CAE9385046}.

69. See Carey v. Population Servs. Int'l, 431 U.S. 678 (1977); Bellotti v. Baird, 428 U.S. 132 (1976).

70. Yoder, 406 U.S. at 209.

71. 406 U.S. at 209–10.

72. 406 U.S. at 211–12.

73. 406 U.S. at 213 (quoting Pierce, 268 U.S. at 535). 406 U.S. at 213–14.
74. 374 U.S. 398, 406 (1963).
75. Yoder, 406 U.S. at 233–34.
76. Yoder, 406 U.S. at 233.
77. 405 U.S. 438, 467 (1972) (Burger, C.J., dissenting). 405 U.S. at 471–72.
78. Yoder, 406 U.S. at 215–16.
79. See 406 U.S. at 216 ("[I]f the Amish asserted their claims because of their subjective evaluation and rejection of the contemporary secular values accepted by the majority, much as Thoreau rejected the social values of his time and isolated himself at Walden Pond, their claims would not rest on a religious basis. Thoreau's choice was philosophical and personal rather than religious, and such belief does not rise to the demands of the Religion Clauses").
80. 406 U.S. at 215.
81. See Brief for Respondents, State v. Yoder, 182 N.W.2d 539 (Wis. 1971).
82. Yoder, 406 U.S. at 229.
83. 406 U.S. at 230.
84. See Braunfeld v. Brown, 366 U.S. 599 (1961). In dissent, Justice Brennan argued that the Sunday closing law, in "put[ting] an individual to a choice between his business and his religion," violated the Free Exercise Clause. 366 U.S. at 611 (Brennan, J., dissenting). He was not impressed with the state's assertion of its interests. See 366 U.S. at 613–14 ("What, then, is the compelling state interest which impels the Commonwealth of Pennsylvania to impede appellants' freedom of worship? What overbalancing need is so weighty in the constitutional scale that it justifies this substantial, though indirect, limitation of appellants' freedom? . . . It is the mere convenience of having everyone rest on the same day").
85. Yoder, 406 U.S. at 221.
86. 406 U.S. at 222.
87. See Brief for the Petitioner at 18–22, State v. Yoder, 182 N.W.2d 539 (Wis. 1971); cf. Joel Feinberg, "The Child's Right to an Open Future," in Whose Child?: Children's Rights, Parental Authority, and State Power, eds. William Aiken and Hugh LaFollette (Totowa: Littlefield, Adams, 1980) 134–35 ("But how is 'the goal of education' to be viewed? That is the question that must be left open if the Court is to issue a truly neutral decision[:] to assume that 'the goal' is preparation for modern commercial-industrial life is to beg the question in favor of the state, but equally, to assume that 'the goal' is preparation for a 'life aloof from the world' is to beg the question in favor of the parents. An impartial decision would assume only that education should equip the child with the knowledge and skills that will help him choose whichever sort of life best fits his native endowment and matured disposition. It should send him out into the adult world with as many open opportunities as possible, thus maximizing his chances for self-fulfillment").

88. Yoder, 406 U.S. at 225.

89. See Blackstone, 1 *Commentaries on the Laws of England*, 435.

90. Yoder, 406 U.S. at 232.

91. 406 U.S. at 231–32.

92. See 406 U.S. at 225–26 ("When Thomas Jefferson emphasized the need for education as a bulwark of a free people against tyranny, there is nothing to indicate he had in mind compulsory education through any fixed age beyond a basic education. Indeed, the Amish communities singularly parallel and reflect many of the virtues of Jefferson's ideal of the 'sturdy yeoman' who would form the basis of what he considered as the ideal of a democratic society") (footnote omitted).

93. 406 U.S. at 236.

94. See 406 U.S. at 233.

95. See, e.g., Parker v. Hurley, 514 F.3d 87, 100 (1st Cir. 2008) ("Tellingly, *Yoder* emphasized that its holding was essentially sui generis, as few sects could make a similar showing of a unique and demanding religious way of life that is fundamentally incompatible with any schooling system"); cf. Mozert v. Hawkins Cnty. Bd. of Educ., 827 F.2d 1058, 1067 (6th Cir. 1987) ("*Yoder* rested on such a singular set of facts that we do not believe it can be held to announce a general rule").

96. Employment Div., Dept. of Human Res. of Oregon v. Smith, 494 U.S. 872, 885 (1990).

97. 494 U.S. at 881.

98. On the meaning of neutrality and general applicability, see generally Church of Lukumi Babalu Aye v. City of Hialeah, 508 U.S. 520 (1993); see also, e.g., Christopher C. Lund, "A Matter of Constitutional Luck: The General Applicability Requirement in Free Exercise Jurisprudence," *Harv. J.L. & Pub. Pol'y* 26 (2003): 627, 633–44; Robin Cheryl Miller, "What Laws Are Neutral and of General Applicability Within Meaning of *Employment Div., Dept. of Human Resources of Oregon v. Smith*, 494 U.S. 872, 110 S. Ct. 1595, 108 L. Ed. 2d 876," Annotation, A.L.R. Fed. 167 (2001): 663.

99. Smith, 494 U.S. at 878–79. To say the least, this assertion did not go uncontested. See, e.g., William P. Marshall, "In Defense of *Smith* and Free Exercise Revisionism," *U. Chi. L. Rev.* 58 (1991): 308, 309; Michael W. McConnell, "Free Exercise Revisionism and the *Smith* Decision," *U. Chi. L. Rev.* 57 (1990): 1109, 1120. But see John P. Forren, "Revisiting Four Popular Myths about the Peyote Case," *U. Pa. J. Const. L.* 8 (2006): 209, 212–15 (disputing "myth" that pre-*Smith* courts vigorously protected religious practices from regulation).

100. Douglas Laycock, "Free Exercise and the Religious Freedom Restoration Act," *Fordham L. Rev.* 62 (1994): 883, 902 ("Justice Scalia had only five votes. He apparently believed he couldn't overrule anything, and so he didn't. He distinguished everything away instead").

101. Marshall, "In Defense of *Smith* and Free Exercise Revisionism," 309 ("The *Smith* opinion itself, however, cannot be readily defended. The decision, as written, is neither persuasive nor well-crafted. It exhibits only a shallow understanding of free exercise jurisprudence and its use of precedent borders on fiction") (footnotes omitted); cf. Kent Greenawalt, 1 *Religion and the Constitution* (Princeton: Princeton University Press, 2006) 105 ("Justice Scalia's treating of *Yoder* as a hybrid resting on two separate legs was not quite creation ex nihilo, but it came close; it is the kind of imaginative reclassification that later courts occasionally perform on earlier cases whose approach does not appeal to them").

102. See, e.g., Parker v. Hurley, 514 F.3d at 97 ("Observers debate whether *Smith* created a new hybrid rights doctrine, or whether in discussing 'hybrid situations' the Court was merely noting in descriptive terms that it was not overruling certain cases such as *Pierce* and *Yoder*").

103. See, e.g., Kissinger v. Bd. of Trs. of Ohio State Univ., 5 F.3d 177, 180 (6th Cir. 1993) ("[T]he *Smith* court did not explain how the standards under the Free Exercise Clause would change depending on whether other constitutional rights are implicated").

104. Church of the Lukumi Babalu Aye, 508 U.S. at 567 (Souter, J., concurring).

105. Thomas v. Anchorage Equal Rights Comm'n, 165 F.3d 692, 704 (9th Cir. 1999), withdrawn and rev'd on other grounds, Thomas v. Anchorage Equal Rights Comm'n, 220 F.3d 1134 (9th Cir. 2000).

106. For a survey of the commentary, see Ariana S. Cooper, Note, "Free Exercise Claims in Custody Battles: Is Heightened Scrutiny Required Post-*Smith*?" *Colum. L. Rev.* 108 (2008): 716, 723 n.55. On hybrid rights and family law generally, see James G. Dwyer, "The Good, the Bad, and the Ugly of *Employment Division v. Smith* for Family Law," *Cardozo L. Rev.* 32 (2011): 1781.

107. See, e.g., Leebaert v. Harrington, 332 F.3d 134, 143 (2d Cir. 2003) ("Given our understanding of the *Smith* statement as dicta, we are not bound . . . to apply some stricter standard of review than the rational basis test to hybrid claims") (citing Knight v. Connecticut Dept. of Public Health, 275 F.3d 156,167 [2d Cir. 2001]); see also Watchtower Bible & Tract Soc'y of N.Y. v. Village of Stratton, 240 F.3d 553, 562 (6th Cir. 2001), rev'd on other grounds, 536 U.S. 150 (2002) (doctrine was dicta and therefore not binding).

108. Kissinger v. Bd. of Trs. of Ohio State Univ., 5 F.3d at 180; see also 5 F.3d at 180 ("[A]t least until the Supreme Court holds that legal standards under the Free Exercise Clause vary depending on whether other constitutional rights are implicated, we will not use a stricter legal standard than that used in *Smith* to evaluate generally applicable, exceptionless state regulations under the Free Exercise Clause").

109. Thomas v. Anchorage Equal Rights Comm'n, 165 F.3d at 704 n.8.

110. See Brown v. Hot, Sexy & Safer Prods., 68 F.3d 525, 539 (1st Cir. 1995).

111. Compare Henderson v. Kennedy, 253 F.3d 12, 19 (D.C. Cir. 2001) ("We also reject plaintiffs' contention that the regulation should receive some heightened scrutiny because they are presenting some sort of 'hybrid claim' resting on both the Free Exercise Clause and the Free Speech Clause of the First Amendment. For this argument to prevail, one would have to conclude that the combination of two untenable claims equals a tenable one. But in law as in mathematics zero plus zero equals zero"), with Richard F. Duncan, "Free Exercise Is Dead, Long Live Free Exercise: *Smith*, *Lukumi* and the General Applicability Requirement," *U. Pa. J. Const. L.* 3 (2001): 850, 858 ("Of course, the concept of hybrid claims is not completely irrational. Although it is certainly true that zero plus zero does not equal one, it is equally true that the sum of a number of fractions—one-half plus one-half, for example—may equal one. *Yoder*, indeed, is a case in which Wisconsin's mandatory attendance laws implicated not only religious liberty interests, but also free speech, association, and parental rights. Even if no single strand of the constitutional interests at stake in a case like *Yoder* is sufficient to trigger heightened constitutional protection, it is possible to argue that the cumulative effect of all these interests is sufficient").

112. Thomas v. Anchorage Equal Rights Comm'n, 165 F.3d at 704 ("Nonetheless, the Supreme Court's repeated references to the Free Exercise Clause in the so-called hybrid cases leave us with little doubt that, whatever else it did, the Court did not rest its decisions in those cases upon the recognition of independently viable free speech and substantive due process rights"). 165 F.3d at 705.

113. See 165 F.3d at 706 (comparing colorable claim to "the traditional 'likelihood of success on the merits' test that governs the issuance of preliminary injunctive relief"); Swanson v. Guthrie Indep. Sch. Dist. No. I-L, 135 F.3d 694, 700 (10th Cir. 1998) ("Whatever the *Smith* hybrid-rights theory may ultimately mean, we believe that it at least requires a colorable showing of infringement of recognized and specific constitutional rights, rather than the mere invocation of a general right such as the right to control the education of one's child").

114. Thomas v. Anchorage Equal Rights Comm'n, 165 F.3d at 707. 165 F.3d at 699.

115. 165 F.3d at 705. The *Thomas* court believed that a colorable claim approach is consistent with Supreme Court precedent, explaining the result in both *Yoder* and *Smith*. To reach this conclusion, the court assumed that the *Smith* plaintiffs could not make out a colorable companion claim. See 165 F.3d at 706. ("The plaintiffs in *Smith* could not have made out a 'colorable claim of infringement' with respect to their free speech rights. Ingesting peyote is certainly not 'speech' in the traditional sense; at best, it is 'expressive conduct.' And the only cases in which the Supreme Court has invalidated laws regulating expressive conduct are

those in which it has concluded that the government has prohibited such conduct 'precisely because of its communicative attributes'") (citing cases). But this is hardly a certain proposition. See McConnell, "Free Exercise Revisionism and the *Smith* Decision," 1122 ("Why isn't *Smith* itself a 'hybrid' case? Whatever else it might accomplish, the performance of a sacred ritual like the ingestion of peyote communicates, in a rather dramatic way, the participants' faith in the tenets of the Native American Church. [Plaintiffs] Smith and Black could have made a colorable claim under the Free Speech Clause that the prohibition of peyote use interfered with their ability to communicate this message. If burning a flag is speech because it communicates a political belief, ingestion of peyote is no less") (footnote omitted).

116. People v. Bennett, 501 N.W.2d 106 (Mich. 1993).

117. People v. DeJonge, 501 N.W.2d 127 (Mich. 1993).

118. Nor had the state used the least restrictive means to achieve its end. See 501 N.W.2d at 137–44.

119. Duncan, "Free Exercise Is Dead, Long Live Free Exercise," 858.

120. See Yoder, 406 U.S. at 237 (Stewart, J., concurring).

121. 406 U.S. at 238 (White, J., concurring).

122. 406 U.S. at 239–40 (White, J., concurring).

123. 406 U.S. at 243 (Douglas, J., dissenting). 406 U.S. at 242; cf. Meek v. Pittenger, 421 U.S. 349, 386 (1975) (Burger, C.J., concurring in the judgment in part and dissenting in part) (denial of state provision of educational services "penalizes children . . . not because of any act of theirs but because of their parents' choice of religious exercise"). 406 U.S. at 245–46. Douglas was equally concerned that the state as educator might make ideological impositions upon children. See Lemon v. Kurtzman, 403 U.S. 602, 630 (1971) (Douglas, J., concurring) ("While the evolution of the public school system in this country marked an escape from denominational control and was therefore admirable as seen through the eyes of those who think like Madison and Jefferson, it has disadvantages. The main one is that a state system may attempt to mold all students alike according to the views of the dominant group and to discourage the emergence of individual idiosyncrasies").

124. 406 U.S. at 244–45. 406 U.S. at 246 n.3 (internal quotation marks omitted). 406 U.S. at 246 n.3. 406 U.S. at 245–46 (footnote omitted).

125. 406 U.S. at 242.

126. In re Gregg, 5 New York Legal Observer 265, 267 (N.Y. Super. 1847). Planned Parenthood of Central Missouri v. Danforth, 428 U.S. 52, 74 (1976).

127. See Philip Greven, *The Protestant Temperament: Patterns of Child-Rearing, Religious Experience, and the Self in Early America* (New York: Alfred A. Knopf, 1977) 27 (internal quotation marks omitted). And it seems that grandparents remained

a problem. Greven writes, "A century and a half [after Robinson's admonition], John Wesley warned mothers that 'Your mother, or your husband's mother, may live with you; and you will do well to shew her all possible respect. But let her on no account have the least share in the management of your children. She would undo all that you have done; she would give them their own will in all things. She would humour them to the destruction of their souls, if not their bodies too.'" Greven, 27.

128. 530 U.S. 57 (2000).

129. See Michael H. v. Gerald D., 491 U.S. 110, 122 (1989) ("In an attempt to limit and guide interpretation of the Clause, we have insisted not merely that the interest denominated as a 'liberty' be 'fundamental'" ((a concept that, in isolation, is hard to objectify)), but also that it be an interest traditionally protected by our society. As we have put it, the Due Process Clause affords only those protections 'so rooted in the traditions and conscience of our people as to be ranked as fundamental'") (footnote omitted) (quoting Snyder v. Massachusetts, 291 U.S. 97, 105 [1934]).

130. Troxel, 530 U.S. at 65. O'Connor was not alone in denominating the right to parent as fundamental. See 530 U.S. at 80 (Thomas, J., concurring in the judgment); 530 U.S. at 87 (Stevens, J., dissenting).

131. 530 U.S. at 67. 530 U.S. at 67 (internal quotation marks and citation omitted). 530 U.S. at 67. 530 U.S. at 69. 530 U.S. at 70.

132. 530 U.S. at 63 (emphasis added). 530 U.S. at 73; cf. David D. Meyer, "Partners, Care Givers, and the Constitutional Substance of Parenthood," in *Reconceiving the Family: Critique on the American Law Institute's Principles of the Law of Family Dissolution*, ed. Robin Fretwell Wilson (New York: Cambridge University Press, 2006) 47, 64.

133. 530 U.S. at 66.

134. Santosky v. Kramer, 455 U.S. 745, 753 (1982) (discussing "[t]he fundamental liberty interest of natural parents in the care, custody, and management of their child"); cf. Quilloin v. Walcott, 434 U.S. 246, 255 (1978) ("We have little doubt that the Due Process Clause would be offended '[i]f a State were to attempt to force the breakup of a natural family, over the objections of the parents and their children, without some showing of unfitness and for the sole reason that to do so was thought to be in the children's best interest'") (quoting Smith v. Organization of Foster Families for Equality and Reform (OFFER), 431 U.S. 816, 862–863 [1977] [Stewart, J., concurring in the judgment]).

135. See Troxel, 530 U.S. at 65–66.

136. Lehr v. Robertson, 463 U.S. 248, 257–58 (1983).

137. 463 U.S. at 261 (quoting Caban v. Mohammed, 441 U.S. 380, 392 [1979]). 463 U.S. at 261. 463 U.S. at 262 (footnote omitted).

138. 463 U.S. at 257 ("[T]he Court has emphasized the paramount interest in the welfare of children and has noted that the rights of the parents are a counterpart of the responsibilities they have assumed").

139. 405 U.S. 645 (1972). For the background facts, see 405 U.S. at 646–67.

140. 405 U.S. at 648. 405 U.S. at 655. 405 U.S. at 652 (internal quotation marks and citation omitted). 405 U.S. at 652–53.

141. 434 U.S. 246 (1978).

142. For the background facts, see 434 U.S. at 247.

143. 434 U.S. at 253.

144. 434 U.S. at 256.

145. 441 U.S. 380 (1979). For the background facts, see 441 U.S. at 382–83.

146. 441 U.S. at 388 (internal quotation marks and citation omitted).

147. 441 U.S. at 389. 441 U.S. at 392. 441 U.S. at 389 n.7 (noting that in *Quilloin v. Walcott* the Court "emphasized the importance of the appellant's failure to act as a father toward his children").

148. 441 U.S. at 397 (Stewart, J., dissenting).

149. Lehr, 463 U.S. at 258. 463 U.S. at 259.

150. Troxel, 530 U.S. at 98 (Kennedy, J., dissenting).

151. 530 U.S. at 90 (Stevens, J., dissenting). 530 U.S. at 88. 530 U.S. at 88. 530 U.S. at 88. 530 U.S. at 86. 530 U.S. at 90. 530 U.S. at 86.

152. 530 U.S. at 86 ("While, as the Court recognizes, the Federal Constitution certainly protects the parent-child relationship from arbitrary impairment by the State, we have never held that the parent's liberty interest in this relationship is so inflexible as to establish a rigid constitutional shield, protecting every arbitrary parental decision from any challenge absent a threshold finding of harm") (Stevens, J., dissenting) (cross-reference and footnote omitted); 530 U.S. at 97 ("To say that third parties have had no historical right to petition for visitation does not necessarily imply, as the Supreme Court of Washington concluded, that a parent has a constitutional right to prevent visitation in all cases not involving harm") (Kennedy, J., dissenting).

153. 530 U.S. at 77 (Souter, J., concurring in the judgment). 530 U.S. at 80 (Thomas, J., concurring).

154. 530 U.S. at 91 (Scalia, J., dissenting); cf. Calder v. Bull, 3 U.S. 386, 399 (1798) (Iredell, J., concurring).

155. Cf. David D. Meyer, "The Constitutionalization of Family Law," *Fam. L.Q.* 42 (2008): 529, 557–58. Meyer advocates a "softer approach" to family privacy rights that "eschew[s] strict scrutiny's focus on compelling interests and narrow tailoring for far more indeterminate, intermediate interest-balancing." Meyer, "Constitutionalization of Family Law," 558–59; cf. also Katharine B. Silbaugh, "*Miller v. Albright*: Problems of Constitutionalization in Family Law," *B.U. L. Rev.* 79

(1999): 1139, 1160; Carl E. Schneider, "Moral Discourse and the Transformation of American Family Law," *Mich. L. Rev.* 83 (1985): 1803, 1858.

156. Sandra Day O'Connor, Remark, "The Supreme Court and the Family," *U. Pa. J. Const. L.* 3 (2001): 573, 575 (citing Santosky v. Kramer, 455 U.S. at 753). O'Connor, "The Supreme Court and the Family," 575–76 (citation omitted).

Chapter 4. Toward Constitutional Parenthood

Epigraph. William Ellery Channing, *The Works of William Ellery Channing* (Boston: American Unitarian Association, 1886) 117–18. Channing writes that parents "are not the only educators of their offspring, but must divide the work with other and numerous agents." In this, they should rejoice "for, were the young confined to domestic influences, each generation would be a copy of the preceding, and the progress of society would cease." Channing, *Works,* 117.

1. See Brief of Plaintiff-Appellant at 18, Leebaert v. Harrington, 332 F.3d 134 (2d Cir. 2003).

2. Leebaert v. Harrington, 332 F.3d 134 (2d Cir. 2003).

3. 332 F.3d at 136–37; see also Brief of Plaintiff-Appellant at 18, Leebaert v. Harrington ("'Character' is something that Mr. Leebaert believes that he alone must teach his sons").

4. Brief of Plaintiff-Appellant at 18, Leebaert v. Harrington. Leebaert thought that the health education curriculum was "anti-religion." See 332 F.3d at 138 ("I believe that the way the school system teaches the subjects to which I sought to opt my son out of, is anti-religion. For one example, it doesn't support a married man and woman together as the basic unit of the family. The school teaches that this unit can be comprised of anything or anyone, that anything you say can be a family. This contradicts my religious beliefs").

5. Leebaert, 332 F.3d at 138.

6. See Brief of Plaintiff-Appellant at 23–27, Leebaert v. Harrington.

7. Brief of Plaintiff-Appellant at 24, Leebaert v. Harrington. Brief of Plaintiff-Appellant at 26, Leebaert v. Harrington. Brief of Plaintiff-Appellant at 18–19, Leebaert v. Harrington. Brief of Plaintiff-Appellant at 15, Leebaert v. Harrington.

8. James C. McKinley Jr., and Sam Dillon, "Some Parents Oppose Obama Speech to Students," *New York Times,* September 3, 2009, at http://www.nytimes.com/2009/09/04/us/04school.html.

9. Stephen G. Gilles, "On Educating Children: A Parentalist Manifesto," *U. Chi. L. Rev.* 63 (1996): 937, 938.

10. Leebaert, 332 F.3d at 139.

11. 332 F.3d at 143.

12. 68 F.3d 525 (1st Cir. 1995).

13. 68 F.3d at 533. 68 F.3d at 533–34 (citations omitted). 68 F.3d at 534. For background on the Common Core State Standards Initiative, see, for example, Diane Ravitch, *Reign of Error: The Hoax of the Privatization Movement and the Danger to America's Public Schools* (New York: Knopf, 2013) 10–18.

14. Swanson v. Guthrie Indep. Sch. Dist. No. I-L, 135 F.3d 694 (10th Cir. 1998).

15. Leebaert, 332 F.3d at 141 (quoting Swanson, 135 F.3d at 699–700). 332 F.3d at 141 (quoting 135 F.3d at 700). Most courts hold that parents have no right to direct how public schools teach their children. See, e.g., Parker v. Hurley, 514 F.3d 87 (1st Cir. 2008) (challenge to books portraying diverse families); Blau v. Fort Thomas Pub. Sch. Dist., 401 F.3d 381 (6th Cir. 2005) (dress code); Littlefield v. Forney Indep. Sch. Dist., 268 F.3d 275 (5th Cir. 2001) (uniform policy); Parents United for Better Sch., Inc. v. Sch. Dist. of Philadelphia Bd. of Educ., 148 F.3d 260 (3d Cir. 1998) (voluntary condom distribution program); Immediato v. Rye Neck Sch. Dist., 73 F.3d 454 (2d Cir. 1996) (community service); Brown v. Hot, Sexy and Safer Prods., 68 F.3d 525 (1st Cir. 1995) (sex education); Fleischfresser v. Dirs. of Sch. Dist. 200, 15 F.3d 680 (7th Cir. 1994) (supplemental reading program); Morrison v. Bd. of Educ. of Boyd Cnty., 419 F. Supp. 2d 937 (E.D. Ky. 2006) (diversity training). But see Alfonso v. Fernandez, 606 N.Y.S.2d 259 (N.Y.A.D. 2 Dept. 1993) (mandatory condom distribution program violates parental rights).

16. Brief of Plaintiff-Appellant at 6, Leebaert v. Harrington. Leebaert, 332 F.3d at 142. 332 F.3d at 138.

17. 332 F.3d at 141.

18. Herndon v. Chapel Hill-Carrboro City Bd. of Educ., 89 F.3d 174 (4th Cir. 1996); Immediato v. Rye Neck Sch. Dist., 73 F.3d 454 (2d Cir. 1995).

19. Littlefield v. Forney Indep. Sch. Dist., 268 F.3d 275 (5th Cir. 2001).

20. Brief of Plaintiff-Appellant at 11, Leebaert v. Harrington (footnote omitted). Brief of Plaintiff-Appellant at 12, Leebaert v. Harrington.

21. Leebaert, 332 F.3d at 137 ("While I do not belong to any institutionalized religion, I have religious beliefs which incorporate, in my view, the best from all religions. The basis of my religious beliefs is Christian, I consider myself to be a Christian and I was baptized a Catholic").

22. Brief of Plaintiff-Appellant at 12–13, Leebaert v. Harrington (citation and footnote omitted).

23. George W. Dent Jr., "Of God and Caesar: The Free Exercise Rights of Public School Students," *Case W. Res. L. Rev.* 43 (1993): 707, 726.

24. Brief of Plaintiff-Appellant at 11, Leebaert v. Harrington.

25. 187 N.W. 100 (Neb. 1922).

26. Kelley v. Ferguson, 144 N.W. 1039, 1044 (Neb. 1914) (Letton, J., concurring in judgment).

27. Leebaert, 332 F.3d at 143. Here, too, the reasoning of the court repeated that of other circuits. In *Brown v. Hot, Sexy and Safer Productions, Inc.*, the First Circuit found that the plaintiffs' free exercise claim was "qualitatively distinguishable from that alleged in *Yoder*." 68 F.3d at 539. The *Brown* plaintiffs could not show—they did not even allege—that compulsory attendance at a sex education program "threatened their entire way of life." 68 F.3d at 539; cf. *Parker v. Hurley*, 514 F.3d at 100 ("[T]here are substantial differences between the plaintiffs' claims in Yoder and the claims raised in this case. One ground of distinction is that the plaintiffs have chosen to place their children in public schools and do not live, as the Amish do, in a largely separate culture. There are others. While plaintiffs do invoke *Yoder*'s language that the state is threatening their very 'way of life,' they use this language to refer to the centrality of these beliefs to their faith, in contrast to its use in *Yoder* to refer to a distinct community and life style. Exposure to the materials in dispute here will not automatically and irreversibly prevent the parents from raising Jacob and Joey in the religious belief that gay marriage is immoral").

28. Ira C. Lupu, "Where Rights Begin: The Problem of Burdens on the Free Exercise of Religion," *Harv. L. Rev.* 102 (1989): 933, 936.

29. See Employment Div., Dept. of Human Res. v. Smith, 494 U.S. 872, 887 (1990) ("'[It] is not within the judicial ken to question the centrality of particular beliefs or practices to a faith, or the validity of particular litigants' interpretations of those creeds'") (quoting Hernandez v. Commissioner, 490 U.S. 680, 699 [1989]).

30. Cf. Fellowship Baptist Church v. Benton, 815 F.2d 485 (8th Cir. 1987) (upholding constitutionality of Iowa state "Amish exception" statute against equal protection challenge brought by Baptist church schools).

31. Smith, 494 U.S. at 888. Illinois ex rel. McCollum v. Bd. of Educ., 333 U.S. 203, 235 (1948) (Jackson, J., concurring) ("If we are to eliminate everything that is objectionable to any of these warring sects or inconsistent with any of their doctrines, we will leave public education in shreds").

32. William A. Galston, *Liberal Pluralism: The Implications of Values Pluralism for Political Theory and Practice* (New York: Cambridge University Press, 2002) 24; see also generally Nomi Maya Stolzenberg, "'He Drew a Circle That Shut Me Out': Assimilation, Indoctrination, and the Paradox of a Liberal Education," *Harv. L. Rev.* 106 (1993): 581. But see generally Stephen Macedo, "Liberal Civic Education and Religious Fundamentalism: The Case of God v. John Rawls," *Ethics* 105 (1995): 468.

33. William A. Galston, "Two Concepts of Liberalism," *Ethics* 105 (1995): 516, 521. For a response to Galston, see Robin West, "The Limits of Liberal Pluralism," in *Moral Universalism and Pluralism* (NOMOS XLIX), eds. Henry S. Richardson and Melissa S. Williams (New York: New York University Press, 2009) 149.

34. Harry Brighouse, "School Vouchers, Separation of Church and State, and Personal Autonomy," in *Moral and Political Education* (NOMOS XLIII), eds. Stephen Macedo and Yael Tamir (New York: New York University Press, 2002) 244, 269; cf. Jeff Spinner-Halev, *Surviving Diversity: Religion and Democratic Citizenship* (Baltimore: Johns Hopkins University Press, 2000) 50 ("If we think that members of restrictive communities need not have a range of options as long as the options are present in the larger society, then liberals need not think they have to open up these communities"); Michael Walzer, *Spheres of Justice: A Defense of Pluralism and Equality* (New York: Basic Books, 1983) 219 ("I don't think that there is any need for a frontal assault on parental choice, so long as its chief effect is to provide ideological diversity on the margins of a predominantly public system").

35. Cf. Rob Reich, "How and Why to Support Common Schooling and Educational Choice at the Same Time," *J. Phil. Ed.* 41 (2007): 709, 721 ("[T]o the extent that educational choice makes it likelier that schools will be divided along religious and moral lines, the prospects of realizing the common school ideal look dimmer"); Martha L. A. Fineman, "Taking Children's Interests Seriously," in *Child, Family, and State* (NOMOS XLIV), eds. Stephen Macedo and Iris Marion Young (New York: New York University Press, 2003) 234, 238; Abner S. Greene, "Why Vouchers Are Unconstitutional, and Why They're Not," *Notre Dame J.L. Ethics & Pub. Pol'y* 13 (1999): 397, 407; Hugh LaFollette, "Freedom of Religion and Children," *Public Affairs Q.* 3 (1989): 75, 85; Walzer, *Spheres of Justice*, 219. But see generally, e.g., Michael W. McConnell, "Governments, Families, and Power: A Defense of Educational Choice," *Conn. L. Rev.* 31 (1999): 847.

36. Brief of Plaintiff-Appellant at 30, Leebaert v. Harrington.

37. Tinker v. Des Moines Indep. Cmty. Sch. Dist., 393 U.S. 503, 506–7, 511 (1969). On the public school as educational monolith, see, e.g., Nadine Strossen, "'Secular Humanism' and 'Scientific Creationism': Proposed Standards for Reviewing Curricular Decisions Affecting Students' Religious Freedom," *Ohio St. L.J.* 47 (1986): 333, 369–70; Stephen Arons and Charles Lawrence III, "The Manipulation of Consciousness: A First Amendment Critique of Schooling," *Harv. C.R.-C.L. L. Rev.* 15 (1980): 309, 317.

38. Susan Svrluga, "7,000 Use Religious Opt-Out of Schools," *Washington Post*, September 11, 2012, at B1 ("Nearly 7,000 Virginia children whose families have opted to keep them out of public school for religious reasons are not required to get an education, the only children in the country who do not have to prove they are being home-schooled or otherwise educated").

39. Andrew Block et al., "7,000 Children and Counting: An Analysis of Religious Exemptions from Compulsory School Attendance in Virginia," 28 (on file with author); cf. Chandran Kukathas, "Are There Any Cultural Rights?" *Political Theory* 20 (1992): 105, 117 ("The wider society has no right to require particular

standards or systems of education within [minority cultural communities] or to force their schools to promote the dominant culture"). Kukathas would accept the possibility of "communities which bring up children unschooled and illiterate; which enforce arranged marriages; which deny conventional medical care to their members (including children); and which inflict cruel and 'unusual' punishment." "Cultural Toleration," in *Ethnicity and Group Rights* (NOMOS XXXIX), eds. Ian Shapiro and Will Kymlicka (New York: New York University Press, 1997) 69, 87.

40. Galston, *Liberal Pluralism*, 23–24. Galston sets forth a third liberal purpose: "the development of . . . 'social rationality' (the kind of understanding needed to participate in the society, economy, and polity)."

41. Galston, *Liberal Pluralism*, 23. K. Anthony Appiah would have the state "step in" only where the parent compromises "the possibility of an autonomous adulthood—as would be the case with a refusal, on religious grounds, to allow one's children to learn to read." "Liberal Education: The United States Example," in *Citizenship and Education in Liberal-Democratic Societies*, eds. Kevin McDonough and Walter Feinberg (Oxford: Oxford University Press, 2003) 56, 72; Jeff Spinner-Halev is "reluctant to force parents to expose children to other ways of life, except in extreme cases where children are not let out of the house or given a basic education." *Surviving Diversity*, 111. But see Will Kymlicka, "The Rights of Minority Cultures: Reply to Kukathas," *Political Theory* 20 (1992): 140, 142 ("A liberal theory can accept special rights for a minority culture against the larger community so as to ensure equality of circumstances between them. But it will not justify ((except under extreme circumstances)) special rights for a culture against its own members. The former protect the autonomy of the members of minority cultures; the latter restrict it") (footnote omitted).

42. See Shelley Burtt, "The Proper Scope of Parental Authority: Why We Don't Owe Children an Open Future," in *Child, Family, and State* (NOMOS XLIV), eds. Stephen Macedo and Iris Marion Young (New York: New York University Press, 2003) 243.

43. Burtt, "The Proper Scope of Parental Authority," 246, 248 (emphasis added), 248, 244, 244, 266, 247.

44. Gilles, "Parentalist Manifesto," 939. At a minimum, Gilles says, a reasonable worldview is one that "acknowledges the importance of human development, embraces civic toleration, and respect for law, and acquiesces in our basic constitutional arrangements."

45. Brighouse, "School Vouchers, Separation of Church and State, and Personal Autonomy," 265–71. In "Civic Education and Liberal Legitimacy," *Ethics* 108 (1998): 719, Brighouse "focuse[s] on the requirements imposed by liberal legitimacy and the independent obligation to provide children with the realistic opportunity to become autonomous persons." His argument is that "civic education can meet the requirements imposed by legitimacy only if tied to autonomy-facilitating education." "Civic Education and Liberal Legitimacy," 744.

46. Brighouse, "School Vouchers, Separation of Church and State, and Personal Autonomy," 268, 271; cf. Macedo, "Liberal Civic Education and Religious Fundamentalism," 476 ("[P]olitical liberals leave the school door open to reasonable fundamentalists, that is, to those willing to acknowledge for political purposes the authority of public reasonableness").

47. Rob Reich, "Testing the Boundaries of Parental Authority over Education: The Case of Homeschooling," in *Moral and Political Education* (NOMOS XLIII), eds. Stephen Macedo and Yael Tamir (New York: New York University Press, 2002) 275.

48. Reich, "Testing the Boundaries," 293. See also generally Rob Reich, *Bridging Liberalism and Multiculturalism in American Education* (Chicago: University of Chicago Press, 2002) 89–112.

49. Reich, "Testing the Boundaries," 299; see also "Testing the Boundaries," 300 ("Some [homeschooling parents] are eager to prevent their children from being exposed to anything contrary to the moral and spiritual values they wish their children to learn").

50. Amy Gutmann, "Civic Education and Social Diversity," *Ethics* 105 (1995): 557, 578. Similarly, Callan would "honor both the commitment to a shared political morality and the accommodation of pluralism that is commonly in tension with that morality." Eamonn Callan *Creating Citizens: Political Education and Liberal Democracy* (Oxford: Clarendon Press, 1997) 9–10. His path through the horns of this dilemma would "give parents substantial latitude to instill in their children whatever religious faith or conception of the good they espouse" and "permit communities of like-minded citizens to create educational institutions that reflect their distinctive way of life, even if that entails some alienation from the political culture of the larger society." Callan, *Creating Citizens*, 9.

51. Appiah, "Liberal Education: The United States Example," 72; cf. John Tomasi, *Liberalism Beyond Justice: Citizens, Society, and the Boundaries of Political Theory* (Princeton: Princeton University Press, 2001) 98 (suggesting that political liberals "find ways of teaching students about the political norms of their society that [do] not unintentionally disrupt students from the ethical worldviews that they have already formed from their experiences within their families").

52. Carefully taught, we are reminded by the song "You've Got to Be Carefully Taught" from the Richard Rodgers and Oscar Hammerstein musical *South Pacific* (1949). It was not an uncontroversial lesson. See Andrea Most, "'You've Got to Be Carefully Taught': The Politics of Race in Rodgers and Hammerstein's *South Pacific*," *Theatre Journal* 52 (2000): 306.

53. 827 F.2d 1058 (6th Cir. 1987). On the background to Mozert, see generally Stephen Bates, *Battleground: One Mother's Crusade, the Religious Right and the Struggle for Control of Our Classrooms* (New York: Poseidon Press, 1993).

54. 827 F.2d at 1069. 827 F.2d at 1067 (citation omitted).

55. Tomasi, *Liberalism Beyond Justice*, 92–93 (footnote omitted).
56. See Mozert, 827 F.2d at 1064 ("[T]he plaintiffs' own testimony casts serious doubt on their claim that a more balanced presentation would satisfy their religious views. Mrs. Frost testified that it would be acceptable for the schools to teach her children about other philosophies and religions, but if the practices of other religions were described in detail, or if the philosophy was 'profound' in that it expressed a world view that deeply undermined her religious beliefs, then her children 'would have to be instructed to [the] error [of the other philosophy].' It is clear that to the plaintiffs there is but one acceptable view—the Biblical view, as they interpret the Bible").
57. 827 F.2d at 1062 (emphasis added). Bowen v. Roy, 476 U.S. 693, 699 (1986).
58. Mozert, 827 F.2d at 1074 (Boggs, J., concurring).
59. Stolzenberg, "'He Drew a Circle That Shut Me Out,'" 591 (footnotes omitted).
60. Mozert, 827 F.2d at 1063.
61. Stolzenberg, "'He Drew a Circle That Shut Me Out,'" 596 (footnotes omitted).
62. See Mozert, 827 F.2d at 1071–73 (Kennedy, J., concurring).
63. 827 F.2d at 1070–71 (Kennedy, J., concurring).
64. 827 F.2d at 1062 (Kennedy, J., concurring).
65. Christopher L. Eisgruber, "How Do Liberal Democracies Teach Values?" in *Moral and Political Education* (NOMOS XLIII), eds. Stephen Macedo and Yael Tamir (New York: New York University Press, 2002) 58, 71–72.
66. Eisgruber, "How Do Liberal Democracies Teach Values?" 62.
67. See Steven Porter, *Wisdom's Passing: The Decline of American Public Education in the Post-World War II Era and What We Can Really Do About It* (New York: Barclay House, 1989) 153.
68. Porter, *Wisdom's Passing*, 153. See Porter, *Wisdom's Passing*, 154 ("As an example [of objectionable material], Frost cited for Judge Hull the story, 'Freddy Found a Frog,' from the second-grade reader. Freddy, finding a frog, asks neighbor Mays what he would do with it. Mays replies he would use it for bait. Freddy then asks Miss Denny, and she tells him that she would cook it. Finally, Freddy asks his mother who says that she would return it to the pond from which it came. This Freddy does and decides that the frog is beautiful there. According to Frost's testimony, this story 'could seduce a child into a belief in disarmament,' because 'if you think it's wrong to kill an animal for food, then the inference could be made that it is wrong to kill a person in war'").
69. Stolzenberg, "'He Drew a Circle That Shut Me Out,'" 597 (footnotes omitted).
70. Tomasi, *Liberalism Beyond Justice*, 93.
71. C.H. ex rel. Z.H. v. Oliva, 195 F.3d 167, 172 (3d Cir. 1999), vacated and reh'g en banc granted by 197 F.3d 63 (3d Cir. 1999), on reh'g en banc 226 F.3d 198 (3d Cir. 2000).
72. In *Troxel v. Granville*, Justice Kennedy suggested that had the Court's due process parenting cases "been decided in recent times, [they] may well have been

grounded upon First Amendment principles protecting freedom of speech, belief, and religion." 530 U.S. 57, 95 (2000) (Kennedy, J., dissenting); cf., e.g., Gilles, "Parentalist Manifesto," 1012. For cases involving religious speech by children in the public schools, see Busch v. Marple Newtown Sch. Dist., 567 F.3d 89 (3d Cir. 2009); Curry ex rel. Curry v. Hensiner, 513 F.3d 570 (6th Cir. 2008); Peck v. Baldwinsville Cent. Sch. Dist., 426 F.3d 617 (2d Cir. 2005); Settle v. Dickson Cnty. Sch. Bd., 53 F.3d 152 (6th Cir. 1995); DeNooyer v. Merinelli, 12 F.3d 211 (6th Cir. 1993); M.B. ex rel. Martin v. Liverpool Cent. Sch. Dist., 487 F. Supp. 2d 117 (N.D.N.Y. 2007); O.T. ex rel. Turton v. Frenchtown Elementary Sch. Dist., 465 F. Supp. 2d 369 (D.N.J. 2006); Duran v. Nitsche, 780 F. Supp. 1048 (E.D. Pa. 1991).

73. 342 F.3d 271 (3d Cir. 2003). "Candy cane" cases are a litigation perennial. See, e.g., Morgan v. Swanson, 659 F.3d 359 (5th Cir. 2011); Curry ex rel. Curry v. Hensiner, 513 F.3d 570 (6th Cir. 2008).

74. 342 F.3d at 274.

75. 342 F.3d at 280. Walz ex rel. Walz v. Egg Harbor Twp. Bd. of Educ., 187 F. Supp. 2d 232, 234 n.1 (D.N.J. 2002).

76. The circuit courts are split on this issue. Compare Ward and Fleming v. Jefferson Cnty. Sch. Dist. R-1, 298 F.3d 918, 926–28 (10th Cir. 2002) (holding that educators may make viewpoint-based decisions about school-sponsored speech), and Ward v. Hickey, 996 F.2d 448, 452 (1st Cir. 1993) (same), with Planned Parenthood of S. Nevada, Inc. v. Clark Cnty. Sch. Dist., 941 F.2d 817, 829 (9th Cir. 1991) (en banc) (applying viewpoint neutrality standard), and Searcey v. Harris, 888 F.2d 1314, 1319 n.7 (11th Cir. 1989) (same). In *C.H. ex rel. Z.H. v. Oliva*, a panel of the Third Circuit held that "a viewpoint-based restriction on student speech in the classroom may be reasonably related to legitimate pedagogical concerns and thus permissible." On a rehearing en banc, the circuit was equally divided on the question. See 195 F.3d 167, 172 (3d Cir. 1999), vacated and reh'g en banc granted by 197 F.3d 63 (3d Cir. 1999), on reh'g en banc, 226 F.3d 198 (3d Cir. 2000).

77. See Sch. Dist. of Abington Twp., Pa. v. Schempp, 374 U.S. 203, 290–91 n.69 (1963) (Brennan, J., concurring); cf. Edwards v. Aguillard, 482 U.S. 578, 584 (1987) (citing cases).

78. See Walz, 342 F.3d at 277; cf. Hazelwood Sch. Dist. v. Kuhlmeier, 484 U.S. 260, 272 (1988).

79. 342 F.3d at 277.

80. 393 U.S. 503 (1969).

81. 393 U.S. 503 (1969); cf. Thomas I. Emerson, "Toward a General Theory of the First Amendment," *Yale L.J.* 72 (1963): 877, 939 ("The world of children is not strictly part of the adult realm of free expression"). The assertion of children's rights can be a heavy tool to wield against young people. In 2012, California banned mental health providers from engaging in "sexual orientation change efforts" ("SOCE") with patients under eighteen years of age. The anti-"reparative

therapy" law was immediately challenged by the Pacific Justice Institute, whose president enlisted the rhetoric of rights—in this case, children's rights—as the basis of his argument: "This new law is an outrageous violation of the fundamental First Amendment and privacy rights of young people." Jason Kandel, "Lawsuit Filed to Fight California Gay Conversion Therapy Ban," 4 NBC Southern California (October 3, 2012), at http://www.nbclosangeles.com/news/local/Lawsuit-California-Gay-Conversion-Therapy-172484671.html. In *Pickup v. Brown*, the United States Court of Appeals for the Ninth Circuit held that the statute was merely a regulation of professional conduct and thus did not violate the rights of SOCE practitioners or minor patients. 2103 WL 4564249, Nos. 12-17681, 13-15023 (9th Cir. 2013).

82. Walz, 342 F.3d at 278. 187 F. Supp. 2d at 241. 342 F.3d at 279. 342 F.3d at 280.
83. Keyishian v. Bd. of Regents of Univ. of State of N.Y., 385 U.S. 589, 603 (1967).
84. On teaching about religion in the public schools, see generally, for example, Emile Lester, *Teaching About Religions: A Democratic Approach for Public Schools* (Ann Arbor: University of Michigan Press, 2011); Warren Nord and Charles Haynes, *Taking Religion Seriously Across the Curriculum* (Alexandria, Va.: Association for Supervision and Curriculum Development, 1998); Warren Nord, *Religion and American Education: Rethinking a National Dilemma* (Chapel Hill: University of North Carolina Press, 1995); cf. also generally Kent Greenawalt, *Does God Belong in Public Schools?* (Princeton: Princeton University Press, 2005).
85. See School Dist. of Abington Twp., Pa. v. Schempp, 374 U.S. at 225.
86. 374 U.S. at 225 ("[I]t might well be said that one's education is not complete without a study of comparative religion or the history of religion and its relationship to the advancement of civilization"); see also 374 U.S. at 300 (Brennan, J., concurring) ("[W]hether or not the Bible is involved, it would be impossible to teach meaningfully many subjects in the social sciences or the humanities without some mention of religion").
87. McCollum v. Bd. of Educ., 333 U.S. at 236 (Jackson, J., concurring).
88. Cf. Stanley Ingber, "Religious Children and the Inevitable Compulsion of Public Schools," *Case W. Res. L. Rev.* 43 (1993): 773, 774 n.4 ("There is an ironic twist to the fundamentalist attack on a 'godless' curriculum. Many textbooks and teachers steer clear of religious references precisely to avoid the wrath of fundamentalist groups or parents who find the specific religious portrayal offensive").
89. Callan, *Creating Citizens*, 133.
90. 427 F.3d 1197 (9th Cir. 2005).
91. 427 F.3d at 1204 (citing Troxel v. Granville, 530 U.S. at 66). 427 F.3d at 1206.
92. 427 F.3d at 1202.
93. 427 F.3d at 1206; see also 427 F.3d at 1206 ("Although the parents are legitimately concerned with the subject of sexuality, there is no constitutional reason to distin-

guish that concern from any of the countless moral, religious, or philosophical objections that parents might have to other decisions of the School District—whether those objections regard information concerning guns, violence, the military, gay marriage, racial equality, slavery, the dissection of animals, or the teaching of scientifically-validated theories of the origins of life. Schools cannot be expected to accommodate the personal, moral or religious concerns of every parent"). 427 F.3d at 1204 (citing Prince v. Massachusetts, 321 U.S. 158, 166 [1944]).

94. 427 F.3d at 1205 (quoting Brown v. Hot, Sexy and Safer Prods., 68 F.3d at 534).

95. 427 F.3d at 1204. 427 F.3d at 1210.

96. Everson v. Bd. of Educ., 330 U.S. 1, 18 (1947).

97. Bd. of Educ. v. Allen, 392 U.S. 236, 245–47 (1968) (emphasis added) (footnotes omitted); see also 392 U.S. at 248 ("[A] wide segment of informed opinion, legislative and otherwise, has found that [parochial] schools do an acceptable job of providing secular education to their students. This judgment is further evidence that parochial schools are performing, in addition to their sectarian function, the task of secular education") (footnote omitted); cf. Runyon v. McCrary, 427 U.S. 160, 178 (1976).

98. On common education, see, for example, Terence H. McLaughlin, "The Burdens and Dilemmas of Common Schooling," in *Education and Citizenship in Liberal-Democratic Societies*, eds. Kevin McDonough and Walter Feinberg (Oxford: Oxford University Press, 2003) 121; Rosemary C. Salomone, *Visions of Schooling: Conscience, Community, and Common Education* (New Haven: Yale University Press; 2000), passim; cf. Reich, "How and Why to Support Common Schooling and Educational Choice at the Same Time," 709–25.

99. Brief of Plaintiff-Appellant at 20, Leebaert v. Harrington.

100. See Minersville Sch. Dist. v. Gobitis, 310 U.S. 586, 599 (1940), overruled by West Virginia State Bd. of Educ. v. Barnette, 319 U.S. 624 (1943).

101. See Ira C. Lupu, "Home Education, Religious Liberty, and the Separation of Powers," *B.U. L. Rev.* 67 (1987): 971; Lupu, "The Separation of Powers and the Protection of Children," *U. Chi. L. Rev.* 61 (1994): 1317; cf. Amy Gutmann, *Democratic Education* (Princeton: Princeton University Press, 1987) 42; Maxine Eichner, "Who Should Control Children's Education?: Parents, Children, and the State," *U. Cin. L. Rev.* 75 (2007): 1339, 1340.

102. See Lupu, "Home Education, Religious Liberty, and the Separation of Powers," 990; cf. Gutmann, *Democratic Education*, 69 ("[P]arents command a domain other than schools in which they can—and should—seek to educate their children, to develop their moral character and teach them religious or secular standards and skills that they value. . . . The discretionary domain for education—particularly but not only for moral education—within the family has always been and must continue to be vast within a democratic society. And the existence of this

domain of parental discretion provides a partial defense against those who claim that public schooling is a form of democratic tyranny over the mind").

103. See, e.g., New Life Baptist Church Academy v. Town of East Longmeadow, 666 F. Supp. 293, 297 (D. Mass. 1987). Several themes run through the cases where parents challenge state regulation of private educational schemes that are pervasively sectarian: first, that exposure to foreign ideas is tantamount to moral corruption, see, e.g., Duro v. Dist. Attorney, Second Jud. Dist. of North Carolina, 712 F.2d 96, 97 (4th Cir. 1983); second, that all subjects should be taught from a religious point of view, see, e.g., Blackwelder v. Safnauer, 689 F. Supp. 106 (N.D.N.Y. 1988); and, third, that the state lacks jurisdiction to regulate private religious educational arrangements, see, e.g., People v. DeJonge, 501 N.W.2d 127, 130 (Mich. 1993).

104. See Meira Levinson, *The Demands of Liberal Education* (Oxford: Oxford University Press, 1999) 58 ("[I]t is difficult for children to achieve autonomy solely within the bounds of their families and home communities—or even within the bounds of schools whose norms are constituted by those held by the child's home community"); cf. Reich, "Testing the Boundaries," 299 ("I submit that even in a minimal construal of autonomy, it must be the function of the school setting to expose children to and engage children with values and beliefs other than those of their parents. To achieve minimal autonomy requires that a child know that there are ways of life other than that into which he or she has been born. Minimal autonomy requires, especially for its civic importance, that the child be able to examine his or her own political values and beliefs, and those of others, with a critical eye. It requires that the child be able to think independently. If this is all true, then at a bare minimum, the structure of schooling cannot simply replicate in every particularity the values and beliefs of a child's home") (footnote omitted).

Before the boom era of the modern homeschooling movement, courts took seriously this concern about schooling that merely "replicate[d] in every particularity the values and beliefs of a child's home"; they routinely upheld state educational regimes that did not permit home instruction. See, e.g., State v. Edgington, 663 P.2d 374, 378 (N.M. Ct. App. 1983) ("By bringing children into contact with some person, other than those in the excluded group, those children are exposed to at least one other set of attitudes, values, morals, lifestyles and intellectual abilities").

105. See, e.g., Emily Buss, "The Adolescent's Stake in the Allocation of Educational Control Between Parent and State," *U. Chi. L. Rev.* 67 (2000): 1233 (suggesting that public education might be required in order to facilitate adolescent associational activity with unlike peers).

106. Cf. Ambach v. Norwick, 441 U.S. 68, 78–79 (1979).

107. Nord, *Religion and American Education*, 203.

108. Nord, *Religion and American Education*, 202.

109. Bruce Fuller, "The Public Square, Big or Small?: Charter Schools in Political Context," in *Inside Charter Schools: The Paradox of Radical Decentralization*,

ed. Bruce Fuller (Cambridge: Harvard University Press, 2001) 12, 14; cf. Bruce A. Ackerman, *Social Justice in the Liberal State* (New Haven: Yale University Press, 1980) 160 ("Surely most parents will refuse to spend 'their' vouchers on anything but 'education' that strives to reinforce whatever values they have—with so much effort—imposed on 'their' children during infancy. Thus, [school voucher plans] legitimate[] a series of petty tyrannies in which like-minded parents club together to force-feed their children without restraint. Such an education is a mockery of the liberal ideal").

110. Lawrence D. Weinberg, *Religious Charter Schools: Legalities and Practicalities* (Charlotte, N.C.: Information Age Publishing, 2007), 2. Weinberg writes that "[t]his [opportunity] may mean as much (or more) to some religious parents as the ability to create a denominational school." *Religious Charter Schools*, 2

111. Robert K. Vischer, "The Sanctity of Conscience in an Age of School Choice: Grounds for Skepticism," *U. Md. L.J. Race, Religion, Gender & Class* 6 (2006): 81, 106.

112. 262 U.S. 390, 401 (1923).

113. Ambach v. Norwick, 441 U.S. at 77.

114. The argument for a more robust curriculum has been made by, among many others, Stephen Macedo, *Diversity and Distrust: Civic Education in a Multicultural Democracy* (Cambridge: Harvard University Press, 2000); Eamonn Callan, *Creating Citizens: Political Education and Liberal Democracy* (Oxford: Clarendon Press, 1997); Walter Feinberg, *Common Schools, Uncommon Identities* (New Haven: Yale University Press, 1998); and Amy Gutmann, *Democratic Education* (Princeton: Princeton University Press, 1987).

115. See James G. Dwyer, "Changing the Conversation About Children's Education," in *Moral and Political Education* (NOMOS XLIII), eds. Stephen Macedo and Yael Tamir (New York: New York University Press, 2002) 314, 334–44 (concluding that, from a child-centered analysis, state funding of private schools is required, but that the state must attach extensive regulations to such funding).

116. 268 U.S. 510, 534 (1925).

117. Cf. Macedo, "Liberal Civic Education and Religious Fundamentalism," 484–85. Macedo would allow accommodations "where public imperatives are marginal and the burdens on particular groups are very substantial." But his position is unapologetically in favor of "[t]he bedrock liberal insistence on toleration [that] is a constraint on the range of religious practices that can be tolerated. . . . Do families have a moral right to opt out of reasonable measures designed to educate children toward very basic liberal virtues because those measures make it harder for parents to pass along their particular religious belief? Surely not."

118. Reich, "How and Why to Support Common Schooling and Educational Choice at the Same Time," 721; see also Salomone, *Visions of Schooling*, 265 ("A varied model of government-supported and -regulated schooling permits each school to

develop a comprehensive curriculum, including core and selected noncore values, that reflects a 'coherent moral-cultural perspective.' This pluralistic approach averts the value dilution that inevitably results when schools strain to be neutral and secular by relying solely on those 'low-doctrine' values that have gained minimal acceptance. . . . At the same time, by prohibiting all government-subsidized schools, whether public or private, from conveying a message or engaging in any activities that are inconsistent with core political commitments, the proposed model suggests political and legal safeguards to preserve those democratic principles which bind us together as a nation").

119. Reich, "How and Why to Support Common Schooling and Educational Choice at the Same Time," 721; cf. Macedo, "Liberal Civic Education and Religious Fundamentalism," 486 ("[S]ome level of awareness of alternative ways of life is a prerequisite not only of citizenship but of being able to make the most basic life choices. This ground alone might well be adequate to deny the claimed right to opt out").

120. Callan, *Creating Citizens*, 5, 133.

121. Nord, *Religion and American Education*, 201; cf. Feinberg, *Common Schools, Uncommon Identities*, 237 ("In order to consider issues on their own merits students need to have available the range of alternatives that acquaintance with different ways of life entails, and in order to be able to choose from different conceptions of the good, students need to be able to consider evidence that may be uncomfortable for the prevailing authority in their own community").

122. Cf. Callan, *Creating Citizens*, 133 ("The essential demand is that schooling properly involves at some stage sympathetic and critical engagement with beliefs and ways of life at odds with the culture of the family or religious or ethnic group into which the child is born").

123. Keyishian, 385 U.S. at 603 (quoting Sweezy v. New Hampshire, 354 U.S. 234, 250 [1957]).

124. Shepp v. Shepp, 906 A.2d 1165 (Pa. 2006). For the background facts, see 906 A.2d at 1166–68.

125. See 906 A.2d at 1166 n.2: "'Mormon Fundamentalism' denotes the beliefs and practices of contemporary schismatic groups that claim to follow the teachings of the Prophet Joseph Smith. The Fundamentalist movement began after the issuance of the Manifesto of 1890, which publicly declared an official end to plural marriage in The Church of Jesus Christ of Latter-day Saints. Fundamentalists held that God requires all 'true' believers to abide by the principle of polygamy, irrespective of Church mandate" (quoting J. Max Anderson, "Fundamentalists," in 2 *Encyclopedia of Mormonism*, ed. Daniel H. Ludlow [New York: Macmillan, 1992] 531–32).

126. See 906 A.2d at 1168 ("Mother's daughter from a previous marriage . . . testified that when she was thirteen years old, Father (who is her stepfather) told her 'that

if you didn't practice polygamy or you didn't agree with it, but mostly if you didn't practice it, that you were going to hell'").

127. 906 A.2d at 1168.

128. Brief of Appellant at 17, Shepp v. Shepp, 821 A.2d 635 (Pa. Super. Ct. 2003). Brief of Appellant at 22, Shepp v. Shepp, 821 A.2d 635 (citations omitted). Brief of Appellant at 22, Shepp v. Shepp, 821 A.2d 635 (citing Zummo v. Zummo, 574 A.2d 1130, 1155 [Pa. Super. Ct. 1990]).

129. See Brief of Appellee at 7–8, Shepp v. Shepp, 821 A.2d 635; cf. Brief of Appellee at 14, Shepp v. Shepp, 906 A.2d 1165, 1173 (Pa. 2006) ("[I]t follows that the Commonwealth of Pennsylvania has the right to enforce, regulate, and prohibit such conduct or speech that may be incidental to such conduct, whether it be the use of peyote, enforcement of social security taxes, or the practice of polygamy").

130. Brief of Appellee at 6–9, Shepp v. Shepp, 906 A.2d 1165. Brief of Appellee at 8, Shepp v. Shepp, 906 A.2d 1165.

131. 821 A.2d at 638.

132. 821 A.2d at 638.

133. 906 A.2d at 1173.

134. 821 A.2d at 638 (emphasis added).

135. 906 A.2d at 1171. 906 A.2d at 1172.

136. See 906 A.2d at 1172–73.

137. Wisconsin v. Yoder, 406 U.S. 205, 215 (1972).

138. Shepp v. Shepp, 906 A.2d at 1173.

139. See Naomi Schaefer Riley, "Interfaith Marriages Are Rising Fast, But They're Failing Fast Too," *Washington Post*, June 6, 2010, at http://www.washingtonpost.com/wp-dyn/content/article/2010/06/04/AR2010060402011.html ("According to the General Social Survey, 15 percent of U.S. households were mixed-faith in 1988. That number rose to 25 percent by 2006, and the increase shows no signs of slowing").

140. See American Law Institute, *Principles of the Law of Family Dissolution: Analysis and Recommendations* (St. Paul, Minn.: American Law Institute, 2002) § 2.12(1)(c) at 335, 338.

141. See, e.g., Zummo v. Zummo, 574 A.2d at 1154–55 ("The vast majority of courts addressing this issue, before and after *Morris*, have concluded that each parent must be free to provide religious exposure and instruction, as that parent sees fit, during any and all period of legal custody or visitation without restriction, unless the challenged beliefs or conduct of the parent are demonstrated to present a substantial threat of present or future, physical or emotional harm to the child in absence of the proposed restriction") (citing cases). See also generally George L. Blum, Annotation, "Religion as Factor in Child Custody Cases," A.L.R. 5th 124 (2004): 203; George L. Blum, Annotation, "Religion as Factor in Visitation Cases," A.L.R. 5th 95 (2002): 533.

142. The harm standard varies in degree of rigor. Courts may require a demonstration of actual harm, see, e.g., Pater v. Pater, 588 N.E.2d 794 (Ohio 1992); or that harm be imminent, see, e.g., Garrett v. Garrett, 527 N.W.2d 213 (Neb. Ct. App. 1995); or that there be a substantial risk or grave threat of harm, see, e.g., Zummo v. Zummo, 574 A.2d 1130 (Pa. Super. Ct. 1990); cf. ALI *Principles* § 2.12 at 311–12, 335–39.

143. ALI *Principles* § 2.12(1)(c) at 304.

144. Kendall v. Kendall, 687 N.E.2d 1228, 1232–33 (Mass. 1997).

145. Shepp v. Shepp, 906 A.2d at 1173–74 ("[A] court may prohibit a parent from advocating religious beliefs . . . only where it is established that advocating the prohibited conduct would jeopardize the physical or mental health or safety of the child, or have a potential for significant social burdens").

146. 906 A.2d at 1173. 906 A.2d at 1167. 906 A.2d at 1174. 906 A.2d at 1179–80 (Baer, J., dissenting).

147. Zummo v. Zummo, 574 A.2d at 84.

148. Cf. Milton C. Regan Jr., *Family Law and the Pursuit of Intimacy* (New York: New York University Press, 1993) 135 ("Rights discourse traditionally has focused on the relationship between the individual and the state, but many family law issues involve conflicting individual rights claims. An emphasis on rights alone offers no basis for resolving such controversies") (footnote omitted).

149. Nonintervention may restrict the liberty of a mother who wants her children raised exclusively in the Jewish faith, see Zummo v. Zummo, 574 A.2d 1130 (Pa. Super. Ct. 1990) (order prohibiting father from taking his children to religious services contrary to mother's faith was improper where mother failed to demonstrate that the belief or practice of father actually presented a substantial threat of physical or emotional harm to the children), or may restrict the liberty of a father who wants to perform a Hindu religious ritual upon his child, see Sagar v. Sagar, 781 N.E.2d 54 (Mass. App. Ct. 2003) (upholding order that ritual should not be performed where father failed to show that the child would suffer physical or psychological harm by not undergoing the disputed ceremony).

150. See, e.g., Chris Cuomo et al., Dad Pleads Not Guilty on Violating Court Order for Taking Daughter to Church, February 16, 2010, at http://abcnews.go.com/GMA/Law/divorce-battle-joseph-reyes-faces-jail-baptizing-daughter-church/story?id=9845919.

151. Begins v. Begins, 721 A.2d 469, 471 (Vt. 1998) (internal quotation marks and citation omitted).

152. ALI *Principles*, § 2.12 at 311, Comment d.

153. Lange v. Lange, 502 N.W.2d 143, 148 (Wis. Ct. App. 1993).

154. Zummo v. Zummo, 574 A.2d at 1141.

155. Zummo v. Zummo, 50 Pa. D. & C.3d 447, 450 (Pa. Ct. Com. Pl. 1988).

156. 574 A.2d at 1142.

157. 574 A.2d at 1142. 574 A.2d at 1142. 574 A.2d at 1157. 574 A.2d at 1138. 574 A.2d at 1157–58.

158. 574 A.2d at 1138.

159. For cases, see D. W. O'Neill, Annotation, "Child's Wishes as Factor in Awarding Custody," A.L.R. 3d 4 (1965): 1396. Here, too, legal scholars are quick to make false historical assumptions. See, e.g., Elizabeth S. Scott, N. Dickon Reppucci, and Mark Aber, "Children's Preference in Adjudicated Custody Decisions," *Ga. L. Rev.* 22 (1988): 1035, 1035 ("Historically, courts usually paid little attention to the child's wishes in deciding which parent should have custody upon divorce").

160. Zummo v. Zummo, 574 A.2d at 1148–49.

161. 574 A.2d at 1152 (footnote omitted).

162. Cf. 574 A.2d at 1159–60 (Johnson, J., dissenting) ("Although of course courts may not render value judgments on the merits of a particular religious belief, they may properly examine the effect of that belief on a child involved in a custody dispute") (citations omitted); cf. Morris v. Morris, 412 A.2d 139, 144 (Pa. Super. Ct. 1979) ("We neither intend to, nor are capable of, rendering a value judgment on the intrinsic truth of the varied religious beliefs [of the parents], but confine our investigation solely to any detrimental effect their practice may have on the development of the child").

163. See Fed. R. Evid. 801(c); cf. Peterson v. Sorlien, 299 N.W.2d 123 (Minn. 1980). In *Peterson*, the plaintiff, a member of a religious group called The Way, was held against her will as part of a deprogramming episode, and she sued for false imprisonment. The court ruled that evidence of The Way's activities and practices was admissible to show defendants' state of mind, which was a question relevant to the assessment of punitive damages.

164. Morris v. Morris, 412 A.2d 139 (Pa. Super. Ct. 1979).

165. 412 A.2d at 143.

166. Zummo v. Zummo, 574 A.2d at 1139–40.

167. Eisenstadt v. Baird, 405 U.S. 438, 453 (1972).

168. Morris v. Morris, 412 A.2d at 144.

169. Johnson v. Schlotman, 502 N.W.2d 831, 834 (N.D. 1993).

170. 502 N.W.2d at 837 (Levine, J., concurring).

171. See ALI *Principles*, § 2.12 at 304–05.

172. Young v. Young, 628 N.Y.S.2d 957, 963 (N.Y.A.D. 2 Dept. 1993) (quoting Daghir v. Daghir, 441 N.Y.S.2d 494, 496 [N.Y. App. Div. 1981]) (alteration in original).

173. Under the "friendly parent" concept, primary residential placement is awarded to the parent most likely to foster the child's relationship with the other parent. For a critique of the doctrine, see Margaret K. Dore, "The 'Friendly Parent' Concept: A Flawed Factor for Child Custody," *Loy. J. Pub. Int. L.* 6 (2004): 41.

174. See, e.g., Johnson v. Schlotman, 502 N.W.2d at 836–37 (Levine, J., concurring).

175. Young v. Young, 628 N.Y.S.2d at 959.

176. Schutz v. Schutz, 581 So. 2d 1290, 1292 (Fla. 1991).

177. 581 So. 2d at 1292.

178. Quiner v. Quiner, 59 Cal. Rptr. 503, 517 (Cal. Ct. App. 1967); see also Mellott v. Mellott, 476 A.2d 961, 962 (Pa. Super. Ct. 1984) (ordering that "it shall be the duty of each parent to uphold the other parent as one whom the children should respect and love").

179. Ex parte Aguilera, 768 S.W.2d 425, 426 (Tex. App. 1989).

180. Schutz v. Schutz, 581 So. 2d at 1291. 581 So. 2d at 1292.

181. See, e.g., Gifford v. Tuggle, No. CA 06–601, 2007 WL 266443 (Ark. Ct. App. January 31, 2007) (warning mother and her fiancé not to alienate child from father).

182. See, e.g., In re E.L.M.C, 100 P.2d 546 (Colo. App. 2004) (considering whether, in custody case, trial court's prohibition against homophobic religious teachings impermissibly invaded mother's constitutional rights).

183. Eugene Volokh, "Parent-Child Speech and Child Custody Speech Restrictions," *N.Y.U. L. Rev.* 81 (2006): 631, 631.

184. Volokh, "Parent-Child Speech," 705, 716, 717, 717–18.

185. Volokh, "Parent-Child Speech," 717.

186. ALI *Principles*, § 2.12(1)(c) at 304.

187. ALI *Principles*, § 2.12 Comment d at 311.

188. ALI *Principles*, § 2.12 Comment d at 311.

189. ALI *Principles*, § 2.12 Illustration 9 at 312.

190. ALI *Principles*, § 2.12 Illustration 10 at 313.

191. 687 N.E.2d 1228 (Mass. 1997).

192. 687 N.E.2d at 1233–35 (alterations in original).

193. 687 N.E.2d at 1235 (emphasis added) (citation omitted).

194. See, e.g., Zummo v. Zummo, 574 A.2d at 1156; Kendall v. Kendall, 687 N.E.2d at 1232; Kirchner v. Caughey, 606 A.2d 257, 262 (Md. 1992).

195. Kirchner v. Caughey, 606 A.2d at 262 (quoting Ledoux v. Ledoux, 452 N.W.2d 1, 5 [Neb. 1990]) (second alteration in original).

196. Kendall v. Kendall, 687 N.E.2d at 1231 (emphasis added).

197. See Zeitler v. Kendall, 780 N.E.2d 157 (Mass. App. Ct. 2002).

198. See Quiner v. Quiner, 59 Cal. Rptr. at 509; Leppert v. Leppert, 519 N.W.2d 287, 289 (N.D. 1994); Kirchner v. Caughey, 606 A.2d 257, 264 (Md. 1991); In re Marriage of Hadeen, 619 P.2d 374, 375–76 (Wash. Ct. App. 1980).

199. Peterson v. Peterson, 474 N.W.2d 862, 871 (Neb. 1991).

200. 474 N.W.2d at 871–72.

201. Bienenfeld v. Bennett-White, 605 A.2d 172, 175 (Md. Ct. Spec. App. 1992). Bienenfeld, 605 A.2d at 182 (quoting Kennedy v. Kennedy, 462 A.2d 1208, 1215 [Md. Ct. Spec. App. 1983]).

202. See 1 Kings 3:24–28.
203. Regan, *Family Law and the Pursuit of Intimacy*, 135.
204. See, e.g., Zummo v. Zummo, 574 A.2d at 1155 ("For children of divorce in general, and children of intermarriage and divorce especially, exposure to parents' conflicting values, lifestyles, and religious beliefs may indeed cause doubts and stress. However, stress is not always harmful, nor is it always to be avoided and protected against").
205. Morris v. Morris, 412 A.2d at 142.
206. Felton v. Felton, 418 N.E.2d 606, 608 (Mass. 1981).
207. Bethel Sch. Dist. No. 403 v. Fraser, 478 U.S. 675, 681 (1986) (citation omitted). Prince v. Massachusetts, 321 U.S. 158, 168 (1944). Bethel, 478 U.S. at 681.
208. 321 U.S. at 163.
209. See 321 U.S. at 171–72 (Murphy, J., dissenting).
210. Brief of Appellant at 34, Prince v. Massachusetts, 321 U.S. 158, 168 (1944).
211. West Virginia State Bd. of Educ. v. Barnette, 319 U.S. at 642. 319 U.S. at 642. 319 U.S. at 633. 319 U.S. at 642.
212. James Madison, "Memorial and Remonstrance Against Religious Assessments," reprinted in *The Supreme Court on Church and State*, ed. Robert S. Alley (Oxford: Oxford University Press, 1988) 18; cf. Thomas Jefferson, "The Statute of Virginia for Religious Freedom" (1786), reprinted in *The Virginia Statute for Religious Freedom: Its Evolution and Consequences in American History*, eds. Merrill D. Peterson and Robert C. Vaughan (New York: Cambridge University Press, 2003) (1988) (xviii).
213. Lee v. Weisman, 505 U.S. 577, 592 (1992); cf. Lawrence v. Texas, 539 U.S. 558, 562 (2003) ("Liberty presumes an autonomy of self that includes freedom of thought, belief, expression, and certain intimate conduct").
214. *Public Opinion* (New York: Harcourt, Brace, 1922) 50.
215. On the psychological and emotional maltreatment of children, see, for example, James Garbarino, John Eckenrode, and Kerry Bolger, "The Elusive Crime of Psychological Maltreatment," in *Understanding Abusive Families: An Ecological Approach to Theory and Practice*, eds. James Garbarino and John Eckenrode (San Francisco: Jossey-Bass, 1997) 10. See generally James Garbarino et al., *The Psychologically Battered Child* (San Francisco: Jossey-Bass, 1986).
216. Ginsberg v. New York, 390 U.S. 629, 649 (1968) (Stewart, J., concurring in the result) ("The First Amendment guarantees liberty of human expression in order to preserve in our Nation what Mr. Justice Holmes called a 'free trade in ideas.' To that end, the Constitution protects more than just a man's freedom to say or write or publish what he wants. It secures as well the liberty of each man to decide for himself what he will read and to what he will listen. The Constitution guarantees, in short, a society of free choice") (citation omitted); Laurence Tribe, 1 *American Constitutional Law* (New York: Foundation Press, 2000) § 15–5, at 899–900 ("The

Constitution has enumerated specific categories of thought and conscience for special treatment: religion and speech. Courts have at times properly generalized from these protections . . . to derive a capacious realm of individual conscience, and to define a 'sphere of intellect and spirit' constitutionally secure from the machinations and manipulations of government").

217. Cf. Richard Arneson and Ian Shapiro, "Democratic Autonomy and Religious Freedom: A Critique of *Wisconsin v. Yoder*," in *Democracy's Place* (Ithaca: Cornell University Press, 1996) 160; Stanley Ingber, "Socialization, Indoctrination, or the 'Pall of Orthodoxy': Value Training in the Public Schools," *U. Ill. L. Rev.* 1987 (1987): 15, 16.

218. Galston, *Liberal Pluralism*, 104.

219. Galston, *Liberal Pluralism*, 104.

220. Cf. Rob Reich, "Multicultural Accommodations in Education," in *Citizenship and Education in Liberal-Democratic Societies: Teaching for Cosmopolitan Values and Collective Identities*, eds. Kevin McDonough and Walter Feinberg (New York: Oxford University Press, 2003) 305 ("It is one thing simply to announce that cultural groups may not forbid their members from exiting; it is an entirely different matter to create the capacity for individuals to exercise this right"). The idea that the child's capacity to form dissenting beliefs should be protected from ideological coercion by state actors finds broad support among First Amendment theorists. On the First Amendment and the protection of belief formation as well as expression, see, for example, Ingber, "Socialization, Indoctrination, or the 'Pall of Orthodoxy,'" 16; Strossen, "'Secular Humanism' and 'Scientific Creationism,'" 370; Tyll van Geel, "The Search for Constitutional Limits on Governmental Authority to Inculcate Youth," *Tex. L. Rev.* 62 (1983): 197, 261; Arons and Lawrence, "The Manipulation of Consciousness," 312.

221. See Joel Feinberg, "The Child's Right to an Open Future," in *Whose Child?: Children's Rights, Parental Authority, and State Power*, eds. William Aiken and Hugh LaFollette (Totowa, N.J.: Littlefield, Adams, 1980) 124. But see, e.g., Burtt, "The Proper Scope of Authority," 243.

222. Cf. generally James G. Dwyer, "Parents' Religion and Children's Welfare: Debunking the Doctrine of Parents' Rights," *Calif. L. Rev.* 82 (1994): 1371. But cf., e.g., Karen Gushta, Should Big Brother Shape Your Child's Soul?, STOP the War on Children (April 8, 2011), at http://stopthewaronchildren.wordpress. com/2011/04/08/should-big-brother-shape-your-child%E2%80%99s-soul/ ("[T]here are those who want to take away the right of custodial parents to determine what influences and ideas their children should be exposed to. This is the heart of education, which by definition is intended, directed learning. The issue at stake is not 'who owns the soul of the child,' but who has the right to shape it").

223. See, e.g., Guinn v. Church of Christ of Collinsville, 775 P.2d 766, 781 (Okla. 1989) ("[T]he First Amendment will not shield a church from civil liability for imposing its will, as manifested through a disciplinary scheme, upon an individual who has not consented to undergo ecclesiastical discipline").

224. See Guinn, 775 P.2d at 779 ("Parishioner voluntarily joined the Church of Christ and by so doing consented to submit to its tenets. When she later removed herself from membership, Parishioner withdrew her consent, depriving the Church of the power actively to monitor her spiritual life through overt disciplinary acts") (footnote omitted); Bear v. Reformed Mennonite Church, 341 A.2d 105 (Pa. 1975) (reversing dismissal of tort suit by former member of church). But cf. Paul v. Watchtower Bible Tract Soc'y of New York, 819 F.2d 875 (9th Cir. 1987) (holding that members of church were free not to associate with former member).

225. See, e.g., Wollersheim v. Church of Scientology, 66 Cal. Rptr. 2d 1 (Cal. Ct. App. 1989); Molko v. Holy Spirit Ass'n for the Unification of World Christianity, 762 P.2d 46 (Cal. 1988); cf. Meroni v. Holy Spirit Ass'n for the Unification of World Christianity, 506 N.Y.S.2d 174, 206 (N.Y. 1986) (dismissing emotional distress claim against religious entity because church member "chose to subject himself to the church's discipline").

226. Cf. Ginsberg, 390 U.S. at 649–50 (Stewart, J., concurring in the judgment) ("I think a State may permissibly determine that, at least in some precisely delineated areas, a child—like someone in a captive audience—is not possessed of that full capacity for individual choice which is the presupposition of First Amendment guarantees") (footnote omitted).

227. On parental narcissism, see generally Alice Miller, *Thou Shalt Not Be Aware: Society's Betrayal of the Child* (New York: Farrar Straus Giroux, 1998); Leonard Shengold, *Soul Murder: The Effects of Childhood Abuse and Deprivation* (New Haven: Yale University Press, 1989); R. D. Laing, *The Divided Self: An Existential Study in Sanity and Madness* (New York: Pantheon Books, 1960); cf. Lupu, "The Separation of Powers and the Protection of Children," 1317, 1326 ("[S]elf-love may be an unusually corrupting force when it comes into play in a parent-child relationship. . . . Because the parent is socially and psychologically reinforced to view her relationship with the child as one of affectionate personal attachment, the parent may be unusually blind to the possibility that self-love is distorting her judgment. Moreover, one can much more easily justify domination of children, who obviously need some degree of care and guidance, than one can justify comparable (mis)treatment of adults").

228. See, e.g., Bette L. Bottoms et al., "In the Name of God: A Profile of Religion-Related Child Abuse," *J. of Soc. Issues* 51 (1995): 85; Clyde Z. Nunn, "Child Control Through a 'Coalition with God,'" *Child Development* 35 (1964): 417, 430.

In his study of the (early American) Protestant temperament, Philip Greven explains how the evangelical "preoccupation with obedience, submission, the denial of self-will and of self" evoked forbidden feelings of anger and rage. He describes the powerful forces released in the evangelical psyche by the denial and suppression of anger: "Deeply buried within their own psyches, rage and rebellion constantly erupted, placing constant pressures upon them which, more often than not, they resisted and rejected. Few passed through childhood without accumulating a deep and unfathomable reservoir of hostility toward their parents and toward the exercise of parental power and authority, feelings of rage that continued to shape their response to themselves, to their God, and to the world in which they lived." Philip Greven, *The Protestant Temperament: Patterns of Child-Rearing, Religious Experience, and the Self in Early America* (New York: Alfred A. Knopf, 1977) 109–10.

229. Cf. Barbara Bennett Woodhouse, "Child Custody in the Age of Children's Rights: The Search for a Just and Workable Standard," *Fam. L.Q.* 33 (1999): 815, 816 ("The law on custody is unique in giving one human being the right to control the body and mind of another, without requiring either the subject person's consent or an individualized finding of lack of capacity. Perhaps this is due to the fact that custody laws have their roots in a social order that established hierarchies of domestic status, treating women, children, and slaves as property of the patriarch"). See also generally LaFollette, "Freedom of Religion and Children," 75–89.

230. *A Letter Concerning Toleration* (J. Brook, 1796) (1689) 14–15.

231. See Galston, *Liberal Pluralism*, 28–29 (noting that for some groups it is a matter of great importance to live in a society "structured by commandments whose binding power does not depend on individual acceptance"); cf. Michael J. Sandel, *Democracy's Discontent: America in Search of a Public Philosophy* (Cambridge: Harvard University Press, 1996) 66–67 ("For procedural liberalism, . . . the case for religious liberty derives not from the moral importance of religion but from the need to protect individual autonomy. . . . But despite its liberating promise, or perhaps because of it, this broader mission depreciates the claims of those for whom religion is not an expression of autonomy but a matter of conviction unrelated to a choice. Protecting religion as a life-style, as one among the values that an independent self may have, may miss the role that religion plays in the lives of those for whom the observance of religious duties is a constitutive end, essential to their good and indispensable to their identity"). But cf., e.g., Wallace v. Jaffree, 472 U.S. 38, 52–53 (1985) ("[T]he Court has unambiguously concluded that the individual freedom of conscience protected by the First Amendment embraces the right to select any religious faith or none at all. This conclusion derives support not only from the interest in respecting the individual's freedom of conscience, but also

from the conviction that religious beliefs worthy of respect are the product of free and voluntary choice by the faithful") (emphasis added) (footnotes omitted).

232. Yoder, 406 U.S. at 211.

233. On children's religious development, see Robert Coles, *The Spiritual Life of Children* (Boston: Houghton Mifflin, 1990); James W. Fowler, *Stages of Faith: The Psychology of Human Development and the Quest for Meaning* (New York: HarperCollins, 1981); see also Christian Smith, *Soul Searching: The Religious and Spiritual Lives of American Teenagers* (New York: Oxford University Press, 2005). For a discussion of the law and the religious life of adolescents, see generally Emily Buss, "The Law's Influence over Children's Religious Development," in *Children and Childhood in American Religions*, eds. Don Browning and Bonnie Miller-McLemore (New Brunswick, N.J.: Rutgers University Press, 2009) 210–22; Roger J. R. Levesque, *Not by Faith Alone: Religion, Law, and Adolescence* (New York: New York University Press, 2002); Note, "Children as Believers: Minors' Free Exercise Rights and the Psychology of Religious Development," *Harv. L. Rev.* 115 (2002): 2205, 2220–25; Buss, "The Adolescent's Stake in the Allocation of Educational Control," 1264–67 (discussing religious identity formation).

234. Yoder, 406 U.S. at 225.

235. Parham v. J.R., 442 U.S. 584, 600 (1979).

236. See Ingraham v. Wright, 430 U.S. 651 (1977); Goss v. Lopez, 419 U.S. 565 (1975); Breed v. Jones, 421 U.S. 519 (1975).

237. Bellotti v. Baird, 443 U.S. 622, 634 (1979); cf. May v. Anderson, 345 U.S. 528, 536 (1953) ("[C]hildren have a very special place in life which law should reflect. Legal theories and their phrasing in other cases readily lead to fallacious reasoning if uncritically transferred to determination of a State's duty towards children") (Frankfurter, J., concurring). In re Gault, 387 U.S. 1, 13 (1967). Tinker v. Des Moines, 393 U.S. at 506–7, 511.

238. Bellotti v. Baird, 443 U.S. at 634.

239. See, e.g., J. Shoshanna Ehrlich, "Shifting Boundaries, Abortion, Criminal Culpability, and the Indeterminate Legal Status of Adolescents," *Wis. Women's L.J.* 18 (2003): 77, 116 ("Respect for the transitional nature of the teen years requires a domain-sensitive approach that takes the developmental process into careful consideration, rather than a simplistic line-drawing approach that disregards it"). For a critique of developmental capacity as the measure of children's rights, see Emily Buss, "What the Law Should (and Should Not) Learn from Child Development Research," *Hofstra L. Rev.* 38 (2009): 13.

240. Parham v. J.R., 442 U.S. 584 (1979).

241. 442 U.S. at 602. 442 U.S. at 603–4. 442 U.S. at 603. 442 U.S. at 604. 442 U.S. at 602.

242. On adolescent medical decision making and the mature minor doctrine, see, for example, Rhonda Gay Hartman, "Coming of Age: Devising Legislation for Adolescent Medical Decision-Making," *Am. J.L. & Med.* 28 (2002): 409.

243. 428 U.S. 52 (1976).

244. 428 U.S. at 74.

245. 428 U.S. at 75; cf. Carey v. Population Servs. Int'l, 431 U.S. 678, 719 (1977) (state may not use police power to enforce its concept of public morality as it pertains to minors).

246. 443 U.S. 622 (1979).

247. 443 U.S. at 635. 443 U.S. at 642. 443 U.S. at 640. 443 U.S. at 647.

248. C. Fried, Correspondence, *Phil. & Pub. Aff.* 6 (1977): 288–89, quoted in Thornburgh v. American College of Obstetricians and Gynecologists, 476 U.S. 747, 777 n.5 (1986) (Stevens, J., concurring).

249. Kenneth L. Karst, "The Freedom of Intimate Association," *Yale L.J.* 89 (1980): 624, 637, 644, 644, 637, 638; cf. Alan B. Kalin, Comment, "The Right of Ideological Nonassociation," *Calif. L. Rev.* 66 (1978): 767.

250. Cf. Yoder, 406 U.S. at 242 (Douglas, J., dissenting) ("Where the child is mature enough to express potentially conflicting desires, it would be an invasion of the child's rights to permit such an imposition without canvassing his views").

251. Compare the regulation of religious worship by slave-owning states: "The slave master may withhold education and the Bible; he may forbid religious instruction, and access to public worship. He may enforce upon the slave and his family a religious worship and a religious teaching which he disapproves. In all this, as completely as in secular matters, he is entirely subject to the will of a master, to whom he belongs. The claim of chattelhood extends to the soul as well as to the body, for the body cannot be otherwise held and controlled. There is no other religious despotism on the face of the earth so absolute, so irresponsible, so soul-crushing as this." William Goodell, *The American Slave Code in Theory and Practice: Its Distinctive Features Shown by Its Statutes, Judicial Decisions, and Illustrative Facts* (1853) (Buffalo: William S. Hein, 2007) 235 (internal quotation marks omitted).

On religion as a matter of generational tradition, see, for example, Stephen L. Carter, "Parents, Religion, and Schools: Reflections on *Pierce*, 70 Years Later," *Seton Hall L. Rev.* 27 (1997): 1194, 1205 ("A religion survives through tradition, and tradition is multigenerational. A religion that fails to extend itself over time is, in this vision, not a religion at all. It might be a set of moral beliefs or a collection of folk tales or a nifty theological idea or a list of interesting rules, but, if it does not exist in this timeless, evolutionary fashion, the one thing it is not is a religion"); Dent, "Of God and Caesar," 738 ("The communitarian tradition is especially relevant to the religion clauses because the survival of religious communities is necessary to make the religious freedom of individuals both possible and meaningful"). But see Kenneth Henley, "The Authority to Educate," in *Having Children: Philosophical and Legal Reflections on Parenthood*, eds. Onora O'Neill and William Ruddick (New York: Oxford University Press, 1979) 262 (arguing that "traditional ways of life have no right to survive . . . at the expense of the liberty of the children who are born into them").

252. Galston, *Liberal Pluralism*, 28–29 (footnote omitted).

253. Galston, *Liberal Pluralism*, 103.

254. William Galston, *Liberal Purposes: Goods, Virtues, and Diversity in the Liberal State* (Cambridge: Cambridge University Press, 1991) 253.

255. Galston, *Liberal Pluralism*, 105 (quoting Callan, *Creating Citizens*, 152–54) (footnote omitted). But cf. Anne C. Dailey, "Developing Citizens," *Iowa L. Rev.* 91 (2006) 431, 484 ("A developmental approach [to caregiving] does rule out the possibility that a commitment to democratic citizenship is compatible with depriving children of the means by which to choose whether to accept or reject family beliefs or practices. The unexamined life—a life premised on faith rather than reason—is a perfectly acceptable choice for adult citizens, but foreclosing children from eventually making that choice for themselves is not compatible with democratic principles or the maintenance of a democratic constitutional polity") (footnote omitted).

256. Galston, *Liberal Pluralism*, 104; cf. Fineman, "Taking Children's Rights Seriously," 234, 240 ("The big question is not whether the state must recognize parents' expressive interest in their children's education, but where we draw the line separating that expressive interest from the *child's* interest in the diversity and independence-conferring potential of a secular and public education").

257. Galston, *Liberal Pluralism*, 105–06.

258. Colin M. Macleod, "Conceptions of Parental Autonomy," *Politics and Society* 25 (1997): 117, 136 ("[A]lthough entrance into the Amish culture by an adolescent is officially a matter of voluntary choice, it is difficult to see such a choice as the expression of genuine autonomy"); cf. Arneson and Shapiro, "Democratic Autonomy and Religious Freedom," 140–41 ("Although the Amish believe that the vow of baptism must be taken voluntarily by a mature person, they go to great lengths in designing their system of education and acculturation to ensure that Amish children will take the vow and join the church").

259. Galston, *Liberal Pluralism*, 95.

260. Galston, *Liberal Pluralism*, 106. On the Amish retention rate, see Donald B. Kraybill, "Plotting Social Change Across Four Affiliations," in *The Amish Struggle with Modernity*, eds. Donald B. Kraybill and Marc A. Olshan (Hanover, N.H.: University Press of New England, 1994) 53. According to Kraybill, "[O]n the average at least four out of five Amish youth will join the church of their birth."

Kraybill, "Introduction: The Struggle to be Separate," in *The Amish Struggle with Modernity*, 1, 10. On Galston's reading of *Yoder*, see Josh Corngold, "Toleration, Parents' Rights, and Children's Autonomy: The Case of Sex Education," 80–95 (Ph.D. diss. Stanford University, 2008) (on file with author); cf. generally Eamonn Callan, "Galston's Dilemmas and *Wisconsin v. Yoder*," *Theory and Research in Education* 4 (2006): 268. But see Chandran Kukathas, "Cultural Rights Again: A Rejoinder to Kymlicka," *Political Theory* 20 (1992): 674, 677 ("[I]f the individual is forcibly prevented from associating with outsiders this would count as a violation of the right to exit. . . . If, however, the individual is prevented from associating with others because the cost would be rejection by the community, this is another matter altogether, although the effective power exerted by the group to deny the opportunity to associate may be just as great. The Amish practice of 'shunning' or, in extreme cases, 'banishing' those members who have violated community norms is an example of the latter kind of 'prevention'").

Michah Gottlieb's description of de facto coercion in ultra-Orthodox Jewish communities could be applied with equal force to other culturally or religiously secluded enclaves: "While the modern nation-state stripped Jewish leaders of the authority to enforce religious norms through threats and punishments, ultra-Orthodoxy has turned to social pressure and disapproval. Non-conformists in ultra-Orthodox communities know that they will find it difficult to arrange their children's marriages. They are also confined to their communities by their poor command of English and lack of secular education. They know how difficult it would be to try to make their way in the alien, outside world. These barriers to leaving the community constitute a powerful de facto form of religious coercion. The paradox is that while the ultra-Orthodox justify their separatism by appealing to religious freedom, they use that freedom to restrict the freedom of their individual members." Michah Gottlieb, "Are We All Protestants Now?" *Jewish Review of Books* 10 (2012): 17 (reviewing Leora Batnitzky, *How Judaism Became a Religion: An Introduction to Modern Jewish Thought* [Princeton: Princeton University Press, 2012]).

261. 406 U.S. at 222; cf. James G. Dwyer, *Family Law: Theoretical, Comparative, and Social Science Perspectives* (New York: Wolters Kluwer, 2012) 511 ("Is the [*Yoder*] majority inconsistent as to the importance of ninth and tenth grade? Responding to the parents' desire to ensure continued adherence to the Amish faith and way of life, the majority treats these two years as crucial; requiring that the children attend school for these two years seriously threatens the Amish community's survival. Responding to the state's desire to ensure an open future, the majority dismisses the two extra years as inconsequential"); cf. Arneson and Shapiro, "Democratic Autonomy and Religious Freedom," 172 ("[T]he Amish defendants themselves seemed to have a lively appreciation of the fact that early adolescence is a crucial period for defining one's identity and one's relation to the values taught as au-

thoritative in one's childhood. If the development of children's minds from ages fourteen to sixteen is not consequential, what is the fuss about?").

262. See Steven V. Mazie, "Consenting Adults?: Amish *Rumspringa* and the Quandary of Exit in Liberalism," *Perspectives on Politics* 3 (2005): 745, 751–53; cf. Reich, "Multicultural Accommodations in Education," 307 ("The costs of exit for children—possibly forgoing the continued love and support of one's parent and family, of suffering shame and ostracism, and so on—are so great that even those with the wherewithal and courage to leave will have powerful reasons to stay").

263. ALI *Principles*, § 2.12 Illustration 11 at 313–14.

264. Ross v. Hoffman, 372 A.2d 582 (Md. 1977). But see In re Hood, 847 P.2d 1300 (Kan. 1993) (denying visitation to "grandparent like" day-care provider).

265. See, e.g., Sacha M. Coupet, "'Ain't I a Parent?': The Exclusion of Kinship Caregivers from the Debate over Expansions of Parenthood," *N.Y.U. Rev. L. & Soc. Change* 34 (2010): 595; Melissa Murray, "The Networked Family: Reframing the Legal Understanding of Caregiving and Caregivers," *Va. L. Rev.* 94 (2008): 385; Laura T. Kessler, "Community Parenting," *Wash. U. J.L. & Pol'y* 24 (2007): 47; Melanie B. Jacobs, "Why Just Two?: Disaggregating Traditional Parental Rights and Responsibilities to Recognize Multiple Parents," *J. L. & Fam. Stud.* 9 (2007): 309; Nancy E. Dowd, "Parentage at Birth: Birthfathers and Social Fatherhood," *Wm. & Mary Bill Rts. J.* 14 (2006): 909; Matthew M. Kavanagh, "Rewriting the Legal Family: Beyond Exclusivity to a Care-Based Standard," *Yale J.L. & Feminism* 16 (2004): 83, 85; Nancy E. Dowd, *Redefining Fatherhood* (New York: New York University Press, 2000) 157–80; Alison Harvison Young, "Reconceiving the Family: Challenging the Paradigm of the Exclusive Family," *Am. U. J. Gender & Law* 6 (1998): 505; Katharine T. Bartlett, "Rethinking Parenthood as an Exclusive Status: The Need for Legal Alternatives When the Premise of the Nuclear Family Has Failed," *Va. L. Rev.* 70 (1984): 879, 947.

This call has certainly not gone uncontested. See, e.g., Lynn D. Wardle, "The Disintegration of Families and Children's Right to Their Parents," *Ave Maria L. Rev.* 10 (2011): 1; June Carbone, "The Legal Definition of Parenthood: Uncertainty at the Core of Family Identity," *La. L. Rev.* 65 (2005): 1295; Elizabeth Bartholet, "Guiding Principles for Picking Parents," *Harv. Women's L.J.* 27 (2004): 323; John DeWitt Gregory, "Family Privacy and the Custody and Visitation Rights of Adult Outsiders," *Fam. L.Q.* 36 (2002): 163; Emily Buss, "'Parental' Rights," *Va. L. Rev.* 88 (2002): 635; David M. Wagner, "Balancing 'Parents Are' and 'Parents Do' in the Supreme Court's Constitutionalized Family Law: Some Implications for the ALI Proposals on De Facto Parenthood," *BYU L. Rev.* 2001 (2001): 1175.

It is already the law in several states that a child may have more than one legal parent. See, e.g., Jacob v. Shultz-Jacob, 923 A.2d 473 (Pa. Super. Ct. 2007); Stitham

v. Henderson, 768 A.2d 598 (Me. 2001); cf. A.A. v. B.B., 83 O.R. 3d 561 (Ontario Ct. App. 2007). For state cases rejecting multiple parenthood, see Laura Nicole Althouse, "Three's Company?: How American Law Can Recognize a Third Social Parent in Same-Sex Headed Families," *Hastings Women's L.J.* 19 (2008): 171, 185 nn.103–11.

266. But see Solangel Maldonado, "When Father (or Mother) Doesn't Know Best: Quasi-Parents and Parental Deference After *Troxel v. Granville*," *Iowa L. Rev.* 88 (2003): 865, 920 ("[A]lthough it is unlikely that a paid babysitter, whose relationship with the child was initially based primarily on financial compensation, will be a quasi-parent, it is possible"); Karen Czapanskiy, "Interdependencies, Families, and Children," *Santa Clara L. Rev.* 39 (1999): 957, 992 ("It would be a rare event under interdependency theory for a paid babysitter to qualify as a caregiver or supporting caregiver, but the possibility should not be ruled out"); cf. Barbara Bennett Woodhouse, "Horton Looks at the ALI *Principles*," *J.L. & Fam. Stud.* 4 (2002): 151, 158–64 (questioning exclusion of de facto parent who has accepted compensation for caretaking).

267. Ross v. Hoffman, 372 A.2d at 585 (quoting In re Bort, 25 Kan. 308, 310 [1881]).

268. 26 Kan. 650 (1881).

269. 26 Kan. at 656. 26 Kan. at 658 (emphasis added).

270. 26 Kan. at 652. 26 Kan. at 652. 26 Kan. at 653. 26 Kan. at 654.

271. In re Murphy, 12 How. Pr. 513, 515 (N.Y. Sup. 1856).

272. Chapsky v. Wood, 26 Kan. at 654.

273. For the background facts, see Ross v. Hoffman, 372 A.2d at 587–90.

274. 372 A.2d at 589 (internal quotation marks omitted). 372 A.2d at 590. 372 A.2d at 586. 372 A.2d at 587.

275. 372 A.2d at 594. 372 A.2d at 593–94 (emphasis added) (footnote omitted).

276. 372 A.2d at 593–94 (emphasis added) (footnote omitted).

277. See, e.g., David D. Meyer, "Parenthood in a Time of Transition: Tensions Between Legal, Biological, and Social Conceptions of Parenthood," *Am. J. Comp. L.* 54 (2006) 125; cf. June Carbone and Naomi Cahn, "Which Ties Bind?: Redefining the Parent-Child Relationship in an Age of Genetic Certainty," *Wm. & Mary Bill Rts. J.* 11 (2004): 1011.

278. See "Visitation Rights of Persons Other Than Natural Parents or Grandparents," Annotation, A.L.R. 4th 1 (2012) (1980): 1270.

279. Meyer, "Parenthood in a Time of Transition," 127.

280. Moore v. City of East Cleveland, 431 U.S. 494, 504 (1977).

281. The Etna, 8 F. Cas. 803, 806 (D. Me. 1838).

282. Joel Bishop, *Commentaries on the Law of Marriage and Divorce* (Boston: Little, Brown, 1852) 526 (§ 643).

283. State v. Clottu, 33 Ind. 409, 412 (1870); cf. State v. Shorey, 86 P. 881, 882 (Or. 1906).

284. See Ellen C. Segal and Jody George, "State Law on Grandparent Visitation: An Overview of Current Statutes," in *Grandparent Visitation Disputes*, eds. Ellen C. Segal and Naomi Karp (Washington, D.C.: American Bar Association, 1989) 5.

285. Writing in 1989, Segal and George reported that thirty-two states enacted grandparent-only statutes; four states allowed both grandparents and great-grandparents to petition for visitation rights, and thirteen states permitted visitation to a broader category of claimants. "State Law on Grandparent Visitation," 6–7.

286. "State Law on Grandparent Visitation," 8–9. Idaho's statute stated that "when a grandparent or grandparents have established a substantial relationship with a minor child, the district court may, upon a proper showing, grant reasonable visitation rights to said grandparent or grandparents." North Dakota's statute was even more open-ended, "grant[ing] visitation rights upon a finding that visitation would be in the best interest of the minor and would not interfere with the parent-child relationship."

287. Segal and George list the following situations: divorce; death of a parent; abuse, neglect, or abandonment; juvenile delinquency; and incompetence or incarceration of a parent. "State Law on Grandparent Visitation," 8–9.

288. "State Law on Grandparent Visitation," 11–13.

289. See Sketo v. Brown, 559 So. 2d 381, 382 (Fla. Dist. Ct. App. 1990); Bailey v. Menzie, 542 N.E.2d 1015, 1020 (Ind. Ct. App. 1989); Spradling v. Harris, 778 P.2d 365, 368 (Kan. Ct. App. 1989); King v. King, 828 S.W.2d 630, 631–32 (Ky. 1992); Herndon v. Tuhey, 857 S.W.2d 203, 208 (Mo. 1993) ; Roberts v. Ward, 493 A.2d 478, 481 (N.H. 1985); People ex rel. Sibley v. Sheppard, 429 N.E.2d 1049, 1052 (N.Y. 1981); Deweese v. Crawford, 520 S.W.2d 522, 526 (Tex. App. 1975). In Campbell v. Campbell, 896 P.2d 635, 644 n.18 (Utah Ct. App. 1995), the court noted that "the vast majority of courts that have addressed the constitutionality of grandparent visitation statutes authorizing visitation if in the best interest of the child, have upheld those statutes as constitutional."

290. See Cynthia L. Greene, "Grandparents' Visitation Rights: Is the Tide Turning?" *J. Am. Acad. Matrim. L.* 12 (1994): 51; see also Joan Catherine Bohl, "Grandparent Visitation Law Grows Up: The Trend Toward Awarding Visitation Only When the Child Would Otherwise Suffer Harm," *Drake L. Rev.* 48 (2000): 279.

291. 855 S.W.2d 573 (Tenn. 1993).

292. 855 S.W.2d at 582. 855 S.W.2d at 578. 855 S.W.2d at 580. 855 S.W.2d at 578.

293. 855 S.W.2d at 579.

294. Compare 855 S.W.2d at 577 with 855 S.W.2d at 579.

295. See, e.g., Evans v. McTaggart, 88 P.3d 1078, 1079 (Alaska 2004).

296. Brooks v. Parkerson, 454 S.E.2d 769, 773 (Ga. 1995).

297. See, e.g., Moriarty v. Bradt, 827 A.2d 203, 205 (N.J. 2003); Camburn v. Smith, 586 S.E.2d 565, 568 (S.C. 2003); Roth v. Weston, 789 A.2d 431, 447 (Conn. 2002);

Blixt v. Blixt, 774 N.E.2d 1052, 1059 (Mass. 2002); Neal v. Lee, 14 P.3d 547 (Okla. 2000); In re Herbst, 971 P.2d 395 (Okla. 1998); Williams v. Williams, 501 S.E.2d 417 (Va. 1998); In re Smith, 969 P.2d 21 (Wash. 1998); Beagle v. Beagle, 678 So. 2d 1271 (Fla. 1996). But see Martin v. Coop, 693 So. 2d 912 (Miss. 1997); Michael v. Hertzler, 900 P.2d 1144 (Wyo. 1995).

298. Moore v. City of East Cleveland, 431 U.S. 494 (1977).

299. 431 U.S. at 495–96.

300. 431 U.S. at 500. 431 U.S. at 500. 431 U.S. at 503 (quoting Griswold v. Connecticut, 381 U.S. 479, 501 [1965]) (Harlan, J., concurring) (footnote omitted). 431 U.S. at 501 (quoting Poe v. Ullman, 367 U.S. 497, 542 [1961] [Harlan, J., dissenting]). 431 U.S. at 503 (footnote omitted). 431 U.S. at 504 (footnote omitted). 431 U.S. at 505 n.15.

301. 431 U.S. at 501 (quoting Poe v. Ullman, 367 U.S. at 542–53 [Harlan, J., dissenting]) (footnote omitted).

302. 431 U.S. at 549 (White, J., dissenting). Even within the biological family, who deserves due process protection is a debatable matter. Do siblings have a fundamental right to visit one another? See, e.g., L. v. G., 497 A.2d 215, 218 (N.J. Super. Ct. Ch. Div. 1985). Half-siblings? See Rivera v. Marcus, 696 F.2d 1016 (2d Cir. 1982).

303. Smith v. Organization of Foster Families for Equality and Reform (OFFER), 431 U.S. 816, 837 (1977). For the background of the litigation, see David L. Chambers and Michael S. Wald, "*Smith v. OFFER*," in *In the Interest of Children: Advocacy, Law Reform, and Public Policy* (New York: W. H. Freeman, 1985) 68.

304. 431 U.S. at 842.

305. 431 U.S. at 842 (internal quotation marks and citation omitted). 431 U.S. at 839. 431 U.S. at 840 (internal quotation marks and citation omitted).

306. 431 U.S. at 857–58 (Stewart, J., concurring in the judgment). 431 U.S. at 857 (quoting Bennett v. Jeffreys, 356 N.E.2d 277, 285 n.2 [N.Y. 1976]).

307. 431 U.S. at 845.

308. Moore, 431 U.S. at 505. 431 U.S. at 845. Brennan also considered that due process protections for foster families would come at the cost of the natural parent's liberty interests. See 431 U.S. at 846–47.

309. Frances E. Olsen, "The Myth of State Intervention in the Family," *U. Mich. J.L. Reform* 18 (1985): 835, 837; cf., e.g., David D. Meyer, "The Paradox of Family Privacy," *Vand. L. Rev.* 53 (2000): 527, 556–57.

310. See Prince v. Massachusetts, 321 U.S. 158, 166–67 (1944).

311. Smith v. OFFER, 431 U.S. at 844. The Court did not decide whether the foster parents had a constitutionally protected liberty interest, resolving the case instead on the constitutionality of the state's removal procedures. See 431 U.S. at 847–57; cf. Rodriguez v. McLoughlin, 214 F.3d 328 (2d Cir. 2000) (holding that foster parents do not enjoy a liberty interest under state law).

312. Moore, 431 U.S. at 507 (Brennan, J., concurring).

313. Arons and Lawrence, "The Manipulation of Consciousness," 325 (emphasis added) But cf. Dwyer, "Changing the Conversation About Children's Education," 327 ("Sometimes the elision of parent-child separateness is manifest in an ontologizing of families. Theorists will speak of 'families' having rights or claims, and of families choosing a form of education, even though it is plainly the case that parents typically do the choosing, with little or no consultation of children, especially when choices turn on basic values or ideology") (footnote omitted).

314. Compare Brief for the Legal Aid Society of the City of New York, Juvenile Rights Division, as Amicus Curiae, at 24, Smith v. OFFER, 431 U.S. 816 (1977) ("Children possess a liberty interest in the preservation of their natural home independent of the parents' right to maintain custody of their children"), with Brief for Appellees Organization of Foster Families for Equality and Reform at 47 ("The liberty interest at stake in this case is of crucial significance. It is a child's interest in maintaining the emotional and psychological relationship with care-taking adults who give the child his or her sense of security and identity").

315. "Partners, Care Givers, and the Constitutional Substance of Parenthood," in *Reconceiving the Family: Critique on the American Law Institute's* Principles of the Law of Family Dissolution, ed. Robin Fretwell Wilson (New York: Cambridge University Press, 2006) 47, 65; cf. Francis Barry McCarthy, "The Confused Constitutional Status and Meaning of Parental Rights," *Ga. L. Rev.* 22 (1988): 975, 1016.

316. 412 A.2d 139 (Pa. Super. Ct. 1979).

317. 412 A.2d at 143.

318. Moore, 431 U.S. at 508 (Brennan, J., concurring).

319. Smith v. OFFER, 431 U.S. at 833. For a latter-day child-saving reform proposal that is certain to raise constitutional hackles, see James G. Dwyer, "No Place for Children: Addressing Urban Blight and Its Impact on Children Through Child Protection Law, Domestic Relations Law, and 'Adult-Only' Residential Zoning," *Ala. L. Rev.* 62 (2011): 887. On family preservation policies, compare Elizabeth Bartholet, *Nobody's Children: Abuse and Neglect, Foster Drift, and the Adoption Alternative* (Boston: Beacon Press, 1999), and Richard Gelles, *The Book of David: How Preserving Families Can Cost Children's Lives* (New York: Basic Books, 1996), with Martin Guggenheim, "Somebody's Children: Sustaining the Family's Place in Child Welfare Policy," *Harv. L. Rev.* 113 (2000): 1716 (reviewing Elizabeth Bartholet, *Nobody's Children*).

320. Brief for Legal Aid Society of the City of New York, Juvenile Rights Division, as Amicus Curiae, at 8, Smith v. OFFER.

321. See Eisenstadt v. Baird, 405 U.S. at 453. Griswold v. Connecticut, 381 U.S. 479, 486 (1965).

322. See, e.g., Hiller v. Fausey, 904 A.2d 875, 886 n.18 (Pa. 2006) (listing cases where courts have applied strict scrutiny); see also Bohl, "Grandparent Visitation Law

Grows Up," 279. See generally Daniel R. Victor and Keri L. Middleditch, "Grandparent Visitation: A Survey of History, Jurisprudence, and Legislative Trends Across the United States in the Past Decade," *J. Am. Acad. Matrim. L.* 22 (2009): 391, 404 n.47; Michael K. Goldberg, "A Survey of the Fifty States' Grandparent Visitation Statutes," *Marq. Elder's Advisor* 10 (2009): 245.

323. Santi v. Santi, 633 N.W.2d 312, 320 (Iowa 2001).

324. Lulay v. Lulay, 739 N.E.2d 521, 531 (Ill. 2000) (emphasis added).

325. Wickham v. Byrne, 769 N.E.2d 1, 4 (Ill. 2002) (internal quotation marks omitted).

326. 769 N.E.2d at 4 (citation omitted). 769 N.E.2d at 6. 769 N.E.2d at 6.

327. In cases involving new reproductive technologies, parenting intentions may become the touchstone of legal parenthood. See, e.g., Marjorie Maguire Shultz, "Reproductive Technology and Intent-Based Parenthood: An Opportunity for Gender Neutrality," *Wis. L. Rev.* 1990 (1990): 297, 302–3; cf. Richard F. Storrow, "Parenthood by Pure Intention: Assisted Reproduction and the Functional Approach to Parenthood," *Hastings L.J.* 53 (2002): 597, 602.

328. Compare In re Custody of H.S.H.-K. (Holtzman v. Knott), 533 N.W.2d 419 (Wis. 1995), and A.C. v. C.B., 829 P.2d 660, 663–65 (N.M. Ct. App. 1992), with Alison D. v. Virginia M., 572 N.E.2d 27 (N.Y. 1991).

329. 100 P.3d 546 (Colo. App. 2004). For the background facts, see 100 P.3d at 549–50.

330. 100 P.3d at 548 (citing N.A.H. v. S.L.S., 9 P.3d 354, 359 [Colo. 2000]).

331. Except in the areas of dental care and religion. See 100 P.3d at 550. The district court also ordered Clark "to make sure that there is nothing in the religious upbringing or teaching that the minor child is exposed to that can be considered homophobic." 100 P.3d at 563. Clark appealed, contending that the order violated her rights under both the Colorado state and the United States constitutions. 100 P.3d at 562–65.

332. 892 P.2d 246 (Colo. 1995).

333. 892 P.2d at 258. 892 P.2d at 256.

334. In re E.L.M.C., 100 P.3d at 552 (citing Troxel, 530 U.S. at 65).

335. 100 P.3d at 559.

336. See, e.g., In re Gallagher, 539 N.W.2d 479 (Iowa 1995).

337. See, e.g., Bupp v. Bupp, 718 A.2d 1278 (Pa. Super. Ct. 1998).

338. See, e.g., Quinn v. Mouw-Quinn, 552 N.W.2d 843 (S.D. 1996).

339. In re Custody of H.S.H.-K. (Holtzman v. Knott), 533 N.W.2d at 421 (footnote omitted). In re E.L.M.C., 100 P.3d at 560. Rubano v. DiCenzo, 759 A.2d 959, 974 (R.I. 2000). 759 A.2d at 974.

340. The influence of the ALI *Principles* goes well beyond its formal adoption by courts, but some courts have explicitly relied on its recommendations. See, e.g., C.E.W. v. D.E.W., 845 A.2d 1146, 1152 & n.13 (Me. 2004); Rubano v. DiCenzo, 759 A.2d at 974–75; E.N.O. v. L.M.M., 711 N.E.2d 886, 891 (Mass. 1999).

341. ALI *Principles*, § 2.03(1)(a) at 117.

342. §2.03(1)(b) at 117. A good-faith belief may be "based on marriage to the mother or on the actions or representations of the mother." § 2.03(1)(b)(ii)(A) at 117. If, after the two-year period, a good-faith belief no longer exists, an individual may be designated a parent by estoppel if he "continued to make reasonable, good-faith efforts to accept responsibilities as the child's father." § 2.03(1)(b)(ii)(B) at 117.

343. § 2.03(1)(b)(iii)–(iv) at 117–18.

344. § 2.03(1)(c) at 118.

345. Meyer, "Partners, Care Givers, and the Constitutional Substance of Parenthood," 65.

346. Cf., e.g., Bartholet, "Guiding Principles for Picking Parents," 323; Gregory, "Family Privacy and the Custody and Visitation Rights of Adult Outsiders," 163; Buss, "'Parental' Rights," 635; Wagner, "Balancing 'Parents Are' and 'Parents Do' in the Supreme Court's Constitutionalized Family Law," 1175.

347. See § 2.01 at 100, Comment b. The intact family may be a two-parent family, parents who merely live together, or a parent who is the child's only parent.

348. See § 2.03 at 122, Comment b. Because a parent by estoppel is to be treated as a legal parent—that is, to be afforded all the privileges of a legal parent—"it is important to limit the category to the most appropriate cases. The objective requirements . . . are designed to identify those parent-child relationships most important to preserve."

349. § 2.03 at 123, Comment b.

350. See § 2.03 at 130, Comment c. A de facto parent may be recognized in the absence of agreement "when there has been a complete failure or inability of any legal parent to care for the child."

351. § 2.03 at 130, Comment c(i).

352. Woodhouse, "Horton Looks at the ALI *Principles*," 155.

353. In re E.L.M.C., 100 P.3d at 561–62. 100 P.3d at 562.

354. 100 P.3d at 562. 100 P.3d at 549. Troxel, 530 U.S. at 67.

355. This was the basis of the *Troxel* Court's objection to the state's visitation statute: "[T]he Due Process Clause does not permit a State to infringe on the fundamental right of parents to make child rearing decisions simply because a state judge believes a 'better' decision could be made." Troxel v. Granville, 530 U.S. at 72–73. The concern is not new. See Foster v. Alston, 7 Miss. (6 Howard) 406, 466 (Miss. Err. & App. 1842) (Sharkey, J., dissenting) (The best interests standard "is destructive of the law, for if the court in all cases may award the child to whom it pleases, this would make the will of the court the law").

356. Helen Simpson, "The Unfit Parent: Conditions Under Which a Child May Be Adopted Without the Consent of His Parent," *U. Detroit L.J.* 39 (1962): 347, 355.

357. Where statutes provide that grandparent visitation merely be in the best interest of the child, state courts have "read into" the law a rebuttable presumption favoring parental decision making. See, e.g., Koshko v. Haining, 921 A.2d 171, 184 (Md. 2007).

358. Vibber v. Vibber, 144 S.W.3d 292, 295 (Ky. Ct. App. 2004).

359. Santosky v. Kramer, 455 U.S. 745, 756 (1982) (quoting Addington v. Texas, 441 U.S. 418, 424 [1979]).

360. State ex rel. Brandon L. v. Moats, 551 S.E.2d 675, 684 (W. Va. 2001) (internal quotation marks omitted).

361. See, e.g., Bolivar v. Waltman, 85 So. 3d 335, 338 (Miss. Ct. App. 2012).

362. See, e.g., State Dept of Social and Rehabilitation Servs. v. Paillet, 16 P.3d 962 (Kan. 2001).

363. See, e.g., Vibber v. Vibber, 144 S.W.3d at 295.

364. R. H. Mnookin, "Child-Custody Adjudication: Judicial Functions in the Face of Indeterminacy," *L. & Contemp. Probs.* 39 (1975): 226, 261; see also Jon Elster, *Solomonic Judgments: Studies in the Limitations of Rationality* (Chicago: University of Chicago Press, 1989) 123–73. Cf. generally Robert H. Mnookin et al., *In the Interest of Children: Advocacy, Law Reform, and Public Policy* (New York: W. H. Freeman, 1985).

365. Feinberg, "The Child's Right to an Open Future," 39.

366. 140 N.W.2d 152, 155 (Iowa 1966). To be fair to the court, it did not base its decision solely on an unfavorable assessment of Painter's lifestyle. With the benefit of expert psychiatric testimony, the court concluded that the child had established a parent-child relationship with his grandfather. In the face of "dire warnings" about the child's welfare, the court decided that it could not "gamble with this child's future." 140 N.W. at 158. See Carl E. Schneider, "Moral Discourse and the Transformation of American Family Law," *Mich. L. Rev.* 83 (1985): 1803, 1859 (citing *Painter* as an example of a "psychiatric turn" in custody law).

367. See the heartfelt essay by Bruce C. Hafen, "Individualism and Autonomy in Family Law: The Waning of Belonging," *BYU L. Rev.* 1991 (1991): 1.

368. Martha Minow, "'Forming Underneath Everything That Grows': Toward a History of Family Law," *Wis. L. Rev.* 1985 (1985): 819, 893–94; cf. Bartholet, *Nobody's Children*, 243 ("There are of course risks that the state, as representative of the larger community, will not do its intervention job right. But there are greater risks involved in continuing to abdicate any community responsibility for our nation's children—in continuing to see the children suffering abuse and neglect as *not* belonging to all of us"). See generally Jennifer Nedelsky, *Law's Relations: A Relational Theory of Self, Autonomy, and the Law* (New York: Oxford University Press, 2011).

369. James G. Dwyer suggests that the law might be changed "so as to restrict [the power of parents to prohibit children's associations] somewhat, perhaps by amending definitions of neglect in child protective statutes so as to prohibit excessive restriction of children's association with nonfamily members or denial of choice in such matters, authorizing involvement of child protective workers in cases where children appear truly to be suffering from extremely isolating or tyrannical parenting practices." *The Relationship Rights of Children* (New York: Cambridge University Press, 2006) 165.

Conclusion

Epigraph. *Alb. L.J.* 9 (1874): 401, 402.

1. Hendrik Hartog, *Man and Wife in America: A History* (Cambridge: Harvard University Press, 2000) 134.
2. Hartog, *Man and Wife in America*, 134.
3. I.iii.96–98.
4. I.iii.181–82.
5. I.iii.185–91.
6. Compare Philip Greven's description of simultaneous rebellion and obedience within the evangelical psyche: "The role of soldier seemed well suited to the temperaments of many evangelicals, since it both liberated and suppressed altogether their sense of individuality and of self. Having experienced the breaking of self-will several times during the course of their lives, and always seeking to ensure that their own wills had been replaced by the will of God, evangelicals could both deny and assert the self simultaneously." *The Protestant Temperament: Patterns of Child-Rearing, Religious Experience, and the Self in Early America* (New York: Alfred A. Knopf, 1977) 124.
7. I.i.46–51.
8. Brief of Appellee, Pierce v. Society of Sisters of the Holy Names of Mary and Joseph, 268 U.S. 510 (1925), in *Oregon School Cases: Complete Record* (Baltimore: Belvedere Press, 1925) 274.
9. See Felicia Sonmez, "Santorum: Obama's College Plan Makes Him a Snob," *Washington Post*, February 27, 2012, at 6.